D1476860

Themes in Right-Wing Ideology and Politics Series
Edited by Roger Eatwell, University of Bath

The Right in the Twentieth Century

Themes in Right-Wing Ideology and Politics Series
Edited by Roger Eatwell, University of Bath

Titles published:

The Right in the Twentieth Century
Conservatism and Democracy

Brian Girvin

PINTER
PUBLISHERS
LONDON, NEW YORK

Distributed exclusively in the United States and Canada by St. Martin's Press

Pinter Publishers
25 Floral Street, Covent Garden, London, WC2E 9DS, United Kingdom

First published in Great Britain in 1994

British Library Cataloguing in Publication Data

A CIP catalogue record for this book is available from the British Library

ISBN 0 86187 981 3

Distributed exclusively in the USA and Canada by St. Martin's Press, Inc. Room 400, 175 Fifth Avenue, New York, NY 10010, USA

Library of Congress Cataloging in Publication Data

A CIP catalog record for this book is available from the Library of Congress

Typeset by GCS, Leighton Buzzard
Printed and bound in Great Britain by
Biddles Ltd, Guildford and King's Lynn

Contents

For my father
Brendan Girvin

List of tables

Preface

This book has its origins in the events of 1968 and the years which followed. As a young political activist who arrogantly believed he knew better than anyone else how the world should operate, I was astonished at the election of various conservative governments with comfortable majorities. Faced with the question of respecting majority decisions at that time, I retreated into the fashionable leftist response of false consciousness, media manipulation or simply ignored the verdict. Yet the question never went away and for a decade I wrestled with it in political terms. By the mid-1970s I had embraced the politics of liberal democracy and had rejected the utopian nihilism of my youth, but an explanation for the successful mobilisation of conservative majorities continued to evade me. Political changes at the end of the 1970s prompted me to look more closely at the dynamics of liberal democracy and especially the role of conservative politics within this. This coincided with the beginning of an academic career, the study of conservatism seemed an appropriate focus for my attention.

This book contains a preliminary answer to the question, which I hope neither insults the conservative voter nor diminishes the need for radical reform. I now share Mill's view that a party of order and one of reform is required in a healthy party system. In this the party of order must eschew reaction while that of reform must avoid utopian radicalism. This is not easily achieved, as can be appreciated by the difficulties encountered by reformers in Russia and by the response of conservatives of all varieties throughout the former soviet block. One important conclusion from this study is that whatever else is required for securing democratic stability, conservatives must be part of the process. If conservatives are excluded or if they refuse to accept the limits which representative government impose, then liberal democracy is unlikely to survive.

Conservatives remain sensitive to what Disraeli called 'outraged tradition' and it is often on that basis that they can mobilise majorities in a democracy. Liberals are often careless when it comes to tradition, especially when tradition is subsumed under prejudice. However, care has to be taken in a democracy to recognise the strength of tradition and the reality that most people dislike change. If modern life is essentially about change, then the place for conservatism will be secured for some time to come. Fukuyama noted this tension and it is one which requires careful attention:

The rational liberal state cannot be brought about by a single election. Nor can it survive without some degree of irrational love of country, or without an instinctive attachment to values like tolerance. If the health of contemporary liberal democracy rests on the health of civil society, and the latter depends on people's spontaneous ability to associate, then it is clear that liberalism must reach beyond its own principles to succeed.[1]

Historically, conservatives have proved more successful than radicals in providing communitarian anchors for society. The problem has been that these have frequently been anti-thetical to tolerance and liberal democracy. As I hope this book shows, it is only in the course of the last forty five years that conservatives in western Europe have found a method to resolve this tension. Whether this outcome is appropriate to other societies remains to be seen.

Although this book is mainly concerned with the twentieth century a word of explanation may be required on its organisation. The first two chapters where written after the bulk of the text had been drafted. During research I found myself being pushed further back historically for an explanation of the origins of conservatism as a political movement and mode of thought. Hence the first chapter attempts to outline an approach to the origins of conservatism in modernity while Chapter 2 focuses on some aspects of its evolution up to 1914. These two chapters I believe help to sharpen the focus for the remainder of the book.

One consequence of this has been considerable delay in finalising the manuscript. I am grateful to Pinter Publishers for their patience which at times must have been exhausted by my failure to meet agreed deadlines. My thanks to the series editor Roger Eatwell for inviting me to write the book and to Iain Stevenson for his initial encouragement. In the later stages Nicola Viinikka was most helpful in her advice and encouragement while I was trying to complete the text.

I would also like to take this opportunity to thank Professor Joe Lee, the head of my department, for his support while working on this book. His interest in the project and the intellectual environment in the department provides a continuing challenge to those working there. I would also like to thank the archivists and staff at the Public Records Office, London; the House of Lords Library, London; the Conservative Party Archives and the Bodleian Library Oxford; Trinity College, Cambridge; the Library of Congress and the National Archives in Washington DC; and the Eisenhower Library in Abilene Kansas. Without the help obtained in these libraries and archives the book would have been more difficult to complete. I would also like to thank the Arts Faculty Research Fund in University College, Cork for awarding me grants to pursue aspects of this work. The American Politics Group also generously awarded me a research grant which allowed me to carry out research in the United States.

A number of people read parts of the manuscript at different stages. Alan Booth read an earlier version of Chapter 5 and offered me useful advice on Britain. An earlier version of Chapter 3 was read at a seminar in the History department in Oxford; the discussion on the paper proved very useful for the development of the argument. Tom Buchanan has discussed many aspects of the book with me over the years, as well as providing me with a place to stay when in Oxford, for which I am most grateful. Nigel Ashford read an earlier version of Chapter 6 and his comments were particularly incisive. Nigel has over the years provided me with a considerable amount of material on American politics and on conservatism generally. I always welcome his comments and his help.

Wolfgang Müller in Vienna alerted me to the complexities of Austrian politics. I have learnt a considerable amount from his own work, and am grateful for the data and published work which he has sent me when I needed it. Paul Lucardie in Groningen has been generous in providing me with data on Dutch politics, in addition to discussing many aspects of Dutch politics with me. Paul also read the penultimate version of the manuscript and offered a large number of incisive comments on it. He and other colleagues at the University of Groningen, in particular Jan van der Harst have provided a stimulating intellectual environment when I taught in the university over the past five years.

A significant proportion of this text was written when I spent a period of research leave at the European University Institute in 1992. I also had the opportunity to present earlier versions of various chapters at EUI seminars and to engage in wide ranging discussions as a consequence. I would like to thank Richard Griffiths for his kind invitation then, and subsequently, to work in an environment so conducive to productive research. Geoff Roberts read the final version of the text. He shares many of the interests reflected in the book which allowed for useful intellectual interaction. Rona Fitzgerald also read the entire manuscript. Her incisive comments were most welcome, as was her knowledge of Christian democracy and particularly the European People's Party. Rona played a special role in helping me to finish this book, it is one that she will be aware of. Notwithstanding all this valuable support, I alone am responsible for the conclusions drawn and for the interpretation.

The book itself is dedicated to my father Brendan Girvin in appreciation of the support he has given me over the years. It is something that I value and I hope that he will find some aspects of the book of interest.

Brian Girvin
Cork, March 1994

Notes

1. Francis Fukayama, *The End of History and the Last Man* (London: Hamish Hamilton, 1992), p. 222.

List of abbreviations

ARP:	Anti-Revolutionaire Partij
BP:	Bayernpartei
BSP/PSB:	Belgische Socialistiche Partij/Parti Socialiste Belge
BRD:	Bundes Republik Deutschlands
CCO:	Conservative Central Office
CDA:	Christen Democratisch Appel
CDU:	Christlich Demokratiische Union
CEDA:	Confederacion Espanola de Derechas Autonomas
CHU:	Christlijk – Historische Unie
CIO:	Congress of Industrial Organizations
CSD:	Conservative Research Department
CPA:	Conservative Party Archives
CSU:	Christlich Soziale Union
DC:	Democrazia Christiana
DDP:	Deutsche Demokratische Partei
DNVP:	Deutsche Nationale Volks Partei
DP:	Deutsche Partei
DVP:	Deutsche Volkspartei
FDP:	Freie Demokratische Partei
FPÖ:	Freiheitliche Partei Österreichs
GB/BHE:	Gesamtdeutscher Block/Bund der Heimatvertriebenen und Entrechteten
GNP:	Gross National Product
IRA:	Irish Republican Army
KPD:	Kommunistische Partei Deutschlands
KVP:	Katholieke Volks Partij
MRP:	Mouvement Républican Populaire
NSC:	National Security Council
NSDAP:	National Sozialistische Deutsche Arbeitspartei
NUR:	National Union of Railwaymen
ÖVP:	Österreichische Volkspartei
PCF:	Parti Communiste Francais
PCI:	Partito Communista Italiano
PDIUM:	Partito di Unita Monarchica

PLI:	Partito Liberale Italiano
PRI:	Partito Republicano Italiano
PSC/CVP:	Parti Social Chretien/Christelijke Volkspartij
PSDI:	Partito Socialista Democatico Italiano
PSI:	Partito Socialista Italiano
PvdA:	Partij van der Arbeid
PVV/PLP:	Paartij voor Vrijheid en Vooruitgang/Parti de la Liberté et dur Progrés
RPR:	Rassemblement pour la Republique
SFIO:	Section Francaise de l'Internationale Ouvriére
SPD:	Sozialdemokratische Partei Deutschlands
SPÖ:	Sozialistische Partei Österreichs
TGWU:	Transport and General Workers Union
TUC:	Trades Union Congress
TVA:	Tennessee Valley Authority
UNR:	Union pour la Nouvelle Republique
VVD:	Volkspartij voor Vrijheid en Democratie
ZENTRUM:	Deutsche Zentrumspartei/Christliche Volkspartei

1 Conservatism and its Confrontation with Modernity

'Change is not made without inconvenience, even from worse to better'. (Dr Johnson)

Introduction

The most striking feature of right-wing politics in the twentieth century has been its democratisation. From its origins as a political movement in the late eighteenth century, and earlier as an ideological counter movement to modernity, conservatism has had an uneasy relationship with representative government, mass democracy and industrial capitalism. Yet at the same time conservatism has functioned as a mirror to and a critic of the modern age, insisting on the existence of alternative ways of mediating politics. At its most benign, conservatism provides, in the useful image of John Stuart Mill, one key element in any viable political system:

> In politics, again, it is almost a commonplace that a party of order or stability and a party of progress or reform are both necessary elements of a healthy state of political life, until the one or the other shall have so enlarged its mental grasp as to be a party equally of order and of progress, knowing and distinguishing what is fit to be preserved from what ought to be swept away.

Mill argued that the strength of each was drawn from the deficiencies of the other. Thus in an imperfect world, there will always be room for a conservative party to offset the imbalances of radicalism without due concern for those who do not share its concerns.[1]

Notwithstanding Mill's positive remarks concerning the need for a party of order, his usage had limited applicability in respect of democratic politics. The political right and conservative ideology for most of its history has been opposed to democracy and to the trappings of modernity.[2] Moreover, Mill was drawing conclusions from the two political systems, Britain and the United States, which complied with his model. This is not to say that he was incorrect in offering it as a political ideal, only that most political systems had yet to adopt such an approach when he wrote. Indeed, the idea of opposition itself had still to acquire legitimacy in most states in Europe, never mind elsewhere in the world where forms of representative institutions existed (Latin America in particular). Even when, subsequently, some legitimacy was accorded to the ideal of opposition, this did not guarantee political succession by the opposition if it won an election. As late as the 1930s, the legitimacy of an opposition becoming a government and receiving the support of the former incumbent was quite restricted, mainly to a limited number of states in Western Europe.[3] Where representative regimes have been extinguished, this has normally been a result of an attack from conservative or right-wing forces on these institutions. In an analysis of sixty-one cases where democratic government ended between 1900 and 1985, the predominant political complexion of the forces opposed to democratic government was conservative or right wing. In only two cases, that of Czechoslovakia in 1948 and Grenada in 1979, can it be argued that the threat came from the left. For the most part military intervention is the cause of terminating democracy (in thirty-six of sixty-one cases), and in almost every such case the military are pursuing a 'right-wing' ideological purpose.[4] This picture of the threat to democratic government emanating from the right or conservative forces is reinforced if the constellation of states examined is restricted to Europe and satellite settler states such as the United States or Australia. Throughout the nineteenth and twentieth centuries, the most serious threat to democratic government, whether to its establishment or its stability, has come from conservative forces. This is not to suggest that left-wing threats to democratic governments did not exist, but it is to argue that whatever instabilities were caused by the left the consistent and long-term challenge to democratic government since the French Revolution has come from conservatives.[5] Thus for most of its political history conservatism has been, at the very least, uneasy concerning the claims of democratic government and in many cases dismissive of them. In the latter cases, conservative elites have mobilised politically against democratic governments, seeking to undermine their legitimacy and existence. It is only after 1945 that the right in Western Europe identifies unquestionably with the liberal democratic system and then under rather unique and unusual circumstances.

Conservatism and change

Why then did conservatism take so long to come to terms with modern democratic government? Mill's belief that a party of order was necessary to political equilibrium was lost on most conservatives outside of Britain and at times even here. If the political development of modern Europe can be identified in terms of a trajectory from absolute monarchy to universal suffrage then conservatives have been slow to embrace any individual step on this particular road. This movement might be traced in the following way: Absolute monarchy; aristocratic parliamentarianism (Britain until 1832); a limited property-based suffrage; representative system with universal male suffrage (perhaps with unequal weightings); and universal and open suffrage. On the occasions when a transition between any two phases is under discussion, the right overwhelmingly sides with the status quo and criticises the changes on conservative or reactionary grounds. While this does not exclusively define the historic differences between the left and right (questions of economy, culture and religion are also important), it does represent an important distinction between those political forces which identify with modernity and those which remain opposed to that logic, though not in every case opposed in principle.[6]

Conservatism is born at the moment of modernity and has maintained an ambiguous relationship to that process every since. Simply in historic terms the concepts 'right' and 'conservative' have their origin in the transformations effected by the French Revolution. Yet the origins of political conservatism are older than this, though both terms achieve salience in the course of the nineteenth century and in opposition to the new forces, political, social and economic, then coming to prominence. Conservatism, or self aware conservatism as we know it, sometimes defensive and sometimes aggressive, came into existence as a reaction to the French Revolution. It defines the polarity between left and right and revolution and order for the subsequent two centuries.[7] The need for a self-conscious defence of existing society, institutions and behaviour is a novel product of modernity however defined. Prior to the seventeenth century there was little need to do so. The need to conserve arises only when radical changes are in prospect. It is on these occasions that the need to justify or defend what actually exists takes priority for some sections of society. Political conservatism has to be distinguished from the simple need to conserve, or the unease associated with change in familiar circumstances. In prehistory and for much of written history change has been an external influence. Environmental change dictated where prehistoric peoples would live and how they would survive. Population increase pushed communities to the margin of their habitat, and then beyond that to seek new resources. Human adaptation for much of history can be understood as a reaction to, usually, uncontrollable pressures from nature. There is a confrontation with nature, but it is one which the human community does not seek, reluctantly accepting it in the face of extinction.[8] It would be mistaken to ascribe a static nature, to pre-modern agrarian societies, but most if not all of them embraced change with reluctance and favoured stability over change. This 'conservatism', or resistance to change, is a product of living in a fairly stable environment and operating in an economic structure which values regularity and repetition. The political dynamics of such societies are far removed from those of the modern world and do not evolve similar conditions.[9]

By the sixteenth century this had changed and divisions between the modern and the classical world were becoming more pronounced. Montaigne in 1580 criticised the new intellectual fashions, evoking the fear of instability. Subsequently the modern and the radical made increasing inroads into the medieval and traditional modes of thought and behaviour. This in turn evoked a more self-consciously conservative response.[10] In 1651 Hobbes, responding to widespread political instability, argued for stabilisation through the reassertion of the status quo, which in effect involved the maintenance of absolutism:

> This desire for change, is like the breach of the first of God's Commandments: for their God says, *Non Habelis Deosalienos*: Thou shalt not have the Gods of other nations; and in another place concerning *Kings*, that they are *Gods*.[11]

Hobbes is but one political response to the encroachment of modernity on the established absolutes of the political firmament. The crisis of the seventeenth century exposed the weakness of absolutist rule and generated forces which,

though contained for the most part, remained influential. The ideological dividing line between the Reformation and the French Revolution was essentially
theocratic: Roman Catholic against Protestant and the various strands of Protestantism against one another. One of the by-products of the wars of religion was a
level of toleration of other religions which ran counter to both theocracy and authoritarianism. Toleration after 1648 was more a cold war than a recognition of
the validity of the alternatives, but it did provide an element of space for believ-
ers in alternative religious views. On this basis a rough and ready pluralism
emerged by the end of the seventeenth century and expands throughout the
eighteenth. The Enlightenment is one logical, though not predetermined, extension of this process. For much of this time the process was one of live and let
live, rather than an acceptance of the equality of the alternative religious view,
but it contained the seeds of a radical pluralism where all beliefs could be accorded equal status. This could generate a form of radical relativism and critics
of toleration argued that such an approach would lead to anarchy not just in religious terms but also in political terms. If the individual had the right to choose a
God, it was urged, then why should one not choose a ruler. These critics were
surely correct in pursuing this point, for it is here that we can locate the fundamental currents which led to modern democracy.[12]

Conservatism, however, appears first as the opponent of change in religious
belief, and the Catholic Counter-Reformation is probably the first
counter-revolution of modernity. The attempt by Catholic powers to reverse the
spread of Protestantism has all the attributes associated with secular
counter-revolutions during the nineteenth or twentieth centuries. There is a refusal to accept any legitimacy on the part of the new social forces, while the
main agency to counter change is violence and extirpation. But these events are
not merely religious, they have a strong political aspect and are closely related
both to the balance of power within Europe and to the claim to sovereignty on
the part of Protestant people such as the Dutch and the English. The characteristic feature of this new era is the transformative effect of it on society. The
explicit defence of existing political authority becomes more necessary by the
beginning of the seventeenth century.

The English civil war in many ways marks the beginning of the modern age in
political terms. When Charles I is executed, this is carried out in the name of the
people; it is not simply the replacement of one monarch by another, but reflects
a significant shift in the nature of sovereignty. Prior to this there are no conservatives at the political level; the consensual nature of the political structure
did not require an act of defence of that structure. Both Catholic and Protestant
powers repressed dissidence, while toleration operated essentially at a state level
rather than within each state. Rulers attempted to contain and control any suggestion of representative government. While the cohesion of early modern
Europe can be exaggerated, it is only when that consensus is challenged that an
explicit conservatism is formulated. What is noticeable is an unease among the
political elites and a reflective defence of the existing order. Conservatism thus
emerged as an attempt to justify what exists and to challenge the advocates of
change.[13]

Absolutism and conservatism

It is perhaps no accident that it is James VI of Scotland (James I of England) who engaged in a vigorous and articulate defence of that traditional order. For James the unquestioning acceptance of authority is the touchstone of political order. James was forced to recognise the threat posed by dissent in Scotland, because the growth of Calvinism there had undermined many existing certainties. The relationship between the monarch and his subject is, James argued, analogous to that of a father to his children; authority is embodied in this patriarchal figure. It would be unnatural for children to kill their father for whatever reason, and it follows from this that no subject can therefore revolt against the monarch. If this reasoning is followed, then there are no circumstances which can justify rebellion or tyrranicide:

> And if it is not lawful to a private man to revenge his private injury upon his private adversary (since God has only given the sword to the magistrate) how much less is it lawful to the people, or any part of them (who are all but private men, the authority being always with the magistrate, as I have already proved), to take upon them the use of the sword, whom to it belongs not, against the public magistrate, whom to only it belongs.[14]

The implications of this claim were far-reaching and reinforced a theocratic underpinning of the absolute monarchy such as evolved in most parts of Europe about this time. There can be no sharing of power: power and authority remain with the monarch whose authority is derived from God and embodied in that relationship. Moreover, the individual remains part of a political order divinely sanctioned, but nevertheless subordinate. By 1610, James follows through the logic of this notion when he claims that the king functions in the secular world as God's lieutenant: 'So it is sedition in subjects to dispute what a king may do in the height of his power'.[15] The argument here is that the political order is divinely sanctioned and consequently political institutions are to be defended in this light. Thus, conservatism in this instance is not so much opposed to democracy, as to all forms of representative institutions which seek to dilute that power. In the short term James's attempts to formulate a conservative theory of divine rule based on theocratic and monarchical precedents was successful. Yet, as his son discovered and as became clear throughout most of the following century, this type of argument proved less and less persuasive, especially to those influenced by the radical Protestant sects and churches. If James was defending the defensible in 1610, this was far more problematic in 1690. Not only had the monarchy been deposed in England, but the Dutch had successfully pursued what was the first war of national liberation in the modern age (if expressed in terms of religious freedom).[16]

Notwithstanding the Restoration of 1660, the Commonwealth marks a point of departure for modern political authority. The events of that era encapsulate the tensions, not only between traditional authority and popular sovereignty, but also, within the popular movement itself, the tensions between notions of democracy, property and representation. It is possible for those who accept popular sovereignty through parliament not to accept political democracy. To execute the king in the name of the people and to establish a republic did not imply an acceptance of political equality. During the seventeenth century two axial points emerged in any discussion of politics, and in any assessment of conservatism. The first, and historically the most important, concerned the nature of governmental power. Was that power to be justified on the grounds of a hereditary monarchical principle, or was it to be based, no matter how loosely, on some concept of popular sovereignty. If the latter, then government required a representative form which was in principle elective, even if the constituency remained narrow. Two governing principles were at variance with one another: one absolutist, the other representative. This is not to claim that the latter form was not based on power or its authority derived from God, only that in contrast to the absolutist, its claim to legitimacy embodied some concept of the people. Charles I expressed a moderate view of the nature of political power just before his execution:

> For the people, and truly I desire their liberty and freedom as much as anybody whatsoever; but I must tell you that their liberty and freedom consists in having of Governments those laws by which their life and their goods may be most their own. It is not having share in government, sirs; that is nothing pertaining to them.[17]

For Charles, as for his predecessors and successor, this was the axial principle of government and one promoted successfully by Louis XIV of France, but also in many other parts of Europe with the growth of absolutism. Unlike his continental fellow monarchs, Charles believed that the rights and privileges of the individual subject could be protected by the monarch, but that the monarch, even while doing so, could not accept that the 'people' should share in that power. Though the claim for representative government was often based on a spurious version of the English past, its power rested on the claim that the monarchy was not absolute, but that authority had been acquired through the people and was consequently contingent on good behaviour. How this was to be defined remained problematic for another two centuries.

In 1683, at the height of the attempt to reimpose absolute monarchy on England, the University of Oxford declared that certain views and opinions were pernicious and should be condemned. Among the views condemned was first that 'all civil authority is derived originally from the people' and second that 'there is a mutual compact, tacit or expressed, between a prince and his subjects, and that if he performs not his duty, they are discharged from theirs'. Thus contingent power is rejected and the absolute nature of the monarchy asserted. Although the Oxford authorities do not attempt to prove these and other propositions wrong, their action is a contribution to the debate at the time of the exclusion crisis and the Rye House Plot. They are a reassertion of the views promulgated by James VI and were expressly reformulated later in the century by Robert Filmer, who consciously argued against power residing in or having its origins in the people. This placed Filmer in something of a quandary, for the logic of his position, and one he effectively endorsed, was that loyalty to a government or monarch should be unqualified. The opponents of absolutism, most famously Locke, countered the appeal to absolutism on the grounds of shared power often based on contract. Limited power is the objective of such thinking. Algernon Sidney, executed in 1683 for holding the views condemned at Oxford, argued that a representative government gave greater security to the people and could consequently command greater loyalty than an absolute monarch. Popular and regular government was the consequence, he urged, of 'filling them [its citizens] with such a love of their country every man might look upon the public cause as his own, and be always ready to defend it'. The popular basis of government justified, for Sidney, the contingent nature of government itself, and the possibility of replacing one ruler with another. In turn such an act would not amount to a rebellion if carried out by a nation: 'there can be no such thing in the world as the rebellion of a nation against its own magistrates, and that rebellion is not always evil'.[18]

The contributors to this debate were rarely democrats. Sidney for example believed that democracy only worked in small communities and under circumstances 'seldom found'. However, the gap between the two views was wide both in intent and in implication. The conservative political view was that of the absolutists; the radical that of the advocates of 'representative' government. For Sidney, Locke and those who re-established the mixed form of government after the Glorious Revolution, representative government meant shared power, but it implied limits and accountability. While not democratic in intent, it did mark the first step away from divine right and towards a secular framework for political authority. This involved some limitations on the absolute power of the monarch and a mixed government; this form of government can be described as aristocratic parliamentarianism. Conservatives were thus aligned against any thought of representation which would limit government and particularly monarchy at this time.[19] Nor were the implications of this lost on the contributors to the seventeenth century debates, whether on the left or the right. If, as Woolton has claimed, the English Civil War is the first modern revolution, most of the themes which have become central to modern political debate can be identified here, and were debated at various times between 1641 and the end of that century. This was recognised by both sides of the debate. Defenders of absolute monarchy warned that representative government would lead to chaos, but the rejoinder was that representative institutions would maintain the status quo, but not the one defended by absolutism. On the crucial issue of the sources of legitimacy, the radicals endorsed a form of representation based on the concept of the people while the absolutists rejected this claim.

However, on the question of the other axial principle – who the people were and what political rights should be accorded to them – the division was quite different. Both absolutists and radicals could be found on the same side when it came to property and its relationship to political representation and democracy. The best known, but also most profound, expression of these differences occurred among those who had won the English Civil War and were faced with the consequences of their actions. Although the King had not yet been executed, sentiment within the New Model Army was moving in a radical direction. But the army itself was divided between those radicals, represented by John Lilburne and the Levellers, who demanded an extensive franchise, though not necessarily a democratic one, and those who wanted a form of representative government circumscribed by property and other restrictions.[20] The importance of the Putney debates in 1647 in affecting subsequent events in England was probably negligible, but they are important in emphasising the centrality of property in alienating radicals from conservatives. It is also one of the first open debates concerning the nature of participatory structures and who should be in a position to influence electoral outcomes. Both sides of the debate, unlike that between absolutists and parliamentarians, were agreed on the source of political authority and legitimacy: the people. What was in dispute was how extensive the franchise would be. The radical democratic position was presented by Colonel Rainborough who claimed that:

> The poorest he that is in England has a life to live as the greatest he; and therefore truly, Sir, I think it's clear, that every man that is to live under a government ought first by his own consent to put himself under that government; and I do think that the poorest man in England is not at all bound in a strict sense to that government that he has not had a voice to put himself under . . .[21]

In contrast, Cromwell believed that anarchy would follow if there were no limits to representation. General Ireton insisted that these limits should be clear-cut and while all Englishmen should benefit from the basic rights available to all, there could be no general right to representation. Ireton is here using the same argument against the left that Charles I used against his critics:

> No person has a right to an interest or share in the disposing of the affairs of the kingdom, and in determining and choosing those that shall determine what laws we shall be ruled by here, no person has a right to this that has not a permanent fixed interest in this kingdom, and those persons together are properly the represented of this kingdom who, given together, and consequently are to make up the representatives of this kingdom; are the representatives who, taken together, do comprehend whatever is of real or permanent interest in the kingdom . . .

This 'real or permanent interest' was based on a property qualification and should not be accorded by right of birth. Birth and residence did grant one specific rights before the law, but this did not include the franchise. The fear of the propertyless, and of those who would be dependent and therefore not free, is palpable throughout and explicitly addressed by Colonel Rich. Claiming that only one in six had a permanent interest, the consequences were such as to threaten the property possessed by the minority:

> If the master and servant shall be equal electors, then clearly those that have no interest in the kingdom will make it their interest to choose those that have no interest. It may happen, that the majority may by law, not in a confusion, you may destroy property. There may be a law enacted, that shall be an equality of goods and estate[s].[22]

Subsequent events relayed the Putney debates to the margin of political evolution. The execution of the King and the establishment of the Commonwealth did not provide the basis for a new stabilisation of political forms. The failure to develop representative institutions under Cromwell meant that continuity was uncertain and the Restoration provided a fallback to traditional political patterns. Notwithstanding this, opinion was not sympathetic to absolute monarchy, whatever the feeling was about monarchy itself. The Glorious Revolution incorporated and confirmed the representative elements inherent in the parliamentary cause by creating a balance between king, lords and commons. This new consensus was based on a narrow electoral base, one solidly resting on landed property and indeed probably narrower than that proposed by Irlton. By 1700 the main tensions inherent in the seventeenth century conflicts had been resolved. Representative government was maintained and while the monarch continued to be influential and powerful, that power was clearly limited by the settlement which followed the deposition of James II and the imposition of William and Mary to the throne. Though not as radical an implication as the execution of Charles I, this action by parliament asserted the limits of monarchical power and the rights of the representatives to withdraw consent to that rule if the king did not fulfil certain obligations. This balance of power was unique in Europe at the time and is in strong contrast to the general trend towards absolutism in most continental states. The 'revolutionaries' also took great care that order would be assured and that continuity would be the key focus of what was a significant political change (there was no Putney debate on this occasion).

In this they were altogether successful, as Burke was to insist a century later.[23] The so called Bill of Rights and the Act of Settlement effectively ended the possibility of absolutism and established the context for representative government within an extremely limited institutional system. This was not conservative and the Whigs who designed it were not so either. What was not an issue at this time was political democracy. To return to the two axial principles, the source of authority is clear and the reformers had won out, but on the issue of a democratic franchise both Whigs and Tories were agreed on the principle of excluding the mass of the population from most aspects of participation. There is a further conservative implication to be drawn from the English experience. Though described as a revolution, the replacement of one monarch by another could be placed in a tradition not unknown in European affairs, the form and much of the substance remained, despite the changes. The Whig view of this, expressed classically by Burke, was that the change was legitimate, but more importantly that with the Act of Settlement there was little to change subsequently.[24]

Conservatism and modernity

The seventeenth century marks the beginning of the transition from the pre-modern to the modern. Although these concepts are slippery in analytical and historical terms, they retain importance for the emergence of conservatism. By the beginning of the eighteenth century the confrontation between the modern and the ancients had become clear, if not yet resolved. This was to be concluded during the Enlightenment, a victory which was to be reinforced by the transformation of Europe during the second half of the eighteenth century. The origins of modernity are surrounded in controversy and there is little agreement about what it means or how it came to be realised. With the arrival of post-modernity in the 1980s questions about what modernity actually is remain controversial. The forces which shaped modernity take form in the seventeenth century with the publication of Descartes', *Discourse on Method* and with the scientific revolutions associated with Galileo and Newton. Moreover, the English Civil War, the stabilisation of British aristocratic parliamentarianism and the establishment of the Dutch state through a war of liberation highlight the political aspects of this process. If for most of this time modernity was a state of mind (literary, philosophical and scientific), it also acquired a political tradition which broke with the older themes, perhaps best reflected in Locke's work at the end of the century.[25] In political terms Britain and the Netherlands were the exception to the successful reinforcement of monarchical and absolutist rule into the eighteenth century. For the most part, the impact of modernity on the political system remained indirect until the end of the eighteenth century. Yet imperceptibly modernity was insinuating itself into the fabric of the older society. It is perhaps no accident that during the eighteenth century the first systematic demands for civil liberty, constitutions and the rule of law are made. By the end of that century Kant could take it for granted that a rational political order would include several criteria which are now associated with republican or liberal politics.[26] A new view of the world was emerging from these considerations, one which assumed with greater confidence that the rational transformation of nature, of the political system and of humanity was not only possible but desirable. The consequence of such thinking was that intervention in society and politics to achieve designated ends was considered appropriate. Whether such was defined in terms of reform or revolution the end product was similar: the transformation of the existing social environment. Such attitudes openly challenged the pre-modern political system which rested its authority on hierarchy, military power and absolutism.

Since the French Revolution, change has become central to the European experience. Consequently Hobbes's dictum no longer applies in its original form, though his approbation does. Indeed in most areas of public life instability has been the most prominent feature of the last two centuries. The world has been turned upside down, but also transformed. In the economy industrialisation and economic development replaced agriculture as the mainstay of growth, while in politics the shift has been from a limited style of politics to an activist and inclusive one. Change, progress and revolution have become acceptable terms to describe the political environment, whereas 200 years ago each of these was still used negatively more often than not.[27] Isaiah Berlin notes that this process began with the Reformation and was accelerated by the Renaissance and the scientific revolutions which followed:

> All of this culminated in the most transforming event of all – the French Revolution, which exploded, or at the very least profoundly altered, some of the most deeply rooted presuppositions and concepts by which men lived. It made men acutely conscious of change and excited interest in the laws that governed it.[28]

The focus is on the shift from one to the other, and on the general rules which govern one system rather than another. This should not be seen in a determinist fashion, but as contextual. Ernest Gellner has recently sought to outline this context:

> Human history is a play in which the cast tends to increase over time and within which constraints seem to be imposed on the *order* in which the characters appear. The theorists of human society cannot introduce them in any old order at will. Some changes are at least relatively irreversible: . . .

Gellner's approach is materialist but not determinist:

in the sense that it assumes and claims that each of the three crucial productive bases – hunting/gathering, agriculture, scientific/industrial production – bestows on the societies which use it radically different sets of problems and constraints, and hence that societies of fundamentally different kinds can usefully be treated as three fundamentally different species. But the argument makes no preliminary assumptions as to which sphere of human activity – production, coercion, cognition – is crucial, either in the maintenance and continuity of societies or in bringing forth new forms.[29]

Capitalist industrialism imposes certain constraints on what a society might easily do or what it might wish to do if and only if it wishes to participate in that particular productive system. However, if a society does participate there are costs as well as benefits in doing so. Some societies will receive considerable benefits while others will be discomforted by the changes which it will have to undergo.

This process is often described as modernity and it is as a process that it has to be understood. Anthony Giddens suggests that a distinction should be made between the traditional state and the modern state. For Giddens the modern state emerged in the late eighteenth century and takes on specific form in the course of the nineteenth and twentieth centuries. For him the absolute monarchies are not modern, though they might contain some features of the modern they remain traditional in a fundamental way. There is a striking discontinuity in this transformation, characterised by the features which have shaped the modern world, 'capitalism, industrialism and the nation state system'. Each of these interact to provide a type of society which is at variance with the previously existing and dominant one. Giddens has conceptualised this by distinguishing between a 'class divided society' (i.e. pre-modern) and a 'capitalist society'. The former is characterised by a ruling class, lack of class conflict, the severance of the political from the economic, low alienability of property, the absence of labour markets, while the main sanction available to the state is the control of the means of violence. In contrast to this the modern age can be characterised in a different fashion. There is a governing class, endemic class conflict, separation of the political from the economic, property is freely alienable as capital, the labour market governs occupational allocation, and the economic necessity of employment is the main sanction.[30]

If discontinuity is the main characteristic of this period, then capitalism, the emergence of a new form of economic organisation, is the main instrument promoting change. Capitalism transformed the way in which economic exchange took place, forcing even the most traditional economies to adapt to the exigencies of the new system. However, for our purposes the economic consequences are not the most important aspect of this process. Far more important are the relationships between this global transformation and the emergence of the modern state and activist politics. Paralleling the growth of capitalism, in part a product of and in part a response to it, it is possible to identify the nation state, popular sovereignty (democracy), and an intrusive state bureaucracy as aspects of this phenomenon.

What is characteristic of capitalism, nationalism and democracy is the transformative power of their appeal. Whether it is the market, elections or national identity each of these challenge the foregoing commitment to stability and continuity. Industrialism not only changes the conditions under which economic activity takes place, it changes the class structure, generates new sources of wealth and power and integrates specific geographical areas into both international and domestic markets. This in turn places new political questions on the agenda, both for traditionalists (how to deal with disruption) and for radicals (how to realise the potential of the changes). It has often been noted that movements for the reform of the British political system existed from the mid-eighteenth century, yet what is rarely remarked is how ineffectual they were. One reason for this is the extent to which Britain, perhaps the most modern of the European states, remained within the traditional state system allowing the old elites to resist the demands for fundamental change.[31]

It may be no accident that reform comes after Britain has experienced the transformative impact of both the industrial and French revolutions. The dominance of market criteria challenged the corporatist assumptions which prevailed in most places, even the most advanced at the end of the eighteenth century. Nationalism provided a secure haven for individuals to associate and create new political identities. Democracy legitimised these new identities and facilitated the inclusion within the polity of excluded majorities. Giddens stresses the notion of a 'capitalist society' and defines it as one where 'industrial capitalism is the main motor of production'. Furthermore, on this analysis the commodification of labour power is one of the fundamental elements of discontinuity, 'that separate modernity from pre-existing forms of socio-economic order'.[32] Modernity on this account should not be equated with modernisation theory, and does not presuppose any specific stages of growth or otherwise. In other words if industrial society is compared with agrarian society, the political and cultural forms which are embedded in it will be as diverse as those embedded in any other system. If, as I would urge in this chapter, capitalism is central to modernity then so also are nationalism and democracy. In one sense democracy does not necessarily entail representative institutions, but political authorities claim to speak in the name of the people and to some particular ideological purpose. Indeed it is nationalism rather than representative democracy which appears to give coherence to this sense of identity, and it is not fortuitous or contingent that nationalism appears at just the same time as revolution, democracy and liberalism. To cite Giddens again:

> The disintegrative impact which is wrought upon preexisting traditional cultures by modern economic and political development creates a search for renewed forms of group symbolism, of which nationalism is the most potent. Nationalism engenders a spirit of solidarity and collective commitment which is energetically mobilising in circumstances of cultural decay.[33]

In response to change, groups which were dependent on the traditional and familiar productive and political frameworks recoiled from the consequences of modernity. Change certainly threatened elites who felt this inconvenience, but also peasants and tradesmen dislocated by the rapidly changing environment. Not only was this change disruptive and cumulative, but because it reflected a new productive structure the traditional methods of responding to the changes were usually inadequate. Even prior to the French Revolution individuals and groups were groping for a way of dealing with the phenomenon which we call modernity.

John Gray has argued, convincingly in my opinion, that liberalism, while having its origins in the seventeenth century, becomes by the early nineteenth century the main carrier of modernity. The main elements of liberalism can be briefly summarised as individualism, egalitarianism in the sense that legal or political distinction based on race or class are unacceptable, a universalist commitment to the moral unity of the human species, and the possibility of improvement and progress. Gray points to the defining features of this ideology as the main contributor not only to the political theory of modernity, but also, though not explicitly, to the disruptive impact of that ideology:

> Its postulates are the most distinctive features of modern life – the autonomous individual and his concern for liberty and privacy, the growth of wealth and the steady stream of inventions and innovations, the machinery of government which is at once indispensable to civil life and a standing threat to it – and its intellectual outlook is one that could have originated in its fullness only in the post-traditional society of Europe after the dissolution of medieval christendom. [34]

Though liberalism in its various forms effectively contested the intellectual dominance of traditional society, that society did not collapse of its own inertia. Indeed, well before the nineteenth century there were those who actively defended that traditional society. The crisis of the late eighteenth century is but the most profound of the series which began with the Reformation and which accelerated towards the end of the eighteenth century. While liberals and radicals were developing their critique of what actually existed, there were those intent on defending the present against the perceived instabilities of the future. It is only when society divides on significant matters that it is possible to identify and locate radicals and conservatives. Those on the right were intent on preserving what actually existed of the traditional society such as the established church, the monarchy, and limited elite political participation. These were specific elements of the old regime, but conservatives were also intent on defending something more basic: the values which underpinned the very nature of that society. Thus, for conservatives crisis and breakdown could be evidence for the value of the older institutions as the anarchy which prevailed did little to improve the overall lot of that society.[35]

The political origins of conservatism can also be located in the continuing presence of pre-modern forces well into the nineteenth, and indeed into the twentieth century. Radicals have generally believed that traditional influence would quickly disappear once exposed by the evidence of their behaviour or actions. If kings were corrupt and the churches venal, all that was necessary was to expose them and the masses, once emancipated from that influence, would be liberated to follow the dictates of reason. At the risk of parody, it is clear that many of the leading publicists in the continental Enlightenment believed this.[36] But what is significant is not whether they were correct or not, but the continuing influence of pre-modern forces and their ability to organise opposition to reform and other elements of modernity. Even after a revolution such as that experienced by France, there remains a strong sense of continuity, though it can be argued that this was more superficial than real as subsequent political changes up to 1848 demonstrate. What is clear is the extent to which conservative forces realign after significant political changes and are able to influence the political evolution of a society, often in the simply negative sense of preventing further change, but also more positively by contributing to change itself and affecting the context of change by their own participation.[37]

The origins of political conservatism must be sought at that moment in historical time when capitalism, liberalism and democracy become contested issues for European politics. After their entry on the political scene there emerges alternative sets of values which, when embodied in political ideology framed the alternating power structures of the nineteenth century. While there is no full resolution of the conflict between conservatism and liberalism by 1914, the parameters of the conflict had been structured and a complex mosaic of political allegiance established. Conservatism is an outgrowth of conflict with liberalism, not as in the twentieth century with socialism. It is the values of the new society, usually described as liberal, which the right and conservatives generally wish to transform, change or destroy. Perhaps the foundation of conservatism can be attributed symbolically to the traditional response to Rousseau's best known if misleading claim that 'man is born free; and everywhere he is in chains'. The claim that the past is tyrannical, or something similar, has been central to the radical critique of actually existing society since then. The response of Edmund Burke reflects a very different sense of what it means to be born into a community: for him each individual owes a debt to the past, and it is one that is carried into the future.[38]

The conservative could counter with the claim that not only are we not born free, but every individual carries a considerable social and intellectual heritage into the world at birth. In traditional societies this did not pose a real problem for the community, and the political environment was rarely if ever questioned. However, with the disruption of the modern age there emerged those who sought to defend what is and the traditions which remained embedded in that community. One of the fears of conservatives during the eighteenth century was that the scepticism of the Enlightenment would lead to the destruction of all authority. The Cartesian method in particular, it was feared, would lead not only to scepticism, but to atheism and anarchy. Reason, when juxtaposed to tradition, rejected the past and with it the institutions, norms and values which many believed sustained order. This unease has both personal and theoretical aspects to it. There will always be individuals, and perhaps groups and nations, who will resist change whatever that might be. This conservatism cannot and is not the basis for political conservatism. However, it reflects an inflexibility towards one's own socialisation, even when the very proponents of such attitudes themselves do deny that they are socialised. Furthermore, it also draws attention to an attitude of mind which has political consequences, the claim that the past or a traditional way of life has merit and should be recognised as such.[39]

To choose to wear a particular hat or tie (or not) may identify the individual as eccentric, but to organise politically to promote the wearing of such may be a political statement. When it is closely associated with the restoration or protection of the king, Church, land and property it can constitute a political programme of some importance. The link between the personal and the political or collective is difficult to make, but does exist. Individuals behave as collective units after they make decisions about themselves. This is not to say that individuals join a counter-revolution merely because they dislike the clothing style of the other side, but it can contribute to it. A dislike of such style can confirm for the individual that life might not be worth living if such people came to power or were allowed to continue in power. Fashion merely symbolises the problem rather than addresses it. Uneasiness concerning change does not always turn into counter-revolution, or into political form. It does so because something tangible is challenged. For some this is property, but it can also involve status or power. While this is certainly a contributing factor, it is not the only one. For example the reaction of the Vendee to the French Revolution and the willingness of the peasantry to wage what was effectively a religious war against the new regime can only in part be attributed to property relations in that area of France. What is detectable even in the work of those who advocate an economic explanation for these events is a complex cultural response mediated as much through religious affiliation as by property and the fear of confiscation or other adverse consequences from the changes taking place.[40]

It is possible to dismiss this, and other examples from Spain and Italy, as merely false consciousness or religious bigotry. However the real reason may rest elsewhere, in the socio-political beliefs which a society has internalised and its refusal to accept a new version of belief. What is at issue here is the past, and the extent to which the past continues to prove acceptable to significant sections of society. If only the elite was disturbed by the political changes taking place they would not be in a strong position to counter the revolution. Alternatively, if the former rulers can count on more than military power they are in a strong position to contest the new disposition. Even at moments of 'intense political mobilisation' the past can have a dramatic effect on the extent to which traditional norms will be defended. Charles Maier distinguishes two components which accompany this shift in consciousness:

> The first (but not necessarily first chronologically) amounts to a change in collective mentality. It involves the discovery of what seems virtually a natural (or at least imposed) order of subordination and hierarchy which has no justification beyond its mere persistence. Accompanying this awareness is the burst of conviction that institutions need not be cages, that people acting together can break out of them and 'make history'.

Maier points out subsequently that this 'anarchistic moment', though vital, is inevitably followed by stabilisation.[41] Stabilisation is usually what conservatives are seeking after the threat or actuality of radical change. But prior to this, the break enumerated by Maier is frequently met by resistance on the part of at least one section of society. The dawn of freedom for the revolutionary appears as the twilight of civilisation for the conservative. This division is frequently cemented into political alignments which lead to stabilisation on terms dictated by one or the other or by a composite outcome.[42]

Conservatism as a mode of political thought

While the sources of stabilisation can be located in the institutions or rule which acquire post-revolutionary legitimacy, another cause is the already embedded sense of traditional order which, while challenged by the revolution, often continues to carry an important resonance for many people. The success of counter-revolution, though often attributed to force, may also be a result of this embedded reality continuing to maintain a dominance at least among a section of divided people. The search for stability, even in revolutionary times, is not always the search for something new. It may be expressed in different form, but it often draws on the past. The example of Napoleon's empire with its use of traditional symbols while continuing to express the main themes of the revolution is but a case in point. In theoretical terms, conservatism continues to maintain the values of the past, its customs, traditions and prejudices in the face of this modernity. Burke comes closest to understanding the attraction of what exists for political mobilisation when faced with revolution himself. He claimed that despite the Enlightenment emphasis on reason 'we are generally men of unthought feelings'. While he did not ignore reason, he concluded that human action was not solely or indeed generally motivated by reason. On the contrary it is prejudice rather than reason which is the main guide to action. As such Burke confronts the whole intellectual basis for the Enlightenment urging:

> that instead of casting away all our old prejudices we cherish them to a very considerable degree, and, to take more shame to ourselves, we cherish them because they are prejudices; and the longer they have lasted, and the more generally they have prevailed, the more we cherish them.

For Burke prejudice has a somewhat different meaning from that which is used today. He concludes that 'individuals would do better to avail themselves of the general banking capital of nations, and of ages'. This is an insistence that the past can offer a guide to the present and that there is no logical reason why an institution should be destroyed simply because it is old. Indeed Burke would argue quite strongly that this is a very good reason for leaving well enough alone. He suggests that if reason is applied to prejudice it is more than likely that the prejudice will be maintained and justified by reason:

> Because prejudice, with its reason, has a motive to give action to that reason, and an affection which will give it permanence. Prejudice is of ready application in the emergency; it previously engages the mind in a steady course of wisdom and virtue, and does not leave the man hesitating in the moment of decision, skeptical, puzzled, and unresolved. Prejudice renders a man's virtue his habit; and not a series of unconnected acts. Through just prejudice, his duty becomes a part of his nature.[43]

Prejudice and bias have negative associations in the modern world. Since the Enlightenment they have come to denote judgements which are unfounded and consequently lack a scientific basis. To say that the world is flat or that creationism is a more adequate explanation for the existence of humans on the earth are examples of bias or prejudice in the sense that the judgements are unfounded and/or unscientific. The basis for this reaction against prejudice lies in the growth of the modern scientific method and philosophically in Cartesian rationalism. According to this method of reasoning, prejudice leads to error because it overly depended on prior authority or leapt to conclusions without adequate investigation. Both were mistaken, especially when applied to scientific endeavour.

This view has been elaborated more recently by Gadamer who observed that this has led to a 'prejudice against prejudice', particularly in the realm of human behaviour, and for the purposes of this argument in the specific realm of politics. Gadamer argues that the pre-Enlightenment meaning of prejudice has only a tangential relationship to the way it has been used subsequently. In English, French and German, prejudice meant to prejudge on the basis of the information available, but without necessarily having all the evidence to hand which would conclusively allow one to draw conclusions from this. It does not mean that the judgement is necessarily false or unsound, though this is now the meaning ascribed to it. The Enlightenment bias against tradition, authority and prejudice prevents the modernist from accepting bias as part of an intellectual framework which is justifiable and worthy of respect. To be value free or objective remains central to most intellectual endeavours which are aimed at securing the truth or falsity of a question. In the natural sciences this claim has been easier to verify as it is in the nature of the process that an experiment can be verified by other workers in the field.[44]

Yet history, which is applied politics, cannot be open to the type of verification which would satisfy the natural scientist. Here the element of subjectivity is stronger and affects the entire process:

> In fact history does not belong to us, but we belong to it. Long before we understand ourselves through the process of self examination, we understand ourselves in a self evident way in the family, society and state in which we live. The focus of subjectivity is a distorting mirror, the self awareness of the individual is only a flickering in the closed circuits of historical life. That is why the prejudices of the individual, far more than his judgments, constitute the historical reality of his being.[45]

These historical realities can be 'legitimate prejudices' when they allow individuals to accept authority which is securely grounded and takes precedence over one's own opinion at that moment in time. Thus Gadamer insists that authority need not be either arbitrary or irrational, but when embodied in a specific tradition can be a positive element in the life of a community and the individual:

> Tradition is not simply a pre-condition into which we come, but we produce it ourselves, in so much as we understand, participate in the evolution of tradition and hence further to determine it ourselves.[46]

What is here identified as a type of dynamic tradition is in fact the sense of continuity that the well ordered society insists on and around which, in times of social change or revolution, and reactionary politics focus. However, to accept this should not lead to the rejection of tradition or the prejudice of accepting it as a normal feature of political division in modern society. When Burke uses prejudice it is in the sense applied here, not in the negative sense acquired subsequently.

In terms of political mobilisation, prejudice becomes imperative at times of crisis. The radical rejects authority and all the intellectual and social associations that go with it. However, if the radical rejects the past, this is not the case for everyone and the source of modern conservatism can be located in the refusal of large groups of individuals to do just that. Prejudice at its best is a provisional response to a political problem. No one can refrain from an opinion when events affect them in whatever context. They will look to their prejudices and prejudge the events in that light. They will further seek to accommodate what is happening within the constellation of beliefs which underlie these prejudgements. If we are unable to match the events to these judgements it does not mean that the judgements are false, but it does mean that rejection is the most likely outcome of that assessment. In most cases accommodation or amendment takes place, but at crucial periods or disjunctures, this proves to be impossible and consequently the individual moves into the conservative camp as a self-conscious partisan of the traditional view against what is now on offer.[47]

There is a further layer to the human condition which affects the growth of a conservative political movement. This occurs when a political movement, an ideology or a piece of legislation runs counter to firmly held views on the part of significant sections of the population. Progressives or radicals often describe this reaction as prejudice in the pejorative sense of that term, and it is frequently the case that the individual or group will not be able to offer a concrete or fully reasoned answer to the legislation or reform (abortion or divorce would be good examples of this). This brings us up against what R.G. Collingwood has called Absolute Presuppositions, those elements which an individual or society have internalised without thinking of their origin or the need to defend them; they simply are. There is accordingly no need to justify absolute presuppositions: 'the distinction between truth and falsehood does not apply to absolute presuppositions'. However, their importance should not be underrated, they are the foundation stones of political and social order and are interfered with at the risk of danger to the stability of that system.[48]

Collingwood was not here concerned with conservatism or indeed with political change. Absolute presuppositions could be religious beliefs, or scientific axioms: in each case they provide the foundation upon which life is lived or study carried out. Yet they seem to fulfil an essential condition for the growth of conservatism, and perhaps in all societies they establish a foundation which is not questioned and consequently provide the basis for stability. When it is challenged, the challenge may be seen as incomprehensible, for it is an instinctive but not irrational source of order. As Collingwood himself pointed out absolute presuppositions change with great difficulty, if at all:

> People are not ordinarily aware of their absolute presuppositions, and are not, therefore, thus aware of changes in them; such a change, therefore, cannot be a matter of choice. Nor is there anything superficial or frivolous about it. It is the most radical change a man can undergo, and entails the abandonment of all his most firmly established habits and standards for thought and action.

It is these circumstances which give rise to the radical challenge to society, but they also mobilise opinion in defence of existing institutions. In politics there is never a clear-cut break with the past, and the confrontation between revolution and counter-revolution or between radical and conservative has to be appreciated as a normal process of political life, even in a non-democratic environment.

Change takes place because of 'strains' which affect the overall structure. In political terms a 'strain' emerges when the absolute presuppositions of a society no longer acquire the near unanimous assent of that society. Collingwood may have been mistaken to believe that absolute presuppositions are never questioned; what may happen is that once they are questioned they cease to be absolute presuppositions, and are then open to contestation by different political arguments and groups. One example of this would be the questioning of the absolute presuppositions of Newtonian physics by the Einsteinean system. Prior to the publication of the theories of relativity, Newtonian mechanics remained the (largely) unquestioned foundation of physics, afterwards a new 'paradigm' emerges. Politics clearly does not work in the same fashion as that of scientific revolutions, but the analogy will serve. However, because human behaviour in politics is not like physics there is greater room for dispute and, consequently, when a new paradigm emerges in politics various groups will align themselves along a continuum from the old to the new. Conservatives and radicals are aligned in this way but, unlike Einsteinean physics which quickly asserted its dominance, there is no guarantee that the new concept will become an unquestioned absolute presupposition.[49]

This is to claim that there is a significant difference in the nature of truth and politics. An ideologist may believe that truth is possible, but the reality seems to be that individuals do not have an internally consistent view of what truth may be. Berlin suggests that this basically utopian approach to politics is inaccurate and is based on a partial view of the way questions above politics are normally addressed. He believes that the tradition which underwrites utopian ideology in the West is flawed by its basic assumptions, which stress the uniqueness of truth. For all its historic importance, rationalism does not provide an adequate explanation for political behaviour, or for the institutions which societies create to give expression to this. It is not therefore possible to translate the axioms of natural science into those of political behaviour. Perhaps the most important reason for this is that cultural values intrude to give different meaning to the behaviour of different groups:

> There are many things which men do have in common, but that is not what matters most. What individualises them, makes them what they are, makes communication possible, is what they do not have in common with all the others. Differences, peculiarities, nuances, individual character are all in all.[50]

This approach does not necessarily lead to radical relativism. In politics it is necessary to appreciate that there may be no single way of obtaining a specific end and that a structure which seeks to propose one over another may ignore all the truths. What this means in the context of the growth of conservative politics is that radicalism tended to dismiss political interests as irrational or as prejudices and this in turn led to a reaction, not just in the immediate response to the specific event but over the longer term. Left and right may not be useful terms in this context if they are taken to mean good and bad or progressive or reactionary. If they designate specific means to problem-solving in a political context then they may be more understandable.

If to 'make history' is to favour change, reform or revolution, what place exists in the political constellation for those who 'resist' history? Traditionalists, conservatives and the right seem, in this context, to be reactionary in their attempt to obstruct progress. In particular, conservatism does not have the transformational qualities of those ideologies which emerge directly from modernity: liberalism, socialism and nationalism. The characteristic feature of modern ideology is its transformational promise, something not shared by conservatism. This, however, does not mean that conservatism is not an ideology, only that it is not transformational in intent. There is an ideological purpose to conservatism which involves limiting the appeal and impact of modernity and to reject, or at the very least modify, its progressive objectives. Conservatism also has a philosophical basis in its scepticism concerning reason, which it counters by its emphasis on culture and history. In social terms it juxtaposes tradition to modernity, while in political terms limited forms of government have been preferred to mass democracy. Despite this, conservatism has a symbiotic relationship with modernity. Though deriving its intellectual strength and political power from pre-modern forces, it cannot be separated from the process of modernity itself. It is the political response of culture and tradition to reason and modernity. While conservatism works against modernity, it also operates within it, and by doing so modifies, influences and changes that structure. The clash of the modern with the traditional does not lead to the victory of one over the other, but in the course of the 200 years since the eighteenth century has led to a blending and influence which has affected both the left and the right and which has had a decisive impact on the evolution of democratic politics.

Although conservatism originates as a reactionary movement seeking to destroy modernity, it has been forced to accommodate itself to some of these forces, though often reluctantly. In turn, to accommodate the assault by conservatives the radical or reformer has had to interact with forces which are repugnant to it, but which in turn modify its force and direction. A further consideration, which will be referred to later in this book, is that the relationship between conservatism (as a political philosophy) and the political right is an historically contingent one. Some recent studies have suggested that in the second half of the twentieth century this contingent relationship has broken down. If this is so, it has profound implications for conservatism and modernity at the end of this century.[51] Notwithstanding this, for most of the period under review here conservatism and right-wing politics do in fact overlap, though the relationship is both complex and fluid. For much of the period conservatism continues to resist modernity. This can be highlighted by the continued resistance of conservative and right-wing politics to the implications of liberal democracy and the problems posed by power and participation in the modern era.

Notes

1. John Stuart Mill, *On Liberty* ed. Gertrude Himmelfarb (Harmondsworth: Penguin Classics, 1974 [1859]), p. 110.
2. As will become clear in the text I believe there are conceptual problems in reducing right-wing politics to conservatism and identifying the two. Not all right-wing political formations are conservative, nor are all conservatives right-wing. For definitional purposes right wing and conservative are used interchangeably in a number of chapters in this book. Where the relationship breaks down I have sought for a redefinition of the terms. Some of the conceptual difficulties are addressed in Roger Eatwell and Noël O'Sullivan (eds), *The Nature of the Right* (London: Pinter,

1989), pp. 47–76; examples of right wing and conservative thought are collected in Robert L. Schuettinger (ed.), *The Conservative Tradition in European Thought* (New York: G.P. Putnams, 1975); Hans Rogger and Eugen Weber (eds), *The European Right* (Berkeley and Los Angeles: University of California Press, 1966).

3. Robert A. Dahl (ed.), *Political Opposition in Western Democracies* (New Haven: Yale University Press, 1966). This difficulty continues into the present as can be seen from the transition to democracy in Eastern Europe and the former Soviet Union.

4. Frank Bealey, 'Stability and crisis: fears about the threats to democracy', *European Journal of Political Research* 15:6 (1987), pp. 687–715; Alan Ware, 'Liberal democracy: one form or many', *Political Studies* XL (1992), Special Issue, pp. 130–45.

5. Robert J. Goldstein, *Political Repression in Nineteenth Century Europe* (London: Croom Helm, 1983), assesses the conditions for democratic government. Bealey, op. cit., reviews the global context in the twentieth century.

6. Jaroslav Krejcí, 'Introduction: concepts of right and left', Luciano Cheles et al., (eds), *Neo-Fascism in Europe* (London: Longman, 1991), pp. 1–18; Albert O. Hirschman, *The Rhetoric of Reaction: Perversity, Futility, Jeopardy* (Cambridge, Mass.: Harvard University Press, 1991).

7. Ted Honderich, *Conservatism* (London: Hamish Hamilton, 1990), p. 1; Michael Freeman, *Edmund Burke and the Critique of Political Radicalism* (Oxford: Basil Blackwell, 1980), pp. 54–83.

8. Jonathan Kingdom, *Self-Made Man and His Undoing* (London: Simon and Schuster, 1993), pp. 94–123. For a different approach which compliments some aspects of Kingdom's see Jared Diamond, *The Rise and Fall of the Third Chimpanzee* (London: Vintage, 1991).

9. John A. Hall, *Powers and Liberties* (Harmondsworth: Penguin, 1986).

10. Tilo Schabert, 'Modernity and history 1: what is modernity?' in Athanasios Moulakis (ed.), *The Promise of History: Essays in Political Philosophy* (Berlin: Walter de Gruyter, 1985), pp. 9–21.

11. Thomas Hobbes, *Leviathan* ed. C.B. Macpherson (Harmondsworth: Penguin, 1968. [1651]), pp. 379–80.

12. W.E.H. Lecky, *Rationalism in Europe* (London: Longmans, Green, 1913 [1865]); Stephen Toulmin, *Cosmopolis: The Hidden Agenda of Modernity and Culture* (New York: Free Press, 1990).

13. Trevor Ashton (ed.), *Crisis in Europe: 1560–1660* (London: Routledge and Kegan Paul, 1965); Charles Tilley, *Revolutions in Europe, 1492–1992* (Oxford: Blackwell, 1993).

14. Cited in David Wootton (ed.), *Divine Right and Democracy* (Harmondsworth: Penguin, 1986), pp. 101.

15. ibid, pp. 107–10.

16. Tilley, op. cit., pp. 52–78 for Dutch revolt and consequences.

17. Cited in Wootton, p. 337

18. Wootton, op. cit., pp. 121, 437–9.

19. Sidney advocated an open form of government, but not necessarily a democratic one, ibid., p. 426.

20. C.B. Macpherson, *The Political Theory of Possessive Individualism, Hobbes to Locke* (Oxford: Oxford University Press, 1962); Mark Kishlansky, 'The case of the army truly stated: the creation of the new model army', *Past and Present* 81 (November, 1978), pp. 51-74; Blair Worden, 'Providence and Politics in Cromwellian England', *Past and Present* 109 (November, 1985), pp. 55-99.

21. Wootton, op. cit., p. 286.

22. The debate can be followed in Wootton, op. cit., pp. 287–97.

23. 'Resolution of the House of Commons, 28 January 1689', cited in B.W. Hill (ed.),

Edmund Burke on Government, Politics and Society (Glasgow: Fontana, 1975), p. 291.

24. J.H. Plumb, *The Growth of Political Stability in England: 1675–1725* (London: Macmillan, 1967); Hill, op cit., pp. 280–86 for Burke's defence of the Glorious Revolution; Conor Cruise O'Brien, *The Great Melody: A Thematic Biography of Edmund Burke* (London: Sinclair-Stevenson, 1992), pp. 440-50, 479–80.

25. Toulmin, op. cit., pp. 5–44; Ernest Gellner, *Reason and Culture* (Oxford: Blackwell, 1992), pp. 1–29; Joseph Schwartz, *The Creative Moment* (London: Jonathan Cape, 1992), pp. 1–34.

26. Immanuel Kant, 'Idea for a universal history with a cosmopolitan purpose' (1784); 'Perpetual peace: a philosophical sketch' (1795–6). Both essays appear in Hans Reiss (ed.), *Kant: Political Writings* (Cambridge: Cambridge University Press, 1991).

27. Noël O'Sullivan, 'An introductory essay: revolution and modernity' in O'Sullivan (ed.), *Revolutionary Theory and Political Reality* (Brighton: Wheatsheaf, 1983), pp. 3–22.

28. Isaiah Berlin, 'The bent twig: on the rise of nationalism', in Berlin, *The Crooked Timber of Humanity* (London: John Murray, 1990), p. 238; E.J. Hobsbawm, *Nations and Nationalism since 1780* (Cambridge: Cambridge University Press, 1990).

29. Ernest Gellner, *Plough, Sword and Book: The Structure of Human History* (London: Paladin, 1991), pp. 13–14, quotation at p. 20.

30. Anthony Giddens, *The Nation State and Violence* (Cambridge: Polity Press, 1985), p. 64. Adapted from Table 2.

31. Albert O. Hirschman, 'Rival interpretations of market society: civilizing, destructive or feeble?' *Journal of Economic Literature* vol. XX (December 1982), pp. 1463–84; Linda Colley, *Britons: Forging the Nation 1707–1837* (New Haven: Yale University Press, 1992), pp. 106–13; George Rudé, *Wilkes and Liberty* (Oxford: Oxford University Press, 1962).

32. Giddens, op cit., pp. 142-3, 145.

33. Ibid., p. 215. For an historical analysis of this process cf. Hobsbawm, op. cit. passim.

34. John Gray, *Liberalism* (Milton Keynes: Open University Press, 1986), pp. x, 82; Stephen Holmes, *The Anatomy of Antiliberalism* (Cambridge, Mass: Harvard University Press, 1993) for an exposition of the liberal case and its critics.

35. Hirschman, op. cit., pp. 1–10, has identified various responses by conservatives to change and upheaval.

36. Gellner, *Reason and Culture*, op. cit., pp. 55-96, discusses these beliefs in detail; P.N. Furbank, *Diderot* (London: Martin Secker and Warburg, 1992); Voltaire, *Philosophical Dictionary* (Harmondsworth: Penguin, 1972).

37. Robert Nisbet, *Conservatism: Dream and Reality* (Milton Keynes: Open University Press, 1986) argues for the continuing significance of a specifically conservative approach to politics in the modern age.

38. Freeman, op. cit., pp. 16–53; Hiram Caton, *The Politics of Progress: The Origins and Development of the Commercial Republic, 1660–1835* (Gainesville: University of Florida Press, 1988).

39. A version of sentimental nostalgia as conservatism can be appreciated in Michael Oakeshott, 'On Being Conservative' in *idem.*, *Rationalism in Politics and Other Essays* (London: Macmillan, 1962), pp. 168–96.

40. Barrington Moore Jr, *Social Origins of Dictatorship and Democracy* (Harmondsworth: Allen Lane, 1967), pp. 92–101; Charles Tilley, *The Vendee* (Cambridge Mass: Harvard University Press, 1964); Simon Shama, *Citizens* (London: Penguin, 1989), pp. 690–706; T.J.A. Le Goff and D.M.G. Sutherland, 'The social origins of counter-revolution in western France', *Past and Present 99*

(May, 1983), pp. 65–87.
41. Charles S. Maier, 'Why stability' in Maier, *idem.*, *In Search of Stability* (Cambridge: Cambridge University Press, 1987), pp. 271–2.
42. The conscious element in the counter-revolutionary should not be underestimated in an analysis of behaviour. It is just as conscious an effort to reject the new as it is to embrace it. Furthermore, the individual acts to make a decision before he or she participates in revolution, counter-revolution or evades participation, only then is collective action possible.
43. Edmund Burke, *Reflections on the Revolution in France*, Conor Cruise O'Brien (ed.) (Harmondsworth: Penguin, 1968 [1790]), p. 183.
44. For example, recent claims that fusion energy could be harnessed were discounted when scientists proved unable to duplicate the findings.
45. Hans Georg Gadamer, *Truth and Method* (London: Sheed and Ward, 1975) p. 245.
46. Ibid., p. 261.
47. For a full treatment of this issue, Gadamer, op. cit., pp. 238–61.
48. R.G. Collingwood, *An Essay on Metaphysics* (Oxford: Oxford University Press, 1940), p. 32; Michael Krausz, 'The logic of absolute presuppositions' in M. Krausz (ed.), *Critical Essays on the Philosophy of R.G. Collingwood* (Oxford: Clarendon Press, 1972), pp. 222–40; Brian Girvin, 'Continuity and change in liberal democratic political culture' in John R. Gibbins (ed.), *Contemporary Political Culture* (London: Sage, 1989), pp. 31–51, for a specific application of this view to liberal democratic states. However, the application need not be restricted to liberal democracy.
49. Thomas S. Kuhn, *The Structure of Scientific Revolutions*, 2nd edn (Chicago: University of Chicago Press, 1970).
50. Berlin, op. cit., pp. 24–34, 39; Jacob Bronowski, *The Identity of Man* (Harmondsworth: Penguin, 1967), p. 36 on the relationship between the search for truth and certainty and the discovery of knowledge.
51. Torbjörn Tännsjö, *Conservatism in Our Time* (London: Routledge, 1990), p. ix; Trevor Blackwell and Jeremy Seabrook, *The Revolt Against Change: Towards a Conserving Radicalism* (London: Vintage, 1993). One of the interesting features of both these books is that the authors are in a left-wing tradition.

2 The Contours of the Right 1777–1914

Introduction

European politics entered a period of sustained crisis as a consequence of the events surrounding the American War of Independence. American independence exposed the strains in the traditional political order, influencing European radical thought for a considerable period. However, the strains in Europe were deeper than this, for the Enlightenment, the scientific revolution and industrialisation all combined with liberal politics to challenge the presuppositions of the political order. This radicalism, though directed at absolutism, also affected the restricted and traditional nature of aristocratic parliamentarianism in Britain and elsewhere. Thus, during the second half of the eighteenth century a political cleavage emerged between the defenders of existing institutions, whether moderate or not, and those who challenged that *status quo*. What is evident is the growth of ideological poles around conservatism and reform, though as yet the terms had not acquired their later meaning. Articulate conservative opinion already prior to the French Revolution had developed an intellectual defence of the existing environment, though until the cataclysm of the revolution this form of thought was on the defensive.

It takes a revolution to clarify the loyalty of individuals and groups. Divisions emerge within states, but also states once hostile to one another find common cause in the face of a new threat. In 1763 two alternative forms of political rule were available to Europeans, absolutism or aristocratic parliamentarianism; by the end of the century a wide variety of forms had been experimented with and were now influential. For the most part, reformers had considered the British model the most adequate alternative to absolutism, but the example of America and later the French Revolution reduced that appeal. The influence of republican and democratic forms of government increased, while traditional forms appeared inadequate to the needs of radicals who now wished to transform the political environment, rather than simply reform it.[1]

Conservatism in a revolutionary era

Ironically, the break with traditional politics occurred in the British Empire which, in 1763, was probably the strongest power in Europe. Its new dominance was challenged, not by the absolutist powers, but by the republican sentiment of its own settlers in North America. While taxation was the cause of conflict, identity and representation were at the heart of the struggle. Within a decade the American colonies were in conflict with the British parliament on virtually every issue of principle. What was identifiable in America was the claim that parliament could not adequately represent the interest of the colonies. The American claim was essentially secular and primarily political, asserting their right to control their own destiny. This was to become the foundation stone of the modern political system. Surprisingly perhaps, these claims were based largely on British precedents, precedents which the British Parliament denied due to its peculiar notion of sovereignty.[2]

If interest is at the heart of politics, then it could be claimed that American interests (never mind the separate interests of thirteen colonies) could not be represented effectively by the representatives of a landed elite in parliament. Consequently, within a relatively short period of time the overall position was transformed. By 1789 the individual states had ratified the constitution of the United States: it established a republic which, though not democratic and flawed by the continuing presence of slavery, was a representative document endorsed by popular support in the states themselves.[3] Moreover the acceptance of the constitution had been achieved by popular debate throughout the states and, most importantly and in contrast to the vicissitudes of the French revolutionary constitutions, accepted by those who were opposed to the specific details of the constitution. The emergence of such a consensus laid the basis for the gradual evolution of the new state towards democracy, though this was not necessarily implied by those advocating the constitution.[4]

In some ways the intellectual basis for the constitution involved a pessimistic view of human nature. The fear of anarchy which had prevailed throughout the seventeenth-century upheavals in Europe returned to haunt those who framed the American Constitution. Many of its sentiments were undemocratic, though not anti-democratic. Despite that, it reflected a revolution in government and political organisation, as prior to the American War of Independence representative government, as reflected by aristocratic parliamentarianism, was limited to Britain and the Netherlands. By 1789 the United States provided the best example of a representative government, which had moved beyond the confines of aristocratic parliamentarianism, and based on popular support operating within a constitutional structure. A number of factors contributed to this. One is the extent to which popular participation in politics had become routine in the colonies. Unlike Europe, American assemblies were answerable to popular opinion and rulers had to face elections on a regular basis. The nature of the economy may also have contributed to this; small producer units predominated and this reinforced both self-sufficiency and independence. Moreover, a free press existed which reflected the views of popular opinion, while politics, especially in urban areas, was of considerable importance. Two other factors played an important role in American developments. Despite the arbitrary behaviour of the British government towards the colonies, they had supporters in Britain such as Burke who believed that the cause of the colonist was just and should be supported. In addition the colonists had inherited a radical political tradition running from the Cromwellian period to the artisan radicalism of Wilkes at the same time.[5]

But the break was more fundamental than the issue of self rule and taxation. The popular political culture of America was transformed by the conflict with Britain. In less than a decade the colonists had fought a war of independence which placed them in a position to regulate their future and they did so in the form of a republic rather than a monarchy. The development of the United States provided the first example of a revolution which successfully stabilised wide-ranging representative and republican institutions on a popular basis. While the colonists may have looked back to the Protectorate and the Glorious Revolution for examples, what they were actually establishing was something uniquely modern and essentially republican in political terms. The constitutions which emerged in the individual states, and the later constitution of the United States, reflected a distinct break from the past, not only the European past, but the American past as well. The new political culture was republican, secularist and participative. It rejected hierarchy and the remnants of feudalism which went with it. American political evolution was posed in terms of experimentation and, while it drew on the past, it increasingly recognised that it was progressive in intent and focus. Finally, though taxation was the issue which brought about the conflict, it was more the occasion than anything else. Americans, and it is possible to call them this by the 1770s, had acquired a sense of identity that at the very least emphasised a sense of separateness which distinguished them from their rulers both within America and without.[6]

Once the authority of a ruler is challenged, the options for both ruler and ruled become fairly limited. The ruler can repress the ruled, reassert traditional dominance and make them subjects once again. In contrast, a new relationship, perhaps one of equality, can be established which enacts a new political compromise. Alternatively, the former subjects can break the connection with the old ruler and establish a new set of institutions which acquire a new legitimacy. This latter option is, of course, the one followed by the American colonists. It was not inevitable, but in the context of the time and in retrospect it was the most likely outcome. The bonds which had held the British empire together were breaking down and, to use a Leninist concept, the American colonies were the weakest link.[7]

However, what is extraordinary about the American revolution is the extent to which it resolved most of the problems associated with both political independence and constitution building. Traditionalists had warned that any break with the narrower aspects of representation would lead to mob rule and anarchy. It was a point of view present in the constitution-making phase of American political life between 1776 and 1788. The traditional argument carried some weight, especially when some of the state constitutions clearly enfranchised the masses, raising the fear of dispossession. The argument during the constitutional process was similar to that of the Putney debates during the English Civil War, focusing on the limits to be imposed on popular control. In most states however, even those which were most conservative, the traditional elites had to come to terms with mass participation in elections or forego influence. This was probably the most unique and revolutionary aspect of the American experience. In New York for example, the candidate of the landed interest for governor believed that losing an election would not prevent the elite from continuing to control the state. In this, he and others were to be radically mistaken. In Maryland a self-conscious elite set about coming to terms with the new forces unleashed by the revolution. Here, as elsewhere, the elites accepted, not always willingly, that financial sacrifices might have to be made to assure stability and some aspects of continuity. Countryman has summarised a number of case studies, concluding that 'by adopting radical policies, conservative institutions were able to take hold'; he further demonstrates the extent to which the demands for equality were met by the elites within individual states.[8] It should be emphasised that the use of conservative here is generic and is placed in opposition to those advocating more radical schemes of government. In the context of the time the actual outcome in America was radical rather than conservative and was seen to be as such by most Europeans. Furthermore, in so far as conservatism can be used in the American context, it reflects on the divisions which emerge after the stabilisation of the Republican regime and cannot be compared with the counter-revolutionary conservatism of Europe after the French Revolution.[9]

The constitutional structure extended political participation. A republican political culture allowed the new state to resolve political conflicts within representative institutions rather than through revolutionary violence or monarchist putsch.[10] This involved more than a reaffirmation of the representative institutions which had been left over from the English experience. It moved the United States closer to the democratic franchise characteristic of the twentieth century. The shift can be seen in the change which takes place between 1760 and 1790. At the beginning of this period democracy is not a widely endorsed notion, and the masses were construed and used as a mob and perceived by the elites as essentially passive in terms of political involvement. During the subsequent decades the mob first become patriots and then citizens. If citizenship is extended to all (except slaves) it becomes increasingly difficult to deny citizens the vote. This is also accompanied by a widespread sense of personal and legal equality which reinforced the notion of political equality. Once this is achieved, it became possible not only to influence political events but to change those who rule in a peaceful and regular fashion. In the United States this lesson was learned in the individual states even before the federal constitution was enacted. In Massachusetts for example: 'a government that the rich had created largely for their own benefit had become something that lesser people could capture and try to use for themselves'.[11]

Yet even within this context it is also possible to note the emergence of conservatism. However, where conservatism emerges within the Republican consensus after the revolution its form is quite unlike the counter-revolutionary ideology of Europe in the nineteenth century. Moreover, different axial principles prevail at different junctures. Prior to and during the War of Independence the main division is between loyalist and patriot. Loyalist conservatism was close to the European variety with the aim of restoration. However, this variety of conservatism – the justification of monarchy and British rule – was effectively neutralised at the end of the war with the expulsion of those who had associated with the enemy. As many as 100 000 loyalists may have left the colonies after the peace settlement.[12] However, once constitution building began, other axial principles operated, dividing people during and after the revolution. These divisions were framed within the Republican consensus and did not have a counter-revolutionary intent.

One such was the extent to which people would have power through the franchise. The state constitutions represented considerable diversity, from the elitist control in some of the slave states to a wide-ranging participation in Pennsylvania. There were those such as Washington, Hamilton and Madison who, while accepting the need for wider representation, did not welcome a democratic form of government. There is a republican conservatism here, represented subsequently by the Federalist party and by Hamilton and his associates. While agreeing on the basic structure of the new state, the revolutionary elite divided on the implications to be drawn from this. The fear among the Federalists was that if sovereignty rested with the people, some method of controlling it should be found. The tradition of republican government had been associated with compactness and accountability, and Americans were endeavouring to generate a republic which would avoid tyranny. That this was achieved through the constitution, the balance of powers and democratic government can be seen in retrospect, but that was not clear when the *Federalist Papers* were written to advocate support for the new constitution. Madison in particular was anxious to demonstrate that republicanism and representative government could function in societies which were not necessarily small or where accountability was immediate. The need for stability was paramount in this argument and almost accidentally political participation through democracy emerged as the answer.[13]

Democracy is not explicit in the *Federalist Papers* and is resisted by the Federalist Party subsequently, but it became the logic of that position within a quarter of a century of the ratification of the new constitution. Madison recognised that faction and dispute were central to any free society, and sought to create institutions which would mediate these differences peacefully. He readily admitted that the real focus of concern was property: 'those who hold and those who are without property have ever formed distinct interest in society', a clear echo of the earlier Putney debates. Consequently he believed that 'the regulation of these various and interfering interests form the principal task of modern legislation and involves the spirit of party and faction in the necessary and ordinary operations of government'. There were, Madison added, many issues on which the public would be divided, and organised groups would seek to influence public opinion in their favour. He accepted that this could not be eliminated, but believed that the effects could be controlled. In contrast to traditional republican theory, Madison did not accept the argument for small self-governing units. Instead, he argued for centralisation and to a large extent succeeded in this aim through the constitution of the United States. The demand for a federal constitution rested on the belief that the thirteen states were unable to provide a basis for stable government without some element of centralisation. A diffusion of power within a large geographical area would, he believed, create the conditions for stabilising the political system. Different majorities and minorities would appear on different issues, but over the longer term a balance could be achieved.

> Extend the sphere and you take in a greater variety of parties and interests; you make less probable that a majority of the whole will have a common motive to invade the rights of other citizens . . .

Though no democrats, Madison and his co-authors were arguing for balanced government within representative institutions underlining a series of checks and balances. In contrast to European developments at the same time, or indeed subsequently during the early nineteenth century, the Madisonian response was to accept popular participation rather than seek to exclude or repress it.[14]

The most remarkable feature of the American Revolution was its ability to function as a democracy in a world of counter-revolution. After 1815 the United States was the only state which survived the revolutionary era with its republican institutions intact. Indeed, between 1789 and 1818 the political system there undergoes a radical transformation due to the collapse of the Federalist Party in 1816 and the emergence of the Jeffersonian Republicans as the main presidential party. Competitive party politics were in place by this time and this form of political action became the dominant feature of the American system with the rise of Jacksonian democracy during the 1820s. By 1828, and the election of Andrew Jackson as president, adult male democracy had been effectively realised. The United States became a liberal democratic political system with competitive elections and an acceptance of the transfer of power. This was not inevitable. There were moments when the idea of opposition continued to be questioned by the incumbent elites: in 1798 at the time of the Alien and Sedition Acts and again during the war of 1812 to 1815 with Britain. Yet, in each case the repressive instinct was harnessed and deflected by the constitution, by elections and by an acceptance of the right of opposition. By the 1820s opposition had become a normal feature of the system. In this the American political system was quite different from those which existed in Europe. In so far as conservatism existed during the nineteenth century, it was framed within a political culture institutionalised by the constitution and hence republican and representative. The conservatism which did emerge concentrated on the defence of existing institutions and property and, with the exception of the slave issue, did not contribute to instability.[15]

The American republic furnished probably the first example of the emergence of conservative divisions within a constitutional system, without the recourse to reaction or counter-revolution. Such was the popular legitimacy of the constitution and the political system, that conservatives were forced to frame their political criticism within that framework. Ironically the defenders of slavery and state rights, such as Calhoun, argued for autonomy on the basis of quasi-democratic rights for the slave system. Elections were considered to be the appropriate method of assuring legitimacy and authority even among the southern planters. A number of reasons contributed to this outcome. The constitution, the balance of powers and the extensive rights available to American citizens forged a consensus which reinforced the republican regime. In addition, America was not just the first 'new nation', it was also the first state to self-consciously adopt the principles of the Enlightenment and incorporate them into its political culture. Moreover, it provided a mechanism for changing rulers unavailable in any other state at that time.

Conservatism and counter-revolution

In Europe the changes proved to be more radical and more difficult. The political order resisted reform, and it is unlikely that changes would have taken place without the French Revolution. A consensus did not emerge as a consequence of the revolution, nor did continental Europe stabilise around the changes which took place. In so far as stabilisation occurs it is in conflict with the aims and objectives of the revolution. Foreign policy and balance of power considerations also entered the European equation. It was thus more difficult to dislodge the existing power structure in Europe than in North America, and once that structure was challenged it responded with its traditional methods of military repression. In turn the terror and its consequences polarised opinion across the continent to an unprecedented extent. The legacy of the revolution was more radical and far reaching precisely because it struck at the heart of the traditional basis of power and authority leaving little grounds for compromise.

Conservative politics emerged in Europe as counter-revolution. The French Revolution itself clearly raised fundamental questions about political order, about traditional institutions and about property itself. In its first overt manifestation, conservatism is closely associated with counter-revolution in an open and formidable fashion. Thus, James Macintosh in 1791 described Burke's *Reflections* as 'the manifesto of the counter-revolution'. Burke himself, despite the reformist character of much of his politics, was clear on the intent of his writing, explicitly supporting the military repression of the revolution:

> We now have our arms in our hands; we have the means of opposing the sense, the courage and the resources of England to the deepest, the most craftily devised, the best combined and the most extensive design that was ever carried on, since the beginning of the world against all property, all order, all religion, all law and all real freedom.

Burke is sometimes mistakenly considered to be a liberal. This confusion is caused by his apparent support for the economics of Adam Smith. This however did not make him a political or a moral liberal, despite an acceptance of economic liberalism. It attests to the complexity of conservative thought, but also to its ambiguity. It may be the case that Burke identified with Smith's economic theories without necessarily recognising the radical consequence for the economy and social structure of such ideas. For Burke, the revolution was a challenge to his fundamental values and as such required extirpation.[16]

The origins of political conservatism can also be detected elsewhere: forces in place prior to and subsequent to the French Revolution itself created the conditions for a defensive, if not counter-revolutionary ideology. Burke's concern for order associated this with the traditional props of a pre-modern society. Axiomatic to this system was that power should be and usually was limited to a land-owning elite which normally possessed control of the means of production, of violence and of the cultural system. In this political environment the state was the vehicle of those in power acting exclusively to marginalise those deemed as non-political. The masses were not considered to be part of the political process and are therefore non-political in the sense that, while they frequently intervene in the political process, this was neither considered legitimate, nor did it usually have more than a short-term impact. The food riot of early modern Europe may have been to these societies what election defeats are to modern governments: a warning, a rejection or the intrusion of a new issue into the political mainstream.

To contemporaries, the 'world turned upside-down' in 1789, as it had previously in America, and the prospect the revolution offered divided European politics in a fundamental fashion. It is not only the moment when revolution appears as a legitimate form of political activity, but it coincided with the transition from agrarian to industrial society. It also coincided with and promoted modernity, unleashed democracy, nationalism and liberalism on the European stage while mobilising the masses and challenging the 'natural' order. The 'twin revolutions', industrial and political, of this era bring about a response on the part of the ruling elites in defence of their values and this sense of order. Though the revolutionary forces in Europe lost the struggle for dominance in 1815, the old order was not unaffected by these events. Eric Hobsbawm has identified the extent to which the traditional forces had to adapt:

> Between 1789 and 1815 few of them had not been transformed – even post-Napoleonic Switzerland was in important respects a new political entity. Such traditional guarantors of loyalty as dynastic legitimacy, divine ordination, historic right and continuity of rule, or religious cohesion were severely weakened. Last, but not least, all these traditional legitimations of state authority were, since 1789, under permanent challenge.[17]

The Restoration of 1815 was not simply a return to the *status quo ante*. Metternich's system was an attempt by the restored monarchies to stay the hand of liberalism, democracy and nationalism. Yet despite its short-term success in reimposing absolutism, the system itself was under challenge almost from the beginning. The British never fully accepted it and at times supported 'liberation' movements under certain conditions. Yet, as with other matters, the apparent successful counter-revolution of 1815 did not last long, nor were the traditional monarchies in a position to dictate the future of European politics. They had to operate in a political climate where their own power increasingly lacked legitimacy or consent, which had not been the case prior to 1789. The modernisation of Europe would have been quite different without the French Revolution. The transformation of Europe established the political environment for future change, though the restoration seemed to preclude such an eventuality. Without the revolution, it is unlikely that the absolutist states would have changed easily in the nineteenth century. Certainly the democratisation of politics in that century is inconceivable without it. The revolution broke the direction of politics and established a new set of presuppositions around which new alignments and cleavages organised. Mass politics emerged with the French Revolution in a startling new form and are channelled in new ways during the first half of the nineteenth century. Nationalism provides the best expression of this new sense of legitimacy opposed to and destructive of hereditary monarchy and the old regime, but industrialisation and liberalism carried similar and more radical challenges.[18]

Conservatives during the first half of the nineteenth century were explicitly reactionary and counter-revolutionary, recognising that concessions to democracy, republicanism or nationalism would undermine their power. Whereas ruling elites in the United States had learned to accommodate such pressures, even the most 'progressive' of European powers maintained opposition to them. Conservatives in Europe were regularly placed on the defensive, recognising the weakness of the system, but unable to reform it and heavily dependent on military means to enforce conformity. Conservatives opposed any change because they recognised the consequences and the transformative effect of the new age.

Conservatives rejected the legitimacy of the new political forms, seeking to mobilise consent for its (now challenged) image of existing order. At the political level conservatism, to cite Burke, claimed that change is not necessarily beneficial and that traditional institutions have a merit, the destruction of which can have unintended consequences for the society. This reflective defence of the past and the existing present is new, but not unique. What is unique is the defensive nature of this conservatism and the self-conscious identification with traditional institutions and power structures. What gives this conservatism its power after 1815 is its successful mobilisation of sections of society around that defence.[19]

The lines of cleavage established by the French Revolution continue to affect our perspective on political organisation. Indeed the very concepts used – left or right, republican or royalist, secular or clerical, revolution and counter-revolution – are products of this era. In terms of the political vocabulary, the French experience has been more influential than that of the United States, and this should caution against the indiscriminate application of such terminology. There can be little doubt that the ruling classes in every state considered themselves threatened by the new forces. In 1793 Arthur Young, a close observer of French events, concluded that these events were, 'the most singular revolution recorded in the annals of mankind'. He had previously supported the revolution in the belief that it would bring about necessary reform. However, the events of 1792/3 convinced him that the revolution was a threat to liberty and property, as it did many other Englishmen. Similar concerns divided American opinion at this time. Young takes Thomas Paine to task for supporting the expropriation of large estates, a policy which would lead, he asserts, to the destabilisation of all ownership:

> that the principal of equality, being once abroad, would infallibly level *all property*; and would give to the beggar, without a loaf, but with a pike on his shoulder, the means of levelling the enormous inequality between his own wallet without a Kernel, and the well-stored grainery of a warm farmer.

Young highlighted what most property owners, then and subsequently, believed to be the main issue of 'popular government'; that if the very wealthy are dispossessed the logic inherent in such a decision would continue down the social scale to be applied to all ownership. Accordingly, the real test of the French Revolution is:

> the quarrel now ranging in that once flourishing kingdom, is not between liberty or tyranny, or between protecting and oppressive systems of government; it is on the contrary, collected to a single point – it is alone a question of property; it is a trial at arms, whether those who have *nothing* shall not seize and possess the property of those who have *something*.[20]

Young's essay was designed to influence those liberal middle class Englishmen, like himself, who had been attracted by the revolution but dismayed by the consequences of its radicalisation. By 1793 it became evident that European events did not correspond to the Glorious Revolution or the American War of Independence, but approximated more to the English Civil War. The juxtaposition of the haves against the have-nots reinforced the fear of democracy, a fear which now appeared justified in the French case. It is perhaps no coincidence that in the year that Young wrote this, the counter-revolutionary revolt by the Vendee should begin. The slogan of the movement: 'Long live the King and our good Priests', 'We want our King, our priests, and the old regime!', can be dismissed as the result of manipulation by priests and nobility of a self-satisfied peasantry. Yet, such slogans appear elsewhere: monarchy and church were not as unpopular as revolutionaries believed, and as the cases of Italy and Spain attest, when linked with patriotism developed a fanatical edge which local sympathisers with the revolution learned to their cost.

Barrington Moore has suggested that one contributory reason for the popularity of counter-revolution was the relative security of land tenure which had been acquired in the Vendee by peasants and that this was threatened by the changes which were taking place. This however is only a partial explanation and Moore further suggests that the attack on the clergy 'was an attack on the linchpin of rural society'. Although he leaves the political consequences of this unclear, Moore's focus after all is quite different, but his brief analysis highlights why counter-revolution can be popular, not just among the middle classes, such as Young or Burke, but also among some sections of the society for whom the revolution claimed to be speaking. The cataclysm is well described by Moore:

> In revolutions, as well as counter-revolutions and civil wars, there comes a critical point when people suddenly realise that they have irrevocably broken with the world they have known and accepted all their lives. For different classes and individuals this momentary flash of a new and frightening truth will come at successive points in the collapse of the previous system.[21]

The rationale for counter-revolution appears more complex than that of revolution, and seems closely connected with the continuing relevance of traditional values and identities for individuals or groups of people. Thus the 'Church in danger' can be a mobilising force for peasants, whereas a threat to property will be for the middle class. The dynamics of this can be attributed to the alienation of sections of the population from the new order. Indeed, it is arguable that the French Revolution never had the unqualified support of a majority; though likewise it is probably the case that the counter-revolutionary armies did not attract majority support. In any event, revolution/counter-revolution depends on violence as a source of legitimacy, not on consensus or accommodation. It is about the politics of crisis and rests on the assumption that a fundamental change has occurred in the consciousness of both revolutionaries and counter-revolutionaries; or as Arno Mayer has argued:

> Counter revolution is a product and stimulant of instability, cleavages, and disorders. It thrives when normally conflictual but accommodating forces begin to abandon the politics of compromise. [22]

What is seen in the Vendee, but which becomes central to right-wing politics throughout the nineteenth century, is the popularity of traditional politics, values and institutions. This does not mean that the *status quo* was actually maintained in any given situation, but that the existence of popular conservatism operated at the political level to restrict the revolutionaries and moulded the political environment in which political action took place.

Popular conservatism is a striking feature of British politics during the revolutionary wars. The British establishment drew on patriotism, loyalism and religion to forge a popularly based ideology which countered the revolutionary ideology of Paine, but especially to that of the French revolutionaries. Burke's *Reflections* sold widely, but was only one example of popular conservative literature during these years. This was part of a widespread movement to defend British institutions against revolutionary threats.[23] Nor can the debate be understood simply in terms of reason versus irrationalism. The conservative case during the French Revolution involved a rational defence of order and one which stressed traditional sources of loyalty. Conservatives concentrated on the differences between nations: history had formed unique communities and the innovations in one cannot (or should not) be introduced in another. George Canning reflected this in *The Anti-Jacobin*, when he reiterated his preferences for 'prejudice':

> It may be thought a narrow and illiterate distinction; but We avow ourselves to be *partial* to the COUNTRY *in which we live*, notwithstanding the daily panegyrics which we read and hear on the superior verities and endowments of its rivals and hostile neighbours. We are *prejudiced* in favour of *her* Establishments, civil and religious; though without claiming for either that ideal perfection, which modern philosophy professes to discover in the other more luminous systems which are arising on all sides of us . . .[24]

What conservatives in most parts of Europe were able to achieve was an identity between patriotism and tradition, without conceding to the revolutionary aspects of nationalism. Those who expressed or supported the ideal of the French Revolution could be easily dismissed as 'Foreigners', holding alien ideas inappropriate to England, Spain or Russia. Although not as yet identical with nationalism, this experience is a formative constituent of the later relationship between nationalism and conservatism. It also draws on an older tradition which feared and criticised the stranger and the other. Indeed the use of foreigner to dismiss radical fellow countrymen has been a significant feature of conservative discourse ever since.[25]

In addition, conservatives insisted on the value of traditional government, of the established Church and the existing structures of power. In particular, they rejected radical claims that the only legitimate form of government was one answerable to the people. Burke objected both to majority rule and to the divine right of kings on conservative grounds, but did not provide an adequate theory of representative government except to claim that the existing system had been tried and tested.[26] The conservative appeal was wide ranging: from an insistence that atheism would lead to chaos, to the belief that the sovereignty of the people could not be acceptable because that majority was transitory. The aim of these conservative theorists was to demonstrate that existing institutions were not only 'necessary and inevitable', 'but also right and good, that is to say corresponding to the true nature of man, then the morality of the existing practices and institutions of civil society would be proven'.[27] Schofield concludes his review of conservative political thought by describing the context in which a conservative political culture emerged:

In this way the perception of an ideological threat led to an ideological counter attack, which in turn helped to justify, if not direct, a course of government action. The intellectual case in favour of stability, made good by legitimating the ethical basis of British society, was instrumental in preserving that stability.[28]

After 1815 it was possible to identify a number of forms of political conservatism. In the United States conservatism involved defending the actually existing institutions (constitution, property, political system, etc.), but without any challenge to the principles of government. In the European context conservatism defended existing institutions which are traditional, and is associated with the belief that the governing principles are in themselves conservative as well. There is another variety which involved the defence of institutions which no longer exist, the object of which was to reimpose these institutions through the re-establishment of the traditional political power structure. The most articulate exponent of this latter view was perhaps Maistre, though Burke also expressed some of these views. As a counter-revolutionary theorist, Joseph de Maistre, unlike Burke, was placed in the invidious position of attempting to justify what no longer existed. In *Considerations on France* (1797) he reiterated what had become commonplace in political theory, that democracy was not an adequate means of ruling a 'large republic'. Though the Federalists in the United States believed they had resolved this dilemma through the constitution, Maistre rejected the American experience as of no significance or importance. Indeed he appeared to consider the spectacle of a republican democracy as an impossibility.[29]

There are a number of reasons for this. The first is that Maistre despised all forms of representative government, and had a particular loathing for constitutionalism. He has usually been considered a Legitimist and while this has validity, Isaiah Berlin's recent claim that Maistre was far more radical in intent than the Legitimists carries considerable conviction. His anti-liberalism is not in doubt, the central motifs of history are tradition and custom rather than natural rights or constitutions. Constitutions are irrelevant and only have meaning in the context of pre-existing and unwritten principles. Maistre stressed irrationality as the motivating force of history and human behaviour.[30] A recognition of the past, however, was but part of a secular tradition. Maistre sought to ground political authority in the recognition that while individuals may act as if they are free they are in actuality 'instrument(s) of God'.[31] This was necessary because Maistre, like Burke, believed that the main cause of the French Revolution was irreligion fomented by the Enlightenment. The counter-revolution, he argued, must then follow on the acknowledgement of the centrality of the sacred: 'Nothing is more admirable in the universal order of things than the action of free beings under the divine hand'. Consequently neither revolution nor counter-revolution can be attributed to the popular activity of the mass of the population. Indeed on this account the people count for very little, if anything only as a passive element in the current of events. Accordingly:

> If the monarchy is restored, the people will no more decree its restoration than they decreed its destruction or the establishment of the revolutionary government.[32]

The translation of this theocratic irrationalism into secular politics had serious consequences for conservatives. Unlike Burke or Hegel, Maistre, though insisting on the religious underpinning of his approach, was seduced by the use of terror to extirpate his enemies. In this sense, as Berlin argues, he is a forerunner of the radical right in the twentieth century and especially of fascism and Nazism. This attitude places him in a position to the right of traditional conservatives, and particularly those such as Hegel then influential on the Prussian state. Maistre believed in an organic state, but not one where people are free in the sense implied by Rousseau. Indeed he insisted that men remain in chains:

> The government is a true religion. It has its dogmas, its mysteries, its priests. To submit it to the discussion of each individual is to destroy it. It is given life only by the reason of the nation, that is by a political faith, of which it is a symbol. Man's first need is that his growing reason be put under the double yoke [of Church and State]. It should be annihilated, it should lose itself in the reason of the nation, so that it is transformed from its individual existence into another – communal – being, as a river that falls into the ocean does indeed persist in the midst of the waters, but without name or personal identity.[33]

The implication is that Maistre was in effect a right-wing revolutionary rather than a counter-revolutionary in the sense that this term was used during the early nineteenth century. There is certainly a totalitarian aspect to this philosophy, a strain of thought, though not action, which is subsequently taken up by right wing revolutionary theorists at the end of the nineteenth century and put into effect during the twentieth. However, in the main Maistre's thought has been influential more on the Catholic conservative and reactionary strains of conservative thought than in the direction of radicalism.

The limits of counter-revolution

Consequently, conservatism emerged from the catalyst of revolution in 1815 as a political force expressed in a number of overlapping ways. The original and most notable is probably that of reactionary conservatism which is the identification with the institutions of the old regime and its political objective that of restoration.[34] It utilised violence, exclusion and repression while its political form is elitist and exclusive. There is a strong dependence within this mode on hierarchy and order with a profoundly anti-constitutional intent. This in turn can be associated with the radical conservatism of a thinker like Maistre, though its totalitarian intent is more residual and its restorationist objectives more real. There is, however, another form of conservatism which is beginning to make an impact during this period. Though associated with Burke, it is not exclusive to him. This, potentially more moderate form of conservatism, is anti-utopian and anti-rationalist to the extent that rationalism is identified with the French Enlightenment and the Cartesian method. It does not, necessarily, exclude constitutional or parliamentary development, though it is elitist in its political implications. The possibility within such a conservatism is for the partial reform of existing institutions, rather than the active promotion of change. It emphasised constitutionalism, but had considerable doubts about radical change. It is not explicitly participatory, although it allows for gradual and cumulative change within the system. It tends to be conservative on property rights and also suspicious about the claims of mass democracy.[35]

Throughout most of the nineteenth century there are various and often contending attempts to work out the logic of each of these modes of conservative thinking and apply them to the organisation of a political conservatism. The right, as distinct from explicitly conservative politics, emerged also in this context. However, it is still to Burke that one must turn for an understanding of the politics of conservatism during the early years of the nineteenth century. He feared, and in this he was joined by most conservatives, that the revolution would undermine the bonds which held societies together. These bonds were, Burke believed, extremely fragile and highlighted the extent to which they are weak and can be easily undermined by rapid change. For conservatives the ultimate objective is to preserve these bonds through authority and control of institutions. The concept of citizenship and with it the idea of popular sovereignty is considered to be unworkable. The outcome of such processes Burke affirmed would be a 'military democracy', which would in turn restore order and authority and preserve the existing property relationships. Although Burke did not have to address the question of how to handle the consequence of the revolution, others did; for despite the widespread consensus among European states that the revolution had to be contained or destroyed this was meshed with the subsequent threat by Napoleon to remake the political landscape of Europe. Revolutionary imperialism however came up against the reality of patriotism and probably contributed to the rise of nationalism as a reaction against the radicalism of French aims in Spain, Prussia and Italy.[36]

Although a restoration took place in 1815 the underlying certainties which Burke and other conservatives wished to preserve remained under considerable pressure. In political terms Britain had undergone severe shocks to its stability between 1790 and 1815: rebellion in Ireland, various conspiracies, the assassination of a prime minister, the Luddite quasi-rebellion of 1811–13. The forms of stability were maintained after 1815, while the repression which continued subsequently confirms the reassertion of traditional values. The pressure for change remained strong and re-emerged during the 1820s. It was not as simple to preserve this sense of stability elsewhere in Europe. After all here is where the revolution had its most direct impact, destroying existing states, overthrowing monarchies and marginalising the established elites in many places.

In Prussia the 1807 reforms which led to the emancipation of the peasantry were a clear response by conservative elites to the trauma of defeat. The subsequent reforms in the education system, the economy and the military reinforced this impression. The reforms, while popular, were instituted by those already in power and can be characterised as precipitative conservatism. This involved a willingness to change certain aspects of the institutional structure while simultaneously excluding 'the people' from any influence over progress. In Prussia the reform movement was dependent on the goodwill of the king and never acquired the independence to have an autonomous influence over developments.[37] The proclamation of March 1813 'An Mein Volk' was also precipitative, seeking to regain control over events which might otherwise have slipped away if action had not been taken.[38] What is noticeable in Prussia is the extent to which by 1813, if only feebly, the monarchy had to address the anxieties of public opinion. It is possible that the survival of the Prussian state was caught up with these actions. Hegel for example recognised that, after the French Revolution, it was no longer possible for the state to function without a popular base, though he like Burke was not in favour of representative government. [39]

The period between 1815 and 1848 is a crucial one for the formation of nineteenth century conservatism. There was no guarantee that any one variety or form of political organisation would emerge, nor that the influence of Burke, Maistre or Hegel (or any of their lesser imitators) would prevail. For the elites who re-established control in 1815, the objective was to secure stability, which in effect meant maintaining the political boundaries fixed at the Congresses of Vienna and Paris: containing any possible French expansionism while controlling the radical aftershocks of the revolution itself in domestic policy. The domestic implications were clear from the immediate post-war years: repression of nationalism, socialism and liberalism (i.e. constitutionalism). This takes various forms, from the refusal of the British parliament to concede Catholic emancipation and the introduction of the combination laws, to the cultivation of a nostalgia for the medieval past. It prompted a return to religion on the part of the British ruling class, while in Prussia Frederick William III strongly supported 'the religious revival that developed in reaction to the Enlightenment and to rationalism'.[40] The reaction was unambiguously anti-liberal in continental Europe and only somewhat less so in Britain. In Prussia restrictions were placed on Jews, while at the same time Prussia organised a common trading area, the forerunner of the Zollverein, but on non-liberal lines. Moreover, by the early 1820s most of the reformers in Prussia had been marginalised by the conservatives.[41]

This reassertion of authoritarianism is not just a German or Prussian phenomenon. Paradoxically, the attack of the French Revolution on religion, especially on the Roman Catholic Church, led to a revival in spiritual commitment. The Church had been stunned by the revolution and put on the defensive by Pope Pius VII's concordat with Napoleon. Yet subsequent events demonstrated that the Church itself had not been destroyed. Radicals believed that reason would undermine the influence of the clergy and the 'people' would be liberated from the noxious influence of religion. Yet the religious revival during the nineteenth century clearly demonstrates the inadequacies of such a view. Napoleon's Italian concordat in 1803 represented a considerable advance for the Church and a recognition of its continuing influence. Moreover, in Spain the French discovered the extent to which conservatism based on religious sentiment could be mobilised against revolutionary principles. After 1808 much of the fervor for anti-French activities within Spain rested on religion; 'the Spanish were the first to identify social war with patriotic war, the resentment of a conquered nation'.[42] Much of this patriotism, however, was refracted through religion; comparison might usefully be drawn between the relationship between priests and people in the Vendee, Spain, and Ireland at this time.[43] The Vendee and Spain in particular draw attention to the failure of radical politics to penetrate stable and traditional systems of loyalty, belief and behaviour.[44] In the circumstances it was perhaps inevitable that the churches would identify so closely with the right after 1815. This however was not a one way influence from the top down. The extent to which popular anti-liberalism existed differed from region to region, but in every state, even France, it maintained continuous influence throughout the first half of the century. In Spain there is an effective restoration and reaction after 1814. The Manifesto de los Persas in 1814 was framed in anti-constitutional and anti-liberal terms, at times coming close to the thought of Maistre. The slogans adopted at the time 'Long live Chains' and 'Death to Liberty' express the failure of liberalism to achieve a popular resonance. This is not to claim that Spanish liberalism had no influence, only that it was faced with a strong opposition from the right. The Carlist movement became the most violent and radical expression of this anti-constitutionalism, and has been described as the first major reactionary movement in the nineteenth century with a mass base. Carlism echoes Maistre in its use of both medieval and crusading symbolism, and looks forward to the mass mobilisation of the right during the twentieth century in Europe.[45] It is perhaps understandable that it is in Spain that one finds the strong assertion of the notion of religion as the stabilising force in a changing world. The conflict between Carlism and Liberalism reflected this division quite well.

But it is the Catholic Church which continues to demarcate its followers from the threat of change and modernity during the nineteenth century. By 1871 the declaration of Papal infallibility, the *Syllabus Errorum* and the Vatican Council combined to place the Church at the margins of political influence. While it retained considerable influence after 1871, this was limited to Catholics and converts. If in 1815 Roman Catholicism could be in the mainstream of European conservatism and acknowledged as such, by 1871 it represented one branch of conservatism closely associated with the more reactionary wings of the right. By this date also considerable changes had taken place in conservative politics, placing the Church in an exposed position. It appeared to follow the logic of the position of Metternich who, while noting the instabilities inherent in the changing environment, could not find an alternative: 'For thirty-nine years I played the role of rock from which the waves recoiled . . . until finally they succeeded in engulfing it. They did not become calm however, afterwards, for what caused their turmoil was not the rock but their inherent unrest.' For the ruling houses of Europe, nationalism, democracy and liberalism remained the primary threat to the social order, yet short of continuous counter-revolution the elites were forced on the defensive in that the political agenda was established by the insurgents and consequently a new consensus based on the old certainties could not be achieved. Metternich captured the dilemma of a statesman who would not concede to reform in normal times and was then faced with how to respond to revolution in times of change.[46]

In domestic terms Berlin and Vienna successfully defended the old order in 1848, but at some cost. In other states this proved more difficult. Although the French restored the Bourbons in Spain in 1822 against the constitutional government, the main consequence of this action was to preclude such intervention in the future. The British refused to endorse the French action and in the following decades pursued a more liberal foreign policy which, though cautious, did not stop short of supporting movements which broke up the diplomatic structure of Europe. The events of 1830/31 confirmed this and the pressures on the traditional powers increased: the July Revolution in France, the secession of Belgium from the Netherlands and the Polish revolt (in addition to insurrections elsewhere on the continent) were followed by a further stabilisation after 1832, but it was in effect an unstable equilibrium.[47]

Between 1830 and 1848 this apparent stability, which involved continuity in personnel rather than political stability, was placed under considerable strain. The revolutions of 1848, though unsuccessful in most cases, were a reminder to ruling elites that the *ancien regime* could not continue in the old ways if it was to continue to rule. Perhaps the weakest link in this chain was France: the constitutional monarchy and especially the July monarchy after 1830 did not stabilise the antagonistic forces within the state. By 1848 the tensions and conflicts of the revolutionary era had still to be domesticated and no one, no more so the elites who commanded power up to 1848, had devised a method of doing so. If, as is probably the case, the lethal nature of the conflicts between Republicans and Legitimists had been considerably modified by 1848, their power to divide had not. The alternation between revolution and repression between 1830 and 1851 are reflections of this disequilibrium. The 1848 Revolution fortuitously resolved the dilemma on how to address the apparently insurmountable cleavages which existed between republican and anti-republican sentiment in France. The April 1848 election which followed the expansion of the franchise from around 250 000 to just over eight million is normally considered to be the first based on effective universal male franchise, and as such can be considered the first democratic representative election of modern times.[48] The decision to institute a democratic franchise had a number of consequences. The first, as reflected in the returns, is that popular opinion was essentially conservative, if not actually monarchist or clericalist. In a turnout of over 80 per cent the Republican left was marginalised, whereas moderate Republicans and Monarchists captured nearly 90 per cent of the seats. The conservative nature of the Constitutional Assembly frustrated the left and prompted the abortive July revolution, which was in turn effectively crushed in the name of the majority. Revolts had been repressed in the past, but this repression was of a fundamentally different character with the forces of order justifying the repression on majoritarian and democratic grounds.[49]

Moreover, in this novel context the peasantry proved to be the advocates of social conservatism, while the military could pose as the defenders of public order. It is at this moment too that the division emerges between the utopian left, which in effect refused to accept the verdict of the electorate, preferring to maintain the purity of the revolutionary act, and those parties which accepted the democratic outcome. Examining this period, Hirschman has suggested that at this moment the vote became the 'only legitimate form of expressing political opinion', and most importantly that while the vote was a right conceded to all, its very existence 'restricted its [the people's] participation in politics to this particular and *comparatively harmless* form'.[50] The elections of May 1849 confirmed both the restrictive nature of universal franchise and its conservative outcome. In an electorate of nearly ten million and a 67 per cent turnout the Party of Order captured 50 per cent of the vote and two-thirds of the seats, giving the right a clear majority. The further revolt in June 1849 provided the pretext to restrict 'democratically' the right to vote of certain categories. This, the election of Louis-Napoleon as president and the subsequent *coup d'état* in 1851 which led to the establishment of the Second Empire, demonstrated the extent to which right-wing forces could command considerable legitimacy even under democratic conditions. The radical belief that the 'people' were on the left was, at the very least, open to question. Although Louis-Napoleon certainly manipulated public opinion, the franchise and parliament, he did not seek to rule without recourse to the electorate. The Empire was ratified by plebiscite and there were competitive elections on a regular basis. Indeed the left increased its vote considerably in the last election prior to the Franco-Prussian War. Universal suffrage was considered by Napoleon to be an adequate method of legitimising his rule, even if his continued power rested more on the military than on parliament. However, that he believed it was necessary to do so, and that he did not seek to abolish the franchise, highlights the recognition by the right that it could compete effectively with the left. Insurrection consequently becomes more difficult to legitimise once a government has received an electoral sanction.[51]

The repression which followed the Paris Commune might suggest another outcome. While the Monarchists won the 1871 election, once the Third Republic was established the franchise was maintained and a moderate republican consensus emerged. To an increasing extent the major disputes of the day (including the acceptability of the Republic) were determined by elections rather than by way of *coup d'état*. The threats to the Republic by General MacMahon in 1877 or General Boulanger in 1889, whatever their authoritarian intent, were initially posed in electoral terms. Defeat in elections led inexorably to the decline of the threat itself. Gambetta argued during the latter crisis that universal franchise was an essentially conservative means to preserve the status quo from revolutionary threat.[52]

It might be suggested that the establishment of universal franchise was 'easier' in France than in other European states because property was protected by peasant proprietorship. This is in part confirmed by the relative stability of the Third Republic until the 1930s. But democratic politics had achieved an autonomy of its own by the 1870s, which politicians in France ignored at their electoral peril. What the French experience clearly demonstrated is that a democratic franchise did not necessarily contribute to radicalism in politics or redistribution in property. The radical left proved to be electorally ineffective while the monarchist right was domesticated. In effect the Third Republic acquired a fundamentally conservative aspect, in part underwritten by regular elections.

Conservative strategies

The French example was not one followed with alacrity by other European states. Between 1848 and 1880 the United States is probably the only other state with an open electoral system similar to that of France. In other cases democracy was still viewed with suspicion and fear. A.V. Dicey could write as late as 1914 that:

> the competition for office which is the bane of the party system, have at last revealed to the electorate the extent of their power, and has taught them that political authority can easily be used for the immediate advantage, not of the country but of class. Collectivism or socialism promises unlimited benefits to the poor. Voters who are poor, naturally enough adopt some form of socialism.

Dicey feared that a growing dependence on the state for income maintenance, old age pensions or protection in one form or another would lead those without property to use the franchise to deprive the property-owning minority of its wealth. This concern extended to the suggestion that in the event of war those dependent on the state would refuse to support the war if this interfered with their entitlement.[53] This fear had been especially strong in Britain where, unlike most other European states, or indeed the United States, the industrial working class were the dominant section of society. Any extension of the franchise would create a situation where this group would also provide the majority of the electorate with unknown consequences.

It is in Britain that conservatives had to confront the threat of modernity in unprecedented fashion. If Burke and the counter-revolutionaries had successfully defended the old institutions, their successors had a much more difficult task. This should not imply that successive governments between 1815 and 1832 were opposed to repression or in favour of either reform or democracy. Lord Liverpool sustained the repression after 'Peterloo', and it was his government which introduced the Six Acts in 1819 in an attempt to destroy the agitation for reform.[54]

The defence of tradition was associated in Britain with Toryism. The governing elite generated a successful conservative political movement during the war with France and maintained effective control for nearly two decades thereafter. Although Britain may have differed in some aspects of its political culture from France, Spain or Prussia, the post-war governing elite shared with their continental counterparts deep reservations concerning the pressures for change. British conservatism and the Conservative Party emerge out of the dynamics associated with industrial change, religious equality, democracy and nationalism. In essence, and not unlike the Prussian monarchy, the Pope or the French Bourbons, British conservatism was deeply suspicious of, and ideologically opposed to, liberalism. Liberalism in whatever form it took promoted change, whereas all varieties of right-wing politics at this stage effectively opposed it. Burke may have believed that a state without the means of changing would not have the means to maintain itself, but his adherents between 1815 and 1825, though possibly subscribing to this view, found it difficult to translate such a formula into political reality. For on each of the issues where matters of principle were involved the right remained opposed to change on principle: parliamentary reform, Catholic emancipation and agricultural protection. Moreover, a commitment to hierarchy, the established Church and a willingness to repress characterised the prevailing ethos for most of the 1820s. In this, therefore, the differences between the British right and the continental right were more nuance than substance. In reality the repression in Britain was less vicious and abrasive than on the continent, but the threat of autocratic government remained potent.[55]

The contrast that should be made between the right in Britain and elsewhere is that, unlike its European counterparts, Britain emerged from the post-war climate of repression not as an authoritarian society but as one committed to, if not united on, reform. Reform versus conservatism divided parliament, the political elite and the society outside this circle. By the early 1830s the control exercised by the right had been weakened, and while Wellington may have commended the traditional order as one beyond improvement, this was no longer self-evident to significant sections of the community. The main contributory factors to the era of reform (1832–84) are well known and do not require documentation here. However, the salient features of the changes are important, for they challenge virtually every aspect of the right's principles. The rise of non-conformism contributed to demands for toleration and generated political hostility to the established church. More radical was the demand for Catholic emancipation, which a Parliament dominated by Orange sentiment was forced to concede by the first effective mass organisation for political reform in the British state. The significance of O'Connell's movement does not stop here: it was not simply a reform, it undermined one of the pillars of the political system and opened up the question of further constitutional reform by demonstrating that what was traditional might not be permanent. It additionally demonstrated the power of nationalism to disrupt the state and to generate loyalties distinct from the state. Finally, the 1832 Reform Act undermined the political basis of the traditional order by changing the nature of representation. Ironically an unreformed Parliament in 1832, as in 1828, had shown itself capable of and willing to reform itself. However, both reforms only took place after a crisis had occurred in the system. In contrast to the continental experience the crisis was resolved in favour of reform.

The December 1832 election which followed reform confirmed the worst fears of the right. The Tories were reduced to a small proportion of Parliament, while those in favour of reform received an unprecedented majority. The choices for the right were limited: they could engage in counter-revolution and continue to oppose change; they could seek to subvert the administration by opposition in Parliament and through the House of Lords; or they could come to some form of accommodation with the new reality. In the years immediately after 1832 the majority of the right, now becoming the Conservative Party, accepted accommodation, though not necessarily on the terms proposed by the reformers. At first, conservatism feared the worst and shared Wellington's assessment:

> The revolution is made . . . power is transferred from one class of society, the gentlemen of England, professing the faith of the Church of England, to another class of society, the shopkeepers, being dissenters from the Church, many of them Socinians, others atheists.[56]

Yet in a remarkably short period of time a political consensus emerged that preserved the new system from interminable conflict, which allowed for regular alteration in government while maintaining prior changes and opened up the possibility for gradual reforms in the future. One reason for this was the moderate nature of the reformers; radicalism was unrepresentative of the new electorate. But it is perhaps the changes on the right which contributed most to this. The Conservative Party did not become the party of reaction, though it did retain strong authoritarian tendencies. It is as if conservatism emerged from the impact with rapid change strongly opposing the changes at every turn and then, once accepted, coming to terms with them. This acceptance of reform was partial, often resulting from the recognition that if the party did not acknowledge the electoral changes and appeal to the new constituency it endangered its own existence. Peel, and here he found common ground with the majority of the party, was not prepared to engage in counter-revolution. Despite the change in the constitution most conservatives continued to operate within the system. If the right accepted that the main focus for political competition remained parliament, this foreclosed the possibility of anti-parliamentary options. Yet the acceptance of change was contingent. Peel made clear in 1834 his acceptance of the new dispensation:

> I consider the Reform Bill as a final and irrevocable settlement of a great constitutional issue – a settlement which no friend of the peace and welfare of this country would attempt to disturb, either by direct or indirect means.

Such a statement of principle is clearly a reflection of Peel's belief that the gap between reformers and conservatives could be narrowed. But Peel saw 1832 as a final as well as an irrevocable settlement. While there could be no going back, neither could there be a 'perpetual vortex of agitation' for further change in constitutional principles. Peel argued that if the spirit of the Reform Act involved:

> promising the insistent redress of anything which anybody may call abuse; by abandoning altogether the great aid of government, more powerful than either law or reason, the respect for ancient rights, and the deference to prescriptive authority . . .

then he would not carry such into effect. If, alternatively, the spirit of the changes involved the correction of real abuses while safeguarding established rights this would pose few difficulties for him.[57]

In essence what Peel was articulating was a view that once constitutional questions were left alone, reform in other areas would be assessed on its merits. In practice this entailed no further extension of the franchise, no repeal of the union with Ireland or significant change to the status of the Church of England. This consensus rested on a coalition of interests between the traditional sectors of British society and the new bourgeois element, an indication of which is the unity against Chartism and the Repeal movement. Nor did the division between Peel and the majority of the party undermine this consensus; indeed the defection of the Peelites helped to sustain it, but neither Disraeli nor Derby questioned the broad outlines of the consensus when they returned to office, albeit with a minority government. What Peel intended, and Disraeli achieved, was an accommodation with the new political culture, while maintaining the political differences between the two political tendencies. Peel failed in this, and his supporters became increasingly indistinguishable from the Whigs. What was more important for the Conservatives, however, was the experience of winning the 1841 election by emphasising religious issues, the Corn Laws and the Poor Law.[58] The conservative in a liberal (or reforming) era could provide what Dicey described as a 'cross-current', that is an opinion which though not dominant could affect and influence the legislation which is promoted by the dominant opinion. By 1841, ironically, Peel had moved away from the 'principles' of his party, in favour of principles more closely associated with the Whigs, thus depriving him of a base in the party.[59]

The division between conservative and Peelites over the Corn Laws was essentially an internal debate between those who sought to reaffirm the primacy of the agricultural interest and those who hoped to generate a wider electoral base for the party. In the short-term Peel failed to do so, but the agrarians also did not prevail.[60] Disraeli was to move away from the protectionist position during the early 1850s and to bring the party with him on the issue during the following decade. In 1858 Derby could express his concept of government in terms not dissimilar to moderate Liberals:

> We live in an age of constant progress, moral, social and political . . . in politics, as in everything else, the same course must be pursued – constant progress, improving upon the old system, adapting our institutions to the altered purposes they are intended to serve, and by judicious changes meeting the demands of society.[61]

The logic of this position appears to have been recognised when Derby and Disraeli introduced the Second Reform Act in 1867 which extended the franchise to a significant proportion of non-propertied males. This in turn opened up the possibility of further reform, a possibility realised in 1884. Yet as late as 1850 the possibility of retrenchment remained strong with the defeat of Chartism in 1848 and with the refusal of Parliament to change the constitutional structure. Disraeli was dismissive of European attempts to bring about reform, believing them incapable of such progress. He shared with Metternich, whom he had met in London after the 1848 revolutions, a suspicion of the masses, modernity and nationality. He also recognised the tensions which resulted from revolution: 'outraged tradition in multiplied forms enfeebles or excoriates the reformed commonwealth'. While this might not justify counter-revolution, it does highlight the continuing significance of what Disraeli describes as 'traditionary influences'.[62]

What had not been attempted prior to 1848 was the mobilisation of tradition to achieve conservative objectives within a changing political environment. Conservatives up to 1850 had in the main been reactionary, responding to political initiatives from radicals and insisting, through their command of superior military force, that no compromise was possible between liberalism and conservatism. This changes during the 1850s for a number of reasons. The first is that traditional elites began to recognise that their position was endangered by uncompromising opposition to change in any form. The recourse to insurrection by nationalists and radicals drew attention to the failure to extinguish the demand for change. Repression might be successful in the short term, but the traditional elites could no longer manage change by repression alone. This was made specific in the context of economic change. The dislocations effected by industrial capitalism were such that even the most traditional state had either to withdraw entirely from economic exchange or come to terms with the new system. This in turn led to a loosening of the mercantilist controls which the state had historically exercised in Europe. A third feature of this change was the recognition that neither democracy nor nationalism were inevitably radical in consequence, as previously believed. Nationalism in particular was potentially a conservative and anti-liberal force, although liberals at first identified with the claims for self-determination on the grounds of freedom.

While nationalism asserted new bonds of loyalty, it was not incompatible with the preservation of a traditional political order. This can be appreciated in the Italian case where Cavour persuaded Victor Emmanuel II to promote the cause of political unity in order to preserve Piedmont from Garibaldi's republicanism and to prevent any radical consequences of unification. Cavour's preventative conservatism was a success in effectively excluding Garibaldi from a share in power, while placing Piedmont and its monarchy at the centre of the unification process. Yet this was not merely a disguised form of traditionalism: Cavour may have been a conservative in his objectives, yet he was innovative in what he achieved. The process of unification demonstrated that a monarchy could provide the basis for political change and that a traditional ruling class could continue to rule once the main aim of unification had been achieved. In other words nationalism need not be radical in its political outcome. By gaining control of unification the right could give form and content to the institutional structure which followed, highlighting the extent to which it could dictate the pace of change and its direction. The right's ability to restrict the franchise subsequently and to control the mechanism of elections until the early twentieth century provides further evidence for this. Moreover, the right was liberal as well as conservative to the extent that though the power and influence of the traditional elites were preserved, the new ruling class was both nationalist and anti-clerical. In Italy, at least, one does not find a clear-cut division between left and right. What Cavour demonstrated was that the right could divide along different lines, depending on the response to nationalism. Whereas on the national issue or on religion the right was not united, it could be on other issues such as land and property. Thus clerical and anti-clerical divisions were imposed on unity and nationalism to give the Italian political system a unique cleavage structure which affected it until at least the time of fascism.[63]

The Italian political elites proved adept at containing the radical intent of nationalism and domesticating it by maintaining effective control of the political system of Italy until the twentieth century. German unification has many similarities with that to Italy: Prussia and Piedmont; Bismarck and Cavour. In some ways, however, Bismarck's political achievement during the 1860s was more radical than that of Cavour. His appointment did not mark a break in the conflict between the Prussian liberals and the autocratic state. Bismarck entered politics as an anti-liberal and was appointed prime minister of Prussia to effect an anti-liberal coup. His success can be measured in the divisions which he subsequently generated among the liberals. His main achievement, and one which had wider consequences for Europe than the Italian experience, was to associate nationalism with conservative politics, while changing conservative politics in the process. His use of the Prussian state and the military to bring about national unity guaranteed control of the new state by conservative elites. Moreover, popular participation in the unification process was marginalised by the use of armed conflict to achieve Bismarck's aims. The new Germany was achieved by extending the Prussian state, but also transforming that structure. Not only did Bismarck break the link between liberalism and nationalism, but by introducing adult male suffrage he was well placed to undermine the liberals' claim to represent opinion in the new Germany. Bismarck believed that the liberals could not mobilise a mass electorate, dependent as they had been on an appeal to a limited sector of the bourgeoisie.[64]

Given the radical import of what he was attempting to achieve, it is not surprising that Bismarck alienated sections of the conservative right in Prussia and elsewhere. As a consequence he was forced to depend on liberal support during the unification and constitution-building process. This alliance was tactical and based on short-term compatibility rather than on a conversion to liberalism on

Bismarck's part. Unlike his critics to the right, Bismarck had recognised that change had to take place if a conservative regime was to remain in power, but the liberals were mistaken in their belief that Bismarck had ceased to be a conservative. Bismarck shifted the right away from the politics of parochialism and reaction to a politics grounded on national unity and new conservative norms. The complicity of the liberals in the Kulturkampf is another case where the apparently 'progressive' nature of a policy was in effect anti-liberal, as was also the case with the anti-socialist laws. One consequence of this was that liberals were becoming a party of order and part of the support base for an authoritarian state.[65]

If Bismarck had led the process of change between 1861 and 1871, his subsequent actions were mainly directed at preserving what had been achieved. While he was prepared to adopt liberal economic policies after unity, this did not make him a liberal as his main aim remained the strengthening of the conservative state. His suspicion of Parliament and of democracy led him to distance his government from the liberal parties and forced them to choose between their liberalism and the state. During the 1870s opinion within Parliament may have been to the left, but Bismarck was seeking to reconstitute his political support base on a right-wing basis. He was able to secure this during the 1880s by settling the Kulturkampf, introducing the anti-socialist laws, discarding free trade and introducing protection.[66]

Although the National Liberals remained crucial to subsequent government formation, it had moved far to the right and away from its essential liberalism under pressure from Bismarck. This liberal participation in a right-wing governmental bloc was to continue up to 1914, despite the increase in Sozialdemokratische Partei Deutschlands (SPD) voting strength and the possibilities which this offered for reform of the system.[67] This was underwritten by a process whereby the 'liberal' political core moved to the right after unification. As Puhle has argued:

> the policies of the National Liberal Party in Germany from the 1880s onwards are much more comprehensible when considered as coming under the general heading of conservative rather than of liberal policy: German liberalism, already structurally weak, had finally split in two, the creation of the Reich and protectionist solidarity having removed the remaining barriers between the right wing of the liberal movement and traditional political conservatism.

Puhle further suggests the use of a 'conservative milieu' to define the political space occupied by those political parties opposed to democratisation of the political system and who feared a challenge to the Bismarckian state, especially after Bismarck. This allows one to include the National Liberals and the Catholic Zentrum within the conservative milieu without necessarily claiming that all these forces are in agreement on every issue. Thus the exclusion of the Zentrum from government does not entail that the party could or would make common cause with the SPD for the further reform of the system.[68]

The common thread identifiable in this 'conservative milieu' is its anti-socialism, its anti-liberalism (in the sense of a commitment to individual liberty and economic individualism), its nationalism and its acceptance of the existing state. While at times it was difficult to manage the electoral system in the interests of this milieu, as late as 1913 it remained the key focus for government formation. What is further distinguishable on the right prior to 1913 and underwritten by both the traditional parties and the new and more radical *volkist* parties is the extent to which they take over the nationalist rhetoric from the left. When war breaks out, nationalism has become a right-wing, and often radical, ideological prop and one that is to be maintained through the inter-war period.[69]

In the encounter with modernity the German right changed to better deal with the challenge of industrialisation, social change and political democracy. To claim that conservative or right-wing forces respond or adjust to change or modernity is not to judge that they have become modern. Germany appears to be a prime case of conservative elites using modernity to capture the leadership of changing political circumstances and utilising what are often seen as progressive issues, such as nationalism or adult suffrage, to generate bulwarks against modernity. Thus for example the fact that the German army adopted advanced technology prior to 1914 can be understood as a passive response by a traditional institution to change or an overt attempt to capture that technology for conservative objectives in an ideologically and politically competitive arena. The ideology or politics of the officer corps does not appear to have changed, but its understanding of how to wage war did. It is more debatable to claim that because of this the Imperial Army could become an instrument of modernisation:

> modernization can also occur when institutions and values are restructured to meet new needs. This is more than uneasy compromising with what cannot be helped. Traditional organizations can be extremely flexible – and this includes armies . . .[70]

This encounter with modernity is not unique to German conservatives; it is detectable in virtually every representative system in the decades prior to the First World War, though of course the outcome differs considerably from state to state. What is highlighted is the successful attempt by the right to capture the political high ground and to influence the political culture in a conservative fashion. This is a dynamic process, but one feature which does become central in most states is the role of nationalism. In Britain the Conservative Party is able to reconstitute its political dominance as a consequence of the Home Rule Crisis in 1886: the party not only achieved long-term electoral strength after the Third Reform Bill but proved successful in asserting its nationalism, imperialism and its defence of the constitution. What is remarkable about the Conservative Party's success is that it is premised on the emergence of a conservative milieu similar to, but not identical with, that in Germany, but which also has some affinities with similar alignments in the United States and in some European states.[71] Nationalism was no longer the prerogative of the left. The right in the second half of the century recognised that nationalism was in many ways as antagonistic to modernity as conservatism. In turn, Liberals became increasingly sceptical about the liberating elements of nationalism.[72]

This move towards a more nationalist policy by the right was reinforced during the response to the long period of economic instability which follows the 1879 slump. Protectionist policies were introduced in a large number of states, and this often prompted a realignment within the political system. In Germany this occurs early with Bismarck's decision to abandon the Liberals and free trade. The new conservative block and its alliance between industry and agriculture was based on the premise that the main component of economic policy should be the protection of the national economy. This is also the case in the United States where the Republican Party is able to fight the 1896 election on the mixed grounds of sound money and protection as a response to recession. In Italy, likewise, the historic commitment to liberal economic policy is eroded with the introduction of a comprehensive tariff policy, a strategy also followed in France and elsewhere.[73]

The common variable here is the nationalist focus, whether in Germany to sustain Bismarck's governing coalition, or in Italy to maintain the basis of an exclusive political system. Each change was based on the need to focus on national objectives. Not all were anti-democratic, but they were assertively anti-liberal. The United Kingdom is the exception to this trend by 1900, though even here changes had occurred. The Liberal split in 1886 not only provided the basis for a coalition between the Liberal Unionists and the Conservatives, but also facilitated the later move to protection by the right. While policy did not change prior to 1914, indeed the Conservative decision to adopt a tariff policy worked to its disadvantage in 1906, what is clear is that the Conservative party moved in that direction but without the success obtained in other states.

The liberal consensus, which prevailed in the United Kingdom from the 1840s, broke down under the pressures of economic change, the Home Rule Crisis and the gradual democratisation of the political system. Liberalism remained the dominant ideology until 1914 but it was no longer uncontested from the 1890s. The challenges came from Ireland, from socialism (more accurately from the working class) and from the reluctance of the Conservative Party to accept the logic (if such it was) of democratic politics. Even after the 1884 Reform Act the Conservatives appear apprehensive concerning the future. In 1883 Salisbury highlighted the twin destabilising elements in the parliamentary system: democracy and nationalism. Though he resisted the implications of these influences as party leader he correctly identified them as the main difficulty for the party. The problem was how to address the demands of an intransigent and alienated national minority within the body politic and how to meet the threat of a non-propertied democratic majority within the state itself. Salisbury's leadership was an attempt to contain if not domesticate these trends. Constructive unionism was one response to the Irish question, but the more problematic one was the challenge from democracy.[74]

The right at the beginning of the twentieth century

Towards the end of the nineteenth century European politics entered a period of instability which, though broken by the First World War, was to continue unabated until 1945. However the two periods, though connected, have to be treated differently. The divisions between left and right by 1890 were complex, but they tended to reflect the continuing conflict over liberty and authority which had characterised liberal and conservative ideology throughout the century. Table 2.1 identifies some of these divisions and links them to the prevailing ideologies. Some of the divisions were blurring by the beginning of the twentieth century, but for the most part they continued to reflect the basic ideological confrontation.

Table 2.1 Lines of division between right and left during the nineteenth century[75]

Attitude to:	Liberal	Conservative
Politics	constitutional	authoritarian
Religion	toleration	clerical/state Church
Economy	individualism	corporatism
Ideology	rationalism	prejudice/tradition
Change	progressive	stability
Identity	nationalism	empire/dispersed

More complex are the political forms which were shaped by these divisions. The European political system had become more diverse, and this multiplicity of regimes is reflected in Table 2.2. This diversity draws attention to the continuing influence of the conservative wing of politics, and its success in restricting the liberal drive for a fully constitutional state. It also reflects the continuing tensions between restricted forms of franchise and the aim of a democratic state. Conservatives defined themselves along the spectrum from absolutism to majority male franchise, but tended to stop short of adult male democracy and universal franchise.

The instabilities present in the European political system are often interpreted as reflections of a fatal crisis in the liberal political order. While the liberal order was under challenge prior to 1914, the actual nature of the threat was more limited than is sometimes thought. Radical insurgency, whether by socialists or suffragettes, involved demands for inclusion in the system, not a rejection of it as such. Inclusion for these groups was a demand that the system acknowledge equality, a demand which in theory, if not always in practice, was quite compatible with liberalism. Nationalist demands were more problematic, but again could be placed within the liberal commitment to liberation and self-determination. Thus the two main threats to the liberal order by 1914 could be met by reform and compromise. This is not to say that on any particular issue the demands would be met, the question of votes for women was especially problematic, but that the demands need not undermine the stability of the liberal order. The real threat to that order came from the radicalisation of the right rather than from the left. This radicalism rejected the further democratisation of society implied by the demands of the insurgent groups. Throughout Europe prior to the First World War, the right increasingly rejected the inclusion of new groups in the power structure and in doing so at times were prepared to jettison the representative features of the existing system. In so far as Europe was in crisis by 1914 this had been prompted by the continuing opposition of the right to democratic politics.

This ambiguous relationship between the right, conservatism, the traditional elites and representative institutions continued until the First World War and beyond. It is reinforced by a tension between the continuing appeal of limited representative systems, still dominated by the right in most countries, and pressures from a resurgent right which underwrote a more authoritarian and

Table 2.2 Regime types *c.*1900

	Composition	Participation	Opposition
Absolute monarchy	exclusive	none	illegal
Aristocratic constitutionalism	elite	exclusive	weak
Restricted parliament	bourgeois	limited	real
Parliamentary rule	majority male	restrictions	real
Male democracy	adult male	extensive	real
Parliamentary Democracy	universal	inclusive	real

anti-parliamentary form of politics. Between 1890 and 1914 the right divided into three categories, each representing different approaches to the question of political order. The main division was between those who continued to accept representative government and the vagaries of electoral competition, and those who began to embrace an authoritarian conservatism which was anti-parliamentary. Within the latter it is also possible to isolate the growth of a radical right which was not only authoritarian, but also rejected constitutional politics altogether. In addition, the radical right recognised the power of nationalism, racism and imperialism as methods of mobilising support for its cause.[76] The primary distinction within the right remained that between the moderate conservatives who, no matter how reluctantly, accepted constitutional, parliamentary and liberal political structures, while maintaining a distinct right-wing agenda, and those who expressed, no matter how reluctantly, a distaste for the developments of modern political life. The reactionary right remained aloof from the organisational, political and cultural imperatives of the modern world, whereas the radical right embraced the forms of modern political organisation, and through its anti-liberal and anti-capitalist ideology shared in the revolt against the complacency of bourgeois society at the beginning of the twentieth century.[77] The cultural crisis of the early twentieth century highlighted these divisions. Nationalism and collectivism it seemed could be utilised by the right as well as the left. This can be seen in racism and extreme nationalism on the one hand and in the renewed interest in medievalism, corporatism and in theories of the irrational on the other.[78]

In contrast, the United States continued to provide the best example of the successful integration of constitutional politics within the political system. The 1896 election confirmed the dominance of the Republican party and the rejection of the Democratic-Populist challenge. Although not a conservative party in 1896, the Republicans were to move in that direction between then and 1912. This occurs in the context of the emergence of a reform movement – the Progressives – which largely dictated the political agenda until the outbreak of the First World War. Although progressives are to be found in both major parties, it is the Republican Party which moves to the right under the pressure of these changes. Under Taft (elected 1908) these divisions split the Party, and at the 1912 election there were two progressive candidates, Roosevelt and Wilson, and one conservative, Taft, (albeit with progressive and reformist antecedents).

In fact Taft and his supporters resist any concessions to the progressives within the party. Writing to William Burnes, Taft stressed that:

> Victory in November is by no means the most important purpose before us. It should be to retain the party and the principle of the party, so as to keep in a condition of activity and discipline, a united force to strike when the blow will become effective for the retention of conservative government and conservative institutions.[79]

What Taft had in mind was the retention of a core of values which could be developed to challenge the progressives. In the interim the Wilson government built a reform coalition which dominated public life until 1916, but subsequent developments undermined this reform bloc and facilitated the revival of Republican and conservative dominance by 1920.[80]

The United States offers an early example of the emergence of a left–right cleavage within an evolving democratic political framework. The same cannot be said for Europe, where the impact of change is resisted by the conservative elites. Trade unions used the general strike as a weapon to advance the suffrage issue in both Belgium and the Netherlands, successfully in Belgium in 1913. In Sweden, often seen as the state with strong consensus politics, the political system was seriously divided by 1914 between those who sought to advance the liberal agenda by extending the franchise and democratising government, and those around the king and the aristocracy who wished to retain a limited form of government. The Dreyfus case in France, though resolved in favour of the republican–democratic forces, demonstrated how potent and divisive both nationalism and anti-semitism could be in a state which had a long tradition of democratic government. Even more questionable was the possibility of continuing parliamentary government in Germany. The Bismarckian system was already dissolving, the SPD success in the 1912 elections did not underwrite a move to parliamentary control of government. The real danger in Germany was that the elites would, in the face of this threat from the left, bypass the political parties and parliament altogether, establishing some form of authoritarian regime.[81] In other parts of Europe, such as Italy and Spain, the traditional power structure was under even more immense pressure, characterised by the radicalisation of both left and right and the failure of the parliamentary system to contain the pressures.

Virtually everywhere in Europe the existing political structures were under pressure by 1914. This should not lead to the conclusion that breakdown was inevitable. The weaknesses, but perhaps also the strengths, of the constitutional system are most evident in the United Kingdom, where the Home Rule crisis compounded tensions arising from labour militancy, feminism and conservative opposition to the policies of the Liberal government. Balfour certainly believed that the 1906 election had radical implications for the distribution of power and compared it with the 1905 Russian Revolution. While his concerns appear exaggerated, the conflicts over the 1909 budget, the 1910 elections and the House of Lords further increased conservative anxiety.[82] It is possible that, individually, each of these conflicts could have been resolved within the parliamentary system, but when taken together and in conjunction with the deep divisions over Ireland, they constituted a more serious threat to the constitutional system. It is surely not simplistic to claim that the war in 1914 saved the United Kingdom from civil strife in Ireland, but possibly also in Britain. Bonar Law broke parliamentary convention and colluded with sections of the military against the government during the so-called Curragh mutiny in 1914. Both sides must share the blame for the deteriorating circumstances in 1914, but it was the right including much of the conservative leadership which questioned the legitimacy of parliament to act in this case. Bonar Law exemplified this and he appears to have condoned an anti-parliamentary stand on the part of his party. Whether he would have precipitated a further deepening of the crisis remains debatable, but if hostilities had been undertaken against Unionist Ulster he would have been placed in a dangerous position.[83]

Arno Mayer may overstate his case that democracy, industrialisation and bourgeois culture were under severe challenge by 1914. To claim that Europe faced a counter-revolution from the traditional elites is too all embracing, especially when employed for those states with some tradition of representative government.[84] Nor was socialist revolution a real threat at this time, despite conservative misgivings. What is evident, notwithstanding this, is that democratic government had not been secured in Europe by 1914. With the exception of the United States conservative elites remained uneasy (the United Kingdom, the Netherlands, Belgium and Sweden) or downright hostile (Germany, Italy, Spain and Austria-Hungary) to the democratisation of the political system. The dilemma for the right has been recently highlighted by Vivarelli who argues, correctly in my view, that the traditional (and often sustaining) props for the conservative regimes were being undermined by modernisation, and this left them with only two choices: either accept democratic government and seek to influence it in a conservative fashion by participating in the competitive arena, or use violence as a means of changing the balance within the system itself by excluding the insurgent movements, whether they be socialist, nationalist, feminist or democratic. The First World War further weakened those traditional influences, opening the way simultaneously for the further radicalisation of the right in some states and its democratisation in others. The war postponed this decision, but it returned in virulent form after 1918.[85]

Notes

1. Simon Schama, *Citizens* (London: Penguin, 1989) pp. 46–7 for the impact of the American War of Independence on France.
2. J.M. Blumsted, '"Things in the Womb of Time": ideas of American independence, 1633-1763', *The William and Mary Quarterly* 31 (1974), pp. 533–64.
3. Gordon S. Wood, *The Creation of the American Republic 1776–1787* (New York: W.W. Norton, 1969).
4. Richard Hofstadter, *The Idea of a Party System* (Berkeley and Los Angeles: University of California Press, 1972).
5. Bernard Bailyn, *The Ideological Origins of the American Revolution* (Cambridge, Mass: Harvard University Press, 1967); J.G.A. Pocock (ed.), *Three British Revolutions: 1641, 1688, 1776* (Princeton: Princeton University Press, 1980); Conor Cruise O'Brien, *The Great Melody: A Thematic Biography of Edmund Burke* (London: Sinclair-Stevenson, 1992) for an incisive analysis of Burke's position during the American conflict.

6. Gordon S. Wood, *The Radicalism of the American Revolution* (New York: Knopf, 1992), which delineates the democratic and radical nature of the changes. John Phillip Reid, *The Concept of Representation in the Age of the American Revolution* (Chicago: University of Chicago Press, 1989) for the crucial link between the defence of British rights and the transformation of these during the War of Independence into much wider rights of representation.

7. In contrast, the British remade the bond in Ireland despite serious challenges to its rule there and succeeded in maintaining its hold throughout the nineteenth century.

8. Edward Countryman, *The American Revolution* (Harmondsworth: Penguin, 1987), pp. 150-53; Wood, *Radicalism*, op. cit., pp. 271–305.

9. Jon Roper, *Democracy and its Critics: Anglo-American Democratic Thought in the Nineteenth Century* (London: Unwin Hyman, 1989), pp. 25–55.

10. Robert A. Dahl, 'The American oppositions: affirmation and denial' in *idem.*, (ed.), *Political Opposition in Western Democracies* (New Haven and London: Yale University Press, 1966), pp. 34–69.

11. Countryman, op. cit., p. 159; Ronald P. Formisano, *The Transformation of Political Culture: Massachusetts Parties, 1790–1840s* (New York: Oxford University Press, 1983).

12. The dilemma for conservatives is discussed in Bernard Bailyn, *The Ordeal of Thomas Hutchinson* (Cambridge, Mass: Harvard University Press, 1974), which explicitly highlights the tension for traditionalists in a revolutionary environment.

13. In addition to Wood, *Radicalism,* op. cit., the nature of the *Federalist Papers* is discussed in Gary Wills, *Explaining America: The Federalist* (London: The Athlone Press, 1981); Bruce Ackerman, *We The People: 1 Foundations* (Cambridge, Mass: Harvard University Press, 1991).

14. Clinton Rossiter (ed.), *The Federalist Papers* (New York: New American Library, 1961), pp. 77–83; 320–24. Wills, op. cit., discusses these aspects of the discussion with considerable care.

15. The essentially democratic nature of American society was stressed by Alexis de Tocqueville, *Democracy in America* (1835). For a criticism of American democracy and its consequences which, in fact had little influence, James Fennimore Cooper, *The American Democrat* (1838). Cooper's conservatism, though influenced by his stay in Europe, was never counter-revolutionary; Roper, op. cit., pp. 56–83 usefully summarises the arguments against democracy. The fear of political enthusiasm and the pressures on the republican elite by mass politics is discussed in detail in Gil Troy, *See How They Ran: The Changing Role of the Presidential Candidate* (New York: Free Press, 1991), pp. 1–60.

16. Cited in Conor Cruise O'Brien, 'Introduction' in Edmund Burke, *Reflections on the Revolution in France*, Conor Cruise O'Brien (ed.) (Harmondsworth: Penguin, 1968 [1790]), p. 60; discussion, pp. 60–63; Koen Kock, 'The first neo-conservative debate: Thomas Paine versus Edmund Burke', in Bob Kroes (ed.), *Neo-Conservatism: Its Emergence In the USA and Europe* (Amsterdam: Free University Press, 1984), pp. 176–89; Cruise O'Brien, op. cit., passim, discusses this question in detail; Robert Eccleshall, 'Conservatism' in Eccleshall, et. al., *Political Ideologies* (London: Unwin Hyman, 1984), pp. 79–114.

17. E.J. Hobsbawm, *Nations and Nationalism since 1780* (Cambridge: Cambridge University Press, 1990), p. 84.

18. I was persuaded of the importance of revolutionary events having unintended or unpredictable consequences of a non-revolutionary nature by Steve McCarthy. He is naturally not responsible for my interpretation.

19. Albert O. Hirschman, *The Rhetoric of Reaction: Perversity, Futility, Jeopardy* (Cambridge, Mass.: Harvard University Press, 1991), pp. 11–42 suggests that one of the earliest intellectual responses of conservatives to change was to assert that reforms

actually made things worse.

20. Arthur Young, 'The example of France, a warning to Britain?', in Marilyn Butler (ed.), *Burke, Paine, Godwin and the Revolution Controversy* (Cambridge: Cambridge University Press, 1984), pp. 103–6. Original emphasis.
21. Barrington Moore Jr, *Social Origins of Dictatorship and Democracy* (Harmondsworth: Allen Lane, 1967), pp. 92, 100; T.J.A. Le Goff and D.M.G. Sutherland, 'The social origins of counter-revolution in Western France', *Past and Present* 99 (May 1983), pp. 65–87.
22. Arno J. Mayer, *Dynamics of Counterrevolution in Europe, 1870–1956* (New York: Harper and Row, 1971), p. 4.
23. The most succinct study of this process can be found in Linda Colley, *Britons: Forging the Nation 1707–1837* (New Haven: Yale University Press,1992), pp. 283–319, 378–81.
24. Cited in Marilyn Butler (ed.), *Burke, Paine, Godwin and the Revolution Controversy* (Cambridge: Cambridge University Press, 1984), p. 216.
25. Linda Colley, op. cit., has explored the emergence of this ideology.
26. Burke, op. cit., pp. 111–12; Cruise O'Brien, op. cit. pp. 220–42.
27. Thomas Philip Schofield, 'Conservative political thought in Britain in response to the French Revolution', *The Historical Journal* 29:3 (1986), pp. 601–22.
28. Ibid., p. 622.
29. Joseph de Maistre, *Considerations on France* (Montreal and London: McGill–Queens University Press, 1974 [1797]), pp. 66–70.
30. Joseph de Maistre, 'On the generative principle of political constitutions' [1814] in Robert L. Schuettinger (ed.), *The Conservative Tradition in European Thought* (New York: G.P. Putnams, 1970), p.274; Isaiah Berlin, 'Joseph de Maistre and the origins of fascism', in Berlin, *The Crooked Timber of Humanity* (London: John Murray, 1990), pp. 91–174; Stephen Holmes, *The Anatomy of Antiliberalism* (Cambridge, Mass: Harvard University Press, 1993), pp. 13–36.
31. de Maistre, 'Generative principle', op. cit. pp. 274–5.
32. de Maistre, *Consideration*, op. cit., pp. 23, 131–2.
33. Cited in Berlin, op. cit., pp. 125–6.
34. Robert J. Goldstein, *Political Repression in Nineteenth Century Europe* (London: Croom Helm, 1983), pp. 89–108.
35. Conor Cruise O'Brien draws a distinction between the Enlightenment and nationalism and suggests that nationalism was responsible for the terror, whereas the Enlightenment was opposed to all forms of fanaticism, 'Nationalism and the French Revolution', in Geoffrey Best (ed.), *The Permanent Revolution* (London: Fontana, 1988), pp. 17–48. Indeed it might be argued that the legitimate child of the Enlightenment is the American Revolution rather than any which occurred in Europe. This is implied, though not directly addressed, in Wood, *Radicalism*, op. cit. passim.
36. Burke, op. cit., pp. 333–49.
37. E.J. Feuchtwanger, *Prussia: Myth and Reality* (London: Oswald Wolff, 1970), p. 131. Thomas Nipperdey, *Deutsche Geschichte 1800–1866* (Munich: Beck, 1983), pp. 31–81.
38. Feuchtwanger, ibid., pp. 132–40; Lawrence J. Baack, *Christian Bernstorf and Prussia: Diplomacy and Reform Conservatism 1818-1832* (New Brunswick, New Jersey: Rutgers University Press, 1980), pp. 24–35. I have used the term precipitative rather than reform to designate a more self-consciousness and dynamic response, though the meanings are similar in intention.
39. J.F. Suter, 'Burke, Hegel and the French Revolution', in Z.A. Pelizynski (ed.), *Hegel's Political Philosophy* (Cambridge: Cambridge University Press, 1971), pp. 52–72.
40. Feuchtwanger, op. cit., p. 144; Ian Bradley, *The Call to Seriousness* (London:

Jonathan Cape, 1976).
41. Nipperdey, op. cit., pp. 272–85.
42. Owen Chadwick, *The Popes and the European Revolutions* (Oxford: Clarendon Press, 1981), pp. 527–28.
43. Brian Girvin, 'Making nations: O'Connell, religion and the creation of political identity', in Maurice R. O'Connell (ed.), *Daniel O'Connell Political Pioneer* (Dublin: Institute of Public Administration, 1991), pp. 13–34.
44. Chadwick, op. cit., pp. 487–528.
45. Stanley Payne, 'Spain' in Hans Rogger and Eugen Weber (eds.), *The European Right* (Berkeley and Los Angeles: University of California Press, 1966), pp. 168–207 for discussion.
46. E.L. Woodward, *Three Studies in European Conservatism* (London: Frank Cass, 1963 [1929]), which deals *inter alia* with Metternich and the reaction of the Catholic Church to modernity. Henry A. Kissinger, 'The conservative dilemma: reflections on the political thought of Metternich', *American Political Science Review* 48:4 (1954), pp. 1017–30.
47. Nipperdey, op. cit., pp. 272–85; 313–19; James J. Sheehan, *German Liberalism in the Nineteenth Century* (London: Methuen, 1982), pp. 7–48; Bruce Coleman, *Conservatism and the Conservative Party in Nineteenth Century Britain* (London: Edward Arnold, 1988), pp. 29–54.
48. The 1828 presidential election in the United States might also qualify, but the exclusion of slaves and other restrictions weakens such a claim somewhat.
49. Alexis de Tocqueville, *Recollections* (Garden City, New York: Anchor Books, 1971 [1893]), for a contemporary assessment of these events.
50. Albert O. Hirschman, *Shifting Involvements* (Oxford: Martin Robertson, 1982), p. 112; Alfred Cobban, *A History of France:1799–1871,* 2nd edn. (Harmondsworth: Penguin, 1965), p. 146.
51. Hirschman, *Shifting,* op. cit. p. 113. Cobban, op. cit., pp. 146–99.
52. Cited in Hirschman, *Shifting,* op. cit., pp. 113–14; J.M. Thompson, *Louis Napoleon and the Second Empire* (Oxford: Basil Blackwell, 1965 [1954]); Theodore Zeldin, *France 1848–1945* (Oxford: Clarendon Press, 1973), I, pp. 504–69; Robert R. Locke, *French Legitimists and the Politics of Moral Order in the Early Third Republic* (Princeton: Princeton University Press, 1974); Robert Tombs, (ed.) *Nationhood and Nationalism in France: From Boulangism to the Great War* (London: HarperCollins, 1991).
53. A.V. Dicey, *Law and Public Opinion in England,* 2nd edn (London: Macmillan, 1914), pp. lxv, xxxiv–v, lxxxvi–vii. In contrast Engels was to complain a little earlier that the surprising feature about the British working class was that they did not use the vote in a class consciousness fashion; Friedrich Engels, 'A working men's party', *The Labour Standard,* 23 July, 1881.
54. Michael Bentley, *Politics without Democracy 1815–1914* (Glasgow: Fontana, 1984); Norman Gash, *Aristocracy and People: Britain 1815–1865* (London: Arnold, 1979); Coleman, op. cit., p. 3 stresses the distinct nature of British conservative ideology.
55. See Coleman, op. cit., pp. 13–25 for an evaluation of this authoritarian instinct.
56. Coleman, op. cit., p. 57.
57. Robert Peel, 'Address to the electors of the Borough of Tamworth' (1834), in P.W. Buck (ed.), *How Conservatives Think* (Harmondsworth: Penguin, 1975).
58. Ian Newbould, 'Sir Robert Peel and the Conservative party, 1832–1841: a study in failure?', *English Historical Review,* July (1983), pp. 529–57.
59. Ignoring what Mill had insisted was the central organising feature of representative systems: a party of order and one of reform.
60. Newbould, op. cit., p. 557.
61. Cited in Coleman, op. cit., p. 86.

62. W.F. Moneypenny and G.E. Buckle, *The Life of Benjamin Disraeli: III 1846–1855* (London: John Murray, 1914), pp. 181; 182–4; P.R. Ghosh, 'Style and substance in Disraelian Social Reform, c.1860-80' in P.J. Waller (ed.), *Politics and social Change in Modern Britain* (Sussex: Harvester Press, 1987), pp. 59–90.

63. Denis Mack Smith, *Victor Emanuel, Cavour and the Risorgimento* (London: Oxford University Press, 1971).

64. Nipperdey, op. cit., pp. 674–748 for a review; Sheehan, op. cit., pp. 79–119 emphasises the inability of the Liberals to translate electoral success into political influence.

65. James Retallack, *Notables of the Right: The Conservative Party and Political Mobilization in Germany, 1876–1918* (London and Boston: Yale University Press, 1988); Hans-Jürgen Puhle, 'Conservatism in modern German history', *Journal of Contemporary History* 13:4 (1978), pp. 689–720; Gordon R. Mork, 'Bismark and the "Capitulation" of German liberalism', *Journal of Modern History* 43:1 (1971), pp. 59–75.

66. Lothar Gall, *Bismarck: The White Revolutionary* (London: Allen and Unwin, 1986), pp. 35–9.

67. Gall, ibid., passim; David Blackbourn and Geoff Eley, *The Peculiarities of German History* (Oxford: Oxford University Press, 1984); Sheehan, op. cit., pp. 181–203.

68. Puhle, op. cit., pp. 693, 695; Gall, op. cit., p. 27. The leader of the Zentrum always insisted that the party was conservative.

69. Puhle, ibid., p. 706 adds that: 'The conservative principles which found the greatest echo during the Republic were not those of the traditional pre-Wilhelminian movement but those of the new volkist nationalism consensus and its public protagonists, the new right and its ideologists.'

70. Flexibility should not however be confused with an acceptance of modernity, which is a political, economic and cultural disposition towards the world. This reflects the considerable confusion which exists between modernisation, which is concerned with bringing an organisation up to date in bureaucratic or technological terms, and being modern in the wider and inclusive sense intended by my use of the term. Dennis E. Showalter, 'Army and society in Imperial Germany: the pains of modernization', *Journal of Contemporary History* 18:4 (1983), pp. 583–618. For a somewhat different view of this Geoff Eley, 'The British model and the German road: rethinking the course of German history before 1914', in Blackbourne and Eley, op. cit., pp. 39–155.

71. Coleman, op. cit., pp. 163–99; Paul Kleppner, *Continuity and Change in Electoral Politics* (New York: Greenwood Press, 1987), pp. 97–120; E.H. Kossman, *The Low Countries: 1780-1940* (Oxford: Oxford University Press, 1978), pp. 310–74, 473–516.

72. Hobsbawm, op. cit. pp. 101–30.

73. Peter Alexis Gourevitch, 'International trade, domestic coalitions, and liberty: comparative responses to the crisis of 1873–1896' *Journal of Interdisciplinary History* VIII:2 (Autumn, 1977), pp. 281–313.

74. Paul Smith (ed.), *Lord Salisbury on Politics* (Cambridge: Cambridge University Press, 1972), pp. 346, 361–7.

75. Table adapted from J.A. Laponse, *Left and Right: The Topography of Political Perceptions* (Toronto: University of Toronto Press, 1981), p. 199.

76. Roger Eatwell, 'The nature of the right 2: the right as a variety of "Styles of Thought"', in Roger Eatwell and Nöel O'Sullivan (eds), *The Nature of the Right* (London: Pinter, 1989), pp. 62–76; Arno Mayer, op. cit., passim for a discussion of the elements of counter-revolution.

77. Eugen Weber, 'The right: an introduction' in Rogger and Weber (eds), op. cit., pp. 2–16; *idem.*, 'Ambigious victories', *Journal of Contemporary History* 13:4 (1978), pp. 819–27; Roberto Vivarelli, 'Interpretations of the Origins of Fascism', *Journal of Modern History* 63:1 (March, 1991), pp. 29–43; Frans Coetzee and Marilyn Shevin

Coetzee, 'Rethinking the radical right in Germany and Britain before 1914', *Journal of Contemporary History* 21:4, (1986), pp. 515–37.

78. Stanley G. Payne, *Fascism: Comparisons and Developments* (Madison, Wisconsin: University of Wisconsin Press, 1980), pp. 14–39. Paul Kennedy and Anthony Nicholls, *Nationalist and Racialist Movements in Britain and Germany before 1914* (London: Macmillan, 1981); Matthew Fforde, *Conservatism and Collectivism 1886–1914* (Edinburgh: Edinburgh University Press, 1990).

79. Cited in John Gable, *The Bull Moose Years* (New York: Kennikat Press, 1978), pp. 15–16.

80. James L. Sundquist, *Dynamics of the Party System* (Washington, D.C.: Brookings Institution, 1983), pp. 170–81; Francis L. Broderick, *Progressives at Risk* (New York: Greenwood Press, 1989); I am grateful to Mr Gary Murphy for discussing the details of this period with me.

81. John C.G, Röhl and Nicolaus Sombart (eds), *Kaiser Wilhelm II: New Interpretations* (Cambridge: Cambridge University Press, 1982); Hans-Ulrich Wehler, *The German Empire: 1871–1918* (Leamington Spa: Berg, 1985), pp. 94–9; 155–62; Wolfgang J. Mommsen, 'Kaiser Wilhelm II and German politics' *Journal of contemporary History* 25:2–3 (1990), pp. 298–316.

82. Balfour to Lord Knollys, January 17, 1906. Balfour Mss: British Library, Add. Mss. 49685. Bonar Law expressed similar views to Joseph Walsh in 1913, House of Lords Record Office, Bonar Law Papers: 33/5/46; Franz Coetzee, *For Party or Country: Nationalism and the Dilemmas of Popular Conservatism in Edwardian England* (New York: Oxford University Press, 1990), pp.107–37; Alan Sykes, 'The radical right and the crisis of conservatism before the First World War', *Historical Journal* 26:3 (1983) pp. 661–76.

83. There is a large literature on Britain before the First World War. Alan Sykes, op. cit. and Robert Blake, *The Unknown Prime Minister: The Life and Times of Andrew Bonar Law 1858–1923* (London: Eyre and Spottiswoode, 1955) both address some of the dilemmas for the right.

84. Arno J. Mayer, *The Persistence of the Old Regime* (London: Croom Helm, 1981), p. 4. However Goldstein op. cit. p. 343. is more cautious on this issue when he notes that democratic governments were maintained in Europe between 1918 and 1939 only in those states where some forms of representative government had been established prior to 1914.

85. Vivarelli, op. cit. for the development of this argument in detail.

3 The Right and the Crisis of the Liberal Political Order, 1914–40

The Impact of war on the right

By 1914 the main political, economic and social questions raised by democracy remained unresolved in Europe and North America. At the centre of all such considerations was how, or if, some type of popular democracy could be created while maintaining much of the old order intact. Conservatives continued to fear the impact of democracy on property and political order, in the belief that the propertyless would expropriate those with 'a stake in the society' and in general engender disorder. Welfare reforms in Britain and the progressive platform at the 1912 Presidential election in the United States heightened these concerns, as did the campaign for progressive taxation elsewhere. These pressures to adapt to democratic influence, indeed in some cases to cultivate and frame it, usually came from the left; whether new-liberal, new nationalist or socialist.

What remained unclear when war broke out was the response of the right to these challenges. This is not to imply that responses were not forthcoming, but that the right was divided in its response. Even in Britain, where it is probable that the Conservative Party would have won an election in 1914 or 1915, the right was seriously divided on tactics, and it is only its continuing hostility to the Home Rule legislation which gave it an appearance of unity. A number of trends are detectable which would have continued whether or not a war had broken out in 1914. It is probable that a number of states including the United Kingdom, the United States, the Netherlands, France and the Scandinavian kingdoms would have accommodated the pressures for change over the next decade. The most likely outcome for these states was a gradual extension of the vote to all men and possibly to women as well. Though this was not inevitable, it was most likely in those states which already had established parliamentary institutions. A tradition had been established in a small number of states where the electoral system was regularly used to influence public and political opinion on controversial issues, such as the suffrage or welfare but also on national identity. In other states these channels were not as readily available, nor was the preservation of parliamentary democracy a certainty. In Russia absolutism appeared intact, while Austria-Hungary appeared close to a nationalist explosion in 1914 despite the extension of the franchise. In Germany, it is difficult to predict the outcome of the domestic tensions in the absence of war. It may be the case that war was embraced in 1914 to offset domestic pressures, yet despite numerous rumours of military intervention prior to 1914, representative institutions remain intact, though not dominant.[1]

Arno Mayer has argued that the period 1914 to 1945 should be characterised as 'nothing less than the Thirty Years War of the general crisis of the twentieth century'. He reminds us that anti-modern forces (not exclusively on the right) remained strong, that democratic institutions were often weak, and that a liberal-capitalist order was neither unchallenged nor in full possession of the means of production. This is a timely and justifiable counter to the traditional view which emphasised a golden age for liberalism, capitalism and democracy in the decades prior to 1914. It also re-addresses the question of the nature of right-wing politics in 1914 and the role of conservative parties in this milieu. Mayer's premises, though not uncontestable, carry considerable weight when he describes the constellation of the 'reactionary right':

> Though losing ground to the forces of industrial capitalism, the forces of the old order were still sufficiently willful and powerful to resist and slow down the course of history, if necessary by recourse to violence. The Great War was an expression of the decline and fall of the old order fighting to prolong its life rather than of the explosive rise of industrial capitalism bent on imposing its primacy. Throughout Europe the strains of protracted warfare finally, as of 1917, shook and cracked the foundations of the embattled old order, which had been its incubator.[2]

Moreover, Mayer goes on to suggest that despite the war, the Russian Revolution and the collapse of other empires, the old regime retained enough strength after the war to continue to destabilise the continent, pushing it into a further war in 1939. He is of course correct to stress that pre-modern forces do not simply disappear to be replaced by those of modernity. This was also true after 1815, but this influence continues into the twentieth century. Unless conservative forces are extirpated by the use of terror, as after the Russian Revolution, it is likely that they will continue to play a political and economic role if not always an effective one.[3] The notion of a crisis sequence is also attractive, as it offers a clear focus for analysis. Originating in the rapid changes which took place prior to 1914, a crisis occurred in the hierarchical and authority structure of Europe. This challenge would not in itself have led to a general crisis without the First World War and the subsequent instabilities which prevailed in much of the world thereafter. It would be dangerous to generalise from this, but it can be claimed that where most or all of the constituent parts are present, it is possible to identify a generalised crisis. While each of the factors enumerated may be contingent, when they come together their interlocking power can lead to a crisis which undermines the foundations of political stability. The war also induced rapid discontinuity among many social groups both directly and indirectly.[4]

While disastrous, the war did not resolve the underlying tensions which led to it. The peace which followed was but an interlude leading to the Second World War, which only then resolved many of the outstanding conflicts. For thirty years Europe was either at war or threatened with war. Furthermore, after 1918 there was no return to the *status quo ante*. France and the United Kingdom, despite appearances, had been seriously weakened, while Germany and Italy, among others, remained disaffected as a consequence of the peace. The basis for revanchism remained strong and contributed to that uncertainty. The uncertainty was exacerbated by the collapse of the main European empires in precipitous fashion in 1917 and 1918. The Russian, German and Austro-Hungarian empires ended in chaos with either revolutionary upheavals, nationalist secession or both. In addition, the Ottoman Empire also collapsed under internal strain and external pressure. Nor was this pressure confined to the defeated states; the United Kingdom began to dissolve as a result of the Irish rebellion in 1916 and the War of Independence which began in 1919. The assertion of sovereignty by the new nation states often contributed to inter-ethnic tension, while the geo-political foundations of many of the new states did not approximate with national identity, language or religion and consequently ethnic divisions were exacerbated. The war also undermined the notion of international order which had prevailed during the nineteenth century, based largely on Pax Britannica. Though seriously challenged prior to 1914, nothing replaced the demise of the British-led world order. All attempts to do so between 1919 and 1929 failed and the nearest to it was Hitler's New Order of the late 1930s. The United Kingdom, France, Germany and Italy were in rough equilibrium, opening up the possibility of coalitions to stabilise the system, but no one power could assert or impose its vision of order as the British had done after 1815.[5] Thus in global terms, but particularly in European terms, this era can be characterised as one devoid of a leading interventionist power which could structure multilateral institutions in such a way as to secure the necessary legitimacy required for conflict resolution between the major powers. In contrast to some recent analysis I would argue that what is required for international order is not necessarily a single power with a global reach, but institutions which have the authority to acquire support from the participating states. Without such structures revisionist and insurgent states will place a premium on reordering the international hierarchy to derive the maximum benefit. In different ways Germany, Italy and Japan sought to overturn the *status quo* and establish new hierarchical structures reflecting their dominance. Such attempts usually lead to war, certainly to considerable instability.[6]

If international disequilibrium and economic depression are global in impact, more discrete and individual factors should not be ignored in this process. Revolution in the Soviet Union changed the nature of power in Eastern Europe, but in turn the existence of a revolutionary state, with active supporters in other states, committed to the revolutionary overthrow of the system posed a new challenge to political order. The domestication of social democracy in most countries was not accompanied by a relaxation of class tension, in fact the most characteristic feature of the inter-war period was class polarisation. In many states unemployment remained high, despite the successful restabilisation of the economy. Although many of the communist parties were small their threat and intention was real: given the opportunity communists would have abolished parliamentary rule and democratic liberties.

Yet in retrospect the greatest domestic challenge was that of political democracy and national independence. The number of independent states on the European continent more than doubled after the war. Most of these new states acquired constitutions, and many established parliamentary institutions for the first time. Moreover, even in states with constitutions, or long-standing representative institutions, significant changes occurred in the realm of political participation. The war provided the opportunity and the stimulus for extending

the franchise to those, usually the working class and women, who had been excluded from participation previously. In a Western European context the
anomalies after 1919 proved to be those states which refused to endorse female
suffrage, though Belgium did follow the unusual course of admitting the mothers
and widows of the war dead to the franchise.[7]

The impact of a democratic franchise can be detailed in the rapid expansion of
those with the vote. In the United States the number of those eligible to vote in
presidential elections doubled between 1912 and 1920, from 25 million to 54 million. In the case of the United Kingdom the change is even more striking: in 1910
some 7 million males were eligible to vote, whereas by 1918 with only partial female franchise, the figure had risen to 21 million; this in turn had risen to 29
million by 1929. In the Netherlands a similar pattern can be detected: the extension
of the franchise to all males in 1917 led to a 50 per cent increase in the electorate,
whereas the decision in 1919 to introduce universal suffrage lead to a trebling of
the electorate over the pre-war figure. Much the same ratio existed in Germany
and the remaining European states. Thus in virtually every state in Europe, and
also in the United States, incumbent governments and political and economic
elites were faced with the very real problem of how to manage an electorate which
was large, democratic and often radicalised. The Italian case provides an example
of mass political mobilisation before 1914 which destabilised the existing system,
a process which was exacerbated by the war itself.[8]

In retrospect, it has become commonplace to recognise that democracy was
indeed an exposed and fragile institution for most of the inter-war period. Many
of the successor states, and other newly independent countries, proved unable to
sustain either democracy or parliamentary institutions. The Soviet Union self-
consciously endorsed an anti-democratic form of political organisation, but so
did Hitler and Mussolini on the right. Liberal democracy remained threatened
throughout Europe for most of this period, yet a surprising number of representative institutions actually survived up to 1940. This also focuses on the dilemma
for liberal democracy at this time. Significant portions of the electorate in a
number of states were opposed to democracy itself, often utilising democratic
forms to destabilise the system and to underwrite the dictatorships which followed the breakdown of the parliamentary system.

The extent to which continuity is real is of importance to the outcome for individual regimes. If, as Mayer suggests, the older forms of deference, order and
power maintained much of their legitimacy up to 1914, they were being seriously challenged by democracy, liberalism and capitalism. The potential for
reaction is not the only factor at work before and after 1914. If it is accepted that
conservatism is part of the process of modernity and that it not only has a justifiable part to play in it, but is an instrumental element in the evolution of the
modern age, then the behaviour of conservatives can be of immense importance
to parliamentary democracy. But even during the inter-war crisis, it is mistaken
to simply equate conservative political aims and tactics with those of counter-
revolutionary or extreme right-wing politics. Indeed, conservatism, as often as
not, provided an obstacle to radicalisation on the right, providing an alternative
means of resolving the crisis on conservative grounds.[9] Therefore, a simple
theory of counter-revolution does not provide an adequate explanation for the inter-war crisis. Undeniably reaction did occur, but not as much as is sometimes

thought. Likewise, traditional elites were compromised with fascism in Italy and Germany, yet in other states this did not happen. Indeed it may be that the crisis of the two European wars (1914–41) can be associated with the failure to find a new stabiliser for European society during the twentieth century.[10] Rapid change and modernisation accompanying destabilisation at the socio-economic, political and cultural levels resulted in the challenge to the old order, but had yet to provide an unchallenged replacement for religion, the land or monarchy as the traditional cornerstones for social and political legitimacy. None of the main elements of modernity did so: the anonymous market could not provide the attractions of the land; rationalism might displace religion, but could not provide an authentic sense of belonging; liberalism, for all its emancipatory force, left the individual isolated and often unable to deal with the challenges. Even democracy as a formal method of aggregating choice could not do so for, as Hirschman has argued, regular elections take the drama out of politics and regularise the process:

> The trouble with the vote, in other words, is not so much that the outcome of voting is stacked, because of the way in which economic and political power is distributed in society; rather, it is that the vote *deligitimizes* more direct, intense, and 'expressive' forms of political action that are both more effective and more satisfying.[11]

One of the striking features of political mobilisation in Europe is the extent to which the traditional stabilisers were either modified or discarded and replaced by new forms of organisation which, though often modern in form and organisation, seemed to answer the need for some type of 'collective' or expressive need. Socialism and the trade union movement often provided this for the working class, but they were neither unique nor isolated examples, though they had limited application for the non-working class. The growth of lower-middle-class organisations in the two decades prior to the war reflected the same need. Even when more traditional forms are adopted, the linkage between religion and nationalism is one such, consociational democracy in the Netherlands another; these are not simply a reassertion of tradition, but methods actively developed by conservatives to meet modernist challenges. In the Irish case, the radical nationalist organisations which emerged prior to 1914 were essentially reactionary in their socio-economic intent, but democratic in form. In the Dutch case the development of conflict resolution institutions reflected older-corporatist norms, yet provided the means for consensual approaches to deep-rooted problems providing for the amendment to the constitution in 1917.[12]

The war did not so much disrupt these developments as exacerbate certain aspects of them. The failure of the European working class to oppose the war has often been remarked on, as if the internationalist or liberal pacifist view of war had been internalised by them. By 1914 Marx's remark that the working class had no nation had proved redundant, and was to continue to be so throughout the twentieth century. Indeed it might be countered that the claim never had relevance to the working class, because nationalism quickly acquired influence over most classes. The war itself enhanced the relationship between nation, state and the mass of the population, both in a jingoistic sense and in a political sense. Popular participation during the first two years of the First World War, though often reluctant and ambiguous, reflected the belief that one should support one's own country when at war, whether the objectives of the state were right or wrong. The argument against the war did not prove attractive to the majority of the belligerents in the face of appeals to patriotism. These appeals may have been transparent, but for a considerable time they carried emotional force for many sections of European society. One potent reflection of this is the 2 million United Kingdom citizens who volunteered for military service by the end of 1915.[13] The link between the masses and the state strengthened throughout the war, and as a consequence of it. Moreover, in representative states this reinforced the extent to which loyalty to the nation and patriotism were strengthened by mobilisation. If in 1914 the tension between nationalism and traditionalism still remained unresolved, by 1919 nationalism had replaced other and older forms of political association and identity as the primary focus for political legitimacy.[14] The war swept away many of the traditional institutional forms which had been influential at the end of the nineteenth century. Indeed what appears archaic in 1919 is the dynastic system of authority. Nationalism, which had been seen as leftist and radical after the French Revolution, became a factor of immense importance for the right. Again, the Italian experience demonstrated that nationalism and conservatism were not incompatible. After 1914, and particularly between 1918 and 1940, nationalism and the right became, if not synonymous then, closely linked to an unprecedented extent. Throughout Europe, left and right realigned in the aftermath of the war and in consequence of this.[15]

The configuration of left and right became more complex once democratic participation had been achieved. The division between left and right on the question of the economy and redistribution remains strong, but there are also divisions within both categories as well as important points of overlap between them. The relationship to democracy supersedes the divisions concerning class, religion and the economy for those parties who accept the constitutional system. Within the right those parties which do so have to be distinguished from the authoritarian-nationalists or radical right who do not. Thus, liberals, social democrats and conservatives share a common commitment to the promotion of constitutional norms, while disagreeing on much else. This divides them from the anti-democratic extremists within their own ideological constellation, whether fascist or communist. The growth of this form of conservatism is an important division within the right throughout the inter-war period.

The right and democratic politics

There are grounds for expecting that on certain issues the constitutional parties will share a commitment to defending political institutions, whereas the anti-democratic forces will have no such ground for consensus. In addition, what is remarkable in the years between 1890 and the 1920s is the movement of many liberal parties to the right and the acceptance by many denominational parties of capitalist market relations. While there is no convergence between liberalism and conservatism, what is detectable is the growth of a political bloc in a number of states which seeks to preserve certain institutions from the left and particularly a common defence of property relations, often associated with opposition to nationalisation and an increase in taxation. Such a realignment is already detectable in the United Kingdom prior to 1914 despite continuing points of conflict between the two parties. In Scandinavia, the Netherlands and in Belgium similar alliances or blocs are also emerging to counter the political threat from the left.

An even more radical distinction needs to be made between those parties on the left and right that accepted parliamentary democracy, and those that did not. What is detectable on the right in particular is the extent to which these parties, and others claiming the same constituency, broke with traditional conservatism, which continues to depend on hierarchy, religion and elite control of the political system to perpetuate its power. In contrast, the radical right utilised modern forms of political mobilisation and violence to achieve its objectives. This was not merely a continuation of the brutality of war, but was also a consequence of the breakdown of the old stabilisers which had given the pre-war right some certainties in the continuation of influence. The effective secularisation of politics, with its modernisation and democratisation in association with war and nationalism, continued to create conditions where many on the right believed that the use of violence was the only means available to preserve its interests. The divisions during the 1920s and 1930s can be best characterised by the extent to which any given party accepted or rejected the parameters of the liberal democratic political order. This claim does not exclude a class analysis of inter-war Europe. Class conflict was a predominant feature of domestic politics, to a greater extent than heretofore; but the dividing line in political terms rested on the method by which such divisions were resolved, authoritarian or democratically, and the extent to which the participants accepted the outcome.[16]

Communism and fascism are the long-standing models of the anti-liberal, anti-democratic and anti-market challenges of the period. Though fascist movements frequently destroy liberal systems, the threat is not explicitly from fascism. Between 1919 and 1940 there is not a single occasion when left-wing revolutionaries successfully overthrew a regime and maintained political power thereafter. To the extent that parliamentary democracy collapsed, this was in every case occasioned by the right rather than the left; whether by fascists, authoritarian nationalists or by the military or an amalgam of all these. That the threat came mainly from the right clearly indicates the unwillingness of the right to accept democratic politics and the liberal order. One element which united the authoritarian right and fascism was a rejection of that liberal democratic order. Although these two movements have separate origins and clear distinctions, they agreed on the need to bypass the parliamentary system and move towards an authoritarian or corporatist resolution of what was considered to be the unnecessary conflicts central to liberalism. It is a profound anti-liberalism which unites the various strands of the anti-constitutional right at this time.[17]

Table 3.1 contrasts those European states which maintained democracy with those which did not. For the purposes of this examination only those regimes overthrown by domestic crisis will be dealt with. The end of democracy in France in 1940 cannot be treated as an example comparable to that of Italy or Germany. In the latter indigenous forces brought about the end of parliamentary democracy, whereas in the former it is military defeat following an invasion. If this is accepted, then the analysis in Table 3.1 identifies twenty-seven sovereign states in Europe and assesses their institutional

Table 3.1 European states which maintained or destroyed
democracy, 1919–40

Maintained	*Destroyed*
United Kingdom	Spain (military coup 1936–39)
Irish Free State	Portugal (military coup 1926)
Norway	Italy (fascist takeover 1924)
Sweden	Austria (authoritarian rule 1934)
Finland*	Germany (Nazi takeover 1933)
Denmark	Poland (authoritarian rule 1926)
Netherlands	Yugoslavia (dictatorship 1929)
Belgium	Hungary (authoritarian rule 1932)
France*	Greece (dictatorship 1936)
Luxembourg	Albania (?)
Czechoslovakia	Rumania (coup 1938)
Switzerland	Bulgaria (coup 1923)
	Latvia (military coup 1934)
	Estonia (dictatorship 1934)
	Lithuania (coup 1926)

Note: *Although these states maintained parliamentary rule,
each introduced restrictive laws which weakened the
institution somewhat.

evolution between 1919 and 1940.

In a European context, twelve states can be considered to have maintained sovereign parliamentary institutions intact by 1940. Some doubt remains concerning Finland and France which have been asterixed and will be dealt with later in this chapter. Of the remaining fifteen, each collapsed under diverse internal pressures establishing one form of authoritarian rule or another. Albania does not appear to have had representative institutions of any sort.

Various explanations for this phenomenon are available. A useful one provided by Ian Kershaw suggests that a number of elements combined at the beginning or the 1930s which either sustained or undermined democracy in individual countries:

> The European democracies which survived the depression and did not succumb to either a conservative-authoritarian or fascist-type takeover from within – the United Kingdom, France, the Netherlands, Belgium, Sweden, Denmark, Norway, Switzerland and Czechoslovakia – had either been neutrals or had fought on the victorious side in the First World War; with the exception of Czechoslovakia had been long established state systems enjoying scarcely questioned legitimacy; had no serious border problems giving rise to deeply felt irredentist demands favouring extreme nationalist movements; had faced no revolutionary threat from the left; and (with the partial exception of Belgium and Czechoslovakia) had experienced no major problems of cultural identity.[18]

While Kershaw's focus is on the reasons for the collapse of Weimar, he does offer a more general explanatory context for evaluating why democracy failed or was maintained during the inter-war period. Yet precisely because the focus is on Germany, there is a danger that this will constrain the assessment of other countries. It is not safe to assume that, because democracy was successfully maintained, there was no threat to it. In a number of states (France in particular, but more dramatically in Finland and Ireland which are not included) there were at times real threats to democratic institutions, threats that were overcome. Moreover, there was considerable tension between the Irish Free State and the United Kingdom over Northern Ireland, including significant civil disturbances in the latter area.

One reason why democracies failed might have to do with the extent to which an individual state had some historical experience of parliamentary traditions and democratic accountability. There would appear to be a correlation between the existence of a weak democratic tradition and the failure to stabilise parliamentary systems after the First World War. Many of the parliamentary systems in Central, Southern and Eastern Europe prior to 1914 were not only weak institutionally, but the institutions themselves often disguised the control exercised by traditional and unaccountable anti-democratic elites. The pre-war German example is but the best documented of these parliamentary facades.[19] Clearly other factors contributed to the instabilities which characterised the inter-war world, including the war itself, but the point which requires highlighting is that these factors may have only exacerbated the opposition of the right to parliamentary democracy.

Taking the constellation of regimes in inter-war Europe, it is possible to plot them on a spectrum from totalitarianism to that of legitimate stable democracy. Between the two poles there are a series of sub-sets, some of which are closer to one end or the other. Thus, while Denmark can be considered a stable democratic state, it ceased to be so only because of invasion. In contrast Poland had already ceased to be a democratic state well before the German invasion in 1939. In addition, there are a large number of states which at one time or another had a form of democratic polity, but as a result of domestic politics this ended during the inter-war years. The majority of states which ceased to be democratic had little experience of parliamentary or constitutional politics. Yet this in itself does not fully address the issue, for it needs to be asked why Czechoslovakia remained a constitutional state, despite the tensions from Sudetan Germans and the divisions between Czechs and Slovaks, whereas Hungary, which has a long parliamentary tradition, did not. Likewise, two other successor states, Ireland and Finland, experienced civil war after independence, each state maintained minorities closely associated with the previous ruling class; yet for the most part both states resisted the temptation to opt for non-parliamentary politics. Lack of familiarity with democracy certainly contributed to political instability for the new democracies, yet Austria, Germany and Italy are important examples of states with a constitutional tradition collapsing under internal pressures. This suggests that democratic stability is not simply a matter of having a constitution or elections, but the continuing presence of these in a political culture.[20]

While no single explanation is possible to cover all the European examples, a key condition for the continuation of democracy is the extent to which the right, however defined, accepted the confines of the parliamentary system for exercising power. Where the right refused to accept electoral outcomes, parliamentary democracy usually ends. In Bulgaria in 1923, Stambolïski received a mandate to introduce agrarian reform, as a consequence he was murdered in a *coup* organised by the traditional elites which was followed by widespread repression of democrats. In contrast Czechoslovakia was not faced with similar challenges; coalition government and crisis resolution marginalised the political extremes until the end of the 1930s, and even then the process of dissolution was a consequence of external intervention supporting internal disruption.[21]

The attitude of the right cannot of course be disassociated from that of the left. Where working-class politics was divided or when left-wing parties did not give unequivocal support to the constitutional system, this not only weakened the system but also helped to promote extremist solutions on the right. The other factor which contributed to the stability of the democratic regimes was the extent to which agrarian and petty-bourgeois elements were either disaffected or satisfied by the political system.[22] Yet on its own dissatisfaction would not destroy parliamentary democracy without the reinforcing impact of the traditional conservative right-wing parties deserting it. This has been recently stressed by Salter and Stephenson who after discussing working-class politics tentatively conclude:

> that the defence of liberal democratic institutions cannot be guaranteed by workers' political action alone; and that an essential bulwark of democracy is a strong conservative party, both capable of defending middle class interests and arbitrating middle class grievances and at the same time committed to the parliamentary process.[23]

During the first half of the twentieth century it is the right and the middle classes which consciously pose the main threat to democratic institutions. In contrast, socialists and the working-class have tended to actively support representative institutions, even when, as during the Kapp Putsch in 1920, the armed forces refused to come to the defence of the German constitution. Alternatively, where working-class movements were revolutionary or equivocated on the constitution, the likelihood of an authoritarian solution from the right increased. Italy and Spain provided the main examples of this. The right were always prepared to defend the state, but not necessarily the constitutional institutions in which it was embedded. Thus the open hostility of the right to Weimar and the disdain for parliamentary institutions by the Italian political elite led to a belief that the state could operate more adequately and fulfil its objectives without the liberal commitment to democratic constitutionalism within a parliamentary context. Despite this, a large number of states maintained constitutional and democratic forms. A distinction should be made however: democracy was under a far graver threat from the right during the 1930s than during the 1920s. Looking back from 1929 Italy is more the exception than the rule of a liberal state becoming authoritarian. Germany, which had by 1929 survived war, revolution, inflation and restabilisation, was not yet on the road to revolution or authoritarian government. If any democratic state was close to resolving internal tensions by authoritarian methods it was Austria, which experienced considerable violence after the Socialist Party increased its representation at the 1927 election.[24] One reason for this is that for the most part the 1920s was essentially a conservative decade.

The revolutionary years of 1917–19 did not have a lasting impact; in most states the extent of the revolutionary challenge was limited if not non-existent. Moreover, after the immediate instabilities that followed the war had passed, conservative or right-wing parties quickly regained control of the political system. In the United Kingdom the 'coupon election' laid the foundation for the Lloyd George coalition and the containment of the Labour Party. In addition the coalition also contributed to the demise of the once dominant Liberal Party, securing the Conservative Party as the main vehicle for right-wing politics. Elsewhere liberal parties also suffered, while the left and radical politics came to be dominated by socialists who were often anti-liberal. In Belgium, the Netherlands and in Sweden liberal parties suffered electoral marginalisation after the war. Notwithstanding this, socialist parties, while improving their vote, did not succeed in influencing government formation to any significant degree. In the Netherlands, for example, the socialists were effectively excluded from government by a coalition of the denominational parties; in Ireland and Finland conservative nationalist blocs dominated and excluded any possibility of left-wing or radical alternatives. In Germany, where the SPD had contributed so much to the Weimar constitution and the defence of the Republic, socialism did not provide a challenge to the system, and from 1920 onwards the centre right increased its dominance. Thus, while the Zentrum was clearly a party of the constitution, it was not a radical party. Its base in a Catholic and traditionalist milieu inclined it towards the right on a large number of issues, only being deflected by the opposition of the Protestant parties to the constitution and Catholicism.[25]

In a number of ways it is the right, rather than the left, which proves more adaptable during the 1920s. Conservative and right-wing parties were faced with a number of unattractive alternatives. They could resist change, attempt to manage it or they could reconstruct themselves on new political foundations. Resistance to change was frequent, but reconstruction fairly rare; the norm was to manage change by taking control of the political apparatus, giving a right-wing colour to the changes that actually take place and sanitising them. This form of response is not necessarily reactionary. Its purpose is to adjust the circumstances working towards change in order that the right rather than the left benefits from the outcome. As examples from the United Kingdom, Scandinavia and the Netherlands clearly show, conservative management does not preclude reform, but it does entail the preservation at a political and economic level of the basic power structure. Some sharing of power may have been inevitable, but the political systems were normally managed to achieve stability on terms acceptable to the right, while assuring conservatives about the system itself without undermining that system. The main objective of all right-wing parties during the 1920s was the stabilisation of the post-war world on terms similar to those that it believed existed in 1914. The return to the gold standard was a major symbol of this and one which was achieved by mid-decade, though not without considerable instability in some states. Closely associated with this was a commitment to a stable currency and the fight against inflation, which in turn was a contributory factor in reducing public expenditure and balancing budgets. The concomitant of these objectives was to exclude the left from political influence.[26]

The right, however, did not offer a simply negative message; it claimed, and with increasing confidence after 1920 successfully, that unlike the left only it could provide solutions to the problems of the 1920s. In political and social terms the right generated an appeal which is considerably wider than that of the left, which was successfully portrayed as a sectional interest group. In contrast, the right was well placed to emphasise the defence of national interest, including patriotism, economic stability, anti-inflation and an emphasis on traditional (usually religious) values and anti-radicalism. When, as in some cases, this approach was coupled with moderate social reform the appeal of the left was restricted and essentially narrow. The appeal to patriotism was reinforced in a number of states by the association between the social democrats and attempts immediately after 1918 to use direct action to force through reforms or to threaten revolution. There is evidence for this in Britain, the Netherlands and Switzerland. In these and other cases the threat itself was enough to bring about a bourgeois electoral bloc to exclude the left from immediate and sometimes long-term influence over the polity.[27]

Socialist failure during the 1920s cannot be attributed simply to defects in the socialist model; it also has to be taken in the context of a successful right-wing political bloc which imposed its political will on the society. More often than not, and most effectively in the core liberal democratic societies, this was not achieved through corporate bias or accommodation, but through successful parliamentary majorities.[28] Right-wing dominance was assured by its capacity to win elections and to dictate the political agenda as a consequence. It took different forms from state to state. In the United Kingdom the Lloyd George coalition 1916–22 underwrote the recovery of the right, while in Germany the decline in electoral support for the Weimar coalition in 1920, especially that for the SPD, weakened the influence of the left. In France, Belgium and Scandinavia much the same conclusions can be drawn. In Finland, where a civil war was fought between left and right, leading to a narrow victory by the right and subsequently fierce repression of the working class, socialist influence was marginalised thereafter by the effective coalition of all non-socialist parties against the possibility of a left-wing advance.

Socialist representation in government throughout the 1920s was either in the form of a national coalition, often as a consequence of the war or constitution building (Germany 1919–20; Austria 1919–20; Belgium 1918–21) or as a minority government dependent on other parties (usually liberals, as in the case of Sweden and the United Kingdom, though in the case of Belgium support was forthcoming from the Catholic party). In virtually every case examined, socialist governments were short lived and unstable. The dependence on other parties imposed serious restrictions on policy innovation on the part of the socialists. A case in point is the 1924 Labour government in the United Kingdom which achieved little in terms of social reform, with the exception of the Wheatley Housing Act. It is likely that if it had not fallen on the communist issue, the Labour Party would not have been able to sustain itself in government, especially if it had attempted to pursue a radical programme. In Sweden, where the socialists were in government on four occasions between 1917 and 1926, the room for manoeuvre was clearly limited by a right-wing consensus on economic policy which precluded any active socialist intervention to solve the unemployment problem. In France and Belgium socialist involvement in government (1924–6 and 1925–7 respectively) did not alter the deflationary policies then being pursued.

Unlike the left, the right could offer homogeneous and viable government in most of these states. At a minimum, as in Sweden between 1926 and 1932, the right could exclude the left even when the socialists were the largest party.[29] In most other cases the right achieved electoral majorities based on conservative policies, which usually excluded any left-wing involvement. On this basis the choice of coalition partners was limited to the centre right. It is the new relationship between the liberals and conservatism which is the most significant departure during the 1920s and helps to explain the success of the 'bourgeois bloc' in many liberal democratic states. Prior to 1914 the liberals were often in alliance with the left on issues such as the franchise, social reform and occasionally on prohibition. By the 1920s these questions had been largely resolved and the main internal division was that associated with redistribution, taxation and property. The right within most of the liberal democratic states, whether these parties be denominational, conservative or liberal, continued to be divided on major issues of principle. Despite this, opposition to left-wing demands provided them with the means to co-operate. This rightward movement on the part of the liberals can be plotted in Sweden, the United Kingdom, the Netherlands and Germany.[30] This basic ideological consensus laid the basis for sustaining a broad-based moderate/right-wing ascendancy throughout most parliamentary systems until the onset of the Depression in 1929. What is clear from this is that throughout the 1920s and in most liberal democratic states a right-wing or bourgeois bloc dominated the political, economic or social environment. In most cases also, the right achieved an electoral predominance which it maintained until the 1930s. In all cases examined, though with differing points of emphasis, the right was able to provide majority government which could implement conservative policies, while the left were unable to do this either in coalition governments or as a minority government dependent on external support. Even when, as in the case of Denmark, the Social Democrats came to power with a majority, this did not guarantee a transformation of the political system or policy.

The right elaborated an effective alliance strategy which brought together all the propertied classes, while at the same time linking the defence of property with that of traditional values, most especially religion. The left could not compete with this, particularly when, as in the Netherlands and Belgium, the Catholic parties succeeded in mobilising a religious constituency and making it virtually immune to the appeal of socialist ideology. The Zentrum in Germany, in quite different circumstances, achieved a similar objective. This move to the right is not only detectable in Europe, it has its counterpart in the United States. The Republican Party dominated American politics between 1920 and 1930. It identified closely with free-market capitalism, prohibition and anti-radical sentiment. There is a complex blending of liberal economics with a commitment to anti-modernist culture and social policy. The revival of the Ku Klux Klan is but one reflection of the popularity of nativism, nationalism and racialist stereotyping. It reached its zenith in the 1928 presidential election, when Hoover faced the Democrat Al Smith. While Smith was no radical, he was considered to be representative of three characteristics which the right openly rejected: urban (and ethnic) mass politics, opposition to prohibition and Catholicism. Although Smith did well in many urban constituencies his socio-economic appeal was not radical. There was little difference between the two parties on economic issues, the campaign centered on the Republican candidate's superior credentials as an American and a Protestant. The election itself reflected more the ongoing tensions between Protestant nativist sentiment and the growing influence of the immigrant population. At the heart of the 1928 election was a socio-cultural divide rather than a socio-economic one, as was the case in most European states at the time.[31] The moral politics of the 1920s were usually based on traditional Protestant issues. The Republicans in 1928 were able to win solid democratic southern and rim states for the first time since the 1870s because moral issues took precedence. The 1928 victory was not an isolated success: throughout the 1920s the Republicans controlled the presidency and Congress was predominantly Republican. The weakness of the Democrats (or the strength of the Republicans) can be demonstrated by their failure to challenge the Republicans in any area outside the South. In the solid South and the border South the Democrats normally overwhelmed the Republican challenge, while elsewhere the Republicans captured the overwhelming majority of House seats: in New England around 90 per cent; in mid-Atlantic 75 per cent; in the Mountain and Pacific region, 75–90 per cent. Consequently at the 1924, 1926 and 1928 House elections the Republican share was respectively 58 per cent; 55 per cent; and 62 per cent.[32]

Even this disguises the extent of Republican influence. The Democrats accepted Republican policy positions on most issues, with the possible exception of prohibition which in fact divided the northern urban Democrats from the dry South. The Republican Secretary of the Treasury, Andrew Mellon, remained throughout an advocate of deflation, low taxation and sound money, policies almost identical to those of his conservative counterparts in the United Kingdom, France or Germany. A wide-ranging pro-business culture prevailed in the United States throughout the 1920s, with only the farming community, the unemployed and certain disadvantaged regions not sharing in the sentiment or the benefits. Prior to the Depression the main lines of cleavage in America were not class or distributional but moral, religious and regional, though clearly inter-mixed with issues of a social or economic character. What this entailed was a governing coalition at federal and state level which agreed (or did not disagree) on broad economic and social policy; but often disagreed on regional and moral issues. The character of American politics retained a separateness which allowed the popular mind and the elite to promote the idea of American exceptionalism.

If allowance is made for the obvious cultural differences between the United States and Europe, the broad framework of policy-making shared a number of assumptions. The attack on the left, the post-war recession and the collapse of the trade unions has parallels in virtually every state in Europe, though the circumstances and timing differed. Among virtually all liberal democracies where no ban on trade union organisation existed, there is a significant increase in the proportion of the work force joining unions between 1900 and 1920. The increase begins before the war, but accelerates between 1914 and 1920 when rough estimates concluded that unionisation had increased in Western Europe from 12 per cent to 36 per cent of the work-force (in the United States 10 per cent to 17 per cent). The peak everywhere comes in 1920, and thereafter a significant decline is recorded, though in most cases the figure remained above that of 1910. In Western Europe as a whole trade union density contracts to 27 per cent, still higher than 1910 but a dramatic drop. The German figure drops from 53 per cent to 34 per cent; the United Kingdom from 45 per cent to 25 per cent. The case of Finland is of particular interest as the collapse in trade union membership follows the civil war, a contraction in the socialist vote, its exclusion from government and a strong anti-union sentiment among the non-working-class majority of the population.[33]

The roll back of working-class power occurs in most countries after the electoral defeat of the left, or more significantly a new right-wing electoral bloc proves to be successful. In most cases the state and the propertied classes reasserted control over the production process and reduced to meaninglessness any corporatist institutions which existed. Indeed, the characteristic form of resolving the post-war instabilities included a reassertion of parliamentary control by a bourgeois bloc, a strong commitment to liberal market economic policy, and the marginalisation of labour as an influence in policy-making. The British case is probably the most significant because of its influence over other European states through the return to gold. There is little evidence for 'corporate bias' at this time. The period after 1920 can be better characterised as one of weakening links between government and labour, rather than the establishment of institutional links between these two groups. While avenues of influence certainly existed between business and government these were rarely institutional and all attempts at such institutionalisation prior to 1939 were partial and ineffective. The main reason for this is that politically the constituency for a collectivist response to economic crisis was narrow and could not generate the political or economic coalition necessary to move beyond the traditional British response, which was the neo-liberal option.[34]

It can be argued that a political coalition existed for an anti-corporatist solution to British economic crisis in the 1920s. Nor was such a coalition displaced by the Labour Party's electoral victory in 1929. Such was the extent of the consensus on free trade, gold, and budgetary strategy that if anything Philip Snowden was the last of the orthodox chancellors of the exchequer. Two factors require attention: the first is that economic crisis in the United Kingdom has traditionally been met by deflationary policies, and second that during various crisis deflationary governments have received electoral mandates to pursue such policies. If the Lloyd George coalition had endured after 1922, and if a form of national government had become institutionalised, it is possible given the thinking of Lloyd George that a form of corporatist intermediation might have in time grown to meet the needs of such a government. This however remains of doubtful provenance as the Conservative Party became the dominant party on the right and its ideology and policy resisted the type of state intervention which underwrote corporatism.[35] Similar patterns to those of Britain are detectable in the Scandinavian states, in Belgium and the Netherlands. In those cases when a socialist party entered government, the right was in a strong enough position until the early 1930s to prevent any experiment in socialisation, or for that matter any intervention in macro-economic policy. The consensual traditions which existed in some of these societies did not in itself give the left access to influence. While elite co-operation became a significant feature of Dutch society, Labour for various reasons was not involved in government formation, but particularly because electorally it remained weak. The denominationally controlled governments pursued policies not dissimilar to those carried into effect in Britain; one which was liberal-deflationist accompanied by mild social reform.[36]

Conservatism and Crisis: 1930–33

When the Depression began in 1929, the universal response to it was the traditional one: balanced budgets, deflation and the defence of the currency. There are two reasons to account for this: the first is based on the agreed economic assumption that the capitalist economies were experiencing a cyclical downturn, and would experience growth if not interfered with. The post-First World War recession provided the model for policy-making in all states. The other reason is the continuing dominance of the right in government, or where this was not the case, as in Britain and Denmark, a continuing reliance on the policy framework previously established by the non-socialist parties. Deflationary policies were pursued by all the major states, including Britain, the United States, Germany and France. The British Prime Minister, Ramsey MacDonald, despite having the advice of Keynes and the urging of Mosley, sided with the inflexible orthodoxy of the Chancellor of the Exchequer. In Belgium and the Netherlands likewise the policy response underwrote a continuing commitment to conservative policy-making, though frequently acting positively on specific issues.[37] Throughout the liberal democratic states there is little evidence that any government seriously considered moving beyond the liberal deflationist strategy; nor is it possible to detect any significant attempt to formulate a counter-cyclical strategy based on deficit spending or public works before 1933.[38]

If at first conservative elites believed that the economic disequilibrium would be temporary, then not only were they to be disappointed, but they found that the economic crisis turned into a major political and social crisis. If there is a decade of crisis in twentieth century European history it is the 1930s. One of the by-products was the drift to extremist politics. Communism or fascism may not have been the only alternatives, but for many, liberal democratic politics offered little in response to the crisis. What is surprising, however, during the 1930s is how few political systems actually collapsed. True, a majority of states between the Soviet Union and the Atlantic were no longer democratic by 1939, but with the exception of Germany and Austria none of the remaining had maintained what can be described as stable parliamentary institutions. Democracy may have been beleaguered throughout the 1930s, but in most cases the core democratic states proved resilient in the face of instability, though they were not unscathed by this experience.

This is not to deny that the crisis was serious: there is a temptation to suggest that those states which survived did so because they did survive and leave it at that. No one would make the same claim for the failure of democracy and say that they failed because they failed. It may be that some states were more prone to authoritarian challenge than others: Poland and Hungary, for example, more than Czechoslovakia; France more than the United Kingdom. What then were the conditions necessary for securing democratic regimes during the 1930s, and to what extent can they be generalised? Arno Mayer has offered one method of dealing with the question, emphasising the behaviour of the right at moments of crisis. Counter-revolution, he claims, is a response by traditional elites to the politics of crisis. During such a moment there is a process of politicisation, mobilisation and remobilisation across the political spectrum. Accordingly the certainties of stable politics disappear, while . . . counter revolution . . . is consequently 'a product and stimulant of instability, cleavages, and disorders. It thrives when normally conflictual but accommodating forces begin to abandon the politics of compromise.'[39]

In an attempt to include all right-wing behaviour in a crisis under the rubric of counter-revolution, Mayer has to distinguish between the politics of equilibrium and that of crisis and conflict. It may be added that equilibrium does not exclude conflict and change, nor does it exclude the possibility of significant change without disequilibrium or crisis.[40] The key for Mayer is the role of conservatives who in times of stability feel no threat and indeed are prepared, within that stability, to make concessions to insurgent groups. Pragmatism and flexibility are characteristic features of this environment, but conservatives cannot adjust easily to the politics of crisis because of the lack of an ideological approach to the ensuing problems:

> Conservative thought is in the nature of an articulated refutation, not of a creative innovation. It is designed to give coherence to the defence of *traditional* social, economic, and political institutions and of *traditional* aesthetics, morals and manners.

While there are divisions in how conservatives respond to crisis, Mayer believes that 'in times of acute crisis conservatives, reactionaries, and counter-revolutionaries look to this common social, ideological, and psychological terrain to provide the foundations for political collaboration among themselves'. Mayer consequently believes that the element of convergence on the right is more important than the differences. Conservatives lose their 'effectiveness and self-confidence', either joining with or, more likely, collaborating with the radical or reactionary right. This leads to the conclusion that:

> In sum, in ordinary times conservatives can afford to be purely practical and empirical in defence of the established order, while claiming special credit for being antidoctrinaire and above partisan politics. In times of crisis, however, the logic of their position forces them into joining, condoning or supporting those advocating an anti revolutionary prophylaxis that is both ideological and aggressive.[41]

The implication of Mayer's approach, dealt with here because it remains the most succinct theoretical statement of the position, is that the relationship between conservatives and political democracy is at best contingent on good times: that conservatives are at best fair-weather democrats. There are many examples of such conservatives, but as one comes closer to political systems with long-standing traditions of representative government, they are rarer. In Germany and Austria, for example, there is considerable support for Mayer's model, but it does not apply to a large number of other liberal democratic states. There is another difficulty associated with this, as it implies that if the conservatives in a political system do not become counter-revolutionary (or at least condone them) then there is no crisis. No allowance is made for an accommodationist resolution to the crisis without recourse to counter-revolution, nor is there an acceptance that the right can take on significant change to the socio-economic structure without moving to anti-parliamentary politics. As Kimber and Dowding suggest, it is not change which causes the problem, but the speed of it.

In a number of European states some if not all of Mayer's conditions are met fully. In Italy, Portugal, Spain and Greece, among others, conservative elites abandon both parliamentary democracy and liberalism, thus facilitating in each case dictatorship or military rule. The Spanish case is illustrative of the process by which the right disassociated itself from parliamentary politics; finally, through its own radicalisation, contributing to the crisis which led to military intervention and the Civil War.[42] The refusal of the right, especially the relatively moderate CEDA, to accept the results of the 1936 election confirmed the contingent relationship to the parliamentary system by most of the Spanish right. The Italian example offers an even stronger support for Mayer's model. Italy has had forms of representative government since unification, though limited and controlled by a liberal elite. Political exclusion, however, remained the main feature of the liberal state until 1909, when the electorate expanded dramatically. Two political blocks were historically excluded and feared by the liberal elite: Catholics and the working class. Their effectiveness at mobilising mass support between 1910 and 1920 challenged the liberal hold on the state apparatus and power. It is at this point that the weakness of representative government and the commitment of the liberal elite to its maintenance became clear. Liberal unease between 1918 and 1922 was enhanced by a number of factors. Liberalism had been anti-clerical and anti-socialist; the two social groups which benefited from universal suffrage. On ideological grounds alone, liberals would have been opposed to this development, but the political system was also unstable. The move from exclusion to mass politics had been extremely rapid, but this in itself was not the cause of instability. What was the cause was the inability of the liberal elite to integrate the new forces into its political system.[43]

Instead of consolidating the system, as proved possible in Britain, Belgium and the Netherlands, universal suffrage and war alienated the liberal elites, because they lost control of the state in the immediate aftermath of the war. When this is added to the disappointment on the right concerning the peace settlement, the maximalist strategy of the socialists and the class war in urban and rural areas which followed the mobilisation of the working class and rural poor, it is perhaps not surprising that the liberals moved towards an authoritarian solution to the Italian crisis.[44] Italy is unlike Portugal, Spain and Greece for a number of reasons. The emergence of the Fascist Party and its takeover was at that moment unique, yet cannot be distinguished from the growth of Italian nationalism and Italy's role as a revisionist state before and after 1914. The recourse to violence on a systematic level and the exclusion of opposition from political life was also new. In this sense alone, Italian fascism was a direct assault on the foundations of the liberal democratic state. While there was no conservative party in Italy which could mobilise a right-wing coalition to defend the system, what is clear is that the move to the right by the liberals, the growing importance of authoritarian nationalism and the centrality of fascism included a stabilisation of right-wing politics within fascism and without a parliamentary structure. What the right wanted to achieve with fascism was to control the process of change and to divert it in directions which suited its own interests. The right was not in principle opposed to change, it was the form taken which concerned it. To achieve this, they believed that the parliamentary system should be dissolved.[45] Perhaps the key to fascist success in Italy, and its system maintaining ability until the Second World War, was the link between its anti-liberal ideology, class conflict and nationalism. In effect, although Italian liberals had historically identified with representative government, it remained a contingent identity and one which did not survive mass mobilisation. In answer to this challenge, a new governing coalition emerged which included traditional conservatives (Church and monarchy), liberals and authoritarian nationalists with the aim of transforming the liberal system by preserving those features which continued to benefit the right, while eliminating those which involved political participation.

Fascist radicalism is contained in Italy for much of the 1920s. It is not until the Depression that the opportunity emerges for Mussolini to attempt to realise some of fascism's radical objectives.[46] In this context the Italian experience remains unique: a society with a parliamentary tradition succumbing to totalitarian party control. In contrast, the comparable dictatorships of Primo de Rivera in Spain, Salazar in Portugal or Pilsudski in Poland were traditional and based on military intervention. None of these had either the radical intent or the exclusive party control over the state which was attempted if not actually realised in Italy.

The emergence of the National Sozialistische Deutsche Arbeitspartei (NSDAP) as the major party on the German right was undoubtedly prompted by the impact of the Depression on conservative voters, but also owes much of its success to the fragmentation of the political system during the 1920s, to the failure of parliament to generate realistic responses to the Depression and to the character of Hitler as well as the motivation of his party. While it is correct to conclude that without the Depression there would not have been a national socialist takeover, this is only a partial explanation of the outcome, it might be said that without the failure of the right to sustain Weimar democracy during the 1920s, then the outcome would have been more problematic. Moreover, as has been noted by Richard Bessell, what is remarkable about Weimar 'is not that it collapsed but that it lasted as long as it did'.[47]

That democracy in Weimar continued until 1930 and then partially up to 1933 indicated a degree of resilience on the part of the political system, but here, as in Italy, liberal democracy as a political system was attenuated fairly early in the life of the republic. In effect, for much of its history Weimar did not receive legitimacy from significant sections of the population. Thus Weimar may have been a model constitutional state in formal terms, but the political culture in which it was embedded did not enhance the necessary reinforcing elements which could have sustained its legitimacy. One contributory factor to this lack of stability was that Weimar was the first case of representative government sustained by parliamentary majorities in Germany. More important, however, was the failure of democratic political parties to maintain their control over parliament after the democratic breakthrough of 1919. The existence of a system maintaining a majority of democratic parties throughout the 1920s might have encouraged the right to accept the overall structure. In particular, the trajectory of the Deutsche Volkspartei (DVP) and the Deutschnationale Volkspartei (DNVP) might have been different. The failure of these parties to give anything more than contingent support to the system weakened it from the outset, but especially from the mid-1920s. In 1924 and 1928 authoritarian and communist parties accounted for around 45 per cent of the vote, a figure which rose to 60 per cent by 1932.

The authoritarian potential remained strong for most of the Weimar period, rarely dropping below a third of the electorate. Anti-system voters often commanded as much as 50 per cent of the vote and during the crucial period of 1930–33 over 60 per cent. In addition to this, neither left nor right was united in support of the democratic system. The Sozialdemokratische Partei Deutschlands (SPD) and the Kommunistische Partei Deutschlands (KPD) remained divided throughout the Weimar period on the legitimacy of the system. The Zentrum and the Deutsche Demokratische Partei (DDP) formed a similar division on the right from the DNVP and the DVP. To reinforce this difficulty, left and right within the democratic bloc were also divided along policy lines, which often undermined their ability to co-operate. Consequently, the idea of fragmentation has considerable strength though, as Lepsius demonstrates, there continued to be a democratic potential which could be realised under favourable circumstances.[48] Furthermore, the process of fragmentation during the later 1920s pushed the DVP and the DNVP further to the right, and into outright opposition to the Republic by the time of the Depression. The relationship between these parties and the Weimar Republic remained contingent, but the contingency was qualified by participation in or support for centre-right governments after 1924. After 1928 this ceased to be the case, and from then until 1933 the characteristic feature of the German political system is the rise in the support base for those parties committed to destroying the Republic (DNVP/NSDAP/KPD).[49] It is necessary to distinguish between the authoritarian bloc, which until 1930 at least contained parties that, though hostile to the Republic, were prepared to participate in government and co-operate, (however reluctantly) in the maintenance of the system, and the 'right-bloc' consisting of the NSDAP and DNVP, which was committed to instituting an authoritarian end to the system itself.[50]

The growth of national socialism can partly be accounted for by the depression, but it was also a consequence of the movement to the right on the part of authoritarian nationalists and sections of the liberal constituency. It is also a case which confirms Mayer's view of the relationship between counter-revolution and traditional conservatism. Though liberalism had always been weak in Germany, it is the war, revolution, the establishment of the Republic and the ensuing chaos concluding with the inflation of 1923–4 that undermined whatever slender links the liberal bourgeoisie maintained to the system. In electoral terms the hold of the centre right parties on their electorate was no longer secure. The short-lived rise of anti-inflation protest parties reflected one aspect of this, while the refusal of the major parties to address the losses experienced by sections of the middle and lower-middle classes enhanced the potential attractiveness of more radical and anti-system parties.[51]

To say that the German party system dissolved is only partly correct. What occurred is that the right-wing parties collapsed in the face of the challenge from the NSDAP. The constituency for the Zentrum remained remarkably stable between 1928 and 1933, but the KPD gained at the expense of the SPD. The real erosion in party strength is concentrated on the parties to the right of the Zentrum and among religious, regional and right-wing splinter groups. The two major electoral blocks maintained their electorates, but there was a redistribution

Table 3.2 Elections to the Reichstag, 1928–33 (%)

	1928	1930	1932 (July)	1932 (Nov)	1933
KPD	10.6	13.1	14.5	16.9	12.3
SPD	29.8	24.5	21.6	20.4	18.3
DDP	4.9	3.8	1.0	1.0	0.9
Zentrum	12.1	11.8	12.5	11.9	11.2
BVP	3.1	3.0	3.7	3.4	2.7
DVP	8.7	4.7	1.2	1.9	1.1
DNVP	14.2	7.0	6.2	8.9	8.0
NSDAP	2.6	18.3	37.4	33.1	43.9
Others	13.9	13.8	2.0	2.6	1.6
Turn-out	75.6	82.0	84.1	80.6	88.8

Source: Thomas T. Mackie and Richard Rose, *The International Alamanac of Electoral History*, 2nd Edn (London: Macmillan, 1982).

within each which contributed to the instabilities of the system. This was most pronounced on the right where dealignment occurs in the second half of the 1920s without realignment. This opened the electorate to the National Socialist appeal and the realignment takes place between 1930 and 1933 (see Table 3.2).[52]

The National Socialists benefited in crude terms from the increase in turn-out; about ten percentage points between 1928 and 1932. This in turn was accompanied by the virtual disappearance of electoral support for the DVP and the DDP, while significantly a substantial section of those who had voted for regionalist or particularist parties also moved to the right. Whatever else one might say concerning the National Socialist breakthrough, its electoral base was no bigger in 1932 than that of the combined right-wing vote in 1928. In crude voting terms liberal, conservative and *mittlestandt* parties had attracted 41 per cent of the vote in 1928; a figure which had dropped to 11 per cent in 1932. Over the same period the National Socialists moved from 2.6 to 37.4 per cent.[53]

One analysis has suggested that a majority of the new voters supported one or other of the parties opposed to the Republic, and that some 10 per cent of the population voted for the national socialists who might otherwise have remained with more moderate right-wing parties.[54] What is clear though is that the National Socialists benefited from the failure of the liberal and right-wing parties to maintain their electoral strength during the early years of the Depression. The Nazi appeal was strongest among constituencies which were in small towns, rural areas and Protestant. The correlation between religion and agriculture is particularly strong, but so is that with the *mittlestandt* and other sections of the Protestant petty bourgeoisie.[55] The extent to which certain sections of the middle classes supported the Nazis between 1930 and 1933 is a matter of serious dispute. Hamilton has argued that the party received disproportionate support from the middle and upper-middle classes, suggesting that the emphasis on the petty bourgeoisie may be overestimated if not actually mistaken. Hamilton also disaggregated the middle classes, showing that different groups within that wide sector behaved quite differently in voting terms.[56] What is important is the extent to which the traditional right wing parties failed in the face of the Nazi challenge. Three factors are of significance. The first is that the Nazis failed to attract Catholic or working-class voters in any significant degree. Second, the Nazis electoral base appears to have been disproportionately Protestant and middle class (whether rural or petty bourgeois); and third, the electoral success of the Nazis facilitated an alliance between traditional conservative elites and radical right-wing politics which allowed Hitler to become Chancellor in January 1933.[57]

Hitler's objectives represented the most radical rejection of liberal society in inter-war Europe. The radical nature of Nazi ideology and its implementation allowed the national socialists to marginalise the conservative elites which had supported Hitler's appointment and to exercise effective political control over Germany. The totalitarian intention of Hitler distinguishes his regime from that of Italian Fascism or the Austrian dictatorship, in which conservative elites maintained considerable influence. Of the major right-wing regimes which came to power between 1918 and 1938 the Nazis are qualitatively the most revolutionary, and there is a fundamental departure from the more limited objectives of both the authoritarian and conservative right. While the Nazis and the Fascists co-operated with other parties on the right, the ideological goals of Fascism and Nazism remained more radical than the limited goals of restoration or corporatist alternatives to liberal democracy. However, considerable differences also continued to divide the Italian Fascists from Germany.[58]

It is possible to identify four variants of right-wing political organisation during the 1930s: Fascism, the radical right, the conservative right and the moderate parliamentary conservative right. A twofold ideological distinction can also be made between the authoritarian nationalism of the first three, and the democratic pluralistic politics of the fourth. If Vivarelli's distinction is valid, that the main dividing line in politics remains that between liberalism and authoritarianism, this also has consequences for means and ends. Whatever sympathy there may have been between the conservative and radical right in terms of their relationship to capitalism, monarchy and religion, the determining difference between them is the acceptance or rejection of liberal democracy. In this sense the authoritarian right is closer to Fascism in terms of means and ends than either is to the moderate conservatives. In turn, moderate conservatives are closer to democratic socialists than either are to any of the totalitarian alternatives.[59]

Democracy and conservatism in the 1930s

Once some parties on the left and right accepted the basic liberal premise that the political struggle for redistribution takes place within a parliamentary framework, with each side accepting the electoral outcome, the nature of the political culture changes and a new axial principle emerges. This view of the distribution of power does not invalidate theories that stress the class or conflictual nature of modern politics. However, what it does insist on is that there are political systems whose overarching sets of values exclude, under most circumstances, the use of violence to achieve political ends, to maintain a particular policy or to change a policy that had been enacted within the parliamentary structure. It does not involve accepting at all times decisions which are arrived at by parliamentary majorities, but it does insist that the bias within the system should always be towards recognising that majority. While recognising that majorities can be misguided, the basic presupposition rests on the principle that all else being equal electoral majorities have a mandate to form governments and attempt to implement policy.

On the right, as on the left, there are varying attempts to come to terms with the process of modernisation. Some of these are authoritarian, while others are liberal. The anti-liberal right sought to mediate the process of modernity by gaining control over it. Because of the crisis in Europe after 1919 there was no certainty that the liberal parliamentary system would outlive the alternatives. Yet, despite the gloomy predictions of the early demise of parliamentary democracy, and the evidence that many parliamentary systems were under severe pressure, relatively few parliamentary systems collapsed because of internal crisis. It was the war rather than the Depression which extinguished parliamentary institutions in most European states between 1929 and 1940. In a comparative context Garraty has argued that radicalism was in short supply throughout the 1930s, advancing the view that:

> most of those who suffered from the depression accepted its burdens and endured its indignities without reacting violently or pressing for basic changes in the economy or in the society. No significant alterations of the capitalist system were made, even in Germany and the United States, where the most important changes in the status quo were attempted.[60]

It is true that if one takes voting patterns, policy formulation and implementation and the role of the state into account, it is possible to exaggerate the extent to which the 1930s experienced radical change. However, it is possible to agree that a revolution did not take place, while at the same time arguing that the changes which took place were significant and important. The most dramatic example of this was the National Socialist takeover in Germany and the extent to which the Hitler regime sought to implement its policies. While the extent to which Germany achieved full employment might be debated, compared to other European states the Nazis formulated a successful economic strategy in terms of its own objectives.[61]

Yet Germany may not be the most appropriate example of either radicalism or change in the 1930s. If the circumstances in Germany were unique, then it is possible that the response to those circumstances was in turn unique: the radical nature of national socialism can consequently be accounted for *solely* in the context of German history. If so, the Depression becomes the occasion for mobilisation, rather than the cause. If the causal relationship between national socialism and the Depression is attenuated (I do not wish to suggest that it had no influence), it is necessary to look beyond economic events to account for the success of the Nazis. The logic of such a position is to further claim that the association between economic downturn and authoritarian takeover may be weak and that individual states may encounter very similar economic difficulties, yet experience a radically different political outcome.[62] In contrast to this view Harold James has suggested that if Britain had experienced the type of upheavals in its economic life that was the case in Germany, it and other democracies might not have been able to maintain political democracy. He also notes that when the parliamentary system worked during the Depression in Germany, the outcome was the appointment of Hitler as Chancellor and the end of democracy.[63] Yet, neither of these claims are conclusive in that alternative political coalitions were possible if circumstances were different. It was not the Depression which led to parliamentary failure, but the underlying authoritarian nature of much of the political system and more importantly the political culture itself. Crucially, it was the collapse of most of the centre right which facilitated Hitler's ascent to power. It was political failure which permitted Hitler to capitalise on the economic crisis that followed the Depression, an incapacity by the political leadership of the traditional parties to agree on a government which generated the conditions for the National Socialist electoral success, and the subsequent drive to authoritarianism.

This also illustrates the extent to which the Depression might contribute to the collapse of democracy. In the case of Austria, which also experienced authoritarian takeover after a brief civil war provoked by the right, the Depression does appear to have been the occasion for decisive action against labour and the socialists in 1934. Even prior to the Depression, however, there had been an escalation of violence against the left by the state and by right-wing paramilitary organisations condoned or supported by the governing Christian Social Party. Moreover, the class basis for politics in the new state led to political confrontation between left and right in politics, urban and rural cultures, and between trade unions and employers. This conflictual context was further exacerbated by the failure of the state to acquire legitimacy, especially from the right. In the cases of Austria and Germany right-wing takeover occurs in a context of a right which is, at the least, ambiguous concerning the legitimacy of the state and parliamentary democracy, and a strong left which is the main defence of the democratic republic. The left is without adequate political means or allies to defend the democratic state against the right, particularly if the right continued to reject the state's legitimacy and is prepared to use violence to exclude other parties from power and influence.[64]

In contrast to these examples, which appear to sustain Mayer's thesis, there are other cases of states where democracy was seriously threatened or where the Depression was destabilising, but where the parliamentary system survived. In Finland what is notable is the failure of the Lapua movement, despite some interim successes, to push the governing elite to an anti-parliamentary resolution of the crisis. The Lapua had most of the characteristics of a mass fascist movement, and even if this were not the case, it is clearly an anti-liberal radical authoritarian nationalist movement. Moreover it grew out of the Depression, formulating a set of political demands, while mobilising a mass extra-parliamentary movement between 1929 and 1930. In addition to this, the movement seduced a significant portion of the right in the short term to such an extent that for a period the parliamentary system was numbed by it and the Lapua-endorsed candidate for prime minister, P.E. Svinhufvud, was appointed. As in Austria, Finland was characterised by deep confrontation between left and right throughout the 1920s, in part attributable to the consequences of the civil war and in part due to the effective organisation of both unions and employers. Parliamentary democracy was threatened by Lapua, yet that threat had been met and overcome by 1932. In the meantime the National Coalition Party, the main conservative party, had been seriously compromised by its close identity with the insurgents, to the extent of forming electoral alliances with the Patriotic Peoples Movement in the 1933 elections. There were a number of reasons for the reassertion of parliamentary control in Finland. The first is that a major aim of the Lapua was secured fairly quickly; the outlawing of the communist party and a more authoritarian style of government after the appointed by Svinhufvud. In response to this the Social Democrats, the largest party after the 1930 elections, strongly defended the parliamentary system, though as a party with 66 out of 200 seats there was little it could achieve in isolation. But the centre right also appeared to have misgivings at an early date. A march on Helsinki in 1930, reminiscent of Mussolini's march on Rome, was neutralised by the non-Lapua centre right represented by Mannheim. The Prime Minister and the main elites in Finnish society opted for democracy rather than authoritarianism after the summer of 1930. A majority of the Agrarian Union, the Progress Party and the Swedish Peoples Party provided a parliamentary basis which could, in alliance with the Social Democrats, marginalise the threat to the system. In turn, despite expectations by the Lapua, neither the paramilitary Civil Guard nor the armed forces supported its anti-system aims, though both had supported the anti-communist aims of the movement.

Thus, while Finland moved to the right between 1929 and 1932, and despite the anti-liberal intent of its anti-communist laws, it was confined to the parliamentary system by the emergence of a liberal bloc which included both left and right. The Social Democrats contributed to this bloc because of its moderate politics and its acceptance, under protest, that the working class would suffer in the Depression as a consequence of right-wing parliamentary dominance. In turn the right could enter the bloc having gained the symbolic defeat of communism, but also a real reversal of working-class influence, reflected in the fall in real income. The main stabilising factor was probably the integration of the rural agrarian sector into the parliamentary system. In turn, the nation state had acquired considerable legitimacy after 1918, including the institutions of the state. The discontent which followed the Depression was very real, but it was quickly diverted from the extra-parliamentary to the parliamentary. The Agrarian Union subsequently recognised that the conservative economic policies did not benefit its supporters, a factor which led later in the decade to the inclusion of the Social Democrats in government and a more left-leaning or interventionist policy style.[65]

Of the political systems which survived as democracies throughout the 1930s, Finland seems to be the one which comes closest to breakdown. The survival of democracy was heavily dependent on the behaviour of conservative and right-wing elites. In some cases, conservatives moved towards the authoritarians, but the majority continued to support the democratic system. The right faced a similar dilemma in Ireland a little later in the decade. In 1932 the conservative Cumann na nGaedheal government narrowly lost the election and was replaced by the radical nationalist Fianna Fáil party which, with the support of the Labour Party, was committed to radical economic, social and constitutional change. One of the consequences of these changes was a significant drop in the income of the exporting farming sector. The Blueshirt movement emerged at this time with two objectives. The first was the need to protect the new opposition party from attacks by the Irish Republican Army (IRA) and other paramilitary groups, but it was also committed to defend the economic status of the farmers. There was considerable debate within the new Fine Gael party on the appropriate response to the government, whether opposition should take the form of paramilitary or anti-parliamentary action. There was some equivocation on the part of sections of the right regarding parliamentary democracy; corporatism was influential and the Italian and Portuguese models gained some sympathy among right-wing and Catholic theorists. Despite this, the overwhelming majority of conservatives opposed any challenge to democracy or parliamentary institutions, subsequently emasculating the Blueshirt movement and depriving it of legitimacy or influence. In response to the authoritarian nationalism of the Blueshirts, traditional conservatives reasserted their own commitment to the parliamentary system and continued to maintain their position as a loyal opposition. They strongly opposed the government's policies, believing that the consequences were disastrous for the state, but were not prepared to move outside the democratic framework to challenge them.[66]

The Irish and Finnish cases share a common characteristic: right-wing elites were, for a time, prepared to sanction paramilitary organisation and pressure, but when that moved beyond pressure and embraced an anti-parliamentary objective the elites combined to exclude the radicals from political influence. In each case the movements withered once the traditional right had opted to defend the existing institutions and oppose the aims of radicals. In both these cases sections of the right were attracted by an authoritarian alternative, very fleetingly in the Irish case, but unlike the Austrian and German examples accepted the confines of the liberal democratic system to resolve the difficulties. Why then do some countries rather than others maintain political democracy in times of crisis? In the context of the German example it might be urged that the seriousness of the crisis made radical alternatives attractive to the electorate. There can be little doubt that Hitler offered a radical alternative, one which was in part implemented. Yet it is possible to exaggerate the uniqueness of the effect of the Depression on Germany and ignore the seriousness of its impact on other states. The United States also suffered serious dislocation, American society was affected in a fundamental fashion. Agricultural and industrial output collapsed, investment dried up and growth plummeted. In addition unemployment in the United States was among the highest in the industrial states, while the welfare net was virtually non-existent.

Between 1928 and 1932 the party system disintegrated and there is evidence that the society was under considerable strain by the middle of 1932. The incumbent president Herbert Hoover (1929–33) followed policies almost identical to those pursued by conservatives everywhere in response to the recession. A comparison with Brüning in Germany and MacDonald in Britain highlights the continuity of policy during the early stages of the recession. While exact comparisons across the industrial states are difficult to make, the United States by 1932 was experiencing a crisis only comparable to that of Germany.[67] To quantify the downturn is less difficult: an estimated 70 000 bankruptcies occurred between 1929 and 1933, some 5000 banks had closed and at least one in four people were unemployed. One estimate suggested that, in 1932, 28 million people had no income in any form. The by-product of this was repossession of homes, farms and consumer goods. Between 1929 and 1933 investment declined by 87 per cent, undermining any possible business-led expansion out of the Depression. GNP fell by 31 per cent and consumption by 19 per cent over the same time.[68]

In common with most politicians on the right, and many on the left, Hoover at first did not believe that a special response was required, but once the crisis became more apparent he attempted to respond more positively. However, his actions were limited by a belief in minimalist government, fiscal conservatism and the nature of the American economy. The State, he argued, could not solve the crisis by intervention; only the voluntary efforts of individuals and the states could achieve this. In February 1931, at a time when the severity of the crisis was attested to, he reiterated his philosophy of how such problems should be treated:

> Victory over the depression and over our other difficulties will be won by the resolution of our people to fight their own battles in their own communities, by stimulating their ingenuity to solve their own problems, by taking new courage to be masters of their own destiny in the struggle of life. This is not the easy way, but it is the American way.[69]

The American way for Hoover included deflation, balanced budgets, voluntarism on the questions of welfare and unemployment. Though Hoover was not a strict ideological deflationist, he was confined within traditional conservative parameters by his own conception of the relationship between government responsibility and the economy. For him, and for the bulk of the Republican Party, federal power should remain constrained and the individual states should act when necessary. The most innovative response to the Depression came in the last year of the administration with the establishment of the Reconstruction Finance Corporation, but it was an isolated response and one introduced under pressure. The real limits to Hoover's policies, as was the case with most traditional conservatives, was that they did not work and in the run up to the November 1932 presidential election the economic and social crisis deepened.

Yet the outcome in the United States was quite different from that in Germany. In contrast to the move to the right in the latter case, the American electorate endorsed a Democratic candidate for the first time since 1916, one advocating a more activist policy towards the Depression. Although Roosevelt was cautious during the campaign concerning his policies, once elected, and with the relative security of a majority Democratic Congress, he enacted a series of counter-cyclical policies which improved conditions, though without eliminating the causes of the Depression itself. The New Deal programmes presupposed active involvement by the federal government in the co-ordination of relief, the regulation of the economy and the maintenance of income and prices at a minimum level. In contrast to Germany or some other European states, there is little evidence that the American electorate, or any section of the Republican Party, was attracted by anti-democratic politics during the 1930s.[70] Garraty has explained the relative stability of the United States in the following terms:

> The relatively high American standard of living meant that people, individually and collectively, had more to fall back upon when hard times struck. And its basically harmonious society enabled the nation to get through the times of troubles with less social discord than many other countries experienced.[71]

American politics in the 1930s was not as harmonious as this suggests, nor were losses as easily contained. Stability in the United States was assured by the absence of an anti-democratic right or by a disloyal opposition. The Republican Party, despite its criticism of Roosevelt, remained loyal and used the electoral system and Congress when attempting to challenge the President's policies. In the United States elections continued to be the vehicle for change, but also for preventing or controlling it. Although the New Deal never ended the Depression, its counter-cyclical policies were effective in stabilising the economy and in preventing anti-democratic outcomes. An activist presidency demonstrated to the electorate that the federal authorities were prepared to respond to public opinion and pressure, though this did not reduce unemployment to less than 17 per cent by 1940. The realignment of the party system in favour of the Democratic Party also reflected the emergence of a class cleavage as the main source of division in the political system during this decade. The Republicans found it difficult to counter this appeal, attested to by the Party's disastrous defeat in 1936 when it campaigned on a deflationary programme.[72] It is only during 1937 and 1938 that the Republicans find issues around which they can reconstitute their conservative appeal, and then only through co-operation with conservative Democrats.[73]

It is more appropriate to compare the American experience of the Depression with that of Britain, Scandinavia and Ireland, rather than that of Germany. The former states all retained democratic institutions, while adapting to the challenge of economic crisis. In contrast to either the radicalisation of the right or the counter-cyclical strategy adopted by the United States, relatively little changed in Britain during the 1930s. The Depression prompted a return to the Conservative Party which reasserted its political dominance throughout the decade. In sharp contrast to a number of other states Britain maintained its traditional deflationary policy, though adjusting to take account of the external crisis. It is conservatism rather than radicalism which reaps the electoral benefit of the Depression in Britain; a right-wing majority government is returned to office in 1931 and 1935. One contributory reason for this was the failure of the incumbent Labour government to respond positively to the crisis. Another was the timing of the British election cycle in contrast to elections elsewhere. Until the end of 1931 opinion considered that the Depression was a reflection of the normal business cycle and the 1931 election in Britain endorsed the parties advocating the traditional approach to it. It is only in the course of 1932 that the full seriousness of the crisis became evident and it is in this year and the following that the major electoral changes take place in Germany, Sweden, Ireland and the United States. These elections transformed their respective political systems and allowed the governments to adopt innovative policies. This was followed in the democratic states by the reinforcement of counter-cyclical majority governments at subsequent elections. In Britain the 1935 election was also a reinforcing one, but one which reinforced conservative dominance rather than a radical alternative. Between 1931 and 1935 the National Government in Britain had also responded to the crisis but had framed its response in a Conservative fashion. The most striking contrast in this process was the acceptance in the United States that deficit spending would be a primary response to economic downturn, as in 1937, whereas in Britain such programmes were never put into effect.[74]

By 1936 the worst effects of the recession were over, and most states had adjusted to its impact. A new equilibrium had been established in domestic policy by then and it subsequently became quite difficult to change the nature of that equilibrium; the failure of the French Popular Front to do so is one case in point.[75] Instability during the second half of the decade came from the expansionism of the Hitler regime and concerned the European balance of power. The domestic equilibrium was one which accepted the continuation of high levels of unemployment, low growth and protectionism. The continuation of such circumstances created a number of problems for the right in liberal democratic states. Though conservative blocs retained power in a number of states, they remained exposed to possible radicalisation from the left or right (Rexism in Belgium for example). In the context of the Depression, it is the democratic right which changed least. The totalitarian left and right could argue that the problems of the Depression had been resolved by them, while authoritarian movements suggested that the abolition of democracy provided greater security to property and status than a commitment to parliamentary structures. In addition, leftist intervention, though it did not solve the problems of unemployment, generated political realignment in a number of states, a process which led to the decline and fragmentation of the right. In these circumstances the actions of conservatives appeared timid and their reassertion of traditional economic and social objectives inadequate. Despite this conservative governments continued in power in a number of states up to 1939, while conservatives in opposition in other states functioned as a loyal opposition.

The real threat to the democratic right, and indeed to liberal democracy, is the breakdown of political and international order in Europe after 1936. Conservatives had adapted well to the crisis after the First World War and had contributed to and benefited from the stabilisation which followed. The response to the Depression had been less successful, but not always inadequate in electoral or domestic terms. It is the growing instability in the second half of the decade which posed the greatest threat to those conservative regimes operating within liberal democratic systems. The challenge from Hitler, from the deteriorating international situation and from the continuing Depression were such that a traditional conservative response proved to be inadequate. One of the consequences of this failure was the Second World War. An indirect consequence of the war was the further transformation of the right.

Notes

1. Fritz Fischer, *Krieg der Illusionen: Die Deutsche Politik von 1911–1914* (Kronberg/ Ts: Athenäum-Verlag, 1978), pp. 145–68, 384–412. Gregor Schöllgen (ed.), *Escape into War?: The Foreign Policy of Imperial Germany* (Oxford: Berg, 1990); David Schoenbaum, *Zabern 1913: Consensus Politics in Imperial Germany* (George Allen and Unwin, 1982).

2. Arno J. Mayer, *The Persistence of the Old Regime* (London: Croom Helm, 1981), pp. 3–4. It is necessary to be cautious concerning the radical, as distinct from the destructive, potential of war and its aftermath. It may be an exaggeration to claim that the old fabric was as rent as this implies. Charles S. Maier, *Recasting Bourgeois Europe* (Princeton: Princeton University Press, 1975). The complex outcomes to war

and its aftermath have been admirably modelled for the United States by Karen Rasler, 'War, accommodation, and violence in the United States 1890–1970' *American Political Science Review* 80: 3 (September 1986), pp. 921–45 who suggests that the outcome depends to a considerable extent on the severity of the crisis which results and the extent to which governments can accommodate the pressures for change.

3. Roberto Vivarelli, 'Interpretations of the Origins of Fascism' *Journal of Modern History* 63:1 (1991), pp. 29–43; A similar argument, though from different premises, has been developed by Ernst Nolte, *Der Europäische Bürgerkrieg 1917—945* (Frankfurt: Propyläen Verlag, 1987).

4. Vivarelli, op. cit., develops this theme.

5. Robert Gilpin, *War and Social Change* (Cambridge: Cambridge University Press, 1981), pp. 1–49, for discussion of hegemonic structures. Paul Kennedy, *The Rise and Fall of Great Powers* (London: Unwin Hyman, 1988) for a complimentary view of the same question. However, for a useful counter to both these approaches; Joseph S. Nye, Jr, *Bound To Lead* (New York: Basic Books, 1990) for a discussion of 'power transitions', pp. 25–68.

6. Kennedy, op. cit.. On the search for domestic stability in Europe, Charles S. Maier, 'The two postwar eras and the conditions for stability in twentieth-century Western Europe' in Maier, *In Search of Stability* (Cambridge: Cambridge university Press, 1987), pp. 153–84.

7. It can of course be argued that this was a profoundly sexist action which refused to acknowledge these women as individuals, but as surrogate males under rather special circumstances. France continued to exclude women in every respect.

8. Vivarelli, op. cit. pp. 29–43. The calculations are derived from Thomas T. Mackie and Richard Rose, *The International Almanac of Electoral History* 2nd edn (London: Macmillan, 1982).

9. Mayer, op. cit., pp. 4–10 for the counter-argument.

10. The First World War and the Second World War up to 1941 were essentially European conflicts. Their origins and most of the fighting occurred in continental Europe, where this was not the case it was but an extension of European imperial concerns. This ended with the entry of the Soviet Union, the United States and Japan into the conflict. It was only after this that the war extended beyond the limits of Europe and took on a global resonance. Geoffrey Barraclough, *An Introduction to Contemporary History* (Harmondsworth: Penguin, 1967 [1964]), pp. 93–123.

11. Albert O. Hirschman, *Shifting Involvements* (Oxford: Martin Robertson, 1982), p. 117; Stephen Holmes, *The Anatomy of Antiliberalism* (Cambridge, Mass: Harvard University Press, 1993), who suggests that one of the reasons for hostility to liberalism is the absence of political passion.

12. Arend Lijphart, *The Politics of Accommodation: Pluralism and Democracy in the Netherlands* rev. edn (Berkeley, Los Angeles: University of California Press, 1975), pp. 103–21; Tom Garvin, *Nationalist Revolutionaries in Ireland 1858–1928* (Oxford: Clarendon Press, 1987).

13. J.M. Winter, *The Great War and the British People* (London: Macmillan, 1986), p. 38.

14. Modris Ekstein, *Rites of Spring* (New York: Anchor Books, 1989); Bernard Waites, *A Class Society at War* (Leamington Spa: Berg, 1987).

15. See the essays in Martin Blinkhorn (ed.), *Fascists and Conservatives* (London: Unwin Hyman, 1990) for a discussion of the linkages between nationalism and the right.

16. Walter Korpi, *The Working Class in Welfare Capitalism: Work, Unions and Politics in Sweden* (London: Routledge, 1978); idem., *The Democratic Class Struggle* (London: Routledge, 1983); Gösta Esping-Anderson, *Politics Against Markets: The Social Democratic Road to Power* (Princeton: Princeton University Press, 1985).

17. Stanley G. Payne, *Fascism: Comparison and Definition* (Madison, Wisconsin:

University of Wisconsin Press, 1980), pp. 3–21 for a discussion of these divisions.

18. Ian Kershaw (ed.) *Weimar: Why did German Democracy Fail?* (London: Weidenfeld and Nicolson, 1990), p. 22.

19. Robert J. Goldstein, *Political Repression in Nineteenth Century Europe* (London: Croom Helm, 1983), p. 343.

20. Michael W. Doyle, 'Liberalism and world politics' *American Political Science Review* 80:4 (1986), pp. 1151–63 defines 'Liberal regimes' following Kant as including: market and private property economies; polities which are externally sovereign; citizens who possess juridical rights; and 'republican' representative government (competitive). Francis Fukuyama, *The End of History and the Last Man* (London: Hamish Hamilton, 1992), pp. 49–50 had adopted Doyle's approach, plotting what he claims to be a significant advance in democratic regimes since 1975. While not disagreeing with his general approach to this question, the evidence from the 1930s would suggest that what is important for democracy is not the establishment itself, but the maintenance of such a regime over time.

21. The contrasting outcomes for individual regimes can be assessed in Stephen Fischer-Galati, *Twentieth Century Rumania* (New York: Columbia University Press, 1970), pp. 29–45; R.J. Crampton, *A Short History of Bulgaria* (Cambridge: Cambridge University Press, 1987), pp. 82–99, 107–14; Joseph Rothchild, *East Central Europe Between the Two World Wars* (Seattle and London: University of Washington Press, 1974).

22. Rudy Koshar (ed.), *Splintered Classes: Politics and the Lower Middle Classes in Interwar Europe* (New York: Holmes and Meier, 1990); Frank Bealey, 'Stability and Crisis: fears about threats to democracy', *European Journal of Political Research* 15:6 (1987), pp.687-715.

23. Stephen Salter and John Stevenson (eds), *The Working Class and Politics in Europe and America 1929–1945* (London: Longman, 1990), p. 8; Dietrich Rueschemeyer, Evelyne Huber Stephens and John D. Stephens, *Capitalist Development and Democracy* (Cambridge: Polity Press, 1992), pp. 79–154.

24. Tim Kirby, 'Austria' in Salter and Stevenson, op. cit., pp. 11–40; Jill Lewis, 'Conservatives and fascists in Austria, 1918–34', in Blinkhorn op. cit., pp. 98-117.

25. Kenneth O. Morgan, *Consensus and Disunity: The Lloyd George Coalition Government 1918–1922* (Oxford: Clarendon, 1979); Martin Pugh, *The Tories and the People 1880–1935* (Oxford: Basil Blackwell, 1985); J.J. Lee, *Ireland 1912–1985* (Cambridge: Cambridge University Press, 1989); Geoff Eley, 'Conservatives and radical nationalists in Germany: the production of fascist potentials, 1912–1928', in Blinkhorn, op. cit.,pp. 50–70.

26. Maier, op. cit., p. 581; Maurice Cowling, *The Impact of Labour, 1920–1924* (Cambridge: Cambridge University Press, 1971); Keith Middlemas, *Politics in Industrial Society* (London: Andre Deutsch, 1979), pp. 152–213; Erik Hansen, 'Between reform and Revolution: Social Democracy and Dutch Society, 1917–21', in Hans A. Schmitt (ed.), *Neutral Europe: Between War and Revolution 1917–23* (Charlottesville: University Press of Virginia, 1988), pp. 176–203.

27. Dan S. White, 'Reconsidering European socialism in the 1920s', *Journal of Contemporary History* 16:2 (April 1981), pp. 251–72, where the notion of a socialist breakthrough is evaluated and found wanting. What White does not assess is the failure of the left in the context of the successful strategy of the right; Peter Baldwin, *The Politics of Social Solidarity: Class Bases of the European Welfare State 1875–1975* (Cambridge: Cambridge University Press, 1990), pp. 55–106 on the constituent parts of such a potential breakthrough.

28. This does not mean to imply that corporatism did not have a place in politics, but only to question its importance. Maier (op. cit.) and Middlemas (op. cit.) take the opposite view on this matter.

29. In 1928 the combined right in Sweden accounted for 56.5 per cent of the vote compared with 37 per cent for the SAP.
30. The German liberals had moved to the right well before the First World War, whereas in the other three cases developments during and immediately after the war provided the catalyst for change.
31. James L. Sundquist, *Dynamics of the Party System* (Washington D.C.; Brookings Institution, 1983), pp. 196–7; Edward A. Moore, *A Catholic Runs for President* (Glouwester Mass: Peter Smith, 1968); Matthew and Hannah Josephson, *Al Smith: Hero of the Cities* (London: Thames and Hudson, 1970), pp. 350–400.
32. Data calculated from Barbara Sinclair, *Congressional Realignment 1925–1978* (Austin: University of Texas Press, 1982).
33. For the comparative figures: Hartmut Knaeble, *A Social History of Western Europe 1880–1980* (Dublin: Gill and Macmillan, 1989), pp. 84-86. For Finland, see David Kirby, 'Finland' in Salter and Stephenson, op. cit., pp. 41–45, where he stresses the predominantly low levels of manufacturing industry, the rural basis of society and the failure of a strong political movement to translate electoral support into economic gains for the working class. Australia appears to provide a 'deviant' case in that union density actually increased between 1920 and 1930 to a very high level of 40 per cent. Of the countries discussed here only Sweden can boast of similar levels, but from a lower base without realising or maintaining the Australian level until the late 1930s.
34. Maier, op. cit., pp. 444–5, 594, for the continental experience; Middlemas, op. cit. pp. 174–213; Alan Booth,'Corporatism, capitalism and depression', *British Journal of Sociology* 33 (1982), pp. 200–23
35. It would be mistaken for example to associate the conservative support for protection with support for corporatism. Samuel H. Beer, *Modern British Politics* (London: Faber and Faber, 1969), pp. 277–309; Booth, op. cit..
36. Hansen, op.cit. pp. 176–303; E.H. Kossman, *The Low Countries 1780-1940* (Oxford: Clarendon Press, 1978), pp. 567–92; Arend Lijphart, *The Politics of Accommodation* (Berkeley: University of California Press, 2nd edn 1975).
37. Sundquist, op. cit. pp. 200–1; Ross McKibbin, 'The economic policy of the second Labour government 1929–1931', *Past and Present* 68 (Autumn 1975), pp. 95–123; Richard T. Griffiths (ed.), *The Netherlands and the Gold Standard, 1931–1936* (Amsterdam: NEHA, 1987), pp. 5–7; Kossman, op. cit., pp. 661–5.
38. Gourevitch has provided a model which outlines a policy sequence for the crisis. They are orthodox deflation, socialist orthodoxy, neo-orthodoxy and demand stimulation. As Gourevitch presents the options, the first is in general usage until 1931, the second is never utilised, the third, which involved adopting tariffs and devaluing the currency, is widespread by the mid-1930s, while the fourth is implemented by a number of states. Peter A. Gourevitch, 'Breaking with orthodoxy: the politics of economic policy response to the Depression of the 1930s' *International Organisation* 38.1 (Winter 1984), pp. 95–129. For a somewhat different approach, John A. Garraty, *The Great Depression* (Garden City, New York: Anchor Books, 1987).
39. Mayer, op. cit., p. 4. Counter-revolution may not be the correct term here, for in most cases right-wing authoritarian/totalitarian takeovers are not counter-revolutionary in the sense that revolutionaries are in power or that there is a threat of revolutionary government. In most cases, as in Germany and Spain, the objective of the right was to displace the parliamentary system itself. Perhaps counter democratic or counter-liberal would be the best term. This however does not satisfy Mayer because he wishes to pose counter-revolution in the context of what he believes is the superior claims of revolution in the twentieth century and of the dynamic of world history. Nor does his varieties of counter-revolutionary forms (p. 86) provide a satisfactory schema when applied to historical sequences. His use of counter-revolution as pre-emptive, posterior, accessary, disguised, anticipatory, externally licensed and externally

imposed have some explanatory power, but are limited in application.

40. The complex relationship between change and stability is addressed in Keith M. Dowding and Richard Kimber, 'The meaning and use of "political stability"' *European Journal of Political Research* 11:3 (1983), pp. 229–43; Harry Eckstein, 'A culturalist Theory of Political Change' *American Political Science Review* 82:3, (September 1988), pp. 789–804.

41. Mayer, op. cit. pp. 50–55; It should be added that Mayer's description is a caricature of conservatism in Europe and North America over the past 100 years or more. Not only has it been consistently and self-consciously ideological, it has also demonstrated a proved capacity to act in crisis. The German experience of 1919–1930, notwithstanding many misgivings, is an example of how conservatives did respond to crisis and change and used it to their own advantage. One is led to conclude that Mayer, like others on the left, wish to condemn all conservatives as part of a 'stupid party'. Moreover the idea of ordinary times assumes that accommodation of interests in that context is less onerous than the politics of crisis, and does not prepare a politician for it. In fact it may be more difficult.

42. Martin Blinkhorn, 'Conservatism, traditionalism and fascism in Spain, 1898–1937' in Blinkhorn, op. cit., pp. 118–37.

43. Joseph Baglieri 'Italian Fascism and the Crisis of Liberal Hegemony; 1901–1922' in Stein U. Larsen, Bernt Hagtvet and Jan P. Myklebust (eds), *Who Were the Fascists?* (Bergen: Universitetsforlaget, 1980) pp. 318–336.

44. Paolo Farnetti, 'Social conflict, parliamentary fragmentation, institutional shift, and the rise of Fascism: Italy' in J.J. Linz and A. Stepan (eds), *The Breakdown of Democratic Regimes: Europe* (Baltimore: The Johns Hopkins University Press, 1978), pp. 3–33: Vivarelli, op. cit..

45. R. Sarti, 'Italian fascism: radical politics and conservative goals' in Blinkhorn, op. cit., pp. 14–30, pp. 21–2 for discussion on this point; Maier, op. cit., pp. 562–4 for discussion on nature of the Italian regime; Stanley G. Payne, *Fascism: Comparison and Definition* (Madison: University of Wisconsin Press, 1980), pp. 42–104.

46. A. James Gregor, *Italian Fascism and Developmental Dictatorship* (Princeton, NJ: Princeton University Press, 1979), pp. 153–61.

47. Richard Bessel, 'Why did the Weimar Republic collapse?', in Ian Kershaw (ed.), op. cit., p. 148. Bessel argues that the uniqueness of Germany can be associated with the extent to which the Weimar Republic was assailed by a large number of serious challenges, each of which on its own would have been destabilising, but coming together made crisis management virtually impossible. Weimar Germany, according to this interpretation:

   had the *most* democratic constitution; it developed the *most advanced* social-welfare system; it suffered the *worst* inflation; it had lost and had to pay for the *most* destructive war fought up to that date; due to its peculiar economic structure and position in the world economy it was *most* savagely affected by the Depression.

48. M. Rainer Lepsius, 'From fragmented party democracy to government by emergency decree and National Socialist takeover: Germany, in Linz and Stepan, op. cit., pp. 33–79.

49. By 1930 these parties captured around 38 per cent of total votes; by 1932 over 50 per cent and in 1933, 64 per cent. It is only in 1933, of course, and in unique circumstances, that the right obtains a majority of votes and appears to legitimise the national socialist takeover.

50. Lepsius, op. cit., passim; Eley, op. cit., pp. 50–70.

51. Larry Eugene Jones, 'Inflation, revaluation, and the crisis of middle class politics: a study in the dissolution of the German party system, 1923–1928', *Central European History* XII:2 (June, 1979), pp. 143–68. Jones suggests that the Saxon state elections of October 1926 remains a 'critical episode in the disintegration of the bourgeois party

system'. The protest parties which gained at that election substantially collapsed and while the voters briefly moved back to the traditional parties, the experience here and elsewhere appears to have generated a political volatility and a floating vote which the national socialists were able to attract later.

52. Stefano Bartolini and Peter Mair, *Identity, Competition and Electoral Availability: The Stabilisation of European Electorates 1885–1985* (Cambridge: Cambridge University Press, 1990), where the concept of block stability is developed.

53. Bernt Hagtvet, 'The theory of mass society and the collapse of the Weimar Republic: a re-examination', in Larsen, Hagtvet and Myklebust., op. cit., pp. 66–117.

54. Lepsius, op. cit. pp. 60–1.

55. Nico Passchier, 'The electoral geography of the Nazi landslide', in Larsen, Hagtvet and Mykelebust, op. cit., pp. 283–300; Thomas Childers, *The Nazi Voter* (Chapel Hill: University of North Carolina Press, 1983); Richard Hamilton, *Who Voted for Hitler?* (Princeton: Princeton University Press, 1982).

56. Thomas Childers (ed.), *The Formation of the Nazi Constituency 1919–1933* (London: Croom Helm, 1986) for a review of the evidence; see also *Central European History* XVII:1 (March, 1984), a special issue on the debate between Hamilton and Childers on the Nazi vote.

57. This discussion does not do full justice to the complexities involved in the voter realignment which took place prior to 1933. It does not address the extent to which either former Catholic or socialist voters actually shifted alignment. However, it does emphasise that the main focus for the realignment was *within* what can loosely be described as the right-wing bloc of voters.

58. Payne, op. cit. for comparison and evaluation; Gilbert Allardyce, 'What fascism is not: thought on the deflation of a concept', *American Historical Review* 84:2 (1979), pp. 36–98.

59. For a discussion and explication see. Payne, op. cit., pp. 16–17; Vivarelli, op. cit..

60. Garraty, op. cit., p.172

61. R.J. Overy, *The Nazi Economic Recovery, 1932–1938* (London: Macmillan, 1982); Charles S. Maier, 'The economics of Fascism and Nazism', in Maier, *In Search of Stability,* op. cit., pp. 70–120; Avraham Barkai, *Nazi Economics: Ideology, Theory, and Policy* (Oxford: Berg, 1990), pp. 158–249.

62. The recession after 1974 has not been accompanied by a move to authoritarianism, in fact in a number of cases the movement has been from authoritarianism to democracy. In the case of Spain, Portugal and Greece democratic institutions have been consolidated during the 1970s and 1980s despite high unemployment and recession. I would not wish to suggest either that there is a causal relationship between recession and democracy, but what does require examination is the view that the 'axial principles' which drive politics, the economy or culture operate differentially and at discrete levels and momentum. See Daniel Bell, *The Cultural Contradictions of Capitalism* (New York: Basic Books, 1982).

63. Harold James, *The German Slump* (Oxford: Clarendon Press, 1986), pp. 159–60, 37; Joseph Lee, commenting on this, has pointed to the need for a comparative approach to the impact of different parliamentary traditions on the Depression. This is to invert the normal approach to this question and it is one which I share in this chapter; see Lee, 'Policy and performance in the German economy, 1925–35: a comment on the Borchardt Thesis', in Michael Laffan (ed.), *The Burden of German History 1919–45* (London: Wiedenfeld and Nicolson, 1988), pp. 131–50; Knut Borchardt, *Perspectives on Modern German Economic History and Policy* (Cambridge: Cambridge University Press, 1991).

64. Salter and Stevenson, op. cit., for numerous examples of this outcome.

65. Risto Alapuro and Erik Allardt, 'The Lapua Movement: the threat of rightist takeover in Finland 1930–32', in Linz and Stepan, op. cit., pp. 122–41; Lauri Karvonen, 'The

Fascist conception of law', in Matti Wiberg (ed.), *The Political Life of Institutions* (Jyväsklä: The Finnish Political Science Association, 1991), pp. 285–6 where the similarities between Lapua and Fascism are discussed.

66. Lee, in Laffan, op. cit. pp. 176–85; Andrew Orridge, 'The Blueshirts and the "Economic War": a study of Ireland in the context of dependency theory', *Political Studies* 31:3 (1983), pp. 351–69; Maurice Manning, *The Blueshirts* (Dublin: Gill and Macmillan, 1970); Brian Girvin, 'The Republicanisation of Irish Society: 1932–48' in J. Hill (ed.), *A New History of Ireland* (Dublin: Royal Irish Academy, forthcoming).

67. Anthony J. Badger, *The New Deal* (Basingstoke: Macmillan, 1989), pp. 11–65 for the extent of the crisis. For a comparative approach see Garraty, op. cit..

68. Thomas K. McGraw, 'The New Deal and the mixed economy', in Harvard Sitkoff (ed.) *Fifty Years Later: The New Deal Evaluated* (New York: Alfred A. Knopf, 1985), pp. 37–68.

69. Albert U. Romesco, *The Poverty of Abundance* (Oxford: Oxford University Press, 1965), p. 129; Sundquist, op. cit., pp. 198–203.

70. Badger, op. cit., pp. 283–97; Seymour M. Lipset and Earl Rabb, *The Politics of Unreason,* 2nd edn (Chicago: The University of Chicago Press, 1978), pp. 150–208 where they discuss the potential challenge to the system by Huey Long, Fr Coughlan and the Liberty League. None of these challenges were serious in the sense that the democratic system was challenged.

71. Garraty, op. cit., p. 124.

72. Samuel H. Beer, 'Liberalism and the national idea', in Robert A. Goldwin, *Left, Right and Centre* (New York: Rand McNally, 1965), pp. 142–69; John W. Jeffries, 'The "New" New Deal: FDR and American Liberalism, 1937–1945', *Political Science Quarterly* 105:3 (Fall 1990), pp. 397–418; Ronald L. Feinman, 'The progressive Republican Senate bloc and the presidential election of 1932', *Mid America* 52:2 (1977), pp. 73–92 for the dilemmas facing liberal Republicans in 1932. In time the liberal Republicans came to distance their progressive politics from the liberalism of the radical Roosevelt. Ronald Feinman, *The Twilight of Progressivism: The Western Republican Senators and the New Deal* (Baltimore: Johns Hopkins University Press, 1981).

73. James T. Patterson, *Congressional Conservatism and the New Deal* (Lexington: University of Kentucky Press, 1967).

74. Alan Booth and Melvyn Pack, *Employment, Capital and Economic Policy in Great Britain 1918–39* (Oxford: Basil Blackwell, 1985), p. 199; Alan Booth, 'Britain in the 1930s: A Managed Economy?' *Economic History Review* XL: 4 (1987), pp. 499–522; Peter Clarke, *The Keynesian Revolution in the Making, 1924-1936* (Oxford: Clarendon Press, 1988); Griffiths, op. cit. for a discussion of the Dutch case which has similarities with that of Britain; Albert V. Romesco, *The Politics of Recovery* (New York: Oxford University Press, 1983), pp. 158–88 for Roosevelt's support for deficit spending; Gourevitch, op. cit. for comparison.

75. Karl G. Harr, Jr, *The Genesis and Effect of the Popular Front in France* (Lanham, MD: University Press of America, 1987), pp. 76–94; 266–75.

4 The Democratisation of the Right in Continental Europe, 1940–60

Introduction: The Impact of the Second World War on the Right

By 1940 the authoritarian right had become the dominant force in European politics. The defeat of France and the victory of the German army and its allies seemed a prelude to a long period of German dominance in Europe. Indeed, the socialist Henri de Man concluded that the German New Order was a superior alternative to 'bourgeois democracy' which he considered to be decadent; and he was not alone in that assumption.[1] The main support for the new order was forthcoming from the right rather than the left, however. Many sections of the right found the German New Order congenial, accepting its dominance if not always collaborating with it. The growing convergence between fascism and the conservative right continued apace for much of the war. In France, despite the opposition of de Gaulle, the Vichy regime represented an authoritarian attempt to resolve the questions of order and power, and one which achieved considerable legitimacy on the right. It was only after 1943, with the perceptible weakening of the German war effort, that sections of the French right began to distance themselves from association with Germany. The fall of Mussolini is the most blatant example of a conservative elite attempting to save itself from the consequences of association, but similar responses can be found elsewhere.[2] In general the right proved to be far more active when it supported fascism than when it purported to oppose it.

The move away from the Axis on the part of the right was an attempt to influence the post-war settlement, by claiming that the right was patriotic, and had not been responsible for the catastrophe of 1940. In some cases this was easier than others. In the Netherlands, the royal family and the government had gone into exile and consequently could maintain legitimacy in the face of criticism. In contrast, the decision of the Belgian King to remain in the country allowed critics to suggest his complicity with the occupying regime. For those who supported Vichy France this proved to be very difficult: the right, including the Catholic Church and the conservatives, were unable to convince a sceptical public of its patriotic motives after 1940. Moreover, as recent evidence has suggested the complicity between French institutions and the Germans was widespread, especially in its attitudes to Jews. Nor was this a by-product of the occupation. The behaviour of Italian and French authorities was significantly different in the treatment of Jews under their control during the war. The Italians generally took a more humanitarian role.[3] In the case of Austria the integration of the state into Nazi Germany was widely accepted on the right, and most Austrians accepted Hitler's authority.

By the early 1940s a large section of the traditional or conservative right was acquiescent with the radical right, most explicitly in Germany, Austria and Italy, but evident throughout Europe. In other states, the commitment of the conservative right to political democracy had been weakened by the experiences of the inter-war era; this is particularly true of France, Spain and Portugal but had resonances beyond this. Only in those states which had a long tradition of representative democracy did the conservative forces remain democratic throughout this period. However, due to the defeat of 1940 the continuing maintenance of a democratic conservatism remained in doubt. It is only the defeat of fascism which changes these circumstances. The end of the war brought to a conclusion what had effectively been a European Civil War which had been openly waged since 1918, but more covertly from at least the 1890s. The instabilities which had prevailed throughout this time were largely a consequence of the failure or unwillingness of the right to accept the consequences of democratisation, industrialisation and liberalisation. As a phase of reaction, the period 1890–1945 can be characterised by two features. The first was the continuing refusal of traditional elites to accept liberal democracy and representative institutions as the normal method of allocating political power and through which power could or should be exercised. The traditional elites would have been helpless without the radicalisation of certain sections of the middle and lower-middle classes by fascism, Nazism and authoritarian nationalism during the inter-war period. What took place was the subsuming and radicalisation of the anti-democratic current of traditional elites thorough the mass mobilisation of the right through nationalism. The second was the collapse of the existing party systems in continental Europe. By 1940 democratic party systems were restricted to the periphery of Europe or to a limited number of non-European states. Liberal democracy by this time was rare and democratic conservatism even more so.

That liberal democratic states actually won the Second World War did not ensure that democratic forms of government would be institutionalised in the post-war world. However, at least in what became Western Europe, this possibility was enhanced by the involvement of the United States and the United Kingdom in the winning coalition. In addition to this, the association of the Free French forces with this victory and the resistance's identification with France's republican tradition also contributed to the restoration of democracy in the post-war period. In the occupied areas, in addition, the war forced the resistance to develop a strategy for the post-war world. In most cases this involved a strong commitment to democratic forms of government and the need to restrict or eliminate the right which had been associated with the occupying forces. However, it also involved serious thought concerning the nature of the post-war world in social and economic terms. Although it is possible to exaggerate this, there is considerable evidence to suggest that the war operated as a significant catalyst for most societies in Europe, leading many to recognise that the distribution of power and resources could not continue as had been the case in the inter-war period.[4]

These tendencies were further reinforced by the commitment of the United

States, Britain and France to bring about the reintroduction of political democracy in the former Axis states and to facilitate its consolidation in the occupied states. Political democracy was only on hold in states such as Norway, Denmark, the Netherlands and Belgium. There is little evidence in these states of widespread collaboration, though clearly some did take place. In the Netherlands between 1 and 2 per cent of eligible voters were disenfranchised for collaborating with the occupation forces; in Belgium extreme Flemish nationalists had collaborated with the occupation forces on nationalist grounds, a phenomenon one finds elsewhere in Europe. Even in states with long histories of parliamentary democracy and liberal institutions, there were those who actively worked with the Nazi occupation, and many of these were drawn from a section of the population which felt uncomfortable with the logic of modernism and democracy. If this attraction was quite limited in the Netherlands and Belgium, it was widespread in states such as France, Italy, Austria and Germany.

In 1945 there was no assurance that political democracy would be stabilised in Europe, even in Western Europe. Although isolated in 1945, Spain and Portugal continued to provide powerful examples for some within the right on what the future might hold for politics. However, these states had now become political anomalies, precisely because their political form was similar to those developed by the right elsewhere in Europe during the inter-war period. While they were not directly attacked by the Allies, they did not provide models which the Americans or the British were prepared to accept. They might not be prepared to aid the resistance to Franco after 1945, but neither were they prepared to offer ideological legitimacy to non-democratic states. The division of Europe, the cold war and the ideological mobilisation which followed further marginalised any thought of a non-democratic solution to European politics. Paradoxically, anti-communism preserved the corporatist dictatorships in the Iberian peninsula, but also increased the need to further the democratic form elsewhere. The defeat of authoritarian nationalism everywhere in Europe made it imperative to secure that victory by installing regimes which would be sympathetic to liberal democracy. The new conflict with the Soviet Union over the future of Europe further contributed to the insistence on democracy. The authoritarian nationalist threat to political democracy had been defeated in 1945, and whatever followed reflected this fact. The Soviet Union, whether authoritarian or totalitarian, was presented as a more insidious threat to democracy, and one against which right and left could unite, as was to be the case.

The attraction of authoritarian solutions did not simply die out in 1945. It is possible to argue that for at least a decade after the end of the war strong authoritarian tendencies remained in the political culture, and the object of politics during that ten to fifteen years was to convince former rightists that a new form of democratic politics could address their requirements and meet their needs. The strength of this authoritarianism has been noted by Ernest Gellner:

> as far as continental Europe is concerned, an ideologically eclectic but politically confident version of right-wing reaction was securely in command in the early 1940s. Continental Europe would have accommodated itself to the New Order. Large segments of it would have done so without excessive reluctance. The philosophical stock of ideas of the continent would have found little difficulty in providing the status quo with a vindication, had it been victorious.[5]

Though it was not victorious, its influence remained for a considerable time thereafter. If the stabilisation of democratic political systems can only be achieved if the right becomes democratic, then the challenge for European politics after 1945 was how to achieve this. In the first place the defeat of fascism provided a window of opportunity for those conservatives who were democrats, and who had opposed authoritarian tendencies on the right. Second, right-wing politics was out of fashion because of its association with fascism. Third, communism appeared to many as a greater threat than democracy, whether at a domestic level or internationally. Yet it would be mistaken to suggest that the move to democracy was easy or smooth, especially in Germany or Italy.

Conservatism and the Catholic Tradition

One of the most striking features of politics in post-war Western Europe has been the disappearance of extreme right-wing political parties as important components of their respective political systems. This has been accompanied, if not promoted, by the long-term stability of a set of political systems previously unstable and characterised by deep, if not murderous, political and social divisions. The disappearance of the radical right is not simply a by-product of its defeat in the Second World War, though this was obviously a contributory factor. At various stages since the 1940s there has been a surge in support for right-wing parties, but until the 1980s these quickly disappeared. This outcome is all the more surprising when the post-war experience is contrasted with the influence exercised by the extreme right during the inter-war decades.[6]

At a formal level the right was transformed after 1945. Prior to this, it was internally divided between democratic conservatives and the authoritarian right which sought to undermine democratic institutions. The change involved the right accepting the limits and discipline of liberal democratic institutions and political competition. Thus, the right during the post-war years accepted electoral competition and the rules of the political game within a pluralistic system. This did not happen all at once or to the same degree. Residual authoritarianism surfaced from time to time, even within governing parties (de Gaulle, Strauss and the Democrazia Cristiana (DC) generally). However, what is significant is the extent to which political crises since 1945 have usually been resolved within the political system and by the traditional methods associated with elections and government formation. By resolving problems within the institutions conservatism distanced itself from the inter-war right which had frequently used extra-parliamentary means to achieve its political ends. In Western Europe at least, and with notable exceptions (such as Greece 1967–74), a liberal democratic political culture became the normal framework for political participation by the right. Thus between 1945 and the early 1960s a band of states in central/southern Europe, especially France, Germany, Italy and Austria, joined the Benelux, Scandinavian and British model of competitive and stable parliamentary systems. The influence of the traditional conservative elites, the military and the state bureaucracy weakens appreciably. While these elites may not have been immediately democratised, their rightist sentiments were constrained by the successful introduction and consolidation of republican constitutional order.

Nor can these developments be seen in a vacuum. New political parties emerge after 1945, while older ones take on new forms or assert a break with the past. On the right each of them seek to reflect conservative political opinion within a new climate of opinion. More fundamentally, the historic association between conservatism and the authoritarian right breaks down to the extent that conservative parties, whatever they may be called, can no longer be considered right wing in the sense that being right entailed opposition to or conditional support for parliamentary democracy. One consequence of these changes was that the main distinguishing features between the right, liberalism and democratic socialism dissolve at this time. A commitment to restricted franchise ends and universal franchise becomes the norm. On economic matters various types of neo-feudal systems are discarded for the free market, while the mixed economy becomes the norm. More generally the right's repressive instincts are replaced by a commitment, in theory at least, to toleration and pluralism.[7] This is a dramatic change which brings the European right into conformity with the conservative tradition in northern Europe. The most important expression of this change, though not the only one, is the rise of Christian democracy as the main representative of the right in continental Europe. Indeed, so radical is the departure after the Second World War that it may be that the term 'right wing' becomes redundant. Christian democracy is similar to the moderate conservatism which prevailed in Britain and elsewhere in northern Europe throughout the inter-war years. Between 1945 and 1960 Christian democratic parties redefined right-wing and conservative politics, placing them firmly within the democratic process in their respective political systems. In a number of cases these parties become the mainstay of government formation for the decades after 1945, influencing over the long term the nature of the post-war consensus and the evolution of the political structures. In addition, it is arguable that the stability which Western Europe experienced at this time owes much to Christian democracy, though it is important to note that there are different forms of Christian democracy, and that it has developed and evolved. For the purposes of this chapter the period from 1945 to 1960 will be examined, while later developments will be taken up in chapter 7.[8]

The change in right-wing politics brought about by Christian democracy has to be appreciated in its relationship to modernity, to the traditional right and to denominational politics. In different ways each of these responses framed the way in which Christian democracy succeeded in establishing a political agenda in a national system (or not as in the case of France). Modern society, it has been urged by Hirschman, is characterised by a 'stubbornly progressive temper', one which rests uneasily with conservatism, whether democratic or progressive. For much of its history the right has condemned progress, providing different grounds for its criticism and opposition, but always remaining critical of the process itself.[9] While these strategies may distinguish the right from other ideologies in its resistance to the logic of modernity, a clear distinction has to be drawn between the conservatism which operates within, but often against modernity, attempting to control its 'progressive temper' and at times directing it in safer ways, and that conservatism which is associated with the right. This latter conservatism, which is at once radical and reactionary, is unlike the former as it seeks not to amend modernity but to transform it by replacing it with one or other imagined past. The two most determined variants of this radicalism in the twentieth century have been authoritarian nationalism and generic fascism, the object of both being to destroy modernity, though fortunately by 1945 their programme had been discredited.

However, a less radical, but no less reactionary force remained on the right in 1945 which had yet to accept the nature of democratic government. That force was Roman Catholicism. Whatever the relationship between Catholics and democracy in individual states, the Church as an institution and in its ideology eschewed quite explicitly the modern democratic world, while its prescriptions for it involved a return to the pre-revolutionary era. In some ways the Catholic criticism of modernity was the most comprehensive provided by the right prior to the emergence of Nazism, and it was one which maintained its power thereafter. The Church's medievalism and neo-feudalist ideology influenced and shaped the contours of Catholic politics from the 1850s until the 1960s. There is a strong ideological continuity in papal teaching, if not always in Catholic politics as such. Central to this was an anti-modernist view of the world which criticised socialism, but also rejected liberalism, pluralism and individualism as functional means of behaviour. Papal extremism, particularly after the first Vatican Council (1869–70), the declaration of Papal Infallibility and the unification of Italy, intensified in relation to the progress of modernity so that at the beginning of the twentieth century the Church remained the most intransigent of the right-wing movements providing opposition to modern politics. This is reflected in the hostility of successive popes to democratic politics and their continuing commitment to pre-modern authoritarian and monarchist political forms. Consequently, until the 1940s for the most part, Catholics remained outside the politics of modernity and shared with the radical and authoritarian right a hostility to its logic. While some Catholics had achieved accommodation with modern political forms, this tended to occur in societies which had a Protestant political culture, such as the United States, the United Kingdom or the Netherlands, or in societies which were unrepresentative of continental Catholicism such as Ireland. Outside of these areas Catholic politics were usually authoritarian and anti-democratic. The experience of the 1920s and 1930s hardened this view for many. De Gasperi (later to be a founder of Democrazia Cristiana (DC)) endorsed the establishment of a one party state in Austria in 1934 on the grounds that the repressed socialists 'were de-christianizing and fanaticizing the young of their country, and using political power to destroy the Family and suffocate the Faith'. Later still in 1937 he argued that German Catholics should support the Nazis in preference to communism.[10] Such sentiments were widespread throughout the 1930s, reflecting a disquiet with the prevailing democratic model, one reinforced by the Catholic experience in the Spanish Civil War which often radicalised Catholic opinion further in favour of the extreme right.[11]

Not only was Catholic ideology opposed to the progressive temper of modernity, but also to its decidedly Protestant and democratic nature which remained antithetical to Catholicism. While some Catholic theorists attempted to find an accommodation between democracy and Catholicism, this proved elusive until the 1940s. Gellner has argued that modern society includes a 'tendency towards species of a generic protestantism, egalitarianism, democracy and nationalism', a tendency which runs counter to much of the ideology of Catholicism since the

French Revolution. Indeed in the twentieth century Catholic ideology identified with those trends in European thought which de-emphasised the individual and emphasised the community, the family and the people. Despite Catholic reservations on the issue of race or the use of violence, papal ideology proved to be more congenial to authoritarianism than to democracy.[12] To this extent Catholic ideology participated in the collectivist reaction to liberal democratic capitalist society during the inter-war years.

The relationship between Catholicism and democracy was a contingent one historically. The Church itself, and many Catholics, continued to prefer a political system which was hierarchical and monarchical. Even in societies such as Belgium and the Netherlands, where Catholic political parties provided important support for the parliamentary system, a residual authoritarianism can be identified until the war. Catholic politics was not open to change for much of this time, retaining a commitment to traditional and conservative norms throughout the inter-war decades. This is also the high point of what Whyte has characterised as 'closed Catholicism'.[13] Catholic politics can therefore be placed with ease on the right in most cases in Europe. It opposed liberalism, socialism and capitalism from the right, its social teaching being based on medieval theological concepts. This anti-modernist approach goes back at least to Pius IX's hostility to the new liberal order which can be detected in his encyclicals *Qui Pluribus and Quanta Cura*. Moreover the latter, published in 1864, contained a Syllabus of Errors which condemned the main elements of the modern liberal order, including toleration. One consequence of this was the prohibition of Catholic involvement in secular politics, a decision which isolated Catholics from influence in the new mass democracies, increased hostility to them from liberal and anti-clericalist forces and separated them from the right in organisational terms.[14] It is sometimes suggested that Leo XIII brought about a radical reappraisal of Catholic ideology in his encyclicals *Rerum Novarum* (1891) and *Graves de Communi* (1901), yet this is to overstate the claim. The social aspects of these encyclicals emphasised either the charity aspects of involvement, or provided a restatement of corporatism as an ideal form of economic organisation. Regarding democracy the most that can be said is that democracy should not be condemned as such, and here, and again in 1918, the papacy seems to be accepting democracy in practice rather than as an ideal or as a theoretically acceptable political system. Prior to the Second World War there is no formal public approval of democracy, indeed the actions of Pius XI and Pius XII undermined democratic political parties in Italy and Germany, while colluding with the authoritarian clericalism of the Catholic party in Austria and Spain.[15] One reason for this was the papacy's obsession with communism. The problem ran deeper, however, embracing a comprehensive anti-liberal sentiment that led to hostility to the political expression of this which was parliamentary democracy.

Prior to 1945 'Christian democracy', where it existed, did not receive full recognition from the papacy, nor had denominational politics moved beyond confessional concerns. Indeed, three of the Catholic parties in the 1920s were led by priests and the impression one is left with is a political subculture still imbued with a traditional ideology. Christian democracy may have its origins in the attempts by Catholics to respond to the industrial and political revolutions of modernity, yet there is no clear progression from its origins in the 1820s to the public involvement of the 1940s. 'Christian democracy' had to be transformed before it became Christian democracy. What this entailed, as Fogarty has noted, was that Christian democracy had to be distinguished from both traditional Christian feudalism and from Catholic Action. Both were embedded in the confessional milieu of traditional Catholic thinking about politics, and neither unreservedly supported democracy as a political objective. Indeed the criticism of Italian fascism and German National Socialism by Pope Pius XI and XII concerned restrictions which the regimes placed on the Church or on Catholic Action, rather than an unreserved rejection of either system of government. Notwithstanding growing tension between the Church and fascism, the papacy had a lot to lose if it openly broke with the totalitarian regimes. The popes believed that fascism was anti-communist, but also that, through the concordats, both regimes had given due recognition to the status of the Church in their country.[16]

It is mistaken to believe that the transition within Catholic politics from conservatism to Christian democracy had, with relatively few exceptions, been completed by the 1920s. In this context, Burgess has suggested that:

> Although depicted essentially as a post-war phenomenon, the success of Christian democracy can be explained only by reference to what occurred both before and during the Second World War.

While the second half of this claim is not in doubt, it is more problematic to see Christian democracy as anything other than a post-war phenomenon. There is little evidence to suggest that Christian democracy was central to either Catholic or denominational politics prior to 1940. It is furthermore somewhat overstating the case to claim that:

> Such was the bitter harvest reaped by the Nazis that virtually all anti-democratic elements within the Church had reversed their positions and looked favourably upon a post-war liberal democratic restoration.[17]

The difficulty here is distinguishing between the Church and Catholic politics as a factor in secular politics. There is some doubt whether the Church actually changed its authoritarian and traditional instincts after the war, though it may not have publicised them as loudly as previously. It is clear, however, that Pius XI sided with the authoritarian elements within Catholic politics when he published *Quadragesimo anno* in 1931. Whyte in his careful study of Catholic politics concluded that the intention of this encyclical was to resolve the conflict between the liberal and conservative wings of Catholic politics in favour of the latter:

> Initially, it appeared to obscure rather than clarify the boundaries between Catholic social thought and other ideologies. This was because fascism, for reasons of its own, had developed a similar attachment to corporatist principles. During the thirties and early forties the boundary between Fascist thought was accordingly blurred. With the downfall of fascism everywhere in continental Europe at the end of the war, corporatism became a distinctively Catholic doctrine. By that time, the word 'corporatism' had fallen out of favour because of its Fascist connotations, but the principle, under the less controversial titles of 'vocational organisation' or 'professional organisation', was enthusiastically endorsed by Catholic thinkers and leaders. The result was that in the

immediate post-war period Catholic social teaching had a more distinctive content than before or since.

This observation led Whyte to conclude that the commitment to corporatism enhanced the tendency for Catholicism to remain closed during the post-war decades, thus closing it off from other political influences. Closed Catholicism is characterised by Whyte as one in which a Catholic party exists and 'which receives the support of all Catholics and no non-Catholics'. This is reinforced by a network of Catholic organisations which are clearly confessional and of which Catholics are expected to be members. Furthermore the Catholic population are under strong clerical influence.[18]

This description can be applied with greater validity to the inter-war years than to the post-war era, for the former was more specifically defined in terms of clericalism, Catholicism and traditionalism and an acceptance of the ghetto in politics, whether self-imposed or imposed by other forces. In terms of papal ideology this perception is also accurate. The Church itself changes little after the war; its anti-communism disguised a continuing hostility to the modern world, though not apparently to political democracy as such.[19] In terms of politics, however, the question is more problematic for Catholics. Along with a number of other writers, Whyte considered 'closed Catholicism' to be a force of the centre rather than of the right or left, a feature also highlighted by post-war writers on Christian democracy and Catholic politics.[20] Yet it might be suggested that a new configuration emerged as a consequence of Christian democracy which, though not coming into conflict with the papacy as such, placed it in a difficult position given the closed nature of that politics. Christian democracy may be deemed to have undermined the 'closed' nature of Catholicism precisely because its leading representatives, though remaining loyal Catholics, increasingly drew a distinction between their roles as politicians in the post-war world and the requirements of papal ideology. This can be appreciated in the decline of political Catholicism and its replacement by Christian democracy. For political Catholicism the emphasis was on the Catholic up to 1945, whereas thereafter both were subsumed under the notion of democracy in a Christian environment.

It is therefore possible to conceive of Catholic politics up to 1940 within a theocratic context with the religious receiving primacy over the political. Political Catholicism was defensive, reflecting the lack of integration and exclusion which Catholics had experienced in a large number of states due to liberalism or anti-clericalism. However, as Hans Maier noted, Christian democracy transcended both political Catholicism and social Catholicism. In terms of contingency:

> Christian democracy comes into being where the intent of political and social Catholicism meets with a historico-philosophical concept which recognizes in democracy, not only the providential form of the state and society of a Christian age, but also the surest guarantee of the security of the church. The natural consequence of such a way of thinking is to obligate the church theologically toward democratic solutions.[21]

Whatever validity this may have for the theory of Christian democracy, the Church itself only accepted it reluctantly. It is commonly thought that the first public endorsement of political democracy comes with Pius XII's Christmas speech in 1944. Yet this has to be appreciated as a strategic speech in the context of democracy. The Pope was faced not only with the liberation of Italy and the defeat of fascism, but with a resistance movement obviously influenced, if not led by communists, and which in the north of Italy could embrace revolutionary and anti-clerical demands. Yet even in this context the approach of the Pope is contingent: If the future belongs to democracy, an essential part of its fulfillment must devolve upon the religion of Christ and the Church'. This statement is ambiguous, and is probably intended to be so. There is little evidence that Pius XII embraced democracy as a matter of principle rather than for strategic considerations. In the same speech he also stressed that the Church could not give priority to one type of party over another, that the Church could not be expected: 'to support one party rather than another among the many different systems which are in opposition to each other, products of their time and dependent on it.'[22]

Another reason for the Pope's statement is that whatever he may have wished in 1944, events were moving outside his power to influence them. Catholics had participated in the resistance movements in Italy, France, the Netherlands, Belgium and elsewhere, one consequence of which was a renewed relationship between Catholic politics and patriotic nationalism. In the unlikely event of the Pope insisting on a closed Catholic polity, similar to the pre-war period, it would have been opposed by Catholics in a number of these states.

This is the weak point of authoritarian Catholicism after 1944. A significant proportion of Catholics now believed that traditional denominational politics were no longer appropriate. In France, Gilbert Dru circulated a political memorandum which insisted that politics could not continue as it had been prior to the war and the collaboration of Vichy. New movements would be necessary including a reformed right without the influence of authoritarianism which had so pervaded it previously.[23] Likewise, though from a less radical perspective, De Gasperi in Italy was making the intellectual move from authoritarianism to democracy. Like Dru he circulated a memorandum in 1943 which expressed the need for a new party and a new beginning: 'Freedom will distinguish the new democratic regime, just as all men who are truly free will be pledged to the acceptance of the method of freedom.'[24] De Gasperi was responsive to the charge that Catholics had not been sensitive to the requirements of democratic government:

> Should not even we be worried, we who lean for support on the Catholics, so amenable to dictatorial government and to Conservative ideas? . . . In the light of Catholic history, we are not justified in asking people to take it for granted that we stand for freedom. Catholics have always divided on this point.[25]

At the 4th Congress of the DC in 1952 De Gasperi drew attention to the trajectory of Catholic thought from the corporatism which had previously characterised it to a greater openness to democracy. This movement, he argued, had been prompted by the experience of the inter-war crisis and the war itself:

> But the conclusion to which experience has led us today is this. The dictatorships of the past, the dictatorship threatened for tomorrow, the unavoidable pressure of the State bureaucracy and of systematic State intervention, have brought to the fore – whatever any theory, reflection, or discussion may conclude – the need to insist on freedom, personal and political.[26]

This insistence on democratic accountability broke the close connection between Catholic politics and the Church. It may also have laid the basis for the changes which the Church itself introduced two decades later.[27]

Why Christian democracy?

Why then did Christian democracy appear at this particular juncture in European politics as a viable political movement? For the most part its history had been one of failure and where Catholic politics had been successful, the particular expression of confessional politics had not been Christian democratic. Though Christian democracy was in inception primarily a Catholic phenomenon, it was also the successor to the specifically Catholic response to modernity. The distinguishing mark of Catholic politics until the Second World War was its continuing belief in the appropriateness of its theology for politics, when most other political parties, even Protestant ones, had secularised. Until the collapse of fascism, the emphasis within much of Catholic politics remained on the religious rather than on the democratic or indeed on the political in a secular sense.

Writing in 1966 Hans Daalder identified a significant difference between those states, mainly in northern Europe, where democracy had become legitimised and those where, even after the Second World War, democratic institutions and norms were correspondingly weaker:

> Right-wing parties in various European countries came to assume basically different attitudes towards the rules of the game of democratic party politics. The acceptance of the substance of democratic ideals and practices is still the clearest criterion with which to distinguish Scandinavian or British Conservatives from, say, the right in France, Weimar Germany, or present day Italy. In the latter the constant presence of potentially or actually anti-democratic parties within the party system has hindered the effective working of democratic politics; it has narrowed the range of democratic rule; it has caused disillusionment to spread to other potentially more democratic groups; and it finally eroded the very existence of democratic regimes.[28]

The tension between the right and democratic politics may have been reduced by objective circumstances after 1945 but, as Daalder insists, it did not go away. In France and Italy, particularly, a strong residual suspicion of parliamentary democracy remained which reflected itself in authoritarian strategies for power within an ostensibly democratic constitutional order. In spite of this there is evidence for considerable change in these and other states, and the appearance of Christian democracy is a reflection of it. The background conditions for Christian democracy can be outlined as the impact of the Depression, the war, fascism and the victory of the Allies and particularly the successful control exercised by the American and British governments in Western Europe after 1945. In addition, a contributory factor, though perhaps not one immediately evident in 1945, was the presence of Soviet Communism as a potential threat to Europe either in the form of the Red Army or in the domestic communist parties in France and Italy, though elsewhere post-war elections demonstrated the limited, but as yet not marginal, strength of the communists.[29]

The resistance facilitated the growth of patriotism in a number of states, and in Italy certainly contributed to the strength of the Communist Party after 1943. It may also have alerted many Catholics to the changing circumstances. There was a growing recognition that the traditional right could not function in the new circumstances of post-war Europe and that new political forces were required. New circumstances evoked different responses on the part of political actors. There is no direct causal relationship between the successful dominance of Christian democracy and the crisis for the right. Most of the leaders of the new parties had their origins in predecessor parties or had been radicalised by the war and the resistance. This was true of France and Italy in particular, while different circumstances prevailed in Austria and Germany. Fogarty suggested, after asking the question what was Christian democracy, that:

> It might be crudely defined as the movement of those laymen engaged on their own responsibility in the solution of political, economic, and social problems in the light of Christian principles, who conclude from these principles and from practical experience that in the modern world democracy is normally best: that government, in the state, the firm, the local community, or the family, should not merely be of and for the people but also by them.

Fogarty drew quite radical conclusions from this, suggesting that Christian revelation provided the foundation for pluralist and personalist principles which informed the thinking of Christian democrats. In turn the Christian democrat could:

> conclude from these that conditions in the modern world call for the widespread use of such techniques as political democracy, joint responsibility in industry, or the withering away of the patriarchal family.[30]

While this radical interpretation might not be shared by all Christian democrats during the 1940s and 1950s, what it does draw attention to is the break with the rightist identity that much of Catholic and religious thought had been associated with prior to this. Thus, it is mistaken to see Christian democracy as simply the conservative right reconstituted as a consequence of the failure of the authoritarian right. Undoubtedly persistence existed, but the break with the past allows one to conclude that the break is the fundamental event and one which establishes the uniqueness of Christian democracy both in ideological terms and in respect of its position within the party system. The Mouvement Républicain Populaire (MRP) leader Georges Bidault, in an oft-quoted phrase, claimed that the purpose of Christian democracy was to 'Gouverner au centre et faire, avec les moyens de la droite, la politique de la gauche' – to govern in the centre and make the politics of the left with the means of the right. There is substance to this claim, especially in France, but more generally the statement reflects the anxiety of all Christian democratic parties after 1945 to distinguish themselves from the past. One reflection of this was the refusal of all the main denominational parties to continue the nomenclature used during the inter-war years. In France, Germany, Italy, Austria, Belgium and the Netherlands, the confessional parties either do not reappear, or, if they do, they have adopted a new title and programme which emphasises the non-confessional nature of the party. Moreover, in each of the six cases examined for this chapter, though with varying degrees of emphasis, the new party seeks to distance itself from the overt control of the Church. In France and Germany this is remarkably successful, while in Italy much less so for obvious reasons. While name changes in themselves may only be symbolic, they do constitute a statement of intent on the part of those doing the changing. In most cases, the political parties pursue policies after 1945 which, though often reflecting their Catholic origins and Christian ideology, are less confessional then hitherto expected from such formations.

Therefore, it may be inadequate to characterise Christian democracy as 'a reaction to the modernisation of European society and politics in the wake of the French (or European) Revolution'.[31] There are four unique features to Christian democracy which cannot be found together in the confessional parties or in the right before 1945. The first of these is the extent to which Catholics associated with the state, experienced and expressed patriotism. This is particularly true in those states which experienced occupation, France being the prime example but also Italy after the collapse of fascism in 1943. The German and Austrian cases are more complex because of the nature of the regime, however it seems that Catholics identified with the war effort to the same degree as other sectors of the society. The second major departure is the liberalisation of Catholic politics by Christian democracy. The acceptance of pluralism, multi-party systems and the end of confessional politics enabled the Christian democrats to accept unquestionably the liberal democratic political culture. This did not involve an acceptance of liberalism as an ideology, but it did involve a significant compromise with the basic framework. This in turn allowed for the positive democratic integration of the Catholic masses, a feature unique to the post-war world and to Christian democracy. For the first time in most states, Catholics participated as political equals with the other political ideologies such as socialism and liberalism. Government participation by Catholics had not been unknown prior to this, but the nature of this after 1945 and the extent of integration marks a break. This allowed for the most radical change of all and one which extended well beyond the Catholic milieu. That is the domestication and democratisation of the European right mainly through the electoral and organisational success of Christian democratic parties. It is largely through the Christian democratic parties that the right comes to accept liberal democracy.

There are a number of contributory factors to this success. The continuation of confessional politics would have limited the influence of Catholic politics. It would certainly have weakened the appeal of the Christlich Demokratische Union (CDU) to non-Catholics in Germany, and would certainly have made it difficult for the MRP to cooperate with socialists and radicals in France. The democratisation of Catholic politics and its de-confessionalisation were thus prerequisites for the emergence of Christian democracy as a mass political organisation in a number of states. This involved the Christian democrats breaking out of the 'closed Catholicism' which had characterised their organisation during the inter-war period. This in turn laid the basis for the breakdown of 'closed' politics throughout Western Europe. What is often neglected in studies on post-war European history is that the continuation of closed political formations cease to be the norm. One reason for this was the common opposition to communism on the part of social democrats, Christian democrats, conservatives and liberals within a constitutional structure. Furthermore the success and appeal of 'catch-all' parties undermined the possibility of continuing an electoral strategy based on the ghetto; for those who did, in particular the communists, stagnation was the result. Moreover, in somewhat different but not dissimilar ways Christian democracy and social democracy moved beyond the ghetto after 1945 and embraced a more open form of politics. The social democrats were slower in doing this in France and Germany, but in time this also happened. In their respective ways social democracy and Christian democracy integrated the former ghettos into mainstream politics, while in the case of the latter it provided the added incentive for the democratisation of the right.

Christian democracy has been treated as something of an anomaly by writers on political parties. It does not fit easily into the narrowly defined left–right spectrum traditionally adopted by analysts. It is not a party of the right in the classical sense, though its place may loosely be seen to be there. Fogarty considered it be centrist, which was its own self image:

> From the point of view of relations with other parties, the parties in this group have found a position in the centre of the political stage, flanked normally by Liberals and Conservatives on one side and Social Democrats on the other . . .[32]

This positioning may be accurate, yet caution is required in utilising a simple left–right spectrum to define what a party is, rather than an objective position. In general terms Christian democracy tended to pursue a collectivist strategy on economic and welfare policy. On such issues it is consistently to the left of liberalism, overlapping somewhat with social democracy. The MRP and Katholieke Volkspartij (KVP) are closer to the left with the CDU closer to the right. On other issues, such as education, colonial policy and defence Christian democracy shifts to the right, though these considerations are not necessarily relevant in every case. However, positioning says little about the internal coherence of such an approach. Left and right, and the distance between them, was quite wide during the inter-war period, but narrowed with the decline of the radical and authoritarian right after the war. To be on the right carried a very different meaning in 1935 than it did in 1950, such a shift is not easily quantified by spatial positioning in terms of left and right. Furthermore, it can be said that the various constituent parts of most post-war party systems agree and overlap on a wide range of issues and that political disagreement, while not insubstantial, is not about the legitimacy of the system or its continuity (France remained the exception). The only major force which resists this consensus is communism, and to all intents and purposes communism is marginalised in Western European politics by 1950. It can therefore be suggested that the importance of left and right is reduced in ideological saliency after the war. This is in part a consequence of the changed nature of the left and right and the ending of the closed nature of much of the European political system. It may also be the case that the traditional use of left and right has merely reflected the viciousness of the conflicts between closed systems. Where this polarisation did not exist, as in Britain, Sweden and the Netherlands, the concepts of left and right had a much weaker meaning, allowing for the emergence of consensual forms of politics even before the Second World War. The left–right spectrum was also affected by the shift to the left prompted by the war, the allied victory and the nature of the post-war consensus. To be 'right' in 1950 is not only different from that of 1935, but it is a right which had been pushed to the left by these events.

Without wishing to abandon the left–right distinction entirely, the success of Christian democracy in providing the main political expression for the right in a number of states changed the equation to a considerable extent. There had to be a redrawing of the relationship between the major political parties along the spectrum. Christian democracy is not simply another conservative party, nor is it simply a party of the right. Moreover, the use of centrist confuses the issue and places it with a large number of parties which have proved difficult to categorise, such as Fianna Fáil in Ireland or the various Gaullist parties in France, and does not permit an understanding of those ideological and political characteristics which make it a distinctive political force in post-war Europe. In electoral terms its focus is on denomination, i.e. its appeal in the widest sense is to those who consider themselves to be members of a denomination. Yet on this basis it also appeals outside the class base of socialist or liberal parties, making the claim to be a cross-class party. It is also a movement rather than a strict party carrying into the post-war world many of the attributes associated with closed Catholicism, such as Catholic-led social and economic movements. These features offer further distinguishing marks for Christian democracy; separating it from liberalism because of its rejection of individualism and from socialism because of its rejection of class. Though Christian democracy may be closer to conservatism in terms of the political spectrum, it can also distinguish itself from this formation because of its denominational and social aspects, which are much weaker in conservatism. Moreover, its mass organisation and electoral appeal moves it well beyond the traditional conservative party as a consequence of its democratisation and mobilisation of the right. Consequently denominationalism provides a clear distinguishing feature for the Christian democracy movement, which when linked to democracy separates it from its alternatives to the left and right.[33]

In ideological terms, Christian democracy can also be distinguished from its democratic competitors. Among the key ideological denominators are personalism in contrast to individualism. Personalism invokes solidarity and the notion of social responsibility and the family. It is no accident that the family has been and remains one of the main areas for concern in Christian democratic policy statements. To a far greater degree than is the case with liberals or conservatives, Christian democrats are concerned with the consequences of individual behaviour for society, whether this is framed in terms of the economy or personal morality. The responsibility of the individual does not end with his or her action, but has to be extended to that individual's relationship with the complex social fabric to which they are a party. Yet the Christian democrat falls well short of embracing a collectivist strategy, especially in economic affairs. It is true that the MRP supported nationalisation of some sectors of the French economy after 1945, but it subsequently reversed this position, refusing to accept the Marxist view on this question. Elsewhere, Christian democrats were opposed to the collectivisation of property on the grounds that this limited freedom, and argued instead for a pluralist approach to the question of ownership and distribution. Central to the Christian democratic view of pluralism is the concept of 'subsidiarity' derived from Pius XI, which insisted on activities been carried out at the most appropriate level. This may be the state, but it could also be the individual, the family, the local region or the privately controlled organisation. In addition it can be argued that Christian democracy, though embodying aspects of conservative thought and action, is not traditionalist. It is not traditionalist in that it has broken comprehensively with the authoritarianism of traditionalism, its identity with monarchy and its hostility to democratic and liberal politics.[34]

The most convincing case for the uniqueness of Christian democracy has been suggested by Kersbergen, who links the distinctiveness of the phenomenon with a concept of social capitalism and the emergence of the welfare state. Kersbergen argues that Christian democracy is as distinct from other currents within liberal democracy as they are from one another. While there is considerable overlap in policy and ideology among all currents there is a 'core' ideology which separates each from the other.[35] Both the distinctive nature of Christian democracy and the extent of overlap, however, has to be appreciated in the context of the political culture of post-war Europe. This involved the acceptance by all political tendencies of the basis of liberal democracy, that is, liberalism as a background condition for political participation. Once this had been achieved, the ground rules were established for differentiating between the various currents and for co-operation between them. This also allowed for the reduction of the ideological distance between the parties which accepted the ground rules and allowed them to exclude or marginalise competitors to the left and right (communists or fascists). Notwithstanding the differences between the main political currents after 1945, a unique feature of the post-war world was the extent to which it was characterised by consensus on the structure of the political system. The distinctive nature of Christian democracy can be established in its religious origins and its dependence on denominational culture to maintain an electorate. However, in addition to this, Christian democracy also had a specific 'Christian' approach to the economy and social welfare, which distinguished it from liberalism and traditionalism conservatism, while its continuing acceptance of 'bourgeois' norms on property, fiscal rectitude, etc. distinguished it from social democracy.

Building on this it might be suggested that Christian democracy can be described as a reformist-conservative political force in the first decade after 1945. Most Christian democrats recognised the need to conserve capitalism by reforming it, in particular to address the structural problems associated with the Depression of the 1930s. But the conservation of capitalism in a reformist fashion was also required by Christian democrats in order that democracy, religious and political diversity could be maintained. While policy was naturally differently conceived in different states, there was also a broad framework of agreement on social and economic issues for much of this time. Furthermore these parties were committed to change in the sense that there could be no return to the 1930s and this involved the need to reform the capitalist system. This justified intervention in the economy, a social market and a significant increase in welfare provision. This form of regulated capitalism was a departure from what had characterised the right previously, but it was not transformational in the sense envisaged by post-war social democrats. The Christian democrats generally are also conservative to the extent that they believe that while change is necessary it can only be introduced in a gradual way; there cannot be a rupture with the past. Continuity for them is also important, otherwise instability consequent on the changes would undermine the substance of reform and return politics to the confrontation of previous years. In addition to this the success of Christian democracy in democratising the right carried a substantial cost for the reformist aspects of its programme. Christian democracy became increasingly dependent on a right-wing constituency for its electoral support, placing it on the centre right rather than on the left. However, this is a new variant on conservatism, breaking the connection with one which is traditional and right wing.[36]

The Impact of Christian Democracy on European Politics

If Christian democracy can be characterised as a reformist-conservative political movement with a distinct ideology and social base, what impact did it make on the European party system after 1945? Table 4.1 provides an electoral profile for six states with experience of Christian democratic parties over roughly fifteen years after 1945. The electoral contours of post-war continental Europe can be readily determined from them. These states provide an opportunity to compare and contrast the alternating national trajectories for Christian democracy during this time. The period from 1945 until the first election in the 1960s has been taken as the focus on the grounds that it is during that period that the West European party system stabilised and takes on the form which it has maintained, though in attenuated form, since then.[37]

One feature that each of these states has in common is the centrality of political parties originating in a religious tradition, and particularly in a Catholic tradition. Throughout this period the Christian democratic party is normally the largest party in the system, or is a major contributor to government formation (as in the case of France). In four out of the six cases the parties are new and owe their foundation to the process of renewal after the fall of fascism. In the other two cases, the name of the party is changed to make them appear less denominational. All insist that they are new parties which have broken with the authoritarian past of Catholic and confessional politics. Two conclusions might be drawn here: the first is that the European party system changed as a consequence of the Depression, fascism and war. The defeat of the authoritarian right provided the opportunity in Italy, Germany, France and Austria for new parties to emerge. In the case of three of these states Christian democratic parties dominated the political system for most of the post-war years. Elsewhere Christian democratic influence is extensive, while in most cases it is the party which dominates the right. The second is that Christian democracy provided the opportunity for the democratisation of the right during the post-war years, facilitating the integration of often anti-modern forces into the modern world. In addition, Christian democratic parties presided over the industrialisation of their states and expansion of the social services, sometimes in conjunction with Social democrats, as in Austria or the Netherlands, but even in states where the right ruled alone as in Germany or Italy.

The importance of Christian democracy can also be measured by contrasting its post-war success with the performance of inter-war confessional and people's

Table 4.1　European electoral patterns, 1945–63

			Austria			
	1945	1949	1953	1956	1959	1962
ÖVP	49.79	44.03	41.25	45.95	44.19	45.43
SPÖ	44.59	38.7	42.10	43.04	44.78	43.99
FPÖ	—	11.66	10.94	6.52	7.70	7.04
KPÖ	5.41	5.08	5.28	4.42	3.26	3.04
Other	0.18	0.50	0.40	0.05	0.0	0.48

			Belgium			
	1946	1949	1950	1954	1958	1961
CVP/PSC	42.5	43.6	47.7	38.5	46.5	41.5
BSP/PSB	32.4	29.8	35.5	41.1	37.0	36.7
PVV/PLB	9.6	15.3	12.1	13.1	12.0	11.1
CPB/PCB	12.7	7.5	4.7	3.6	1.9	3.1
Volksunie	—	2.1	—	2.2	2.0	3.5

			France				
	1945	1946	1946	1951	1956	1958	1961
MRP	23.9	28.2	25.9	12.6	11.1	11.1	8.9
SFIO	23.4	21.1	17.8	14.6	15.2	15.7	12.6
Radicals	10.5	11.6	11.1	10.0	15.9	8.3	7.8
Conservatives	15.6	12.8	12.9	14.1	15.3	22.9	9.6
RPR	—	—	3.0	21.6	3.9	19.5	31.9
PCF	26.2	25.9	28.2	26.9	25.9	19.2	21.7
Other	0.4	0.4					

	Germany (Federal Republic)			
	1949	1953	1957	1961
CDU/CSU	31.0	45.2	50.2	45.3
SPD	29.2	28.8	31.8	36.2
FDP	11.9	9.5	7.7	12.8
KPD	5.7	2.2	—	—
BP	4.2	1.7	0.5	—
DP	4.0	3.2	3.4	—
Zentrum	3.1	0.8	—	—
GB/BHE	—	5.9	4.6	—
Others	4.7	1.1	1.0	2.7

The Right in the Twentieth Century

Italy

	1946	1948	1953	1958	1963
DC	35.2	48.5	40.1	42.4	38.3
PRI	4.4	2.5	1.6	1.4	1.4
PSDI	—	7.1	4.5	4.6	6.1
PLI	6.8	3.8	3.0	3.5	7.0
PDIUM	2.8	2.8	6.9	4.9	1.7
MSI	5.3	2.3	2.7	1.5	1.5
PSI	20.7	*	12.7	14.2	13.8
PCI	18.9	31.0	22.6	22.7	25.3
Other	5.8	2.3	2.7	1.5	1.5

The Netherlands

	1946	1948	1952	1956	1959	1963
KVP	30.8	31.0	28.7	31.7	31.6	31.9
ARP	12.9	13.2	11.3	9.9	9.4	8.7
CHU	7.9	9.2	8.9	8.4	8.1	8.6
SGP	2.1	2.4	2.4	2.3	2.2	2.3
VVD	6.4	8.0	8.8	8.8	12.2	10.3
PvdA	28.3	25.6	29.0	32.7	30.3	28.0
CPN	10.6	7.7	6.2	4.8	2.4	2.8
Others	1.1	2.9	4.7	1.4	2.0	4.4

Note: *The PCI and PSI fought the 1948 election on a joint list. The PSDI originated in a split within the PSI over this and related issues.
Source: Thomas T. Mackie and Richard Rose, *The International Almanac of Electoral History,* 2nd edn (London: Macmillan, 1982).

parties. Table 4.2 compares the vote for Christian democratic parties in the immediate post-war years, the early 1960s and for its predecessor party in the last pre-war election.

The most significant changes are to be found in Germany, France and Italy, where there is a Christian democratic breakthrough after the war. The electoral fit between pre- and post-war is much closer for Belgium, the Netherlands and Luxembourg, as is the case for Austria. However, in the latter case, it is possible to identify the growth of a new party quite explicitly making a break with its predecessor. The question of continuity and change is quite problematic on this issue. If the vote for the right, as distinct from predecessor parties, is taken then the fit is much closer than Table 4.2 shows. In the case of Austria the vote for the right in the last pre-war election is over 50 per cent, though this includes the Fatherland Front and the National Socialists. In Germany also the right, including the National Socialists and the German National People's Party, command over 50 per cent of the vote at the November 1932 election. In the French case, the National Front alliance attracted 42.7 per cent of the vote at the 1936 election. While these approximations are crude they do demonstrate an electoral

Table 4.2 Votes for Christian democratic parties

	Pre-war	Post-war 1	Post-war 2
Austria	35.7 (1930)	49.8 (1945)	44.2 (1959)
Belgium	32.7 (1939)	42.5 (1946)	41.4 (1961)
France	10.0 (1936)*	23.9 (1946)	11.1 (1956)
Germany	13.0 (1932)	31.0 (1949)	45.3 (1961)
Italy	20.4 (1922)	48.4 (1948)	42.3 (1958)
Luxembourg	44.0 (1937)	41.4 (1945)	35.9 (1959)
The Netherlands	28.8 (1937)	30.8 (1946)	31.6 (1959)

Note: *Estimate, no direct equivalent for France. Predecessor parties as follows: Austria: Christlich-soziale Partei. Belgium: Catholic Party. France: Estimated vote based on Parti Democrate Populare and Conservatives and Independents. Germany: Zentrum and Christian Social Peoples Service. Italy: Partito Populare Italiano. Luxembourg: Parti de la Droite. The Netherlands: Rooms-Katholieke Staatspartij.

catchment area for the right which though splintered in some cases, as in Austria and France, or disintegrated in others, Germany and Italy, were available to new political parties competing on the centre right of the political spectrum after 1945. However, the distinguishing feature between the pre-war situation and that which prevailed after the war was that prior to 1939 the right was divided between those parties that displayed a liberal democratic commitment and those that did not. Thus the Austrian Christlich-soziale Partei cannot be considered a democratic party of the right, whereas the Rooms-Katholieke Staatspartij can. Moreover, within individual party systems some parties on the right were conservative but not anti-democratic, while others on the right were decidedly anti-democratic; the most striking example is the contrast between the Zentrum and the National Socialists in Germany. After 1945 the anti-democratic alternative was much weaker, even when neo-fascist parties were not outlawed. Even though a case might be made that there is considerable continuity between the electorate for the right in the pre-war and post-war party systems, this case has to be modified by the evidence that in most cases the dominant parties on the right accepted the broad contours of the liberal democratic political system and to all intents and purposes imposed this order on their supporters. This does not mean that fascist or authoritarian nationalist sympathisers did not exist, but that politically their focus came to be identified with the new parties rather than with extremist parties.

The Christian democratic breakthrough is based on two contrasting factors. The first of these is its success in overcoming the confessional nature of Catholic politics while integrating Catholic voters into the new party. The second involves its ability to integrate much of the right, whether Catholic or not, into its electoral constituency. The continuing importance of denomination can be appreciated from Table 4.3, which shows the proportion of Catholics in seven European states and links this with religious practice and voting for a Christian democratic or Catholic party.

The Right in the Twentieth Century

Table 4.3 Catholic Voting Patterns *c.* 1960

	Nominal Catholics in population (%)	Practising Catholics among nominal Catholics (%)	Practising Catholics in total population (%)	Votes for Christian Democractic or Catholic party at general election nearest to 1960 (%)
Austria	89	40	36	44
Belgium	96	50	48	41*
France	91	25	23	12
Germany (BRD)	45	50	23	45
Italy	95	45	43	42
Netherlands	40	80	32	32
Switzerland	41	50	21	23

Note: * Whyte uses the 1961 figure for Belgium. However, it may be more accurate to use the 1958 figure of 46.5% which reflects the effective mobilisation of almost the entire Catholic vote due to divisions between clerical and anti-clerical sentiment. *Source*: John H. Whyte, *Catholics in Western Democracies* (Dublin: Gill and Macmillan, 1980) Tables 2 and 5, pp. 93, 144.

It can be seen that in some cases the fit between practising Catholics and voting for Christian democratic parties is quite close. The correlation is strong in the case of Italy, the Netherlands, Belgium and Switzerland. It seems weaker in France where less than half of practising Catholics voted for the MRP in 1958. The German case offers evidence to suggest that the appeal of the CDU/CSU went well beyond that of practising Catholics or former Zentrum voters to encompass a wider constituency. A similar claim can be made for Austria, which by the end of the 1950s had successfully attracted right-wing anti-clerical voters as well as Catholics. Notwithstanding these observations, the Catholic vote remained crucial for the success of Christian democracy. In the French case the failure of MRP to command the support of even practising Catholics contributed to its weakness by the mid-1950s and to its eventual decline as a force in French politics.[38]

The relationship between religion and voting patterns can be best appreciated in the case of the Netherlands (see Table 4.4), where the closed nature of political organisation had been institutionalised in 1917, arrangements which had contributed to the stabilisation of its political system thereafter. This fit is remarkable and in many ways unique in Western Europe. In many ways it reflected the unique political structure which existed in the Netherlands for much of this time. However, the relationship between religious practice and voting for a Christian democratic party is quite strong elsewhere. In Germany in 1953 the Catholic component in the CDU/CSU is based, in part, on the party's ability to attract practising Catholics, though as is evident from Table 4.5 its reach is wider than in the comparable Dutch case.

Table 4.4 Voting preference by religious groups, The Netherlands, 1954

	Roman Catholic	Dutch Reformed	Gereformeerd	No preference
KVP	87	1	—	1
ARP	—	13	82	2
CHU	—	27	2	1
PvDA	7	41	4	72
VVD	1	14	2	13
Communist	—	1	—	10
Other	5	3	10	1

Source: G. A. Irwin, 'Patterns of voting behaviour in the Netherlands', in Richard T. Griffiths (ed.), The Economy and Politics of the Netherlands since 1945 (The Hague: Martin Nijhoff, 1980), p. 208.

Religious practice provides a strong indication of support for Christian democratic parties. In Germany, practising Christians are more likely to vote for the CDU/CSU than for any other party. Likewise, in Italy the DC received the overwhelming support of those who regularly attended church, a particular advantage during the 1950s when an estimated two-thirds of the adult population did so regularly. In France the position is more complex, but here the correlation between voting for the MRP and church attendance is also strong. These findings can be reinforced by evidence from Belgium, the Netherlands and Austria.[39]

Gender also played an important role in securing Christian democratic dominance. In most political systems between 1945 and the 1960s women tended to vote for the right rather than the left. One estimate has concluded that in Italy the PCI and PSI would have received an electoral majority if the franchise had been limited to male voters.[40] The importance of the female vote for Christian democracy is attested to in Germany, France, Austria and Belgium during this period. There are two contributory elements to this outcome. The first is that

Table 4.5 Religion and party support, Germany, 1953

	CDU	SPD	FDP	KPD	Z	BP	DP	No preference
Catholic	63	38	28	37	92	81	29	39
Protestant	35	55	69	53	6	19	67	56
Other	1	1	2	–	–	–	–	4
No religion	1	6	1	10	2	–	4	4

Source: Juan J. Linz, 'Cleavage and consensus in West German politics: the early fifties', in Seymour M. Lipset and Stein Rokkan (eds), *Party Systems and Voter Alignment* (New York: The Free Press, 1967), p. 303.

women had not had the vote in Italy, France or Belgium during the inter-war years and consequently their participation in electoral politics had been constrained by this. Second, women were more likely to be practising Catholics than men. In addition, both factors are associated with women's identity with traditional conservatism on social and moral matters and this was translated into support for conservative politics. Not surprisingly therefore Christian democracy was heavily dependent on women for its political success. While estimates vary, in general women usually accounted for over 60 per cent of the vote received by these parties.[41]

The other contributory factor was the extent to which Christian democracy penetrated and captured the traditional right-wing sectors of the electorate. In crude electoral terms, this proved to be the case with the ÖVP, the CDU/CSU and the DC. In each case the party dominate the centre right, usually receiving between 40 and 50 per cent of the vote and maintaining significant electoral leads over right-wing competitors. In the German case the CDU/CSU occupy the electoral ground from the centre right in alliance with the liberal FDP contributing to the coalition's dominance of the bourgeois and right-wing vote. In each case its main strength is derived from those sectors of the electorate traditionally allied with the right: property owners, rural areas, small cities and towns, and sections of the administrative elite. In so far as Christian democracy has a working-class component, which in the case of Germany, Italy and Belgium is quite large, the support is based on religious considerations. While the actual figures differ from country to country the trends reinforced the Christian democratic claim to be inter-class, precisely because the movement's appeal was not based primarily on class, but on a diffused religiousness. In contrast, the French MRP – the one Christian democratic party that was unable to command the support of the right, most practising Catholics or to marginalise competition to its right – failed to make the breakthrough to political dominance or stability. Its vote immediately after the war was a conservative one and correlates strongly with pre-war conservative and Catholic strength. However, even this advantage is quickly eroded by its failure to maintain voter loyalty, as can be appreciated by the collapse of its vote by 1951. Voter loyalty was weak and the MRP was susceptible to challenge from its right, and especially from the nationalism of Gaullism.[42]

The failure of the MRP highlights the difficulties which could prevent a Christian democratic party from achieving success. While Christian democrats in Belgium and the Netherlands could depend on existing voter loyalty and a democratic tradition, this was not the case in Germany or Italy. In both these cases it was to take some time for the political system to stabilise around the centre-right alternative, and for the Christian democrats to secure their position as the key component of government. In Germany it is possible to detect an almost inexorable increase in the vote for the CDU after the 1949 election, which by 1959 had ended all effective competition on the right. However, this was to take almost a decade to achieve and was based on the appeal of Adenauer and his government's successful economic and foreign policy. That this was achieved here and elsewhere was based on different strategies in each case, as the party had to accommodate or frame different national conditions.[43]

This new conservatism takes a number of forms during the decade and a half after 1945. By 1960 Christian democracy appears to have reached its electoral limits, or, as in the case of France, has been absorbed by other parties. Thereafter, Christian democracy plays a less autonomous role in the European party system, though a continuing important one. However, what has been undervalued has been the contribution of Christian democracy to the post-war consensus.[44] The spectrum of Christian democratic parties, though on the right because of its conservatism, also has within it a number of variants running from left to right. A three-fold typology can be generated for Christian democracy and its relationship to post-war structures. In the first place there are those states where Christian democracy and social democracy are in coalition for most of the fifteen years after 1945: the best examples of this are Austria and the Netherlands, where shared power between these two blocks is the normal feature of both reconstruction and economic growth. The second involved what might be described as consensual competition within the state: examples of this are Germany and Belgium. Coalition government between left and right is not the normal feature of the political system, but there is intense competition between the two for working-class votes. The third variant is the most complex, present in Italy and France. Here the left is fragmented with a strong communist party which is excluded from government. While social democrats participate in government they do not represent the majority of the working class and cannot deliver on the social consensus which is a feature of most of the other states. Furthermore, in France Christian and social democracy are undermined during the 1950s and replaced by Gaullism, which embodied a more authoritarian form of conservatism, one which continued to exclude the left from participation, competing with it for working-class votes. In Italy this is taken further with the development, implicitly, of Christian democratic (one party) rule, though within an anti-communist coalition or bourgeois bloc. The post-war Italian experience seems to be closer to that of inter-war Austria than to the other examples of Christian democracy. In Italy the right continues to have a contingent attitude to democracy, partly because of the presence of a strong Marxist electoral bloc, but also because of the pervasive presence of the DC in power and the necessity to counter pressure from its right.[45]

The possibility for co-operation is established at the electoral level. Table 4.6 details the combined vote of Christian democrats and social democrats and the governmental relationship between them during the period under review.

Consequently there are a number of combinations which led to significantly different outcomes in terms of policy. Austria and the Netherlands adopted a genuinely consensual approach to governmental power, while maintaining normal competitive politics. The *Proportz* system in Austria and the older *verzuiling* system in the Netherlands were both methods of conflict resolution between blocs, which during the post-war reconstruction period and into the 1950s narrowed the divisions between the two largest political blocs in each state. This consensual approach to policy had the effect of legitimising policies for economic growth, welfare and long-term co-operation between formerly hostile electoral blocs. In contrast, though the Belgian parties agreed to a reform programme for the post-war period, some of which was immediately introduced, that system facilitated a return to former divisions by the early 1950s. The conflict over the monarchy and schools seemed to revive the older clerical\anti-clerical cleavage. However, what is of interest is that each of the

Table 4.6 Combined vote of Christian democrats and social democrats, 1945–60

Austria	94	Coalition Government throughout.
Belgium	73	In competition generally, but intermittent coalition.
France	49	In coalition 1945–58.
Germany	74	In competition throughout.
Italy	55	In competition throughout*
The Netherlands	56.6	In coalition generally, though intermittent competition.**

Notes: * The figure for Italy is a result of combining the DC with its social democratic allies, but does not include either the PCI or the PSI.
** This figure is the result of combining the labour and Catholic vote, but does not include either of the two Protestant parties.

conflicts was resolved by pacts between the blocs, though not after considerable bloc-electoral mobilisation. It is only in 1961 that a Catholic–Socialist coalition structure is established in this context, but by then the traditional grounds for conflict between Catholic and socialist had been resolved, allowing the two parties to exclude the liberals.

In the German case there was considerable nostalgia for the authoritarian tradition and experience until the mid-1950s at least. Surveys carried out at the time found that there was a considerable body of the population which considered Germany to have been well off during the Hitler period, while democratic periods were universally rejected (see Table 4.7). While there can be no simple correlation between those who favour the two authoritarian periods and support for Nazism or rightist politics, the fact that 87 per cent of those asked favoured one of them is suggestive of a strong reservoir of authoritarian sentiment in politics. The 1959 figures are illustrative of a learning curve in the German case, though even at this stage some 46 per cent support one of the authoritarian alternatives. The evidence reinforces the view that, for a decade or more, a significant section of the German electorate approached democracy in a contingent fashion. Thus in 1949 some 40 per cent considered themselves indifferent to the new constitution of the Federal Republic, a third of the electorate favoured introducing monarchy in 1951, while in 1955 40 per cent believed that a working person gained higher esteem during the Third Reich than in the Federal Republic. Such

Table 4.7 When in this century do you think Germany has been best off?

	1951	1959	1963
Federal Republic	2	42	62
Third Reich (1933–39)	42	18	10
Weimar Republic	7	4	5
Empire (pre–1914)	45	28	16
Other	4	8	7

Source: Conradt, p. 226; Noelle and Neumann, p.1950.

findings have to be placed in the context of other findings: in 1951 nearly two-thirds of those asked believed that it was better for the country to have two or more parties, though it should be added that 27 per cent believed that it was better to have one or no party to assure unanimity. It might be concluded that this percentage is the upper limit of those with authoritarian sentiment in the Federal Republic at the time of its foundation and for perhaps a decade thereafter. More importangly, those with such sentiments decline fairly rapidly from mid-decade, settling at around 10 per cent by 1961.[46] Moreover, these changes cannot be interpreted as an example of cohort replacement, there are important changes among those who formerly rated the authoritarian periods highly.[47] In France and Italy there is also evidence for voting patterns which reflect sympathy for authoritarian politics. In Italy however the vote for the radical right was rarely above 12 per cent, while in the case of France it fluctuated from election to election but there is little evidence for a return to fascist-type sympathies.

The traditional denominational and right-wing electoral support for Christian democracy should not disguise the reforming intention of most of the parties. Fogarty insisted in 1957 that Christian democracy was a conservative, but not a traditional movement. He recognised that the voters attracted to the parties after 1945 were those most associated with traditionalist values and political behaviour. Yet he argued that the new parties had broken with the monarchist and clericalist themes central to traditionalism. Christian democratic parties were, he added, reformist in their relationship to capitalism, welfare and the post-war consensus. Summarising the conclusions of the analysis of member parties at the Bruges congress of the NEI in 1954, Fogarty found that the majority of the responses reflected a view that 'in principle at least they felt the priority should go not to preservation but to change'.[48]

In most cases the party programmes offered considerable reformist promise immediately after the war, but had been attenuated considerably between then and the early 1950s. The utopian enthusiasm of the immediate post-war period was replaced by a more sober assessment of the possibilities for change, but also a recognition of the existing constraints. Some of these were electoral, and a need to satisfy a conservative electorate, while others were a response to the more immediate difficulties posed by the European crisis, both political and economic, of 1947 and 1948. It is certainly the case that by 1950 the policy framework envisaged by Christian democratic parties had become more conservative. In the case of the CDU this process has been described as an evolution from Christian socialism to the social market economy, a path which can be traced from 1946 through the Ahlen programme in 1947, the Düsseldorf programme in 1949 and the 1953 Hamburg programme. What is noticeable is that the programmatic emphasis changed from the implicitly corporatist, redistributionist and anti-capitalist sentiments of the early documents, to one where the emphasis is placed on growth within the capitalist economy, but modified by welfare considerations.[49] This view is widespread among the Christian democratic parties, by the early 1950s virtually all of them are committed to economic growth within an expanding market economy in co-operation with the United States.

Notwithstanding this consensus there are considerable differences between the parties in implementation. The DC in Italy is the least progressive of the

Christian democratic parties, not only in programmatic terms but as a consequence of policy implementation also. While Germany and Italy both pursued growth policies under the aegis of Christian democratic governments the consequences for the poor and the working class in each is quite different. Italian growth is quite close to that of Germany during the 1950s and welfare as a percentage of GNP grows quickly in each state. However, the consequences of policy are quite different. Welfare coverage is wider in Germany than in Italy, in addition to which real wages increase in Germany but not in Italy. While the benefits of growth are distributed unevenly in both states, the disparity between rich and poor widens in Italy while it narrows in Germany. One reason for this is that the post-war Italian experience is closer to a one-party state than is the case in Germany. While the DC was unable to enter into a right-wing government with the neo-fascists, or to effectively manipulate the electoral law as in France, electoral competition was to a large extent limited by the presence of the PCI. Furthermore, during the 1950s the DC retained the closest connections with the Church and in terms of its ideology and political practice retained much that can be considered confessional.[50]

The effective absence of an alternative government in Italy reduced the reality of competitive politics and consequently affected the level to which policy and welfare would address the requirements of the community as a whole and not simply those of the dominant classes. If the characteristic features of Christian democracy are associated with introducing a new democratic constitution, the return to party politics and the rule of law, the DC fail to meet each of these criteria. The 1948 constitution was partisan and reflected confessional concerns, effective party competition was weak if not non-existent, while the rule of law has remained in doubt throughout the history of the Italian republic. There is little doubt about the commitment to democracy on the part of the founders of the DC, but the trajectory of the party took it far from the original promise. In this sense it is difficult to compare it with the experience of the other five examples given here.

Nau has suggested that there is a tendency for centre-right governments to favour more conservative economic and monetary policies, usually emphasising growth over redistribution, whereas centre-left governments favour more interventionist policies to promote full employment, even when this forces up inflation. Nau calculates that between 1947 and 1967 centre-right governments were in power for 70 per cent of the time in the G7 states. If France, Germany and Italy are taken as a group then the figure increases to 83 per cent.[51] This view overlaps with other work which suggests a link between the ideology of a government and its policy output. While the correlation is not foolproof, it does suggest that all else being equal conservative governments will favour policies that will control inflation while leftist governments will opt for full employment or reducing unemployment as a priority.[52] The United States and Sweden provide the most striking confirmation of this view during the 1950s. The former accepted higher than average unemployment under Eisenhower as one cost of controlling inflation and spending, while the social democratic governments in the latter virtually eliminated unemployment throughout this period.[53] Yet for the most part all else was not even. The presence of Christian democrats in a government appears to have made a difference in policy outcome as compared with pure conservatives. Stephens, for example, has noted in his study of the influence of social democracy on the post-war consensus that: 'Catholicism weakens socialist rule. But independent of its negative effect on socialist rule, it has a positive effect on welfare state development.' Though Stephens' intention is to explain differences based on socialist incumbency, his analysis also leads to interesting conclusions concerning Christian democracy.[54] In fact there is a complex relationship between the influence of Christian democracy and the nature of the post-war welfare state, a relationship which is implied but not quantified in Stephens' analysis. Table 4.8 highlights expenditure on social services in 1960.

What is significant in Table 4.8 is that the first six of these states all have strong Christian democratic or Catholic parties actively participating in government after the Second World War. Paradoxically, those states usually identified with the social democratic consensus, such as the United Kingdom and Scandinavian states, exhibit lower levels of expenditure on social services than those with a Christian democratic component. It is of course true that absolute figures tell little about the intention of policy or the direction of expenditure. A case could be made for high levels of expenditure which are channelled disproportionately towards the middle classes and not to the working class as would be the case with a social democratic regime. Yet it is also clear that the self-image of the Christian democratic parties during the post-war years was not wedded to the austere economic and fiscal policies that had traditionally characterised the right. Though crude, these figures, and other studies, suggest that while a pure left or right government will attempt to formulate policy in a partisan fashion, this was not always possible.[55]

If allowance is made for national contexts, what Christian democracy shares with social democracy in this first phase of post-war economic reconstruction and expansion is a commitment to economic growth, to industrialisation and to economic modernisation within the context of European integration. For Germany, the social market economy model offered a distinct approach to the instabilities associated with economic growth, while the close co-operation in government between the Christian democrats and social democrats in Austria and the Netherlands is similar in intent if not in structure.[56] This distinctness is

Table 4.8 Expenditure on social services as percentage of GDP, 1960

Austria	15.4	Denmark	11.1
Germany	15.4	Sweden	10.9
Belgium	13.3	United Kingdom	10.8
France	13.2	Norway	9.4
Italy	11.7	Ireland	9.3
Netherlands	11.1	Finland	8.8

Source: Kees van Kersbergen *Social Capitalism: A Study of Christian Democracy and the Post-War Settlement of the Welfare State,* unpublished doctorial thesis, Department of Political and Social Sciences, European University Institute, Florence, 1991 p. 163 drawn from ILO statistics. I have excluded non-European examples from the table.

evident though in weaker form in the other three cases discussed. However, they also share a commitment to the introduction of the welfare state in a number of states. If the function of social democracy historically has been to socialise capitalism from the left, it is possible to argue that Christian democracy has contributed to this process from the right. In effect, Christian democracy offered an alternative to the socialist welfare state model, one which proved to be less redistributive in form and which maintained many of the traditional social divisions intact. Although this involved a move to the left for conservative politics between 1945 and 1960, Christian democracy had a preservative and not a transformational strategy in relation to social change. However, in transforming the European right Christian democracy sought accommodation with liberalism, capitalism and democracy. In successfully achieving this goal in a number of states, it domesticated and democratised the right and consequently contributed to the stability and consensus that prevailed throughout the 1950s.

Notes

1. Lutz Niethammer, *Posthistoire: Has History come to an End?* (London: Verso, 1992), pp. 82–90.
2. The extent to which the right actually opposed fascism in any meaningful way is questionable. Einaudi insists that the existence of Catholic Action in Italy provided a centre of opposition to fascism, but adds significantly that 'even by doing nothing, and this is what it did for the most part, it was anti-Fascist by reason of the simple fact of not being Fascist'. Mario Einaudi, 'Christian democracy in Italy' in Mario Einaudi and Francois Goguel, *Christian Democracy in Italy and France* (Notre Dame, Indiana: University of Notre Dame Press, 1952), p.26.
3. Roger Austin, 'The Conservative right and the far right in France: the search for power, 1934–44' in Martin Blinkhorn (ed.) *Fascists and Conservatives* (London: Unwin Hyman, 1990), pp. 176–99. The comparative perspective can be best seen in the work of Susan Zuccotti, *The Italians and the Holocaust: Persecution, Rescue, Survival* (New York: Basic Books, 1987); and *The Holocaust, the French, and the Jews* (New York: Basic Books, 1992).
4. For recent discussions on this theme see the essays in M.L Smith and P.M.R. Stirk (eds), *Making the New Europe: European Unity and the Second World War* (London: Pinter, 1990); David W. Ellwood, *Rebuilding Europe* (London: Longman, 1992), pp. 3–28; Patrick T. Pasture, 'The April 1944 "Social pact" in Belgium and its significance for the post-war welfare state' *Journal of Contemporary History* 28:4 (October 1993), pp. 695–714.
5. Ernest Gellner, *Plough, Sword and Book* (London: Collins, 1988), pp. 242–3. Gellner suggests that the New Order 'may not have been *the* destiny of Europe, but it certainly was *a* possible destiny'.
6. In this chapter right or conservative usually refers to those conservative parties which accept constitutional government, unless otherwise specified.
7. Jaroslav Krejčí, 'Introduction: concepts of right and left' in L. Cheles, et al., (eds), *Neo-Fascism in Europe* (London: Longman, 1991), pp. 1–18.
8. This chapter is not meant to be exhaustive and examples will be selected to illustrate the overall developments rather than the detail in every individual case.
9. Albert O. Hirschman, *The Rhetoric of Reaction* (Cambridge, Mass: Harvard University Press, 1991) for the argument.
10. Cited in Paul Ginsborg, *A History of Contemporary Italy* (London: Penguin, 1990), p. 49.

11. There is also a need to distinguish between the ideological disposition of the papacy, Catholic politics whether democratic or not, and the support given by Catholics to radical right-wing movements.
12. Ernest Gellner, *Plough, Sword and Book: The Structure of Human History* (London: Paledin, 1991), pp. 262–3, 245–6 for explication of these matters.
13. John H. Whyte, *Catholics in Western Democracies* (Dublin: Gill and Macmillan, 1980), pp. 7–8; Michael P. Fogarty, *Christian Democracy in Western Europe 1820–1953* (London: Routledge and Kegan Paul, 1957), pp. 101–2 for discussion on traditionalist basis of Catholic politics.
14. Hans Maier, *Revolution and Church: The Early History of Christian Democracy, 1789-1901* (Notre Dame: University of Notre Dame Press, 1969), pp.12-13.
15. Peter C. Kent, 'A tale of two Popes: Pius XI, Pius XII and the Rome–Berlin Axis' *Journal of Contemporary History* 23:4 (1988), pp. 589–608.
16. Ibid., pp. 603–8.
17. Fogarty, op. cit., pp. 5, 309; Michael Burgess, 'Political Catholicism, European unity and the rise of Christian democracy' in Smith and Stirk, op. cit., pp. 142–55, 146–47.
18. Whyte, op. cit., pp. 7–8, 84–5 for quotation.
19. Gene Burns, 'The politics of ideology: the papal struggle with liberalism', *American Journal of Sociology* 95:5 (March 1990), pp. 1123–52 for a detailed discussion of the continuing hostility of the papacy to liberalism.
20. Whyte, op. cit., p. 121; Fogarty, op. cit., p. 311.
21. Maier, op. cit., pp. 21–2.
22. Cited in Andrea Riccardi, 'The Vatican of Pius XII and the Catholic Party', *Concilium* (October, 1987), pp. 37–51; Burns, pp. op. cit., 1141–3; Klaus von Beyme, *Political Parties in Western Democracies* (Aldershot: Gower, 1985) p. 84.
23. Cited in Francois Goguel, 'Christian democracy in France', in Einaudi and Goguel, op. cit. pp. 119–20.
24. De Gasperi, *Idee Ricostruttive della Democrazia Cristiana* July 25, 1943, cited in Einaudi, op. cit., p. 29.
25. Cited in Riccardi, op. cit. pp. 49–50.
23. Cited in Fogarty, op. cit., pp. 132–3.
27. Whyte, op. cit., pp. 100–17 where he traces the circumstances of the decline of closed Catholicism after 1960.
28. Hans Daalder, 'Parties, elites, and political developments in Western Europe', in Joseph LaPalombara and Myron Weiner (eds), *Political Parties and Political Development* (Princeton New Jersey: Princeton University Press, 1966), pp. 43–77; citation at pp. 59–60.
29. It should also be noted that despite Soviet occupation of Austria until 1955, this did not prevent the growth and expansion of the Christian Democratic party there, though it probably contributed to the successful coalition strategy pursued by the socialists and the Christian Democrats.
30. Fogarty, op. cit., p. 5.
31. Paul Lucardie and Hans-Martien ten Napel, 'Between confessionalism and liberal conservatism: a comparative analysis of Christian democratic parties in Flanders, Germany, Italy and the Netherlands', Paper presented at the ECPR joint sessions University of Limerick (1992), p. 2. These authors suggest that: 'The major aspects of modernisation: an industrial (capitalist) market economy, a secularized and individualistic culture, and some form of representative mass democracy, are accepted by Christian democracy with substantial qualifications.' Though not disagreeing with this description I will suggest later that it is the extent to which Christian democracy accepts modernism that constitutes both its uniqueness in ideological terms and its (partial) break with anti-modernist sentiment. I am extremely grateful to Paul Lucardie for discussing these matters with me, and for permission to cite from this unpublished

manuscript.

32. Fogarty, op. cit., p. 311.
33. Maier, op. cit., pp. 41–2 who details these featues in a careful fashion; Whyte, op. cit. passim; R.E.M. Irving, *The Christian Democratic Parties of Western Europe* (George Allen and Unwin, 1979). A distinction should be drawn between conservative parties in continental Europe and the Conservative Party in Britain. The latter has been a mass party since the nineteenth century and has been integrated into the democratic process for most of its history. In this respect the Christian democratic parties overlap more with the British party than with other conservative parties; Philip Norton and Arthur Aughey, *Conservatives and Conservatism* (London: Temple Smith, 1981).
34. For a comprehensive discussion of these features *see* Fogarty, op. cit., passim; Irving, op. cit., pp. 29–57.
35. Kees van Kersbergen, *Social Capitalism: A Study of Christian Democracy and the Post-War Settlement of the Welfare State,* (unpublished doctoral thesis, Department of Political and Social Science, European University Institute, Florence, 1991. *Idem.,* 'The distinctiveness of Christian democracy', ECPR joint sessions, University of Limerick, 1992, for discussion of these themes.
36. The different strategies pursued by individual Christian democratic parties can be appreciated in Irving, op. cit., passim, and Zig Layton-Henry (ed.), *Conservative Parties in Western Europe* (London: Macmillan, 1982).
37. Richard Rose and Derek W. Urwin, 'Persistence and change in Western party systems since 1945', *Political Studies* 18:3 (1970), pp. 287–319; this study concluded that the tendency in the party systems was towards stability up to 1969.
38. The French case will be treated in more detail in Chapter 7.
39. Juan J. Linz, 'Cleavage and consensus in West German politics: the early fifties', in Seymour M. Lipset and Stein Rokkan (eds), *Party Systems and Voter Alignment* (New York: The Free Press, 1967), pp. 283–321; Mattei Dogan, 'Political cleavage and social stratification in France and Italy', in Lipset and Rokkan, op. cit., pp. 129–195; G.A. Irwin, 'Patterns of voting behaviour in the Netherlands', in Richard T. Griffiths (ed.), *The Economy and Politics of the Netherlands since 1945* (The Hague: Martin Nijhoff, 1980), pp. 199–222; Robert Leonardi and Douglas A. Wertman, *Italian Christian Democracy* (London: Macmillan, 1989), pp. 164–75.
40. Dogan, op. cit., p. 161; Leonardi and Wertman, op. cit., p. 174.
41. The distinction between male and female participation in church activity can be appreciated from a 1956 poll in Italy. While 69 per cent of respondents went to mass regularly, when this figure is disaggregated for sex it breaks down as 57 per cent of men and 80 for women. In addition the relationship between religious participation and support for DC can be seen in the 86 per cent of their supporters who attend mass. Pierpaolo Luzzatto Fegiz, *Il Volto Sconosciuto Dell'Italia,* Seconda Serie: 1956–65 (Milano: Giuffre, 1966), p. 1283.
42. R.E.M. Irving, *Christian Democracy in France* (London: George Allen and Unwin, 1973), pp. 74–105; Philip M. Williams, *Crisis and Compromise*, 3rd edn (London: Longman, 1964); Compare Maps 5, 6, 8, 13, 14, and 20 for distribution and overlap of vote. Jean-Pierre Rioux, *The Fourth Republic 1944-1958* (Cambridge: Cambridge University Press, 1987) for further discussion. Wolfgang C. Müller and Barbara Steininger, 'Party organisation and party competitiveness: the case of the Austrian People's Party, 1945–92', *European Journal of Political Research* (forthcoming: 1994) (I am grateful to Dr Müller for letting me see a pre-publication version of this article); Ian D. Connor, 'Social change and electoral support: the case of the CDU/CSU, 1949–87', in Eva Kolinsky (ed) *The Federal Republic of Germany: The End of an Era* (New York: Berg, 1981), pp. 83–118.
43. Linz, op. cit. pp. 305–16.
44. This point is made particularly strongly by van Kersbergen, op. cit., which is the best

available discussion of this theme currently available.

45. However, it should be added that whatever misgivings the DC may have had about democracy since 1945, its presence in the political system weakened the threat from the right though not eliminated it.

46. Elisabeth Noelle and Erich Peter Neumann, *The Germans: Public Opinion Polls 1947–1966* (Westport, Conn: Greenwood Press, 1981), pp. 227, 346, 395 for further details; Gerard R. Boynton and Gerhard Loewenburg, 'The development of public support for Parliament in Germany, 1951–1959', *British Journal of Political Science* 3, (1973) pp. 169–89.

47. David P. Conradt, 'Changing German political culture' in Gabriel Almond and Sidney Verba (eds), *The Civic Culture Revisited* (Boston: Little Brown, 1980), pp. 212–272, pp. 225–7 for discussion of this point.

48. Fogarty, op. cit., pp. 101–11 which refers to party documents and programmes to illustrate this point.

49. Ute Schmidt, 'Die Christlich Demokratische Union Deutschlands', in Richard Stöss (ed.), *Partein-Handbuch: Die Partein der Bundesrepublik Deutschland 1945–1980* (Opladen: Westdeutscher Verlag, 1983), pp. 490–660; see pp. 516–44 for discussion on programmes. Geoffrey Pridham, *Christian Democracy in Western Germany* (London: Croom Helm, 1977).

50. Article 7 of the 1948 Constitution incorporated the concordat which had been agreed with Mussolini. See Einaudi and Ginsborg op. cit., pp. 141–209. Severino Galante, *La Fine Di Un Compromesso Storico: PCI e DC nella crisi del 1947* (Milano: Angeli, 1980), pp.73–122; Adenauer and De Gasperi's contribution to post-war Europe can be appreciated in the essays in Umberto Corsini and Konrad Repgen (eds), *Konrad Adenauer e Alcide De Gasperi: due esperienze di rifondazione della democrazia* (Bologna: Mulino, 1984).

51. Henry R. Nau, *The Myth of American Decline* (New York: Oxford University Press, 1990), pp. 41–2; 48–9.

52. Douglas A. Hibbs, jr, 'Political parties and macroeconomic policy' *The American Political Science Review* 71:4 (December 1977), pp 1467–87 for the most succinct development of this view.

53. See Chapter 6 for a discussion of the American context.

54. John D. Stephens, *The Transition from Capitalism to Socialism* (London: Macmillan, 1979), p. 103. However, for Stephens' the role of Catholics is residual:

    The relationship of the percentage of Catholics in a country to the level of welfare spending is complex. Our rationale for including this variable was that it seemed possible that anti-capitalist aspects of Catholic ideology – such as notions of a fair wage or prohibitions on usury – as well as the generally positive attitude of the Catholic Church towards welfare for the poor might encourage government welfare spending.

    This view seems to be based on a contingent relationship rather than on an active response to the problems of post-war reconstruction as will be argued below.

55. Francis G. Castles, *The Social Democratic Image of Society* (London: Routledge and Kegan Paul, 1978) , pp. 68–76 for an alternative reading. In contrast to the data used in Table 4.8, Castles' data are concentrated in the 1970s, after the surge in spending during the 1960s. What I wish to suggest is that up to the 1960s the presence of Christian democrats in government contributed to the post-war expansion; see van Kersbergen *Social Capitalism*, op. cit., for a sophisticated argument for the Christian Democratic case.

56. Jeremy Leaman, *The Political Economy of West Germany, 1945–1985* (Basingstoke: Macmillan, 1988), pp. 43–107; Erik Bloemen, 'Hard work! Ideology and interest in Dutch economic policy at home and abroad between 1945 and 1951', *Economic and Social History in the Netherlands* 2, (1990), pp. 135–48; Albrecht Langner (ed.)

Katholizismus, Wirtschaftsordnung und Sozialpolitik 1945–1963 (Paderborn: Ferdinand Schöningh, 1980); Peter Gerlich and Wolfgang Müller (eds) *Zwischen Koalition Und Konkurrenz: Österreichs Parteien seit 1945* (Vienna: Braumüller, 1983).

5 Conservatism and Consensus in Post-war Britain, 1945–64

Introduction: The Basis for Consensus, 1940–50

Neville Chamberlain's resignation in 1940 was the British equivalent of the collapse of the old conservative order in continental Europe. Chamberlain's gamble at Munich that he could stabilise the European balance of power had clearly failed. His replacement by Winston Churchill, the formation of a coalition government and the enhanced position of the Labour Party marked the beginning of a new phase in British politics. While winning the war remained the main objective of the coalition, in Britain no less than in occupied Europe the shock of defeat and war led many to believe that the post-war world would have to depart radically from the experience of the inter-war years. By 1943 there is a detectable shift in public opinion, a shift which is clearly identified with the reformist intentions of the Labour Party rather than the Conservatives.[1] As early as 1940 Rab Butler had urged the need for a radical conservative response to the challenge of war. For the most part, however, the mainstream of the party remained distant from such suggestions. The general response within the party to reforming initiatives, such as the Beveridge report, was critical of the collectivist assumptions involved.[2]

Moreover the Conservative Party adopted a very cautious policy towards the post-war world, even as late as the 1945 election campaign. There was little difference in substance between the domestic policies advocated by the party in 1945 and that in 1939. The party leadership, a majority of its MPs and its core electorate, continued to believe in the priority of low taxation, limited commitments on social welfare and a sound monetary policy. Consequently, the Conservatives were unable to counter the ambitious domestic programme published by the Labour Party in 1945, with its commitment to full employment, expanded welfare and economic growth. The electorate were asked to choose in 1945 between a Conservative domestic policy which only modified slightly the priorities of the 1930s, and a left-wing programme which promised a clear break with that experience. Britain was not alone in choosing to break with the past, and the 1945 election is not simply a victory for the Labour Party, it also involved a rejection of the policy framework and ideology of the Conservatives. The mandate which the incoming Labour government received was substantial both in terms of its size, and in the extent to which it changed the priorities of government.[3]

The 1945 election did not provide the basis for a post-war consensus in Britain. The Conservative Party remained opposed to the direction of the Labour government for some time thereafter. Nor had the basis for consensus been laid during the Second World War, as is sometimes thought.[4] Despite co-operation, the two parties remained divided on domestic issues. The post-war years began in Britain on the basis of conflict rather than consensus. In this, Britain was not that different from the United States or other liberal democratic states at the time. This is not to claim that a consensus did not emerge in Britain or elsewhere, but to say that it was not in existence in 1945. A consensus was in place by 1950, by which time the Conservative Party had to come to terms with the changes which had been enacted by the Labour government. This acceptance was slow in coming, as late as 1947 the Conservatives were only in the process of re-evaluating their post-war policy on the major issues. The symbolic shift in attitude was the acceptance by party conference of the *Industrial Charter* in 1947, a document which is intentionally ambiguous in objective, probably just as well because Churchill only reluctantly accepted the document as party policy. Notwithstanding the intention of the document's authors, Butler noted in 1948 that it had not attracted working-class support for the Conservatives, who continued to value the high level of security assured by Labour policy.[5]

There was a growing recognition within the party that unless the Conservatives could assure working-class and floating voters of its willingness to maintain the welfare state and full employment, it was unlikely to be returned to government. Some confirmation of this was available to them by 1949 when it was recognised that the party had not defeated the government in a single by-election for a Labour-held seat; this despite the unpopularity of the austerity measures introduced by the government. Thus, while the government was un-popular there was little drift to the Conservatives. This in turn led to the party adopting a high profile on the major changes which had taken place since 1945. Prior to the 1950 election the Conservatives confirmed their intention to main-tain what had been achieved by Labour, though it insisted that some aspects of nationalisation would be reversed. This latter promise was a safe one, as floating voters were not strong identifiers with the nationalisation question in any event.

It is thus necessary to modify the question of consensus in post-war Britain. It is mistaken to believe that no consensus emerged, or that it was already in place in 1945. What occurs is a swing to the left on the part of the electorate which en-dorsed the policy package offered by Labour in 1945. This policy package was implemented and institutionalised over the next five years. By 1950 the changes had been accepted by a large section of the electorate, even those not closely identified with the government. This shift placed the Conservative Party in a dif-ficult position. It could continue to oppose the measures introduced, seeking to reverse them when returned to government. This would entail maintaining a strong right-wing ideological profile, one more extreme than most European conservative parties at that time. Given the nature of public opinion, pursuing such aims would have led to the exclusion of the party from government for some time. The alternative was to come to terms with the changes, criticising the detail and implications of some aspects of them, but generally accepting that it was not possible to move back before the changes themselves. By 1950 the balance of opinion within the party had moved to the latter view, and it is at this point that it is possible to accept that a consensus had been achieved. But having a consensus does not mean that differences have simply been accommodated. The acceptance of the consensus was on Labour's terms and amounted to a defeat for the traditional Conservative Party.[6]

The remarkable revival of Conservative fortunes in 1950 was a reflection of the change in emphasis within the party, though as yet some sections of the electorate continued to have reservations about the party's commitments. In turn, the 1951 election proved to be crucial for the future of right-wing politics in the United Kingdom. If the Labour Party had secured a further majority at that election, it is probable that it would have remained in office for a full term, benefited from the better economic conditions which prevailed from mid-decade while increasing Labour's ideological influence over policy-making. Failure to return to office in 1951 could have had a serious impact on the fortunes of the Conservative Party and on its influence over policy and policy-making. It would be exaggerated to suggest that such a failure could have led to the eclipse of the party, but it was a fear shared by a number of leading party members and by Central Office.[7] A general election victory is not necessarily a mandate for change, nor is it the acquisition of real power. What it offered the Conservatives in 1951 was an opportunity to influence the policy framework in the short term, to modify policy in the medium term and to secure the conditions for a return to power thereafter.

Reaching these objectives was not inevitable. The electoral victory had been narrow and there is a sense that the electorate had placed the party on probation. The existing consensus was also a constraint which could not be ignored. Churchill, however, could form his cabinet in an optimistic mood from a political perspective. The British political system appeared to be stabilising in its classic two-party alignment. Within that system the Conservatives had acquired a number of advantages. Its vote had increased by over 1 million between 1950 and 1951, while the increase for Labour was in the region of 700 000. Table 5.1 shows the shift in support for the parties between 1945 and 1951. Moreover, the collapse of the Liberal Party between the two elections worked to the advantage of the right rather than the left. Despite Churchill's insistence on a formal alliance with the Liberal Party the anti-socialist alliance which emerged did not include them, but reflected the long-standing co-operation between the National

Table 5.1 General election results, 1945–51 (% [seats])

	1945		1950		1951	
Labour Party	48.0	(393)	46.1	(315)	48.8	(295)
Conservatives	36.8	(199)	43.4	(298)	48.0	(321)
Liberal Party	9.0	(12)	9.1	(9)	9.1	(6)
National Liberals	2.8	(11)	–		–	
Others	3.4	(25)	1.4	(3)	1.4	(3)
Turn-out	72.6		83.6		81.9	

Liberals and the Conservative Party. The Conservative Party in 1951 and there-after dictated the terms of the anti-socialist message without compromising its own principles, which had been feared if a formal arrangement had been agreed.[8] This placed the Conservatives in a strong position to attract former liberal voters disenchanted with liberalism or who recognised the futility of voting Liberal in a manner which allowed a Labour candidate to win. In turn, the failure of the Liberal Party to contest more than 109 constituencies reduced dramatically the number of three-corner contests. Conservative tacticians were confident that in the event of a two-sided contest former Liberal voters would move to the right rather than to the left. One party analysis estimated that if 75 per cent of former Liberals voted Conservative then the party could hope to win around thirty-three extra seats, but if the vote dropped to 66 per cent then the number would half to around eighteen. Retrospective analysis assumed that the breakdown between the two parties was 60/40 and that this accounted for eight of the Conservative gains in 1951.[9]

Post-election analysis by Central Office confirmed that the most significant movement to the right occurred in constituencies which had shifted from three-corner contests to straight fights between the main parties. In London the swing was 1.2 per cent, in the English boroughs 2.08 per cent, and in Wales 4.24 per cent. The average swing in the country was 1.1 per cent and it is therefore not surprising that the party gained seats in each of these areas. There was, further-more, a strong correlation between the size of the Liberal vote in 1950 and the swing to the Conservatives in 1951. The contrast is quite striking: where the Liberal vote had been less than 7 per cent, the median swing was 0.8 per cent, whereas where that vote had been in the 15-30 per cent range the swing was 3 per cent.[10]

The impact of the Liberals on Conservative gains was asymmetrical according to Pierssene. In some cases Liberal votes had helped the party, whereas in others it had obstructed its progress. Nevertheless he concluded that:

> A process of attrition has been at work on the flanks of the Liberal Party for many years. The Right Wing and a number of moderate Liberals have come over to us. The Labour Party has swallowed much of the Left Wing. What is left is a hardcore of die hard Liberals who are traditionally at least as anti-Tory as they are anti-Socialist. At this election the Liberal voter was reinforced by a large number of 'doubtful' voters who had no Liberal tradition but supported the Liberal Party as a half-way house between Socialism and Conservatism.[11]

The halfway house argument has limited application in 1950 or 1951. The Labour Party maintained its core constituency and indeed increased its overall vote. In the case of the Liberals its vote increased by 400 000 between 1945 and 1950, but then disintegrated. In so far as the 1950 increase can be attributed to former Labour voters, this is likely to be affecting middle-class voters who do appear to have switched over this period.[12]

It is possible to overestimate the significance of Liberal defection, given the amount of attention paid to the party by some leading Conservatives. Other factors also influenced the 1951 success. The Labour Party maintained an opinion poll lead for most of 1950, remaining high until December 1950. The government's popularity may have been under pressure, but its demise was not inevitable. It is during 1951 that significant slippage occurs: Labour's approval ratings drop to around 30 per cent, while around 50 per cent indicate that they would vote for the Conservatives. A number of factors contributed to this; including divisions within the party, the Korean war and weariness at the leadership level. With a six seat majority and loss of confidence it was clear that the Labour government could not continue without a further mandate.[13]

Conservative appeal between the two elections can be attributed to the attractiveness of its housing policies and its commitments to controlling the cost of living. This had proved effective during the 1950 campaign and the party was considered by Gallup to have been more successful than Labour in its propaganda campaign. After that election Churchill concentrated his criticisms on the 'evils' of nationalisation, reaffirming his commitment to repeal the iron and steel nationalisation programme. Yet the Conservatives had to proceed with caution. Churchill might condemn socialism and complain about the widening ideological gap between left and right, yet his party still had to appeal to a section of the electorate which was attracted to the benefits of socialism. Gallup estimated that over 50 per cent of those voting Conservative in 1950 were of working-class origin, while at least 25 per cent of trade union members were also Conservative voters (6.75 million and 2 million respectively). Significant majorities opposed the nationalisation of iron and steel, but this did not imply any more radical offensive against socialism as such.[14]

Nationalisation had not been a matter of great concern for the electorate even in 1945. Except for Labour Party activists and those immediately affected by the programmes, public opinion remained either neutral or hostile. During 1950 opinion polls found that most respondents identified the cost of living as their major concern, while the Conservative housing policy was the policy which generated most interest. Full employment hardly rated a mention, while nationalisation generated a response rate of around 5-6 per cent. However, on specific questions relating to state intervention a more differential approach is detectable. State provision of medical services was approved by 72 per cent, while 53 per cent believed that the nationalisation of the coal-mines was a positive development. In stark contrast, majorities disapproved of the consequences of state control of the railway industry and the energy industry.[15]

By early 1951 the Conservatives had established the grounds for an effective challenge to the Labour Party. Deprived of victory in 1950 the party redoubled its efforts during the first half of 1951, sensing the government's weakness and its own opportunities. It also believed that public opinion was moving to the party in ways that could work to its advantage. The Korean war and the accompanying anti-communist mood provided a certain respectability for hostility to socialism and collectivism. Commitments to 'free' the economy proved to be attractive in what was still an 'era of austerity'. Promises to provide greater choice in consumption terms reinforced this. At one level this was the politics of nuance rather than substance, and such a conclusion confirms the now traditional view that the incoming Conservative government endorsed the prevailing consensus.[16]

Without dissenting from this view it is important to evaluate the extent to which nuance reflected substance, though in attenuated form. It is often claimed that the denationalisation of iron and steel is a minor exception to the Conservative acceptance of this consensus. However, the insistence on denationalisation is important, for it reflects a deeper ideological commitment to halting any further collectivisation of the economy. It can also be seen as an ideological marker for the party itself, as a method of distancing itself, often only at a rhetorical level, from the left. It is also a signal to the party activists of a continuing commitment to an individualistic and market-led political philosophy. Although constrained by the shifts in the political culture since 1945, the Conservative party by 1951 was attempting to retrieve a liberal individualistic philosophy from collectivist encroachment, while maintaining the commitments to welfare. There remained a basis for this; liberal economic philosophy continued to be influential not only among Conservatives, but in the wider political system.[17]

The 1951 Election and the Reinforcement of Consensus

The Conservative document *Britain Strong and Free*, published in 1951, conceded much to the Labour-defined consensus, but stopped short of embracing a social-democratic philosophy. As with the Christian democratic parties on the continent after 1945 the Conservatives recognised that their world had changed, but wished to influence its further evolution. The commitment to denationalising iron and steel reflected a continuing desire to limit collectivism and endorse individuality. It emphasised the need for a strong and stable currency which, it implied, could be achieved by the return of a Conservative government. The conservatives also criticised the ready availability of credit on easy terms, the inflation of the currency and the weakness of productive activity. The emphasis was on saving and production rather than on a consumption-led expansion (which would not necessarily result in the purchase of British produced goods). In a retrospective analysis on the 1951 election, prepared by the Conservative Research Department, Michael Fraser isolated the October 1951 balance of payments crisis as the major cause of concern for the party prior to the election. The Labour government policies were restricting the economy's room for manoeuvre at a time when it required flexibility to respond to change in the world economy. Therefore the incoming Conservative government had to adopt policies in circumstances which highlighted a classic dilemma for the right:

> Any government in the modern world must try to ensure that general demand is strong enough to provide full employment but not so strong that inflation develops. Conservatives believe that such general control of the economic climate should be exercised by monetary policy as well as by fiscal methods. The use of budgetary policy and fiscal controls alone was proved to be inadequate in the years of inflation between 1945 and 1951. The present government has, therefore, returned to the use of a flexible monetary policy, controlling credit through the use of the Bank rate.[18]

Inflation continued to be the party's main concern after it returned to government. Fraser claimed that continuing price increases would endanger not only the currency but the social changes which had occurred since 1945. Moreover the Conservative Party was well placed to reverse these trends:

> Since the middle of 1952 the rise in the cost of living has been checked and prices have been relatively steady. At the same time a high level of employment has been

maintained. Conservative policy has involved a complete break with the tradition of ever increasing taxation to which we had become accustomed in recent years.[19]

Despite this natural concern with inflation the party also had to recognise that it could not simply revert to the policies of the 1930s. By 1951, whatever its short-term responses to immediate problems such as inflation, the party leadership had accepted the post-war commitments to full employment and were reluctant to concede this sensitive issue to the Labour Party. After all in 1950 and 1951 the party went to considerable pains to offset Labour's claim that the welfare state would not be safe in the Conservatives' hands. Yet the road to this had been painful, especially the degree to which full employment as an objective should be endorsed. Between 1944 and 1951 the emphasis on this issue shifts percepti-bly. At the 1945 general election the Conservatives simply reiterated the commitment of the 1944 Employment Act to a 'high and stable level of employ-ment'. During the following years Conservatives were not prepared to expand on this, or to make specific commitments on the level of unemployment which would be compatible with this objective. With the publication of the *Industrial Charter* (May 1947), the party reiterated its continuing agreement with the 1944 White Paper, but added that it would 'in some respects go further to ensure that the demand for goods and services is always maintained at a level which will of-fer jobs to all who are willing to work'.[20]

In 1949 the party went close to endorsing a full employment strategy. While warning that the real danger to Britain's future rested with inflation rather than deflation, a clear commitment to intervention was given:

> We repudiate the suggestion that deliberate creation of unemployment is necessary to maintain high production and industrial discipline. A Conservative government will do all in its power to safeguard the country from internal fluctuations, by the wise use of the Budget and the Capital investment programme . . .[21]

By the time of the 1950 election any reservations had been abandoned: 'we re-gard the maintenance of full employment as the first aim of the Conservative Government'.[22] The 1951 manifesto, while not explicitly making a commitment to full employment, continued this line of reasoning, but linked it to expanding 'national output' to secure that end.[23] Once the party had become committed to avoiding unemployment, it had accepted the terms of the consensus. The diffi-culty in policy terms, and one which was to plague it until 1964, was how to achieve this while avoiding inflation and unnecessary pump priming. Prior to 1951 there remained a residual fear that government action to offset unemploy-ment would have inflationary consequences.

A report on the 'industrial worker' prepared by the party subcommittee on political education concluded that the working class should be assured without ambiguity that its interests would be protected by a Conservative government. However it warned against a 'bread and circuses' strategy on the grounds that such an approach would only attract the 'shiftless and idlers', while alienating the more self-reliant and intelligent sections of the working class who would be attracted by Conservative policy. While party strategists concluded that the Con-servatives could only hope to attract, at the outside, around 40 per cent of working-class votes it could appeal to these voters along Conservative lines:

Conservatives do not believe in equality of wealth, but in the greater equality of opportunity. We believe that it is for the individual to make the best use of his talents, and that harder work and higher skill should receive a higher reward. The wage differential between the skilled and unskilled worker is fundamental to this belief. The Social Services would provide a minimum standard below which no one through adversity or misfortune should fall. They should not be used to stifle initiative by bringing down the enterprising to the level of the idle and shiftless.[24]

This view also helps to explain why the Conservative government after 1951 was reluctant to challenge the trade unions. If the party hoped to appeal to skilled workers, most of whom were trade union members, then it could not be seen to be demanding restrictions on trade unions. Another reason for refusing to pursue an anti-union line concerned fear that if moderate trade unionists were alienated by Conservative policy then communist militants would take over as leaders. In addition to this, open hostility to unions could lead them to oppose the party electorally and in the workplace if the Conservatives returned to power.[25] Nor were such fears misplaced: between October 1951 and June 1952 Conservative support declined significantly while that of Labour increased. It was noted that much of the fall off in support could be accounted for by the defection of working-class voters from the party.[26]

Churchill's political interest concentrated almost exclusively on foreign policy, and his intervention in domestic policy or on individual ministries was relatively limited and frequently ill informed. Moreover, he was usually dissuaded from promoting alternative domestic policies which might have proved attractive to the right wing of the party, but which the reformers feared would have a negative impact on the party in government. Churchill, despite his age, was neither senile nor stupid in 1951 or thereafter. During the 1952 economic crisis he pressurised Butler to reduce government expenditure to a substantial extent, in addition to which income tax should be reduced and the surtax limited. Churchill, fearing a Keynesian treasury, suggested that the Chancellor should adopt a total figure for expenditure and impose this upon departments. Butler's own response remained ambiguous and it is clear that he feared the effect of Churchill's nostalgia reflected in the Prime Minister's view of the consequences of the Labour Party's tenure in government after 1945:

> The 1945 election put the Socialists in possession of an elaborate Government machine, and an unprecedented level of revenue, which had been created to manage and finance the war-time economy. They were glad to continue these and to use them for their own purposes. Among the legacies to us are a swollen bureaucracy and a level of taxation previously undreamt of in time of peace. *It would of course have been much easier for us to slash these back immediately the war ended, if we had then been returned to power.* It is more difficult now. But the effort, though greater, must be made.[27]

Economic Constraints and Political Priorities, 1951–5

The defence programme of the outgoing Labour government had been based on the assumption that if war occurred in 1954 Britain could provide half to two-thirds of the armaments required, with the United States making up the difference. However, by late 1951 the 'whole structure of economic assumptions current when [the] defense programme [was] adopted has been falsified by developments of last twelve months'. This was based on the assumption that balance of payments difficulties had been finally resolved by the successful post-war production drive. The Labour government had undertaken an expanded defence programme in the belief that it would not encounter any major difficulties. A number of unexpected events, including a significant increase in imports, a shortage of steel, and the nationalisation of the Anglo-Iranian Oil Company, contributed to new external pressures. Consequently the demands on production appeared too great for the economy to bear. In a sense all governments are faced with the classic dilemma of choosing between 'guns and butter', or at least how much butter and how many guns; but unlike other states the United Kingdom was in a particularly difficult position particularly the incoming Conservative government. The classic response would have been to reduce imports, increase exports where possible and expand production. This in turn required controlling consumption which in the circumstances remained politically difficult. The Conservatives were committed to abolishing controls, while maintaining a high standard of living and an accelerated housing programme. As the Central Economic Planning Staff warned there would be competition between defence requirements, and those of the private sector, especially those engaged in housing.[28]

These tensions can be seen more clearly in the Cabinet Committee on the Economic Situation. The Permanent Secretary to the Treasury circulated a note to the Committee suggesting that concerted action be taken to avert the deteriorating economic situation. The Chancellor also argued that reducing imports should be the main aim, an objective which, if realised, would have led to various commitments not being fulfilled. Butler continued that cuts in public expenditure would be necessary, but warned that 'they would wish to consider the political implications of the various types of reduction in Government expenditure'. Macmillan's response to this was clear:

> He did not object to the proposal to limit imports of timber to what was required to maintain present consumption, provided that enough timber was available to carry out the programme of building 200 000 houses and that a decision on this sense would not be regarded as standing in the way of subsequent enlargement of the housing programme.

He insisted that in any public statement on cuts, it would have to be made clear that the number of houses to be built would not be affected. Lord Woolton, like Macmillan, was concerned that any cuts would not have a negative impact on the working class. He pointed out that the working class were buying expensive tinned hams because they could not buy enough fresh meat due to rationing, adding that 'the nation could not obtain the increase in production upon which our economy depended unless it had enough to eat'. These concerns were uppermost in the minds of cabinet ministers when they met on 1 November to decide on policy. Though ministers agreed that the primary aim was to maintain confidence in sterling, many ministers, but particularly Macmillan, were just as concerned with short-term political aims. Macmillan carefully agreed with the objectives of cutting imports and expenditure, but insisted that the cabinet accept his priorities: 'it should be made clear in the Chancellor's statement that the Government were determined to expand the housing programme by every possible means, conventional or unconventional, as soon as we could see our way through our immediate economic difficulties'.[29]

Macmillan's success in achieving his political and domestic aims illustrates the extent to which the Conservative Party had shifted its perspective between 1940 and 1951, and how unrealistic Churchill's demand for retrenchment had been. The Chancellor of the Duchy of Lancaster and the Minister for Materials, Viscount Swinton, recommended that the government should set clear priorities for the use of steel which would involve 'a substantial switch of production from home investment and other uses to indirect exports'. Butler was sensitive to the competing demands for steel from the Commonwealth, defence requirements and the domestic economy. Little could be done for the Commonwealth, he believed, and those countries would have to accept lower deliveries than hitherto. In the conflict between defence and domestic requirements, the Chancellor argued that there could be no automatic priority for defence: 'he could not agree that defence requirements should now or subsequently be accorded an overriding priority irrespective of the needs of other sectors of the economy'. Or as Macmillan put it bluntly, if he did not receive his allocation of steel the houses would not be built.[30] Macmillan's political strength rested on the crucial place which the housing programme held for Conservatives. There was a widespread belief that it offered a window of opportunity for the right to dislodge the left in the competitive electoral arena. Macmillan had two objectives in this: the first was to fulfill the Conservative election commitment to provide 300 000 new houses per year which, taking the 1951 figure as a baseline would lead to a 50 per cent increase. The second involved shifting the weight of investment away from publicly generated housing to a larger share by the private sector. This was in part an ideological commitment, but it also reflected the belief that local authority housing estates became Labour Party ghettos, whereas there was a greater likelihood of home-owners favouring the Conservatives. These objectives were in fact realised. By 1953 the number of house completions had passed the 300 000 target. In 1951 privately built houses accounted for 12 per cent of total completions, while by 1954 the figure had risen to 26 per cent and by 1955 35.8 per cent. However, the number of local authority houses built was greater in 1955 than in 1951 due to the general expansion of construction. This success in fulfilling a commitment had a number of consequences for the party. It may have contributed to its electoral success in 1955, it certainly placed the party at the political centre in its appeal while not alienating its own right wing (the emphasis on private construction meant that the strategy was not incompatible with the ideological predisposition towards a 'property owning democracy'). Furthermore the general expansion of housing meant that while the government emphasised its preference for private building, the public sector was not neglected, thus depriving the Labour Party of political ammunition (indeed the Labour Party had to make similar commitments subsequently). Moreover, the general expansion of construction assisted the government's commitment to maintain the lowest levels of unemployment.[31]

In addition to this the successful implementation of the housing programme provided Macmillan with the means to advance his own political career and con-solidate his position as a (if not the) representative of the moderate/progressive wing of the party. In doing so he demonstrated an adroitness and cunning lack-ing in his chief rival Butler. Butler was placed in the invidious position of a progressive politician implementing a regressive policy at the Treasury. Macmillan proved adapt at neutralising the Treasury's attempts to restrict imports which would be used for the housing programme. The Cabinet meeting of 20 December 1951 agreed to a number of cuts in health, education and related domestic expenditure. Macmillan objected to any reduction in expenditure which would affect his department. At subsequent Cabinet meetings it was agreed that while investment levels for 1952 would be held at those of 1950, a special case would be made for housing. Prior to these meetings Macmillan had defended his department vigorously, arguing that it was necessary for psychological reasons, as well as for economic and political ones, to maintain investment:

> In my experience, if the idea gets around that there is a danger of the building (or any other) industry suffering from unemployment, the tempo of work will rapidly decrease. If it is decided not to build more houses in 1952 than in 1951 there is no justification for the Minister of Housing, and the Government as well as the Minister will be discredited.

The housing policy, furthermore, was not only popular within the party itself, but party officials believed that it gave then a political advantage. One Area Publicity Officer summed up this view in quite disarming fashion:

> Although economists may frown, the promise of a 300 000 a year housing programme has done more to ease the path of the doorstep canvasser than any Charter, however profound, farseeing and progressive. It has given Conservatives something to bite on in debate with socialists.

As Macmillan escalated his demands for resources Butler attempted to hold back the number of houses built to a minimum:

> I believe we must get the 300 000 houses. But I understand that the current rate of starts, taken with the large number of houses already approved but not started (and therefore beyond effective control), and the freedom accorded to private building, suggests that the programme will go well above 300 000 in 1954 unless, as you have stated to me is the intention, steps are taken to reduce the rate of approval drastically from now on. You will remember that last Autumn my advisers estimated that 300 000 houses would be built in 1953.

In the event the number of houses built exceeded the target set in 1953, 1954 and 1955, although in the latter year a process of deceleration had set in. Despite his concerns with the impact of defence and housing expenditure on the economy, Butler remained sanguine about his ability to affect these figures.

> It appears that we shall do the Housing Grand Design. This means longer for me to reestablish the Finances fundamentally (i.e. no election for some time). I have decided that I must face this duty. I cannot go on putting things off unto the Budget of 1955 and hoping things won't be too bad in '54.

Despite the inflationary consequences of the housing programme and Butler's worries about the reserves, Churchill continued to support Macmillan's objectives. In July 1952 Churchill insisted, in a letter to Butler, that he was not prepared to consider cutting the housing programme. Though Butler replied this was not his intention, the tone of his letter and the substance of his argument led logically to such a proposal, even though on political grounds he was unable to do so.[32] Macmillan's insistence on pursuing the housing programme had both ideological and electoral motives which could be placed within the party's commitment to private property and a property-owning democracy. In the case of social services there was always unease about this spending, in the belief that the beneficiaries would be Labour rather than Conservative supporters. In this matter the consensus took priority.[33]

Trade Unions and the Conservative Party: The Framework of Consensus?

One way of measuring the extent of the post-war consensus is to assess the influence exercised by the trade union movement on the government, and the levels of real consumption by the working class. The trade unions had been marginalised up to 1939 and unemployment remained a real threat to workers' living standards. The inclusion of trade unionists within the corporate arrangements and the removal of the fear of unemployment had been a real gain for the industrial working class. By way of contrast, in post-war Italy and Germany the politics of production understandably took precedence over those of consumption for a longer time. However, in both of these states it was not merely the needs of the economy which led to the emphasis on production, it also resulted from the disposition of political forces. The dominance of Christian democracy throughout the immediate post-war years meant that policy considerations could be and were framed in a different atmosphere, one in which trade union influence was weaker and concern for full employment had less priority than other areas of policy.

Circumstances could not have been more different in Britain. Writing in 1956 John Strachey argued that the working class had made significant gains in real wages, ancillary benefits and consumption levels. This he attributed to political change, the growing influence of trade unions and the role of the State.[34] These changes can also be detected primarily in the relationship between the incoming conservative government and the trade unions particularly, but also in the government's concern with the working class generally. As noted above the party was dependent on working-class votes to win elections, but the political culture itself had become permeated by social democratic presuppositions relating to the economy, welfare, affluence and growth. Despite this the party's approach to the trade unions lacked a clear purpose. Churchill may have appointed Lord Monckton to the ministry of labour to keep the unions placated, but there is little indication from Churchill or Monckton on how this was to be achieved or to what purpose. Heathcoat-Amory did chair a Home Affairs committee which sought to give effect to a 'workers' charter'. The committee discussed the possibility of introducing a code of conduct for management and the labour force which would, it was hoped, stabilise industrial relations. The committee made a number of recommendations including conditions of service, training, profit-sharing and disclosure of financial information. These proposals, though fairly uncontroversial, were opposed by the Conservative Parliamentary Labour committee. Furthermore, the committee accepted that the proposals would lose the goodwill of trade unions if they were not consulted on the issue. In addition no sanctions were to be applied if the code was ignored or evaded:

> If the trade unions would not co-operate, it would not be possible to take the proposals further, but every effort should be made to get them to co-operate. What was now proposed might tend to take the matter out of the political field and give it more chance of general acceptance. But it should continue to be borne in mind that the Government were seeking to implement a pledge made by them when in opposition.[35]

The apparent incoherence disguised a deeper ambivalence in government. Successive governments attempted to allay the traditional fears of the trade union movement concerning the intentions and behaviour of Conservatives. Despite the serious economic situation in 1952 the Minister of Labour reported to the Cabinet that in his opinion a wage standstill could not be realistically implemented in the absence of trade union co-operation with the government, which was not forthcoming. The government concluded that a firm position should be taken on wage policy but that it would not intervene directly, while unofficial strikes should be allowed to take their own course. Accordingly:

> the situation would remain delicate and it was important that nothing should be said publicly which might be interpreted as encouraging or even countenancing a breach of restraint on any sector of the wages front.[36]

What such an approach meant in effect was that very little was done to influence wage rates. A series of meetings between the Chancellor of the Exchequer and the Trades Union Congress (TUC) during 1951 and 1952 left the government in no doubt as to the attitude of the Labour movement to its policies. The TUC representatives criticised the decision to review the investment programme, recording their worry over the possibility of unemployment and, in a later exchange, suggesting that the government's commitment to denationalisation did not create favourable conditions for co-operation between the government and the TUC. Butler believed that the initial meetings had established a friendly atmosphere, but recognised that the TUC was not in a position to break the current cycle of wage increases. He believed that the escalation of wage demands could be prevented if co-operation between the government and the TUC became firmly based. After the 1952 budget Arthur Deakin claimed that the TUC was disappointed, that the tax concessions would have little impact on the wage earner, but that the fear of future unemployment was present and real:

> While they were glad to have had the Chancellor's assurance that it was not the government's intention to use the Bank rate as a weapon for the creation of unemployment, they feared in fact, that it might have that result.

Deakin remained concerned that the government would not act decisively in the event of rising unemployment.[37]

The TUC maintained its opposition to any suggestions that wage restraint should be considered by its members:

The General Council could not risk another rebuke from Congress. Apart from any question of prestige, it would not be helpful to the cause the Chancellor had in mind nor to the national interest.

The differences between the two sides were clear: the Chancellor insisted that the central issue for the government remained the value of the pound, whereas the TUC believed unemployment and the price of food were the determinants for its members. Lincoln Evans believed that the TUC was conscious of the impact of wage increases on the economy, but would not support a linkage between prices and wages such as prevailed between 1948 and 1950. He argued that trade unions were in large part moderate and responsible, therefore:

> The matter would have to be left to the good sense of the movement. The Economic Committee could not recommend the TUC to make any specific recommendations or produce any formula, but they could and would issue in due course, a statement on the general economic situation in which the facts would speak for themselves.[38]

Throughout the 1950s Conservative governments sought to achieve a balance between their traditional concerns with inflation, a stable money supply, balanced budgets and the demands of the welfare state. Churchill's thinking on the matter was usually ambiguous. In a speech to Conservative trade unionists in 1949 he reiterated the Conservative pledge to recognise collective bargaining and the right to strike, but commended trade unionists to remain outside party politics. On a more practical level the party leadership did not welcome rank and file pressure to take a hard stance with trade unions. The appointment of Lord Monckton as Minister for Labour reflected Churchill's concern that the trade unions should be conciliated. When Anthony Eden recommended in 1954 that a special Cabinet standing committee should be established, to consider what he believed to be a deteriorating industrial relations situation, Monckton opposed the suggestion on the grounds that this would appear provocative:

> He feared that the appointment of a formal body, if it became known, would invite the criticism that a Conservative Government was seeking to intervene in the conduct of wage negotiations. It would be disastrous if this impression were created.

Monckton believed that private or informal approaches to the unions could be of benefit, but that any other action by the government would be construed as support for employers in their conflict over wage claims. During the following year these pressures were further highlighted when Butler circulated two Treasury memoranda to the Industrial Relations committee of the Cabinet. The memoranda concluded that full employment was contributing to the inflationary spiral because employers and trade unions had no incentive to act responsibly and consequently passed on wage increases to the consumer as price rises. However, Butler was not prepared to recommend deflationary policies, warning that the consequences of using budgetary or monetary policy to offset the wage–price spiral would be 'so severe as to destroy the state of full employment'. Therefore, 'if price stability were made an over-riding objective the policy of high and stable employment would have to be abandoned'.[39]

Subsequent events suggest that neither the government nor the TUC actively pursued a policy which would contain a wage explosion. By 1955 the government could point to a significant rise in wage rates during its first term in office. According to figures prepared for Eden, 'actual earnings' increased by 10 per cent between October 1951 and October 1954, whereas the comparable figure for the three years up to October 1951 was 1 per cent. In addition, whereas under Labour prices rose faster than wages, in contrast under the Conservatives the retail price index rose by 16 per cent between October 1951 and June 1955 while wages increased by 25 per cent. It was implied that the wage increases could have been contained during the first post-war decade because of global shortages and reconstruction, but with the rise of more competitive conditions this no longer proved possible. What was now required, the government affirmed, was the closest possible correlation between wages and productivity. This was based on the realisation that the disparity which had occurred between productivity and the rise in money income was undermining the competitiveness of British exports, a factor which in turn now affected the domestic economy and the individual worker.[40]

If Eden believed that 'spelling out' the economic facts would make an impression on the unions he was mistaken. His Minister of Labour, Walter Monckton, in one of his last exchanges with the Prime Minister expressed his disappointment that the Transport and General Workers' Union (TGWU), which he claimed had hitherto supported the objective of wage restraint, had now come out in opposition to the government's budgetary strategy. The shift in position by the TGWU, however, was not merely a short-term response to a Conservative government, but reflected a more profound questioning of the market order and economic individualism. The Union rejected the link between wages and productivity, arguing that the standard of living could not be dependent on higher levels of productivity. Political considerations were foremost in this belief:

> While it is not the wish of the council to chase an inflationary wage spiral, it is equally not prepared to accept the principle that the proper living standards of the members of the Union should wholly be dependent on higher productivity and particularly so when it is appreciated that productivity, in the accepted sense of the word, cannot be applied to the large sections of union membership employed in road transport and ancillary fields.

The particular case being made by the TGWU had wider implications. They posed a serious threat to any Government, but especially a Conservative one attempting to regulate income rises without creating institutions of coercion. Each of the three Conservative prime ministers during the 1950s was committed to voluntarism in wage policy, hoping that economic reality would influence trade union behaviour.

It appears justified to conclude that none of them fully appreciated the change which had occurred in the relationship between the trade unions, the economy and the government. Churchill made numerous speeches about the working man and advised Conservatives to join trade unions. Macmillan openly accepted a new role for the trade unions, but even Anthony Eden recognised the political imperative of conciliating trade unions. One method of dealing with the trade unions would have been to openly attack them as an arm of the Labour Party, seeking to restrict their political activities. Such an approach, occasionally recommended by the right wing of the party, was not shared by the Conservative Research Department (CRD) or most of the party leadership. The logic of this approach would be to politicise the relationship between government and unions in a fashion which would be essentially confrontational and which would have given the government relatively little in return. Each successive government between 1951 and 1964 studiously avoided any such confrontation.[41]

The Politics of Full Employment in the 1950s

Despite continuing concern with wage policy, international competitiveness and inflation, the Conservative government between 1951 and 1955 never came to terms with the social and political (as distinct from the narrowly economic) consequences of full employment and the welfare state. Woolton remained adamant that whatever government policy might be on public expenditure, any cuts should not lead to a reduction in the standard of living for the mass of the population. He urged Churchill not to act precipitously on reducing taxation because:

> We will find ourselves in politically difficult waters if we begin by making serious cuts in the social services or in the standard of living of the general public and leave ourselves open to the charge that what we have saved by this means we have later spent in the reduction of taxation.

One consequence of this was that Woolton offered his resignation following the Budget in March 1952 in the belief that he had made a commitment prior to the election not to reduce subsidies on food. While he was dissuaded from this action by Churchill, it is illustrative of the sensitivity with which consumption issues had come to be treated by the Conservatives.[42]

One of the better contemporary expressions of this view was given by the former Labour Cabinet Minister John Strachey, who concluded that politicians' attitudes had been radically changed by the Depression and the war, suggesting that it was political suicide for any politician to allow unemployment to rise and return to conditions of depression.[43] What Strachey identified was a set of beliefs to which most politicians now subscribed, leading them at one and the same time to sustain full employment while avoiding economic stagnancy. Nor was such a view restricted to left-wing intellectuals. Woolton himself expressed just such sentiments to Churchill in 1953. He maintained that hitherto (especially inter-war) governments approached the question of unemployment in a remedial fashion: what was now required, he asserted, was prevention which could only be achieved if the government planned for such eventualities. In a subsequent memo to the Cabinet Woolton warned of the risks to 'the country, and the party', if a depression occurred. He believed that full employment was more apparent than real, resting on short-term success and higher taxation. Decisive action should be taken, he added, because 'if severe unemployment comes again under a Conservative government, as it did in the 30s, we can be certain of a serious defeat at the next election'. Woolton insisted that the commitment to 'a high and stable level of employment', required planning to combat the threat of unemployment. Plans for dealing with unemployment were readily available and should be used, he concluded.[44]

Woolton also recognised that wage patterns and pricing policies were placing Britain at a competitive disadvantage. He believed that the 1952 recession in the textile industry was a consequence of high prices. Thus, unemployment could be a consequence of both lack of government action and uncompetitive pricing due to wage increases. The Conservative government slowly appreciated its dilemma which was how to conciliate Labour, while at the same time insuring that British industry remained profitable and competitive. The government had also to be aware of the growing discontent among its own supporters, many of whom believed that the corporate relationships between government, business and labour had a detrimental effect on those receiving fixed incomes, pensions and the self-employed. Anthony Seldon in his study of the Churchill government has noted that contemporaries were puzzled at the ease with which the Conservative Party accepted the 'socialistic' and/or reformist trends within the government. He attributed this in part to natural deference, but more especially to a new Middle Class Conservative member of parliament more open to 'progressive' views. There is considerable validity in this; it is probably safe to conclude that the party leadership manipulated the party conference to suit its objectives throughout this period.[45]

Despite this, Conservative MPs' social background may have made them susceptable to pressures from their constituencies, to an extent unlikely with their upper-middle-class predecessors. It may also be the case that middle-class concerns were not incompatible with traditional upper-middle-class traditions in the party. The question of inflation, full employment and the trade off between the two is a case in point. Duncan Sandys claimed, in a note to Monckton, that the government had not acted decisively enough to prevent wage increases during 1952, citing engineering employers to the effect that wage increases would not have been as high if government had not influenced the outcome. Monckton rejected this and pointed out that the employers themselves were anxious to come to an arrangement with the unions. Such were the perceived difficulties in 1952 that it was concluded by one group of treasury officials that continuing wage claims could lead to a major economic crisis in 1953.[46]

The question of the relationship between income, inflation and competitiveness was not one which was easily grasped by those still influenced by the memory of the 1930s. Unemployment appeared immediate, while inflation's impact was gradual and differential. Also, those who feared inflation or were disadvantaged by it did not have the institutional resources to influence government decision-making at this time. Ian Macleod noted in 1956 that inflation continued to suit significant sections of industry, the cost to trade unions and managers could be avoided by passing it on to the consumer. Macleod also believed that this particular process was at an end and the cost of the behaviour was now known to both sides of industry. This belief was all too optimistic, as subsequent events were to demonstrate; in effect he had recognised a problem rather than addressed it or offered a solution. Macmillan had suggested that the TUC leadership was powerless to act, although recognising the difficulties which high wage claims could cause:

> In their hearts the Trade Union leaders know that another round of wage increases will bring their own people nothing but trouble and may wreck the whole economy. A few

of them who are Communists know this, and are using the wage increase as a method of destroying the economy. The mass are unable to give a lead in any other direction.

Macleod rejected this analysis arguing that the most important union leaders, including Frank Cousins of the TGWU and Jim Campbell of the National Union of Railwaymen (NUR), were quite aware of what they were doing:

> These people are well to the left of the first group although they are in no sense Communist, but they are not persuaded of the necessity for a halt to wage increases and unfortunately, they had unions to which the productivity argument has little application.

Macleod believed that real power rested with the individual trade unions rather than with the TUC. As a body he concluded it had 'little power of persuasion or authority', suggesting that the TUC leadership were 'amiable, weak and ineffective men'. He refused however, to advocate legislation which would restrict the 'traditional rights' of the trade union movement, while recognising that their behaviour reinforced right-wing opinion on these matters within the party.[47]

The Political Economy of Consensus

It is perhaps fair to judge the Conservatives halfway into their period of office on the basis on the dilemmas facing a right-wing government operating within a social democratic climate. Mysterious are the ways that ideas permeate the political consciousness, but they do have an impact. Enoch Powell was later to describe the intellectual problem for Conservatives with his usual incisiveness:

> In the last analysis all power rests upon opinion. The great object of the Socialist is therefore to get people to believe that management, ownership and control by the state are inevitable. . . Once that belief has taken hold in a sufficient part of the nation, the task is done. The safest prisoners are those who are convinced that they could not live outside the jail . . .[48]

While platonic references may not be adequate for politicians, the extent to which Conservative governments were trapped by opinions established elsewhere in the political system can be readily detected by the response of the Conservative Party to creeping inflation during the 1950s. By 1956 the differential between the retail price index and wage increases was widening in favour of the latter. Wages increase more rapidly than prices in the decade after 1945, most of these increases occurred between 1952 and 1956.[49]

The dilemma for post-war governments was captured in a comment on full employment policy by the Central Economic Planning Staff: 'the Government, in intervening in economic questions, is not using instruments of unlimited power'. It added that:

> full employment is not a condition which is automatically maintained by the action of market forces. On the contrary, the government must ensure by its budgetary policy that an adequate but not excessive general level of demand is maintained, and must be prepared to reinforce this by appropriate policies in related fields, e.g. by the keeping down or stimulation of investment.

The incoming Conservative government was not unaware of these difficulties, Churchill in particular appreciated the potential incompatibility between policy aims. He requested that a 'State of the Nation' be prepared to facilitate the government in its decisions on economic policy. This request was in response to the warnings by Treasury and other officials of the catastrophic nature of the economy at the end of 1951. It was proposed to publish a White Paper to highlight the difficulties (also to condemn Labour policies). In the event the circulation of a draft White Paper convinced the Cabinet that policy implementation after 1945 had not been as destructive as believed. In fact the report concluded that the 'real situation' was good, growth had been maintained and inflation contained. On a more somber note this progress was believed to be insecure; the crisis of late 1951 had highlighted the exposed position of the British economy, in particular its heavy dependence on imports to underwrite growth. The report warned in conclusion that whatever the external constraints, domestic policy had 'to follow a narrow path avoiding the danger of inflation and of deflation'.[50]

The government thought it unwise to publish this White Paper, but the problems exposed did not disappear. Underlying difficulties concerning balance of payments could be resolved in time, what was to prove much more difficult was the political economy of the 1950s. The Conservatives inherited a policy framework which had shifted sharply from that implied in the 1944 White Paper to a comprehensive commitment to full employment by December 1951. However, by the mid-1950s unemployment levels in the United Kingdom were among the lowest in Europe, comparable to more successful economies such as Sweden and Switzerland. The constraints imposed by change in the United Kingdom were highlighted during an exchange between President Eisenhower's adviser on economic affairs, Gabriel Hauge, and Sir Robert Hall. The civil servants were discussing alternative interpretations of Articles 55 and 56 of the United Nations Charter, which Hauge considered to be quite limited in application:

> I, for example, would not conclude from the language of those articles that the United States is *committed* to *maintain* full employment. I would say that the United States, together with other member countries, has undertaken to *promote* employment.

In his reply Hall conceded that Hauge's interpretation reflected the greater success of the United States in handling the problems of inflation and full employment. This he attributed in part to higher productivity in the United States, but also to the fact that the Eisenhower administration 'can get away with a rather less uncomfortable definition of full employment than we have been able to do'. Hall recognised that the British government in the White Paper was promising to obtain and maintain full employment, whereas the United States and the United Nations was promising to try and secure these conditions. He concluded by claiming that the Treasury's aim was to 'promote less over-full employment'.[51] In one case a Conservative government was in a position to introduce policies which would be unthinkable for another right-wing government.

In an analysis of full employment just after the Conservatives took office, J.R. Downie concluded that the theoretical possibility of full employment identified in the 1944 White Paper had been realised between 1945 and 1951. He argued, in addition, that full employment would facilitate economic growth and expansion, but that the community had to accept the responsibilities that such a commitment generated.[52] There is a detectable shift in emphasis subsequent to the Conservative return to power. Inflation now becomes a serious concern, prices and wages and the link between them contribute to a fear that there is now a phenomenon of 'national overspending'. There is also a shift in how to assess the problem. In the original draft the solution is posed in terms of production, whereas in the later one there is a move towards fiscal and monetary solutions. The emphasis changes from the benefits of full employment to the potential risks:

> Full employment is very important to everyone: it is also important that everyone should know the risks as well as the benefits which are at stake.[53]

A national consensus was required it urged, to bring prices, wages and production into line; 'what is needed is primarily a new outlook to match the new condition of full employment'. The Minister of Labour objected to the tone of the draft, offering a number of amendments which would in effect have emasculated the thrust of the statement. Bridges, in addition, feared that the sentiments were expressed too simply, and that the left-wing press and 'sophisticated union members' would be opposed. Lincoln Evans of the TUC confirmed these doubts insisting that while the trade unions recognised the problem, 'the matter would have to be left to the good sense of the movement'. Further drafts, including one influenced by a memorandum from Butler, refined the earlier arguments. Inflation is given the primary focus and fear is expressed that wage increases would limit profits significantly. Yet, despite a recognition that full employment had generated new conditions for the economy and problems to go with it, the recommendations were surprisingly restrained:

> But prices cannot be kept down without reasonable restraint in wage increases. This cannot be secured by central direction and administrative fiat.

Subsequently, the focus shifted towards controlling rising prices, in the belief this contributed to the decline in the United Kingdom share of world manufactures between 1950 and 1954. Notwithstanding this, it was conceded that full employment was 'second to none among the objectives of post war economic policy'. In these circumstances the Conservatives' reluctance to become involved in wage determination or accept higher levels of unemployment probably condemned the country to inflation and low productivity for the remainder of the decade.[54]

While this was not inevitable, there is a note of fatalism in much of the documentation which reflected a belief that while there were clear advantages to be obtained from a closer relationship between unions and government, these would not be acceptable to the trade unions:

> The government is asking the Trade Unions to go back on some ideas which have been axiomatic since Trade Unionism started. It is not unreasonable, and is one of the ways of carrying conviction, to show itself ready to do the same thing on its side.[55]

Some type of national consensus on wages and prices was required because of the success of a full employment policy which had removed the fear of subsistence level standards for most workers. One consequence of this change was that the main area of debate concerned living standards and their level rather than the levels of poverty prevailing among the working class.[56] The insecurity usually associated with industrial relations had now disappeared, but the behaviour of trade unions tended to reflect that insecurity despite this.[57] Notwithstanding this, the Treasury remained loath to recommend deflation as a policy to control wage claims. This was a realistic recognition that no government was prepared to accept an unemployment figure higher than 2 per cent. In addition, it was believed that the trade unions had not used their full market power to achieve their economic objectives. This was attributed to a certain caution on the part of union leaders, to objective market factors and to value judgements by those involved:

> But if a government were suspected of policies deliberately intended to increase the power of market forces to the prejudice of the Trade Unions these would be quick to see the challenge and react to it. If the unions were encouraged or provoked into using their strength more fully than on the average they have done, they would probably get bigger increases than the average of recent years.[58]

Rejecting deflation left two options: the first involved some form of incorporation through the creation of corporatist institutions, the second relied on 'persuasion' which essentially meant little action and little influence. The Conservative government appeared paralysed before the trade unions, unable either to incorporate them or persuade them to accept the reasoning of officials on the connection between wages and inflation. Michael Fraser at the CRD rejected the deflation option on the grounds that the subsequent unemployment would lead to an election defeat for the party and that a Labour government would adopt inflationary policies. Despite this general appreciation of the consequences of unemployment, he recommended that among its objectives the party should aim for limited deflation, a reduction in direct taxation, the removal of subsidies and a move towards a more selective welfare state.[59]

Butler circulated two papers to the Cabinet committee on Industrial Relations during 1955 which highlighted the government's dilemma. The first of these concluded, after highlighting the inflationary spiral since 1947, that the level of unemployment should be pushed higher. Inflation, it argued, suited both employers and employees who remained unaffected by the consequences of their action. The paper recognised that if 'price stability were made an over-riding objective, the policy of high and stable employment would have to be abandoned'. The accompanying paper complemented this and concluded pessimistically that:

> we have not found the way to reconcile political freedom, price stability, and full employment. As the first is not at risk, one or other of the remaining two will go on being sacrificed until a solution is found.[60]

The CRD discussions and those of the Industrial Relations committee prompted the government to draft a White Paper on full employment which was published in 1956.[61] Yet without a government commitment to coercion or to engage in corporatist intermediation, the continuing dynamics of free collective bargaining produced instability in industrial relations. The Minister of Labour continued to council caution on industrial relations even when, as in the summer of 1955, there was a major rail strike. The government was placed under pressure by its own supporters to act decisively and in particular to introduce legislation, such as secret ballots, which would limit such action in the future. The Minister of Labour recommended that no action be taken, reiterating what had become a commonplace for inaction on the part of his ministry since 1951:

> It is, in my view, essential that any government initiative in the field of industrial relations should carry the greatest possible measure of TUC approval and concurrence. Unless we carry with us the responsible elements, who are at present in a majority, we run the risk of uniting the whole movement against us.

The most that Monckton would offer was to meet the members of the TUC informally and let them know that while the government had no wish to regulate them it was under pressure to do so. Others, such as Salisbury, were not so sanguine and urged Eden to act decisively, but Macmillan advised him that a cautious approach to the whole question was probably best. In this the Prime Minister concurred.[62]

By the time Eden replaced Churchill as Prime Minister, and shortly afterwards led the party to its electoral victory in May 1955, the leadership appeared unable to break with this tradition of compromise on the main welfare and wage issues. Despite evident disquiet among sections of the Conservative Party, the party leadership continued to pay close attention to the administrative needs of the mixed economy, the welfare state and to the political demands of labour.[63] The government had been pursuing a complex policy with some success, simultaneously accepting the mixed economy, while shifting the emphasis away from the regulatory framework established by the previous Labour government:

> Any government in the modern world must try to ensure that general demand is strong enough to provide full employment but not so strong that inflation develops. Conservatives believe that such general control of the economic climate should be exercised by monetary policy as well as by fiscal methods. The use of budgetary policy and physical controls alone was proved to be inadequate in the years of inflation between 1945 and 1951. The present government has, therefore, returned to the use of a flexible monetary policy, controlling credit through the use of the Bank rate.

This strategy, it was claimed, had allowed the Conservatives to break the inflationary mentality which had prevailed since the war, strengthen the currency and facilitated a break with the previous government's policy of increased taxation.[64]

Over the same period, despite a difficult economic climate, the Conservative governments popularity improved. The leadership attributed this to the positive impact government policies were making on the electorate, a conclusion party officials believed was confirmed by by-election successes in 1952 and 1953. This success was based on the attractiveness of Conservative policy and the inability of the Labour Party to offer a strong enough alternative.[65] Though Woolten worried that the rising cost of living in 1954 could affect the government's chance of re-election, Butler concluded that it had successfully broken the socialistic command economy and was well on the way to establishing the 'normal conditions of peace time'. Butler's optimism proved accurate in the election that followed, though there was also a recognition by him, and his associates, that the party appeal had to balance between attracting a mass electorate while continuing to receive support from the traditional right wing of its core constituency. After the election, Butler came under pressure from sections of the party who believed that their standard of living had declined while that of the working class had improved relative to them. While Butler was concerned at this he was not prepared to jeopardise the moderate approach to policy, nor the working-class voters which such a policy would continue to attract.[66] The party faced an anxious dilemma by the mid-1950s. It could with considerable justification claim that its electorate was more representative of the general population than that of the Labour Party which was heavily dependent on working-class support. However, this meant that, unlike Labour, the Conservatives had to balance very carefully between the often conflicting demands of its middle-class and working-class electorate. Thus while the Labour Party certainly required middle-class votes to win an election, it was far less dependent on the middle class than the Conservative Party was dependent on the working class to win elections. In this, the Conservative Party faced some of the same difficulties which their Christian democratic counterparts experienced with their inter-class constituency.[67]

By 1955, the Conservatives' political strategy aimed to contain any possible erosion of working-class support and the maintenance of its dominant position among the middle classes and professionals. The April 1955 budget was not simply an expansionist budget, it was one designed to achieve this objective in addition to preparing the ground for the subsequent election. Such an approach was also facilitated by the premiership of Eden who was anxious to maintain the consensus that prevailed, but tended to accept Butler's judgements on economic issues which allowed the chancellor considerable flexibility. This could have its disadvantages as can be detected in the reception of Butler's second 1955 budget in October, which offset the positive impression of the earlier one. Eden's interest in economic matters was limited in any event. Having regretted appointing Macmillan to the Foreign Office, he then appointed him Chancellor of the Exchequer in December 1955, a position Macmillan did not wish to hold. However, once there Macmillan hoped to develop a reformist political style.[68] Macmillan's tenure at the Treasury did not last long (December 1955–January 1957), and he had little opportunity to display any reforming zeal or dynamism. Indeed for most of the time prior to the Suez crisis, he sought to cut government expenditure and consequently came into conflict with Eden and the expansionists.

The government recognised during 1955 that Britain's competitiveness was being eroded in export markets by the emergence of a revived Germany and Japan, and by rising prices, attributed to wages rising faster than productivity in Britain. Eden, however, could not convince the trade unions of the relationship between productivity and wages while the subsequent import surge in November 1955 confirmed the government's worst fears.[69] Peter Thorneycroft at the Board of Trade urged Eden to act decisively:

> The solution in my view must be to reduce the total demand on our resources right across the board. The prime need is to reduce the total of monetary demand, rather than to attempt to restrain demand in certain selected fields, a process which would only leave the money to be spent elsewhere. In the private sector this calls for a steady continuance and perhaps intensification of our monetary policy (the credit squeeze).

Thorneycroft also recommended that government expenditure be curtailed to facilitate a more restrictive economic strategy, 'even though it will certainly involve a definite increase in unemployment in comparison with the present quite fantastically low level'. These views reflected a growing concern within the party, even among expansionists, that full employment had generated circumstances which were affecting the stability of the economy by weakening sterling and the balance of payments. All of which the Chancellor of the Exchequer considered to be a consequence of 'the present excessive home demand'. Macmillan quite explicitly recommended deflation of the economy, as Thorneycroft had done, arguing that it was relatively easy to reverse deflation but not inflation:

> Public opinion is not only ready for resolute action but expects it. If we fail now, we shall be discredited as a Government. If we succeed, it will make all the other things we hope to do during our present term of office very much easier.

Butler disputed Macmillan's analysis urging that the economy was not overheated, but in fact required further expansion and growth. Eden, Butler continued, was committed to a policy of 'no return to unemployment', which a policy of deflation would undermine. Butler advised the Prime Minister to advocate 'voluntary restraint', which he believed could be achieved. Eden appears to have been influenced by this and refused to countenance action by Macmillan prior to the budget. In February 1956 Macmillan threatened to resign if his policy was not supported by the Prime Minister, but after an ongoing series of exchanges accepted Eden's assurances as a compromise.[70]

Nor did this conclude the argument. Throughout 1956 Macmillan pressed Eden on the issue of expenditure, recommending, ironically, a substantial cut in housing, a request which Eden curtly rejected. Somewhat earlier he had requested that Macmillan not produce any 'further deflationary thunderbolts', adding a little later: 'short of taking deflationary measures to a length which is politically not tolerable, I do not see how we can hope to limit wage claims by removing pressure on the labour market'. Eden believed that wages followed prices and hoped to persuade employers to resist demands.[71] The Suez crisis and consequent political debacle exacerbated the country's economic difficulties, but simultaneously postponed any realistic strategy for dealing with the underlying problems of economic decline, wage push and full employment. Political and strategic concerns became paramount and these were not to be resolved until after Eden's resignation and Macmillan's successful bid for the premiership in early 1957.[72]

Macmillan and the Extension of the Consensus, 1957–63

Macmillan had shared with Thorneycroft in 1956 the belief that a certain amount of deflation was necessary. However, unlike his new Chancellor of the Exchequer, he was a Keynesian rather than a monetarist at heart. This not only reflected his radical phase during the 1930s, but was based on the belief that while governments could not achieve everything, they could make an important contribution to economic expansion. He was quick however to draw a distinction between the basic Conservative philosophy, based on property owning, and that of the Labour Party which he believed to be essentially collectivist:

We believe that unless we give opportunity to the strong and able, we shall never have the means to provide real protection for the weak and old . . .

Thus capitalism and individual initiative were essential ingredients for the maintenance of the welfare state. This differentiation remained important to Macmillan, reflecting his belief that an area of competence and policy-making could be controlled by the Conservatives. Because of this he also sought to distance himself from the more traditional elements in his party, asserting quite categorically his vision of the party: 'I intend to run it . . . as a *centre* party. I was not prepared to run it on an extreme right wing basis.'[73] The latter claim is easily sustained on issues as diverse as nuclear disarmament, decolonisation and on domestic reform. In a number of crucial ways, the Macmillan's government prepared the ground for the technocratic reformist Labour government which followed after 1964.

For this he was criticised by right-wing opponents at the time, and more recently by the dominant Thatcherite wing of the party. While moving the party further to the left between 1957 and 1963 Macmillan has been accused of not following through on his claim to differentiate between socialism and Conservatism in government. On one point the critics are correct, Macmillan cared more about the political economy of full employment than about the apparent decline in the British economy. Furthermore he did not always make a connection between the two. Whether he can be correctly characterised as the administrator of Britain's decline is another matter. At first the diagnosis agreed upon prior to Suez was maintained during the first nine months of 1957 with considerable success. In September Thorneycroft was still in a position to maintain that deflation would remain the government's main policy instrument. In contrast David Eccles warned that care had to be taken if unacceptable levels of unemployment were to be avoided. At this stage Macmillan took a more active role in economic policy formation, having been absorbed by foreign affairs issues for most of the preceding months. He insisted, for example, that a statement on the economy should reflect Cabinet views and be issued by the prime minister's office. This did not involve serious disagreement with the Chancellor at this time, only that Macmillan had decided to pay close attention to economic issues.[74]

One reason for this may have been a note from Michael Fraser highlighting the decline in government popularity since the general election. Fraser believed that Suez and the Rent Act had contributed to this outcome, but that inflation was the real problem. The government's success in stabilising prices had been welcomed, but the actions taken to achieve it had not been. In addition, the recent bout of inflation after a period of price stability had caused further dissatisfaction.[75] Inflation was, as Fraser noted, a complex phenomenon and one that did not respond readily to prescribed solutions. In these discussions the Prime Minister suggested that government expenditure should be held at the 1956 or 1957 level, rather than be further reduced. Despite this, the marginal difference between Macmillan and Thorneycroft remained slight, but the underlying differences were greater than this implied. Thorneycroft believed that the inflationary policies pursued by the government were alienating the party's core constituency, and that this could prove disastrous in an election:

The Tory party may lose the next election anyway. What matters is not whether it loses it, but why. If we are thrown out because we are thought to have been too tough in defence of what we conceive to be our national and imperial interests and have allowed a modest growth in unemployment, we shall be returned again, perhaps quite soon. If we are thrown out because we have flinched from our duty and allowed our economy to drift into disaster, I see no particular reason why we should ever be asked to resume control.

For Thorneycroft hardship through unemployment was preferable to inflation and his policy proposals reflected this.[76] Macmillan claimed to be puzzled by what the middle-classes wanted from a Conservative government, whereas Thorneycroft was in essence claiming that an orthodox deflationary policy was what was required. However, on one thing Macmillan remained adamant. He was not prepared to alienate 'organised labour', or to see unemployment increase, though he did insist 'that the strength and stability of sterling were a precondition of the maintenance of a high level of employment'.[77]

Macmillan's difficulty was how to achieve price stability while defending free collective bargaining between employers and trade unions. For the deflationists this did not pose the same difficulty, and Thorneycroft, Powell and Birch at the Treasury were prepared to accept the consequences of cutting or containing public expenditure. The difference between Thorneycroft and Macmillan can be interpreted in a number of ways. On one reading the amount involved was slight and Macmillan himself was rather bewildered that the Chancellor should resign on this particular issue. An alternative view is that Thorneycroft had become a captive of Powell's intellectual brilliance and was lead down his mentor's path. Yet another view is that Thorneycroft was reflecting real concerns in the City, the party and among sections of the electorate about the threat from inflation and the influence of organised labour on economic policy. In a sense each of these explanations has some validity. The amount was small, Powell was intellectually influential and crucial groups did wish to see inflation curbed, even if this increased unemployment. The insistence that economic expenditure be held constant can be seen as a doctrinaire stand, or it can supplement the other explanations as an attempt to reverse the changed balance of power which had existed since 1945. If government expenditure was held constant and if unemployment resulted without the government taking countervailing action then the post-war consensus would be over. Thorneycroft was prepared to accept this, refusing to agree to a 1 per cent increase in expenditure. For him cutting expenditure was the key to economic success. Macmillan believed that the differences were minimal, but that the Chancellor should accept the collective will of the Cabinet, warning that the Chancellor's proposals, if implemented fully, would lead to economic stagnation and industrial disorder. In effect, Macmillan insisted that there was a political limit to what the Chancellor ought to attempt. Notwithstanding that, the Cabinet agreed on the need to curb inflation and defend sterling, but it was unwilling to do so if this undermined the consensus. Under such circumstances Thorneycroft had little option but to resign.[78]

Macmillan continued to accept that the threat of unemployment was more serious than that of inflation. During the second half of 1958 he became concerned that unemployment was increasing and while inflation had been contained, 'the pendulum is now swinging a little too far in the opposite direction'. It worried him that unemployment had gone above 500 000 for the first time since the war. Macmillan feared that a recession was possible, and that counter-cyclical measures were required to offset this. His recommendations came after he had read a Treasury paper which advised against using public expenditure as a short-term response to unemployment. He had written 'absurd' next to various paragraphs and minuted to the effect: 'this is a very bad paper. Indeed a disgraceful paper. It might have been written by Mr. Neville Chamberlain's government.' Shortly after this Macmillan recommended that the Minister of Health bring forward to 1958 orders that had been placed for the year 1959/60. Moreover, the Cabinet Committee on Employment, on which the Prime Minister played an active, if not decisive part, accepted the need for increased public sector expenditure to prevent a recession in 1959. By the end of 1958 public sector investment was increased by £150 million over the previous year.[79]

Macmillan had now committed the party openly to an expansionist strategy, one that he was determined to follow over the next five years. To do so he not only accepted Thorneycroft's resignation, and was later to replace Amory with Selwyn Lloyd whom he believed would be more pliable to his expansionist moods. Enoch Powell insisted that 1958 marked a point of departure: that it was the occasion when a Conservative government increased government expenditure as a proportion of national income after seven years of decline in that relationship. Moreover, this expansionist mood was to continue over the next twelve years and beyond.[80]

Powell's position remained unrepresentative within the party throughout most of the 1960s. Macmillan's electoral victory in 1959, when the party achieved an unprecedented third consecutive term, reinforced his belief that 'the great thing is to keep the Tory Party on *modern* and *progressive* lines', and secured the dominance of the expansionists. Moreover, even in the light of stagflation during the early 1960s the movement within the party was towards greater intervention, as the CRD noted in 1961, 'we have virtually exhausted the neo-liberal seam in economic policy'. Ian Macleod observed that the electorate was in an expansionist mood and disliked pay pauses and restrictive regulations.[81] Although he had not fully developed it before leaving office in 1963, Macmillan had begun the process of deepening the institutional arrangements surrounding the welfare state, the commitment to full employment and the strategy for growth. Nor were the British alone in this: the mood in much of the liberal democratic world was towards planning, albeit indicative and based on Keynesian principles. Economists, public opinion and politicians agreed that government responsibility for the economic well being of the nation was primary, and in societies as diverse as France, the United States and Ireland the 1960s can be characterised in terms of this drive towards intervention. In Britain the differences between the Labour and Conservative parties on economic issues (indeed on most issues) continued to narrow, so much so that the 1964 election was fought and won on personality as much as on policy. For the Conservative Party, however, this movement towards collectivism (if not socialism) was fraught with difficulties. It principally marked the point when the party ceased to be a traditional conservative party and embraced fairly wholeheartedly the politics of social democracy. As with other liberal democratic states at the time, although in a more pronounced fashion,

Britain had reached the limits of accommodation with a new-liberal mixed economy which would assure productivity, rising living standards and full employment. What is interesting is the extend of the hold that the consensus maintained over opinion, in that the options considered open to policy-makers were not deflation but further intervention in the economy and the elaboration of forms of corporatist intervention.[82]

Conclusion

By the time Macmillan resigned in 1963 the main thrust of the consensus remained in place, while in the 1964 election campaign the gap between left and right was nearly indistinguishable (see Table 5.2). The General election results demonstrate the capacity of the Conservative Party to extend its appeal after forming its first government in 1951. The 1955 and 1959 results, like those in Germany at the same time, were endorsements of economic success by the electorate. Macmillan believed that if growth and affluence were not available then the Conservatives were unlikely to continue to appeal. The difficulties which the party faced between 1962 and 1964 were associated more with mismanagement and scandal than with any break with the consensus. Indeed, it is the Labour Party which changes in response to the electoral success of the Conservative Party. There was a real fear in the Labour Party after the 1959 election that the Conservatives were unbeatable. A survey carried out after that election found that crucial sections of the working class identified strongly with the Conservative Party. This was not necessarily an ideological identification, though the level of ideological identification with either party was weak in any event, but rested on a belief in competent government and leadership, the provision of prosperity and a scepticism concerning the Labour Party's ability to provide them. In addition, a majority of younger voters leaned towards the Conservatives.[83] Over the next four years the Labour Party responded to this challenge, and in doing so narrowed the difference between the two parties. If the Conservatives had to jettison much of its ideological baggage to return to power in 1951 and to sustain it thereafter, the Labour Party had to use a similar means in the early 1960s. To a large extent the Labour Party emulated the Conservatives by absorbing much of what successive governments had achieved during the 1950s. While the Conservative decade might be at an end its influence continued in the saliency of issues into the 1960s.

Table 5.2 General election results, 1951–64

	1951	1955	1959	1964
Conservatives	48.0	49.7	49.4	43.4
Labour Party	48.8	46.4	43.8	44.1
Liberal Party	2.6	2.7	5.9	11.2
Others	0.6	1.1	0.9	1.3
Turn-out	81.9	76.8	78.6	77.1

Notes

1. Paul Addison, *The Road to 1945* (London: Jonathan Cape, 1975), pp. 229–69.
2. Conservative Pary Archives (CPA) Bodleian Library, Oxford: CRD 2/28/1, 'Restatement of war aims' 28 August 1940; CRD 2/28/6, 'The Beveridge Report Committee'; See also Crookshank Papers, MS Eng 600, Bodleian Library, Oxford; diary entry for 3 June 1943.
3. The qualified nature of the Conservative commitment in 1945 can be seen in 'Mr Churchill's Declaration of Policy to the Electors' (Conservative Party, 1945); CPA: CRD 2/28/9, '40 years of progress', which insisted on the success of inter-war Conservative policies. Martin Gilbert, *Never Despair: Winston S. Churchill 1945–1965* (London: Heinemann, 1988), for Churchill's role during the general election.
4. Addison, op. cit., for the clearest expression of this position. For revisionist qualifications of this view, Stephen Brooke, 'The Labour Party and the Second World War', in Anthony Gorst, Lewis Johnman and W. Scott Lucas (eds.), *Contemporary British History 1931–1961* (London: Pinter, 1991), pp.17–31; Kevin Jeffreys, *The Churchill Coalition and Wartime Politics, 1940–1945* (Manchester: Manchester University Press, 1991).
5. Anthony Howard, *The Life of R.A.B. Butler* (London: Jonathan Cape, 1987), pp. 15–56; CPA: CRD 2/9/7, 'Factors in the 1945 election'.
6. I have dealt with this question in more detail in two unpublished papers: 'The conditions for the post-war consensus in Britain, 1940–1951'; 'Bread and circuses: aspects of domestic policy in Britain 1945–1964'. They are obtainable from the author.
7. K. Middlemas, *Competition and the state: Britain in search of balance 1940–1961* (Basingstoke: Macmillan, 1986), p. 202. Alistair Horne, *Macmillan* (2 vols). volume 1, *1984–1956* (London: Macmillan, 1988), pp. 326–332.
8. M. Baines, 'A united anti-socialist party?' in *Contemporary Records*, 4: 3 (February 1991), pp. 13–15.
9. Hereafter CPA: CCO 150/2/1/1, S. Pierssene, 'Review of 1950 election', 15/3/1950. For a discussion of this aspect of the election see David Butler, *The British General Election of 1951* (London: Macmillan, 1952), pp. 247–270.
10. CPA: CCO 150/2/1/1, Clarke to General Director, 27/12/1951; see Butler op. cit., pp. 270–71.
11. CPA: CCO 150/2/1/1, 'The Liberal vote' 15/3/1950.
12. J. Bonham, *The Middle Class Vote* (London: Faber & Faber, 1954), pp. 124–25.
13. K.O. Morgan, *Labour in Power 1945–1951* (Oxford: Clarendon Press, 1984), pp. 479–86.
14. CPA: CCO 180/3/3 which contains a Gallup report on the 1950 election. For Churchill's remarks see Gilbert, op. cit., pp. 507, 516. The use of socialism here applies to the bundle of policies, such as the welfare state, usually associated with post-war social democracy.
15. Data derived from CPA: CCO 180/1/4, 'The swing to the right'.
16. For a recent endorsement of this view see Dennis Kavanagh and Peter Morris, *Consensus Politics* (Oxford: Basil Blackwell, 1989), p. 17.
17. Alan Booth, 'Corporatism, capitalism and depression in twentieth century Britain', *British Journal of Sociology* 33, (1982), pp. 200–23.
18. *Britain Strong and Free* (London: Conservative Party Publications, 1951), pp. 14–15; Butler papers, Trinity College, Cambridge: H36, Fraser to Boyd-Carpenter, 4 December 1953.
19. Ibid, Fraser to Boyd-Carpenter.
20. *The Industrial Charter* (May 1947), p. 16.
21. *The Right Road for Britain* (July 1949), p. 14.
22. *This is the Road* (1950), p. 8.

23. *The Election Manifesto* (1951), p. 3.
24. CPA: CRD 2/7/6; 'Report of the Working Party on the approach to the industrial worker', 20 July 1950.
25. CPA: CRD 2/7/6; Clarke to Chapman Walker, April 5 1950.
26. CPA: CCO 180/2/2, Public Opinion Summary No. 37, June 1952.
27. Public Records Office, London (hereafter PRO), Prem 11/129 Draft Minute to Butler, September 1952; Butler to Churchill, 8 October 1952; Churchill to Butler, 13 October 1952. Emphasis mine.
28. PRO: T 229/402, 'Urgent economic problems', J. Downie, 21 November 1951.
29. PRO: CAB 130/72, GEN 388, 'The economic position', 30 October 1951; 31 October 1951; 2 November 1951.
30. PRO: CAB 130/72, GEN 391/1 'Allocation of steel', 23 November 1951.
31. Anthony Seldon, *Churchill's Indian Summer: The Conservative Government 1951–55* (London: Hodder and Stoughton, 1981), p. 254–6; Michael Pinto-Duschinsky, 'Bread and circuses? The Conservatives in office, 1951–1964', in Vernon Bogdanor and Robert Skidelski (eds) *The Age of Affluence 1951–1964* (London: Macmillan, 1970).
32. Anthony Howard, *RAB: The Life of Rab Butler* (London: Jonathan Cape, 1987), pp. 184–85; PRO: CAB 134/856, EA(E) (51) 22, 13 December 1951, memo by Harold Macmillan; CAB 128/23, cc(51)19, 20 December 1951; cc(51)20, 29 December 1951 for Cabinet decisions; CPA: CCO 180/2/2; PORD, Confidential Supplement to Public Opinion Summary No. 22, November 1950; Butler Papers: G.26, Butler to Macmillan, 2 May 1953; Butler to Bridges, 3 September 1953; PRO: T 229/747: Churchill to Butler, 9 July 1952; Butler to Churchill, 11 July 1952; Horne, *Macmillan*, vol. 1, op. cit., pp. 335–6.
33. Harriet Jones, 'New tricks for an old dog? The Conservatives and social policy, 1951–5', in Gorst, Johnman and Lucas, op. cit., pp. 17–32.
34. John Strachey, *Contemporary Capitalism* (London: Victor Gollancz, 1956), pp. 131–51.
35. PRO: CAB 134/936; Home Affairs Committee; Sub-committee on the workers charter; HA(WC)(52), 4 July 1952; 9 July 1952; 30 July 1952; 12 September 1952.
36. PRO: CAB 128; cc57(52), 29 May 1952; cc75(52), 31 July 1952.
37. PRO: T 229/405, 'Economic discussions with TUC', 8 November 1951; Butler to Churchill 12 November 1951; Meeting with TUC, 1 April, 1952.
38. Ibid., 24 June 1952.
39. PRO: CAB 130/99, GEN 453, 'Informal meeting in Foreign Secretary's room', 19 January 1954; Seldon, op. cit., p. 201–4; PRO: CAB 134/1273, Industrial Relations Committee, 23 July 1955.
40. PRO: Prem 11/1082, 'Wages policy', Tiffin to Eden, 20 July 1955; Draft Reply 15 August, 1955. For a devastating critique of government policy during the 1950s and beyond see S. Pollard, *The Wasting of the British Economy* (London: Croom Helm, 1982).
41. PRO: Prem 11/1082; TGWU to Prime Minister 9 December, 1955, Minister of Labour to Eden 9, December, 1955. Richard Lamb, *The Failure of the Eden Government* (London: Sidgwick and Jackson, 1987), pp. 40–58; Gerald A. Dorfman, *Wage Politics in Britain: 1945–1967* (London: Charles Knight, 1974), pp. 73–96; Leo Panitch, *Social Democracy and Industrial Militancy* (Cambridge: Cambridge University Press, 1976), pp. 41–64; on the notion of a social contract, Samuel H. Beer, *Modern British Politics* (London: Faber and Faber, 1969), pp. 318–51.
42. MS Woolton 25: Woolton to Churchill, 28 December, 1951. Woolton to Churchill, 18 March 1952; Churchill to Woolton, March 1952; Woolton to Churchill, 19 March 1952.
43. Strachey, op. cit., pp. 205–6; for a more recent and quantitatively sophisticated approach to the same question Douglas A. Hibbs, jr, 'Political parties and

macroeconomic policy', *American Political Science Review* 71:4 (1977), pp. 1467–87.

44. MS Woolton 26: Woolton to Churchill 24 April 1953; 'The problem of stable employment', 30 April 1953. There is now a growing literature on the political dynamics of growth in the post-war world, David W. Ellwood, *Rebuilding Europe* (London: Longman, 1992), pp. 205–42.

45. Seldon, op. cit. Andrew Gamble, *The Conservative Nation* (London: Routledge and Kegan Paul, 1974), pp. 61–86 for a discussion of these tensions. For a contemporary, but still valuable, analysis of the middle class and their influence, see Bonham, op. cit.; Seldon, op. cit., p. 423.

46. PRO: LAB 43/184, Duncan Sandy to Monckton, 22 December 1952; Monckton to Sandy 13 January 1953; see also T 230/309 'Economic situation', 29 May 1952.

47. PRO: LAB 43/276, 'Wage claims' memo, by Ian Macleod, 11 September 1956; Macmillan to Macleod, 3 September, 1956; Macleod to Macmillan, 4 September 1956.

48. Speech of 18 November 1966, cited in R.Lewis, *Enoch Powell* (London: Cassell, 1979), p. 65.

49. PRO: LAB 43/276, Memo by Macleod, 11 September 1956.

50. PRO: T 229/417, Central Economic Policy Staff, 'Economic Planning', 3 November 1951 and revised version May 1952; T 230/242, 'State of the nation'. Report on UK situation on change of government 1951, 6 December 1951; further notes by author D.M.B. Butt, 16 July 1953.

51. References to the White Paper *Economic Implications of Full Employment* (March 1956) Cmd 9727; PRO: T 230/301, Hauge to Hall, May 29 1956; Hall to Hauge, June 4 1956.

52. PRO: T 230/296, 'Problems of employment policy', draft 10 December 1951, based on earlier draft White Paper, 16 February 1951. This draft recommended that an Advisory Council on Wages be set up to promote a wage policy: 'This time we want not just another grudging assent by leaders to the pleas of authorities-in-a-jam but a conviction by the majority of unionists that the policy proposed is a simple permanent institution.' Bridges to Downie, 12 October 1950; T 20/294; see also T 20/295. The TUC opposed an advisory council and any attempt to regulate wage claims: T 230/295; Note 7 February 1951 on TUC refusal.

53. PRO: T 230/296, draft White Paper on inflation, 2 January 1952.

54. PRO: T 230/296 Minister of Labour to Cabinet Office, 4 February 1952; Bridges to Downie, 16 January 1952. T 230/298, 'The rise in unemployment', R.L. Hall 28 May 1952. Lincoln Evans to Butler, 24 June 1952; memo by Butler, 18 April 1952 on Labour note above and new draft; T 230/299, 'Full employment and price stability', 18 June, 1954.

55. PRO: T 239/91, Leslie to Bridges, 3 September 1955, 'Full employment and its implications'.

56. PRO: T 239/91, Strath to Butler, 29 June 1955.

57. It is difficult to pinpoint the moment when this sense of insecurity actually disappeared, but in Britain it probably dates from the 1959 election and somewhat later for continental Europe.

58. PRO: T 234/91 Leslie to Sir Bernard Gilbert, 23 March, 1955.

59. CPA: CCO 150/2/3/3, Industrial Relations Committee, 11th meeting, 23 November 1955; 15th meeting, 22 December 1955.

60. PRO: CAB 134/1273, *Industrial Relations*: IR(55)9, 23 July 1955. ;'Full employment and wage policy', R.L. Hall. 'Economic publicity on Full Employment and Wage Policy', S.C. Leslie.

61. Keith Middlemas, op. cit., pp. 226–37.

62. PRO: Prem 11/921, 'Industrial relations 1955', memo 2 June 1955.

63. Gamble, op. cit., pp. 70–81 offers one explanation for this; for a somewhat different

analysis of the same period see Beer, op. cit., pp. 352–85.

64. Butler papers: H36, Fraser to Boyd Carpenter, 4 December 1952 commenting on the document *Britain Strong and Free* (1951).

65. CPA: CCO 120/2/4; CCO 120/2/8; CCO 120/2/11. MS Woolton 22, 23/9/54; Butler papers: H36, notes for a speech at Sheffield, 14 May 1954.

66. Butler papers: H36, Frazer to Butler, 10 October 1955.

67. Bonham, op. cit. pp. 168–72; Jean Blondel, *Voters, Parties, and Leaders*, rev. edn (Harmondsworth: Penguin, 1967), pp. 56–69.

68. Howard, op. cit., p. 214; R. Rhodes James, *Anthony Eden* (London: Weidenfeld and Nicolson, 1986), pp. 415–16, 420–21; Horne, *Macmillan*, vol. 1, op. cit., p. 377.

69. PRO: Prem 11/1082, Arthur Tiffin (TGWU) to Eden, 20 July 1955; draft reply, 15 August 1955; TGWU response, 9 December 1955. For export figures, PREM 11/1324, '1956 Financial policy'.

70. PRO: Prem 11/1324, Thorneycroft to Eden, 6 January 1956; Memo CP(56)7, Chancellor of the Exchequer, 6 January 1956; Butler to Eden, 6 January 1956; CP(56)17, 21 January 1956 'Economic Situation' by Harold Macmillan; Butler to Eden, 22 January 1956; Eden to Macmillan, 29 January 1956; Macmillan to Eden, 29 January 1956; CM(56), Harold Macmillan, 10 February 1956; Macmillan to Eden, 11 February 1956, on resignation; Eden to Macmillan for alternative; further exchange, Macmillan to Eden, 13th and 14 February 1956 accepting Eden's terms.

71. PRO: Prem 11/1325, Macmillan to Eden, 1 June 1956, with Eden's note on text; Prem 11/1402, Macmillan to Eden, 23 March 1956; Eden to Macmillan, 24 March 1956; Macmillan to Eden, 27 March 1956; reply 11 April 1956; conclusions of meeting in the Prime Minister's office noted, May 1956.

72. There has been an exhaustive discussion on the Suez crisis and its impact on the Conservative party. Representative views can be found in Howard, op. cit. Rhodes James, op. cit.; Lamb, op. cit.; Horne, *Macmillan*, vol. 1, op. cit.

73. Alistair Horne, *Macmillan* (2 Vols), volume 2, *1957–1986* (London: Macmillan, 1989), pp. 17, 37 for citations.

74. PRO: Prem 11/1824, Thorneycroft to Macmillan, 13 September 1957; Eccles to Macmillan, 14 September 1957; Macmillan to Thorneycroft, 15 September 1957.

75. PRO: Prem 11/2248, Fraser to Macmillan, 20 September 1957.

76. PRO: Prem 11/1824, alternative statement by Macmillan, 16 September 1957; C(57)195, 7 September 1957.

77. PRO: CAB 128/31, CC(57)71, 7 October, 1957.

78. PRO: CAB 128/31, CC(57)77, 31 October 1957; CC(57)86, 31 December 1957; CAB 128/32, CC (58)1, 3 January 1958, 11 am; CC(58)2, 3 January 1958, 4.30 pm; CC(58)3, 5 January 1958. For the decision to increase government expenditure 75 million pounds, see CC(58)7, 20 January 1958; Horne, *Macmillan* vol .2, op. cit., pp. 62–79.

79. PRO: Prem 11/2311, 'Future economic prospects following recession'; 'Public investment and reflation' 23 October 1958; Directive by Prime Minister, 27 October 1958; for the Chancellor's unwillingness to reflate memo see (58)211, 'Economic Situation', 21 October 1958; CAB 134/1734, Cabinet committee on employment for discussion on expenditure.

80. Cited in Horne, *Macmillan*, vol. 2, op. cit., p. 76.

81. Harold Macmillan, *Pointing the Way* (London: Macmillan, 1972), p. 15; Horne, *Macmillan*, vol. 2, ibid., pp. 247–336.

82. Kavanagh and Morris, op. cit., passim, for assessment; Beer, op. cit., pp. 386–432.

83. Mark Abrams, Richard Rose and Rita Hinden, *Must Labour Lose?* (Harmondsworth: Penguin, 1960).

6 The Refashioning of American Conservatism, 1940–60

Introduction: Conservatism, Consensus and Stability

American conservatism had been weakened by the New Deal and the electoral realignment which had accompanied it. Roosevelt's political success was based on the party's response to economic crisis, and the New Deal coalition was formed and sustained in respect of social, welfare and economic issues. Despite Roosevelt's personal popularity, the liberal seam in American politics was remarkably weak. By 1938 liberalism was under pressure, while the Second World War challenged much of what had been achieved during the 1930s. In contrast to the European experience, the right emerged from the Second World War stronger than previously and with a commitment to push back what was considered to be the dangerous leftism of the Democratic administration. Nor was the right mistaken concerning the ambitions of the Democrats to extend the New Deal agenda after the war. While recognising the constraints under which the president had to operate, both Roosevelt and Truman hoped to introduce new and comprehensive federal programmes which would extend the government's reach and competence. If American politics is considered to be exceptional, then the post-war experience lends some substance to such a claim.[1]

In contrast to Europe the United States did not move to the left after the Second World War. American politics from the mid-1940s to the mid-1950s can more accurately be characterised in terms of a move to the right which also sustained a period of political reaction against liberalism and the left generally. The main trend during the war involved growing opposition within Congress to Federal involvement in the economy and in society. This momentum was maintained during the post-war years. The failure to introduce a full employment bill in 1945 is symptomatic of this. The Employment Bill (1946) was a weak compromise which offered little by way of a Federal commitment to sustain full employment. In turn the Taft-Hartley Act (1947) eroded much that had been obtained by organised labour during the 1930s, signifying the end of the expansion of the trade union movement. The congressional elections in 1946 confirmed the rightward movement, and President Truman was faced with sustained opposition to all his interventionist proposals during the following two years. Truman's election victory in 1948 contained but did not reverse the trend. His administration's inability to implement its domestic policy indicated that, in effect, there existed an anti-New Deal coalition in Congress. This coalition was made up of Republicans and southern Democrats, and while the reforms of the 1930s were not reversed, there was little basis for new reforms.[2]

Conservatives were placed in a dilemma during the immediate post-war years. They were in a position to prevent the introduction of policies to which they were opposed, while occasionally they were also able to implement their own favoured policies. The presidency in contrast appeared to be outside their reach, Truman appealed in 1948 to those who feared that the Republicans would undo what had been achieved. While opinion had moved to the right on a number of issues there was no mandate for unreconstructed conservatism. Henry Cabot Lodge noted after the 1948 election that the electorate was not prepared to trust the Republicans because the party was still identified with reaction. Thomas Dewey, the Republican candidate, recognised the limits of his appeal after the shock defeat, and appealed to Eisenhower to run in the next election:

> We must look around for someone of great popularity and who has not frittered away his political assets by taking positive stands against national planning, etc....Elect such a man to Presidency, *after which* he must lead us back to safe channels and paths.[3]

The search for stability in post-war America worked to the advantage of the right rather than the left. Rapid change, both domestically and abroad, generated feelings of insecurity and in these circumstances the party of stability offered more than the party of change. At a general level then the Republican Party appeared well placed to optimise its opportunities in this context. This position was reinforced by a number of other factors. The cold war heightened anti-collectivist sentiment, while McCarthyism generated widespread fears concerning internal subversion. By 1950 American was at war again, and this time with a Communist state. Moreover, a consensus on domestic policy had emerged which placed the emphasis on the right rather than the left. While economic growth was considered to be a major objective of policy, this was to be generated by private investment, deregulated markets and decentralised business decisions. The other aspect of this consensus was that the basic welfare reforms of the New Deal would remain, but would not be extended. The 1950 mid-term elections confirmed the movement to the right, with the Republicans gaining five seats in the Senate and increasing its representation in the House from 171 to 199. Between 1950 and 1952 this move to the right continued, with public opinion displaying anti-liberal sentiment for much of the time.[4]

The Republican Party platform for the 1952 election was a careful balance between traditional right-wing concerns and the need to persuade the electorate that voting for a Republican would not turn the clock back. The choice of Eisenhower as candidate fulfilled most of the conditions required to do this. In contrast to other contenders for the nomination, Eisenhower was considered to be a moderate on most issues, in fact the general public appear to have had a vague view of Eisenhower's ideology.[5] Furthermore, the decision to nominate Richard Nixon as vice-presidential candidate allowed the appeal to be balanced between centre and right without alienating either the floating voter or the right-wing activist. Despite this, Eisenhower was a traditional conservative, one who identified closely with the norms and values of the Republican Party. What distinguished him from the right of the party was his recognition that in the modern age it was not possible to return to the self-sufficiency of the nineteenth century. He criticised those within the party, such as Hoover, who demanded an end to New Deal programmes on the grounds that modern life was more complex than heretofore and limited state intervention could be justified. In addition, Eisenhower was an internationalist in the sense that he believed the threat from communism required America's involvement in the world and especially in Europe. His internationalism did not imply a liberal intention, except in the limited economic commitment to free trade. His importance to the Republican Party in 1952 was that he could attract former Democratic voters without alienating the isolationist wing of his own party. His commitment to stabilisation and the status quo further enhanced his appeal to an electorate which sought a degree of certainty after two decades of change.[6] Eisenhower's commitment to stability identified him with the conservative wing of politics. On domestic and foreign policy issues he wished to secure a conservative stability. This is evident in his reluctance to intervene in domestic issues, but it also underwrites his cautious approach to foreign policy. Although strongly anti-communist he was unwilling to act in a fashion which would in his opinion destabilise the balance of power in Europe or elsewhere. Such caution remained the hallmark of his administration for eight years, his appeal for much of that time rested on similar considerations.

Conservatism as a Preventative Philosophy

Eisenhower's commitment to stability reflected a deeper belief in conservative approaches to policy. His complex conservatism included preventing outcomes to which he was opposed taking effect. However, in contrast to traditional conservatives Eisenhower was prepared to act decisively to bring about these outcomes.[7] In an exchange with one of his former military colleagues, who questioned the President's conservative commitments, he tartly rejected the appeal to unreconstructed conservatism: 'I believe that the true radical is the fellow who is standing in the middle and battling both extremes'. Eisenhower concurred in rejecting the influence of radical ideologists such as Rousseau but believed that in the modern world governments had to bear some responsibility when economic change affected individuals 'through no fault of their own'. Moreover, the social problems of a mass society were not amenable to solutions which would have been appropriate to the nineteenth century. Eisenhower defended a specific concept, which he described as middle of the road Republicanism. One, he added, which:

> preserves the greatest possible initiative, freedom and independence of soul and body to the individual, but that does not hesitate to use government to combat cataclysmic economic disasters which can, in some instances, be even more terrible than convulsions of nature.[8]

Eisenhower's willingness to accept a certain level of government intervention distanced him from those in the party who believed that the 1952 election victory provided the opportunity to transform not just the political agenda, but aspects of the political culture itself. Barry Goldwater believed in 1953 that the 'nation was still moving left', and that conservatives hoped to 'free the country from Roosevelt's economic, social, and political engineers'.[9] Whether this meant the dismantling of the New Deal is unclear, but the original intent was certainly reactionary as Goldwater became increasingly critical of what he believed to be Eisenhower's inactivity, despite the replacement of New Deal activists by Republican appointees. This is not to say that Eisenhower was insensitive to the right, only that his view of political reality was more complex than that of Goldwater, Brikker and others. Thus he believed that, whatever the disposition of a party, it was impossible to act precipitously:

> to attain any success it is quite clear that the Federal government cannot avoid or escape responsibilities which the mass of the people firmly *believe* should be undertaken by it. The political processes of our country are such that if a *rule of reason* is not applied in this effort we will lose everything . . . even to a possible and drastic change in the constitution. . . . Should any political party attempt to abolish social security, unemployment insurance, and eliminate labour laws and farm programmes, you would not hear of that party again in our political history.[10]

This is conservatism for an era of competitive party democracy. Eisenhower recognised the need to preserve what is in place in order to assure stability and to prevent innovative action by the Democrats. It is these considerations which disposed him to counter the knee-jerk reaction of the traditional American conservative. The President was anxious to distance his administration from those he considered to be reactionary:

> the forces of reaction . . . have *not* been allowed to gain control over policy or to exert undue influence over leaders in the Administration, but they have been defeated, in some of their most determined efforts.[11]

Even when Eisenhower was uneasy about the existing situation he urged caution. In response to pressure to place social security on a voluntary footing he claimed that the federal system had been examined by 'hard-headed conservative individuals', and that their conclusions had convinced him of the need to maintain its compulsory nature. There was, for Eisenhower, a stark choice: 'We must keep it on that basis or else abandon it entirely.' The only conclusion that Eisenhower would draw from this was the one which sustained the existing programmes:

> It would appear logical to build upon the system that has been in effect for almost 20 years rather than embark upon *the radical course of turning it completely upside down and running the very real danger that we would end up with no system at all.*[12]

Many of the same criteria prevailed when Eisenhower considered a return to the gold standard. On the advice of his officials he concluded that the best strategy at that time was to maintain the *status quo* on the grounds that if America acted unilaterally the results would set back the possibility of multilateral trading arrangements, the success of which he believed would provide the incentive to convertability. In any event Eisenhower was suspicious of the advocates of the gold standard believing that they were either motivated by isolationist sentiment or were in possession of the metal. Eisenhower's own attitude to gold is significant here: 'while I started out with an intense hope that such a thing would be possible, I was forced to accept the conclusion reached by my expert advisors'. The fear of adverse consequences, the advice received from officials (and Eisenhower did not necessarily accept expert advice unless he agreed with it), and the possibility that precipitous action would destabilise world trade and co-operation, all combined to enhance the existing structures.[13] The basis for a possible reactionary politics was also undermined by his belief in the function of democracy:

> A living democracy needs diversity to keep it strong. For survival, it also needs to have the diversities brought together in a common purpose, so fair, so reasonable, and so appealing that all can rally to it.[14]

Despite this, it would be mistaken to conclude that Eisenhower had embraced the philosophy of the liberal democrats associated with the New Deal. If liberal is used for those advocating activist government along the lines normally associated with the social democrats in Europe, then Eisenhower remained a conservative. Following a discussion with Goldwater in 1957 Eisenhower accepted the Senator's claim that he was not a conservative but a 'true liberal'. Here and elsewhere Eisenhower endorsed the distinction between modern liberalism, which he believed to be intrusive, coercive and collectivist, and liberal individualism which he considered to be central to his own world view. Liberalism is used by the President in a restricted fashion and it is a philosophy which overlaps with, although it does not share all the nuances of, the conservative philosophy which prevailed before the 1930s.[15] Nor was Eisenhower as far apart from the right of his party as one might expect from this. At times the isolationist and reactionary wings of the party infuriated him because of its lack of realism, but he was closer to them than sometimes appeared. Not only was Richard Nixon his vice-president, but he was quick to deny that differences between the President and the right were fundamental. He insisted that he and Senator William Knowland, often a critic of administration policies, were agreed on most major issues:

> He and I agree that we are conservatives. While I have recognised the necessity of the Federal government undertaking functions and responsibilities that far exceed those in which it was engaged 40 years ago, yet I have consistently fought against the needless and useless expansion of these functions and responsibilities. Senate members of the so-called 'right wing' have voted similarly.

For Eisenhower 'modern republicanism' meant 'Republicanism adapted to the problems of today'. What this entailed in detail was opposition to centralisation and dependency on the federal government, a reluctance to maintain subsidies for agriculture or to provide special benefits for interest groups. It also involved a reinforcement of spiritual values linked to sustained opposition to communism and dictatorship. In policy terms it required the protection and promotion of private property while sustaining the conditions for economic growth and fiscal responsibility.[16] Eisenhower's criticism of conservatives in the party rested on their failure to recognise the balance between reality and ideology. His own commitment to preservative conservatism would be better served if the conservatives recognised and devoted 'their efforts to helping stabilise the situation rather than criticizing efforts which recognise that you cannot return to the days of 1860'.[17]

In a speech to the Business Advisory Council in 1955 Gabriel Hauge outlined what he considered to be the essence of the Eisenhower philosophy. Hauge cited the presidential use of 'dynamic conservatism' to describe the administration, though he himself preferred to use modern conservatism. Eisenhower commended Hauge on his speech adding that 'it is the most lucid and the best statement of the Administration's philosophy of government that has yet been set forward'. Hauge systematises the balance between maintaining a commitment to traditional objectives and accepting limited government activism in certain areas. The latter commitment to minimum welfare provides the basis in the modern world for the successful functioning of the former.[18]

Eisenhower's realism did not prevent him from identifying with conservative aims. Goldwater's claim that Eisenhower was essentially a New Dealer was basically mistaken. He wished to change the political environment, but his realism forced Eisenhower to recognise the limits of such objectives:

> The most that anyone . . . even if he is supported by a good majority in the Congress . . . could do would be gradually to stop the trend in this direction, slowly to bend the rising curve towards greater socialism and eventually to flatten it out so that further advance in this dangerous direction would be prevented.[19]

Unlike most other liberal democratic political systems, that of the United States is extremely sensitive to public opinion. In effect the president and Congress, at different levels, are always accountable for their respective actions and behaviour. In Eisenhower's case his own majority was comfortable in 1952, but that of the Republican Party was not. The Republicans had won the election because of disenchantment with the Democrats and despite the buoyant state of the economy. Though 1952 provided a mandate, it was limited and dependent on the new administration simultaneously securing stability, peace and economic growth. The difficulty was how to achieve these aims while at the same time securing Eisenhower's position as an independent political actor, free especially from the Republican Party which, if allowed, would have insisted on a more reactionary approach to policy-making.[20]

Senator Henry Cabot Lodge, one of Eisenhower's closest advisers, argued that Eisenhower should impose his will on the party, while at the same time utilising the presidency to dominate public opinion through the media. This would give the President considerable autonomy, and allow him to distance the presidency from a possible Republican defeat in the 1954 mid-term elections. While not inevitable, Lodge continued, if it did occur it would not necessarily be disastrous. Democratic control, he continued:

> need have no effect whatever on the President's popularity, provided he goes ahead and runs his own show, does not allow himself to be used to bolster a lot of shopworn Republicans, and doesn't get his own prestige deeply involved in a Republican victory.

Lodge believed that the Republicans tended to run negative campaigns against the Democrats; this he considered to be counter-productive. The danger he believed was that communism would become the main issue in the 1954 elections. This would not only be negative, but might lose the election in much the same way that Republicans had lost every election since 1932. The reasoning behind Lodge's caution was that while the Democrats had been turned out in 1952 on what were negative slogans, this approach in itself could not assure them of further success unless a more constructive approach was adopted. Although Lodge claimed that he was not advocating it, he did suggest that consideration be given to an alternative strategy which highlighted the armistice in Korea, and emphasised the Republicans' role as peacemakers.[21] Eisenhower reinforced this message during the 1954 campaign by warning prospective candidates that he could not support every candidate irrespective of whether that candidate supported the policies of the administration or not. In particular Eisenhower demanded that candidates looking for his endorsement should make explicit their position on the Brikker amendment, emphasising that his main contribution to the party was his ability to 'appeal to Independents and "intelligent Democrats".'[22]

The run up to the mid-term elections was the first major test of Eisenhower's domestic policy and the reality of 'modern conservatism'. In July 1953 the United States had effective full employment; between then and March 1954, one and a quarter million jobs were lost and the economy experienced a severe recession. The cause of the recession can be ultimately traced back to the end of the Korean war and the cut-back in expenditure which resulted from this, though the role of the Secretary of the Treasury George M. Humphrey, an advocate of severe credit restrictions, also contributed to the outcome.[23] Whatever else Eisenhower received by way of mandate in 1952 it was not one to bring about a recession. Humphrey may have wished to return to the halcyon days of Andrew Mellon, and his actions during the first half of 1953 confirmed the worst fears of those Democrats who believe that a Republican administration could not manage the economy without high unemployment. However, despite Humphrey's innate conservatism on fiscal matters, he was unable (indeed unwilling) to promote a return to the policy conditions of the 1920s.[24]

By early 1954 unemployment had more than doubled over the previous year, prompting Eisenhower to declare that he was not another Hoover. Indeed the President recognised that 'now is the time to liberalise everything we can, because the fear in America is not the fear of inflation; it is the fear of deflation, of going down, not up'. Yet despite this and the regular discussion concerning the possibility of counter-cyclical action, Eisenhower remained cautious about using federal expenditure to bring an end to the recession.[25] Lodge warned the President at the same time that unemployment was the most dangerous threat to his administration. He contemptuously dismissed those Republicans who courted party popularity by evoking images of 'sound money' and 'balanced budgets', adding that:

Cutting government expenditure is popular unless you cut the expenditure with which the individual happens to have a profitable connection. The lowering of taxes is fairly popular, but not nearly as popular as some Republican Congressmen think.[26]

Arthur Burns shared the President's caution during the recession. Both believed that precipitative action was unwarranted unless the danger of a slide from recession into depression threatened. In April 1954 at the height of the recession, Burns outlined three counter-cyclical options. These included, in ascending order of seriousness: easing monetary and credit conditions, deep cuts in taxation, and expansion of government expenditure. What was paramount, he believed, was that the public should be aware of the government's contingency plans:

> If it became known that the Administration lacked an anti-depression policy, public confidence might be shaken. It is vitally important that the policy proposed by the Council, or some satisfactory alternative, be generally understood and accepted within the Administration, and that rough agreement be reached regarding the type of governmental action called for by the policy.[27]

Burns argued that the public reception of the recession was unique, despite economic dislocation confidence remained high. This he attributed to a general belief concerning government responsibility for economic management:

> This feature seemed to result from the confidence of the people that the Government is both committed and able to maintain the stability of the economy simultaneously with its basic belief in private enterprise. The delicacy of such a factor suggests extreme concern as to what might happen if confidence were weakened by any indication that the Administration was timid or impotent in dealing with this subject.[28]

Nor was Burns mistaken in his analysis of public psychology. The Gallup poll confirmed this point of view during early 1954. Between January and August 1954 large pluralities (ranging between 43 and 55 per cent) believed that unemployment would continue to rise during the subsequent six months. When asked what they thought caused the recession, most attributed it to the end of the Korean war or a cut-back in expenditure, only 8 per cent believed it was a normal business cycle. By March unemployment was the main concern in most regions and the opinion polls reflected the accompanying unease. Yet the attitude of the public appears contingent on government action. In January, 71 per cent of those polled believed that America would not experience a depression similar to that of the 1930s. Moreover, even in a depression only 28 per cent believed that the economy would have been better under the Democrats if that party had been re-elected in 1952, whereas 46 per cent perceived no difference between the two parties and 18 per cent concluded that it would have been worse.[29]

The electorate may have waited on government action in the belief that the federal authorities had considerable influence over the management of the economy. While most people may not have blamed government action for the recession, government inaction could have a destructive impact on Republican fortunes. This action was limited throughout the first half of 1954. There was considerable discussion in the Cabinet on possible policies which might stabilise employment. The Secretary of the Treasury consistently urged a cautious approach whereas Nixon and Stassen believed a more forthright response should be adopted. Humphrey believed that some unemployment was inevitable once government expenditure had been reduced but that the reaction to this could be held to a minimum. In May some public works expenditure was recommended by the President who also approved the implementation of some spending plans which would not otherwise have been put into place until the following year. The difference of opinion in the Cabinet was highlighted during an exchange as the recession began to bite late in 1953. The President:

> recalled the campaign pledges of all Republicans to use the full government power to prevent "another 1929", and he asserted the only item in question is the Republican desire to assure the maximum of activity by the individual.

In stark contrast, Humphrey sought to persuade the Cabinet that tough decisions were necessary:

> that because of all the record 'highs' now present the only way for the economy to go is 'down', and a few readjustments are not to be feared. He felt unemployment can decline for 6 or 7 months without becoming critical. The critical levels cannot be detrimental now because of so many variable factors.

In the event policy was never as passive as Humphrey recommended, but it was rarely as active as Eisenhower seemed to imply. Continuing confidence, though qualified, allowed the administration to adopt a wait-and-see approach for much of 1954.[30]

Yet for some sections of the population a wait-and-see approach was not enough. The recession mobilised trade union discontent. The powerful United Steel Workers of America attempted, unsuccessfully, to persuade the President to adopt an ambitious programme of expansion which, it asserted, would restore the economy to full employment.[31] Although Eisenhower chose to ignore this advice, by doing so he alienated sections of the trade union movement. Between 1950 and 1954 the Democrats gained around two and a quarter million extra votes on a turnout which had increased by only about one-third of a million. Post-election analysis by the Republican Party concluded that most of this increase could be attributed to the 'unprecedented efforts of organised labor'. In a number of individual states this intervention proved decisive, while in virtually every other state the contribution of labour added significantly to the Democratic vote:

> In terms of cause and effect, the big Democratic turnout was the *effect*; labor's role was the cause. Unquestionably, the most important factor revealed by the 1954 Congressional elections was the startling display of strength by labor organizations, particularly those with leftist leadership.[32]

This evidence led some Republican strategists to believe that the 'labour' factor could prove decisive in 1956. This may have been putting too pessimistic a gloss on what was a set-back for the party. However, Eisenhower's own authority and prestige remained intact because, as Lodge had pointed out, the mid-term election was not national, nor need it be considered as a vote of confidence in the President.[33]

Nixon's analysis of the elections suggested that the outcome was a 'dead-heat', and that the losses could be explained by contingent circumstances. He believed that this meant that moderate programmes which eschewed extremes could assure the party success in forthcoming elections. Humphrey worried that a Democratic congress would advocate programmes which would induce inflation. Eisenhower concluded that there was a split in the Democratic Party and this would be heightened by having to run Congress, but warned his colleagues that: 'He thought the next two years extremely critical because the Republican theory of moderation remained to be proved sufficiently to wean the people back from ideas dependent on wartime emergencies.'[34]

Immediately after Eisenhower's re-election in 1956 Burns wrote claiming that: 'A grateful nation went to the polls yesterday.' Burns pointed to a dramatic upturn in the economy between autumn 1954 and the November 1956 election. In political terms Eisenhower benefited from the expansion of the economy, a success which neutralised the opposition of labour and made ineffectual Adlai Stevenson's appeal from a liberal democratic perspective. Nor should it be ignored that similar conditions facilitated the return of conservative governments in a number of states between 1955 and 1957.[35] The most telling statistics are those for inflation, unemployment and disposable income. Unemployment in September 1956 stood at 2.9 per cent, well below the average for the previous ten years. Inflation was also low in comparison with the period of Democratic incumbency. This is clearly reflected in income which rose 8 per cent in real terms after tax between 1952 and 1955. This view is further reinforced by the increase in family ownership of consumer products, among many others, such as automobiles and televisions.[36]

To an extent the upswing was fortuitous and owed relatively little directly to the actions of the Administration. One reason for this was that Eisenhower was reluctant to act precipitously even if this resulted in his unpopularity or loss of votes, but another reason rested on his assumption that the period of readjustment would be short and that the economy itself remained sound. In addition the Cabinet shared the view that privately led expansion should receive priority from the Administration rather than invoking the state whenever a downturn occurred.[37] However, the close attention paid to the management of the economy throughout the recession indicates an alertness to the need to act if necessary. If the fluctuations had become serious it is probable that more overt action would have been taken. The Council of Economic Advisers (CEA), though cautious certainly recognised the need to act once the economy had reached a certain low. In this sense the electorate was not mistaken in its belief that any economic fluctuation would not be as serious or prolonged as those experienced during the 1930s. By 1955 over 75 per cent of respondents considered the country to be prosperous and most believed that it would continue to be so. Furthermore, 55 per cent believed that a depression was not inevitable after a period of high prosperity, whereas 22 per cent believed this to be inevitable. Even more strikingly, 72 per cent believed that it was the responsibility of government to secure this prosperity, with only 17 per cent taking what might be described as the conservative view.[38] There were clear limits politically to what a conservative administration could achieve, otherwise it would have to pay the price for inactivity as was the case in 1954. Alternatively by 1956 the United States had experienced unprecedented prosperity and this was attributed to successful actions by the Administration, even if this was not actually the case.[39] The recession and the mid-term elections demonstrate that an Eisenhower administration was prepared to postpone action, but not to advocate non-intervention, which was the most likely outcome of Humphrey's policy rec-ommendations. Politically the Republicans may have been conservative, but it was one which was defined within an environment not of its making and one which the Administration had to cultivate carefully if it was not to fall into the po-litical trap of appearing to sustain a more reactionary policy than acceptable to public opinion.

Conservatism and Macro-Economic Policy

One of the characteristic features of the first three decades of the post-war era is the extent to which governments intervened in the economy to secure the multi-ple objectives of growth, full employment and rising incomes. There was an open consensus on these objectives if not on the means to achieve them: America remained on the conservative end of the spectrum, with Sweden and the United Kingdom on the left, and West Germany roughly between the two extremes. However, the Eisenhower Administration shared in the commitment, but believed that these ends could be achieved without sustained government in-tervention. Indeed Eisenhower believed that such intervention was dangerous for the well being of the economy and individual liberty. Despite this Eisenhower was not in favour of dismantling the main institutional arrangements related to the New Deal; what he hoped to achieve was a balanced budget, low taxation and a reduction in federal expenditure. In particular he was reluctant to endorse any extension of government programmes if this entailed either deficit spending or increased expenditure by the Federal authorities. He remained alert to the need to be seen to be acting in a positive sense even while maintaining broad conservative objectives:

> I am personally convinced that, in a number of fields, this administration will have to come forward, at a reasonably early date, with a constructive programme that will be designed to meet, in a well rounded and imaginative way, the constantly increasing needs of a growing population.[40]

One suggestion developed subsequently was to support an ambitious high-ways programme which would be high profile and have an immediate impact on the public. Eisenhower's commitment to reducing expenditure was consistent, even to the extent of reducing expenditure on defence. His defence of such a strategy relied on his belief that reasonable taxation, low inflation and a sound monetary system were necessary to secure the conditions which would promote savings: 'The foundation of a capitalist system.' This could not be secured un-less expenditure was controlled. Despite his fears about communism the President urged General Guenther, Chief of Staff of Supreme Headquarters Al-lied Powers Europe (SHAPE), to support him on this issue in the belief that:

> ... organised, effective resistance [to Communism] must be maintained over a long pe-riod of years and that this is possible only with a healthy American economy. If we should proceed recklessly and habitually to create budget deficits year after year, we have with us an inflationary influence that can scarcely be successfully combatted. Our particular form of economy could not endure.[41]

This view is not incompatible with Eisenhower's stated belief that 'security is more important that balanced budgets', but it highlights the dilemma he faced. The need to control expenditure had priority, but it should be maintained in a context where security would not be impaired; yet this was not always possible to achieve.[42]

At the institutional level Eisenhower acted quickly to impose conservative norms. The CEA, which under Leon Keyserling had maintained a strong advocacy of Keynesian expansionary economics, was 'depoliticised'. Its functions were closely regulated by presidential advisers and the channels of influence, which had been implicit in its origins, were severely restricted. Such action was reinforced by conservative appointments at the Treasury and the Bureau of the Budget. In the CEA itself the appointment of Burns as Chairman and Saulnier as consultant confirmed the conservative trend, as did the appointment of Hauge as Administrative Assistant to the President for Economic Affairs. What was at issue in the appointments was the extent to which conservative personnel were in place, though they could not always, as Humphrey hoped, achieve their conservative ends.[43] In a memo circulated just after Eisenhower took up office, Saulnier warned that there was a danger that recession would occur if credit policy proved too restrictive. While endorsing the necessity for some restrictions, he drew attention to the need to keep consumer spending high. Failure to do so, he maintained, could tip the balance of the economy into decline unless other factors offset it. For a conservative economist Saulnier took an extremely pragmatic line at this time:

> However much one may wish to see our federal budget brought into balance it must be recognised that this accomplishment in itself will remove from the economic situation one force which has so far been persistently supporting high and rising levels of money income.

This analysis did not lead to an advocacy of intervention as such, as the response to the 1953–4 recession confirmed, but it, and subsequent advice from the CEA, reflected a concern with sustaining growth in the economy.[44]

Eisenhower was sensitive to this advice. In a memo to Dodge at the Bureau of the Budget, he advocated a number of projects concerned with slum clearance, water resources and conservation. Additionally he recommended that initiatives be taken on social security and old age pensions, the aim of which would be to :

> put ourselves clearly on record as being forward looking and concerned with the welfare of our people. In addition, to give substance to our words I should like to see *no* reduction . . . possibly even a slight increase . . . in housing appropriations. The same applies to a few *small* public works projects . . .[45]

This was also a view endorsed by Hauge who recommended an activist programme, but one which did not entail significant spending increases.

For Hauge it was imperative that Eisenhower placed himself in a position to 'have a good story to tell' in his 1954 State of the Union Message:

> The American people simply are not going to be content with budget balancing and

sound money. The American people are a building people, a doing people, and for better or worse, they see Government as having a significant role in this matter.

Such an attitude certainly constrained any government committed to fiscal responsibility and restraint. Whether the Administration had a good story to tell at the beginning of 1954 is debatable given the continuation of the recession, but what does stand out is the anxiety of Eisenhower's policy advisers that he get the political message right, but without committing the Administration to detailed spending programmes.[46] By the end of 1954, and the set backs at the mid-term elections, the general outline of an Eisenhower strategy can be detected. In principle the Administration wished to achieve a balanced budget, a tax cut and a reduction in federal expenditure when possible. The first of these received priority, but if other goals such as security or domestic programmes were endangered then the priority might not be carried through. Moreover, this was reinforced by a reluctance to pursue activist programmes, even during a recession. There was a recognition that the Administration should carefully balance the contending pressures between growth and inflation. All, however, were agreed that growth should be maintained primarily by private means, with the federal authorities operating in a subsidiary position contributing to maintaining stability at particular levels of growth.[47] Thus, just as the recession was ending Hauge could write optimistically to Humphrey that unemployment was down below 5 per cent, and that personal income was at an all-time high. This confirmed Hauge's assertion that while variations were part of the capitalist system such fluctuations 'need not grind on relentlessly into great depressions'.[48]

By early 1955 the Eisenhower Administration was confident that it had achieved the balance between growth and stagnation. Expansion might not be assured in any given year, but the cost electorally or in terms of presidential popularity could, it was concluded, be contained. This, however, did not imply that the Republican Party had embraced the New Deal. On the contrary, in individual matters the party maintained its commitments to the business community and its interests, especially the long-standing hostility to organised labour. This dovetailed with the recognition by Eisenhower and his advisers that generally labour supported the Democrats, and curtailing trade unions could be popular among the party members. Alternative approaches were quickly discarded. According to Sherman Adams, Eisenhower had been attracted by Walter Reuther of the Congress of Industrial Organizations (CIO) but was dissuaded by the party from developing any contact with him. Likewise, while the first Eisenhower Cabinet contained one trade union official, Martin Durkin, as Secretary of Labor he was unable to introduce an amendment to the Taft-Hartley Act which he believed had been the point of his appointment. Durkin was in fact quickly out-maneuvered by the opponents of the amendment, and after an angry altercation with Eisenhower, resigned. He was succeeded by James Mitchell who, though sympathetic to union criticism, was never in a position to significantly alter the legislation.[49]

Although Eisenhower was unwilling to adopt a pro-union position on Taft-Hartley, he also had to placate those Democrats who had voted for him in 1952 and whom he wished to retain as supporters. What Eisenhower described as 'moderate-progressive' Republicanism was dependent on attracting both Democrats and independents, and he recognised that both traditional Republicans and McCarthyites could not achieve this. Yet at the same time Eisenhower did not wish to be seen as a president caving in to Democratic pressure. In June 1955, after the Democratic mid-term success, he noted the difficulties facing him: 'although the Administration had already done a lot of things for which it was being called "New Dealish" despite the fact those things were justified, he was certain the Administration could just not get into a game of who will outbid whom'.[50] Despite criticism by the Republican right, Eisenhower did adhere to a set of policies which set his administration apart from his democratic predecessors or successors. Throughout his two terms in office he resisted what he described as the 'inflationary psychology' which he concluded still retained a strong hold over the electorate. In addition, he opposed any extension of the Tennessee Valley Authority (TVA) into other regions of the south, and resisted any further federal involvement in the husbanding of natural resources.[51]

It is, however, on macro-economic policy that the main contrast between Republican and Democratic administrations appears. Eisenhower was hostile to any suggestion that Keynesian deficit spending would resolve America's economic problems. This is not to claim that he did not wish to achieve full employment, but he was not prepared to promote 'inflationary' policies to achieve this end. It was a matter of priorities: if all else was equal then a policy which promoted both low unemployment and low inflation would commend itself to the Administration. However, this is rarely the case and if a choice had to be made then Eisenhower chose low inflation over both economic dislocation (recession) and unemployment. The President was very clear about this and was anxious to avoid an:

> unwarranted increase in the supply of money . . . which, of course, also means avoiding great deficits in the Federal budget . . . we can establish the strategy that will keep people saving their money and anxious to indulge in long term investment.[52]

Eisenhower explicitly articulated a concept of 'stable economic growth', the aim of which would be to 'maintain prosperity with price stability', an aim which 'is one of the prime objectives of this administration'. Furthermore, this would have to be achieved without undue state interference which if pushed too far would lead to a garrison state thus defeating the purpose of democratic government:

> we are defending a way of life, not merely property, wealth and even our homes. That way of life, over the long term requires the observance of sound fiscal policies, and wise distribution and use of the fruits of our productivity so that the system may continue to work primarily under the impulse of private effort rather than by the fiat of centralised government.

The emphasis was clearly placed on the autonomous action of the private entrepreneur operating within a market system. Unlike European governments at the time, this market was never social, but emphasised limited government whose only function was that of maintaining minimum order to enhance the working of the system rather than one of reinforcement or regulation.[53]

It was a policy framework that laid considerable emphasis on production rather than consumption in the sense that incentives should be provided for business to expand output rather than enhancing purchasing power. If output was expanded and more people were employed then consumption would take care of itself.[54] In the short term this strategy worked well: the economy expanded rapidly, leading Burns to report to the Cabinet that the economy was performing at 'virtually full employment' by the autumn of 1955 with GNP approaching $400 billion per annum.[55] By the summer of 1956 Burns was able to demonstrate that real income had increased while consumption, investment and output were at historically high levels.[56] Although the economic statistics were positive, there remained an underlying unease among the electorate concerning their welfare. Between 1952 and September 1955 over half of those interviewed consistently reported that in terms of income and cost of living they were doing 'just fair'. However, whereas between November 1952 and July 1954 between one-fifth and one-quarter considered themselves to be having a hard time, by September 1955 this had declined to 18 per cent. The most positive response to the economy comes from upper income groups (44 per cent doing well), whereas it is among lower income groups that one finds the negative responses (29 per cent considered they were having a hard time). What is striking is that the perceived beneficiaries of the economic upturn correlates with the most active supporters of the Republican Party, proprietors, managers, professionals and white-collar workers, which constitute around 38 per cent of respondents and the core Republican constituency.[57]

One of the dilemmas for the Administration was how to reconcile conservative objectives such as low tax, balanced budgets and a non-inflationary environment with the demands of a welfare state and the requirements of the military. The CEA under Burns and Saulnier recognised that traditional objectives would have to be supplemented with a commitment to security which in itself would distort the economy. To achieve these expanded objectives need not, Saulnier insisted, involve a return to the Keynesian expansionism implicit in the approach taken by National Security Council (NSC) 68:

> There is no inconsistency, either, between the goal of maximum sustainable economic growth and the maintenance of economic stability, a goal to which we are equally committed. On the contrary, the two are mutually reinforcing. An inflationary boom makes for no real improvement in living standards; all it does is to press unduly on the use of economic resources and produces an increase in prices and money values generally without increasing the output of goods and services.

Yet to maintain expansion it is not enough to provide a positive environment for business. The federal government, Saulnier urged, must also provide against deflation and the consequent erosion of the work-force and its skill. Confidence for business meant primarily securing a positive business environment; for the worker and others it meant guaranteeing employment opportunities and income. However, the recognition that such should be the case did not, in Saulnier's opinion, legitimise pervasive intervention on the part of the federal authorities. In general terms federal activism should concentrate on areas where its impact would have an immediate stimulatory impact, but not so that inflation would be promoted or business opportunity suffocated.

Scientific research, the cultivation of natural resources and the use of anti-trust laws are instances which would fall into such a category. In another context the decision to promote the interstate highway also contributed to this end by providing employment, investment opportunities and perhaps also help to stimulate the consumption of the motor car industry. This infrastructural investment, even if undertaken by the federal government, would not invalidate the more open commitment to private industry as the main motor for American economic expansion:

> Economic growth depends heavily on the undertaking of enterprises involving high degrees of risk; from such ventures often come the advances in technology that raise most dramatically the productive capacity of labour.

To assure this environment four conditions had to be met: economic development had to be directed largely by the private sector through market incentives; a credit policy must be designed to provide the finance necessary for this and to control an 'inflationary credit expansion', which would be detrimental to investment; this in turn necessitated a level of interest on savings which would secure those savings and allow the capital to be productively utilised; finally all of this presupposed a tax system which raised revenue for the government's requirements but which also had 'the least restrictive effect on the process of productive investment'. The aim of all of this was to assure the long-term expansion of the economy, the success of which would allow for a more adequate response to short-term disequilibrium, such as occurred in 1953 and 1954:

> maintaining economic stability over the short run is vastly simpler in an economy in which the force of growth is strong and continuous than in one in which that force is weak and failing. When the growth forces are present and operative, short period declines below the long-term level of growth are less likely to develop into full fledged depressions, and the impulses making for recovery, which may arise from the natural operation of the economic system or from government policies aimed deliberately at stimulating economic recovery, are more likely to come to a fruitful end.[58]

One consequence of such a strategy was to control public expenditure, if not actually to cut it back. Federal expenditure as a percentage of GNP actually increased from 16.1 per cent in 1950 to 18.5 per cent in 1960. Payments to individuals, however, which in 1950 accounted for 5.2 per cent of the total, had fallen to 4.9 per cent a decade later, whereas the figure for defence had almost doubled over the same period from 5.2 per cent to 9.7 per cent.[59] In these terms it was not very successful in achieving its aims. Yet, as Hauge noted this did not mean that the United States was moving in a socialist direction as some economists, notably Galbraith, were insisting. In response to the argument that convergence between the capitalist and communist systems was taking place, Hauge emphasised that between 88 and 90 per cent of United States National income was generated privately, in contrast to the centralised Soviet economy or indeed some of the mixed economies in Europe.[60] Yet the heavy dependence on private initiative to generate national income had some drawbacks. Hauge argued plausibly that the business cycle could not be abolished in a free market economy, thus recognising that recessions, if not depressions, had to be accepted in the policy-making process. Even more worrying for Hauge was the threat posed by prosperity to administration policies. Hauge identified a full employment psychology among both employers and employees which he believed was affecting the open international trading system. Hauge had been surprised to find that prosperity had not removed protectionist sentiment, indeed he highlighted pressures on the administration and Congress to act to prevent competition which in the minds of a particular industry was threatening their prosperity.[61]

During 1955 Burns alerted Eisenhower to the dependence of the economy on credit for expansion. The boom was fuelled by credit expansion especially for house-buying and consumer products such as cars.[62] By 1956 these concerns were joined by worries about Eisenhower's re-election. Burns advised against invoking a cooling-off period for a steel strike as the waiting period would expire just before the election. His belief in credit restriction had now become explicit, but was rejected by Harold Stassen who claimed that there was a threat of unemployment if action was not taken. Stassen believed this was not necessary as the economy was sound, investment potential good, and consumer demand and confidence high, in addition to which the international economy remained buoyant. Accordingly, 'prompt, dramatic, confidence building action can catch the recession before it really takes off'. Despite Burns' wariness, action was subsequently taken to ease credit for home-buyers and builders in October, in time for the run up to the election.[63]

The economy remained buoyant until the end of 1956, contributing to the re-election of the President. The opinion polls placed Eisenhower well ahead of Stevenson throughout the campaign. While there may have been some uncertainty concerning the President's health, there were no reservations about the man. Moreover, trends within specific areas appeared to secure Eisenhower's position well in advance. Between 1948 and 1952 the Republican Party had increased its support significantly in five border states analysed prior to the election, a trend which continues into the 1956 campaign. In addition to this, and despite arguments to the contrary, Republican strategists concluded that Taft-Hartley would not lose Eisenhower votes. Indeed Secretary of Labor Mitchell had judiciously balanced the continuing commitment to Taft-Hartley with the increased minimum wage and other concessions to the labour force. To reinforce this Eisenhower's personal popularity remained high throughout his tenure, only once dropping below 60 per cent.[64] Furthermore Mitchell argued that the Democrat-controlled 84th Congress killed amendments to Taft-Hartley which had been introduced by the Administration. More generally the Secretary of Labor was in a strong position to argue that under the Republicans employment had remained high, real purchasing power increased, while social security had been extended.[65]

Economic issues had not been central to the 1956 campaign, but it is arguable that if the economy had not been performing as well as it had this could have discomforted the President. The sensitivity of the electorate to recession or economic downturn becomes more evident during 1957 when signs emerged that the economy was in difficulty. In March 1957 Burns warned Eisenhower that the economy was encountering some difficulties, but that this was more a process of readjustment than a significant threat to the economy. Burns believed that the time was ripe to cut expenditure and to lay the basis for a tax cut.[66] By October however the CEA reported that there was a danger that unemployment would increase if conditions continued to deteriorate; yet Eisenhower's main concern remained inflation.[67] In December Saulnier advised Eisenhower against increasing expenditure, but to work towards eliminating the deficit during the following year. Later in the same month he reinforced Eisenhower's fears by advising the Cabinet that 'the problem of inflation remained critical', and would require constant attention. Both he and Anderson concluded in pessimistic tone that recovery from a downturn in 1958 might not be as easy as in 1954, nor might it be prevented as in 1956.[68] In December Saulnier forwarded Adams a number of suggestions which involved expenditure of about $5 billion, but which he believed would reverse the recessionary trends. The most important of these included relaxing credit restrictions, bringing forward some investment on roads and urban renewal, in addition to considering the possibility of providing relief on taxation.[69] Although the Administration recognised the danger inherent in the situation, no one appeared anxious to act precipitously. Under pressure from labour Hauge set out a clear but passive response to the recession. He believed that only a general economic recovery could bring about high levels of consumption. A rapid recovery could not be justified if it provoked inflationary tendencies.

> As for the standard union recovery formula . . . increased wages and purchasing power . . . this is only a partial approach at best. Higher wages, if they do not decrease employment, may well raise purchasing power and even total spending but they also raise costs, thereby threatening profit margins in a buyers market and thus dampening down business confidence in rebuilding inventories and expanding capital expenditures. We need a balanced, not a lop sided recovery programme.

This cautiousness was to prevail throughout 1958; the Administration recognised that the recession was serious, deeper than that of 1954, but action proved difficult.[70] Between December 1957 and March 1958 more than 1 million more workers became unemployed, bringing the rate to 7 per cent.[71] In February Eisenhower had predicted that the recession would bottom out in March. This may have been a vain attempt to avoid action on his part. Saulnier warned that demand had reduced significantly in all areas, the consumption of cars which had acted as a spur to expansion previously was particularly badly affected. The danger for Eisenhower was that the Democrat-controlled Congress would put together an anti-recession package which the President could not support. However, Eisenhower was not willing to authorise public works on the grounds that the upturn would occur before projects could have an effect. His argument centred on his fear that the federal government should not act with undue haste, even if the recession proved to be worse than at first thought. This, he added, 'would not cause him to abandon his principles of keeping the country on a sound basis, but he was sufficiently flexible to give the economy a little boost when it needed it'. By early March there was little evidence of such a boost. What was evident was the political imperative of neutralising any Democratic attempt to impose a radical programme to counter the recession. Eisenhower questioned whether a tax reduction at that time was the proper response despite the advice of leading Republicans to adopt such a policy. By late March the economic position had deteriorated further, yet the President continued to pursue the politics of procrastination. Senator Knowland continued to alert the President to the political damage that his inaction was causing, yet Eisenhower in common with most members of the Administration, continued to believe that the states rather than the federal authorities should be the focus for action. Eisenhower probably reflected moderate conservative opinion on the issue when he concentrated on the growth in the budget deficit, a prospect he clearly feared more than unemployment. In addition he remained opposed to any strong interventionist action:

> And if the Federal government went into the countercyclical business on a huge basis, there would be inflation such as the country had never had before. So, he felt, it was imperative to channel hysteria and demagoguery into areas where 'we' can exert some reasonable control. One way to do this is by keeping the States to the forefront.

To do this might reaffirm Eisenhower's own conservative convictions, yet public opinion ran strongly against the party. It was reported in April that unemployment had become the main concern in many parts of the country, while Charles Halleck concluded at the same time that the Republican Party was 'in serious political trouble' and predicted that the political impact would be worse than in 1954.[72]

The recession was over by the end of the summer and attention quickly returned to the problem of inflation. However, the political damage had been done and the Republican Party experienced serious reverses in the 1958 midterm elections. Samuel Lubell concluded that a number of factors contributed to the Republican set-back, including Sputnik, Little Rock and the recession. However, he cautioned at limiting the analysis to these immediate factors, urging that the electorate itself had changed. Unlike his earlier analysis, which stressed the desire for stability, he now drew attention to 'the strange new restlessness of the American voter, which has quickened voting change to a tempo never before known in our history'.[73] John Hamlin, Executive Assistant in the White House, doubted that inflation or the threat of it had been a major constraint on the economy, arguing that in so far as inflation had taken place this could be attributed to service costs rather than to wage increases. The real dilemma for the government, he inferred, was its opposition to expanding federal expenditure both on principle and in general. According to Hamlin the Administration had 'accomplished the double misfortune of alienating the conservatives without winning the liberals.' In effect the Administration was not expansionary enough for those Democrats affected by the recession or dependent on federal support, while at the same time the expanding federal budget alienated the conservatives.[74]

Eisenhower also expressed disappointment at the outcome. In a conversation with Harold Macmillan he criticised the 'desire of the people of our country to depend more and more upon the government'. This attitude helps to explain the Republican defeat, but this he believed was not positive as the electorate 'do not seem to understand that more governmental assistance inevitably means more governmental control'. In response to this and other discussions with Nixon and the defeated Knowland, among others, Eisenhower sought to consolidate the party to prepare for the 1960 election. Eisenhower appears to have concluded that the difficulty was organisational, and partly financial, whereas his remarks identify a deeper and more political problem.[75] Jim Hagerty, the presidential press secretary, suggested an approach which stressed national defence and the communist threat, while linking these concerns to domestic policy. Thus fiscal responsibility, he suggested, should be closely linked to the avoidance of national bankruptcy, which deficit spending and inflation would promote. Hagerty invoked the Roman concept of the President as the 'Tribune of the People', urging Eisenhower to promote specific issues 'over the heads of Congress', and consequently lead a debate rather than respond to it. Hagerty was not recommending new policies, but insisted that the President promote existing ones more forcefully. It was imperative, he added, that this presentation should be structured in terms of the national interest:

> I do not think that there is a general realization that the programs the President proposes are not for his own personal aggrandizement or political gain but rather for the American people as a whole.[76]

Harold Stassen offered a more pessimistic assessment, stressing the distance opening up between the Republican Party and the electorate. He emphasised that while Eisenhower remained a popular president the party itself had been 'decisively rejected' in three consecutive congressional elections. This decline would continue unless Eisenhower recognised that the Republican Party leadership was hostile to the policies being pursued by the Administration:

> I do not believe that you realize the extent to which the official Republican Party machinery has endeavored to foreclose all other considerations except the nomination of Richard Nixon, and the extent to which the great majority of the people of the country have rejected this programme.[77]

Stassen's attempt to distance the President's policies from those of the Republican Party are disingenuous and probably owes more to his hostility to Nixon than to political reality. Prior to the 1958 election Meade Alcorn had circulated a memo, drawn up after prior Cabinet agreement, which focused on the major issues to be confronted. Alcorn's election tactic was to expose liberal dominance of the Democratic Party, and to reiterate the dangers of deficit spending in macro-economic policy. There was no dissent from Eisenhower for this approach. In a post-election analysis for the President, Alcorn confessed his irritation at the outcome. While noting that there were a number of explanations for the reverses, he highlighted the fact that economic 'recovery came too late to aid us politically'. Despite persistently better economic conditions under the Eisenhower Administration than had prevailed under the previous Democratic Administration, the electorate rejected the record of the Administration and the party. 'This is a political phenomenon for which I have been given no plausible explanation.' While this may be so, there are a number of factors which contributed to the negative outcome for the party. In many areas Democratic success was strongly correlated with high levels of unemployment, urban constituencies and strong support from labour. Alcorn cites the Indiana case to demonstrate the effect. What is striking about the 1958 election is that it is not just a mid-term swing but seems to be, as Lubell claimed, a more open and decisive rejection of the philosophy of caution and stability which had prevailed since 1950. Though the elections did not change the seniority system in Congress, it did shift the balance to the left within the Democratic Party and placed the two major parties further to the ends of their respective ideological spectrum than before.[78]

Eisenhower believed that he had become more conservative during his second administration. There is in fact little evidence for this assertion, his administration is no more conservative between 1959 and 1961 than it had been between 1953 and 1955. On most issues, but especially on economic policy, there is a strong element of continuity throughout his eight years in office. What does happen is that the Administration finds itself under policy siege during its last two years. Whereas between 1953 and 1958 Eisenhower could depend on a 'conservative coalition' in Congress to achieve his objectives, or to prevent the realisation of policies to which he was opposed, this proved more difficult after November 1958. What had occurred was that Congress and public opinion had become more liberal, while Eisenhower remained conservative and the conservative nature of his policies became more public and contested. Despite Hagerty's best efforts Eisenhower was unable to promote his policies in such a way that they could be presented in national rather than partisan terms. The result was policy stalemate with the President using his veto to neutralise liberal legislation from Congress.[79]

Despite the growing evidence that public opinion welcomed greater activity on the part of the Administration, Eisenhower was not prepared to change his fundamental approach. He remained obsessed with the national debt, believing that an upturn in the economy justified paying it off. In this context he asserted in 1959: 'Perhaps the time had come for the government to stop trying to provide the best possible services in such things as delivery of the mail or anything else not absolutely necessary.' Eisenhower took a particularly strong line on taxation, arguing that an increase could be justified only as a means to reduce the national debt. The main focus for concern remained inflation and credit-led consumer spending which it was believed contributed to this.[80] These themes were reiterated both privately and publicly during the election year. Saulnier, in particular, urged the need to break what he described as the 'inflation psychology' with high interest rates. While reporting that the federal budget was now in surplus once again, Saulnier concluded that there would be significant advances during the coming year. Nor, he asserted, could one conclude from the evidence that the economy was experiencing a recession. On the contrary most of the economic indicators were positive, despite some adverse international and domestic factors (such as the summit failure, Cuba, racial problems and the talk of recession itself). This in turn led the Administration to condemn John Kennedy's economic policy, arguing that his policies and those of the Democratic Party would have serious inflationary consequences.[81] The Republican Party may have feared Kennedy's liberalism but public opinion appeared to be running in favour of the Democrats: 46 per cent of those interviewed in July believed that the Democrats would do a better job of keeping the country prosperous, while only 26 per cent believed the Republicans could do so.[82]

Moral Politics and Conservatism

Public opinion changes slowly in democracies and politicians need to accommodate both the changes and the elements of continuity. A fine line will usually be drawn in the search for advantage. Arthur Schlesinger Jr condemned the Eisenhower presidency on the grounds that it lacked moral purpose, and that 'moral leadership' should be a central dimension of the modern presidency. Likewise after the 1958 elections Hagerty urged Eisenhower to pursue an active civil rights policy because it is 'one of the great moral issues here at home'.[83] Eisenhower proved unwilling to pursue such a course of action and this rests uneasily with his claim to be devising a form of 'moderate republicanism'. It was not difficult for Eisenhower to generate a political coalition around his policies on defence, communism or indeed, for most of his time in office, on economic issues. The administration was criticised on particular issues of policy, but in general terms the political distance between the Democrats and the Republicans was not wide during the 1950s. McCarthyism and civil rights are qualitatively different questions and highlight on the one hand the strong authoritarian streak in Republican politics, while on the other there is, at the very least, a residual racism. One reason for Eisenhower's equivocation on these two issues relates to his policy style. As Greenstein has argued Eisenhower did not seek to be overtly partisan in his presidency: this was due in part to his dependence on Democratic support in Congress, but more importantly because of what he believed to be the nature of the presidency itself. Presidential politics for Eisenhower had to be couched in national terms eschewing any direct partisan appeal. In public at least his 'discourse was scrupulously not political'.[84]

This in itself was a political tactic which had conservative consequences. It could be used to justify inaction on domestic issues, as well as demanding cross-party support for the President's actions on foreign policy. On domestic issues the appeal to non-partisanship and national interest was not easy to sustain, as Eisenhower's growing irritation with the Democrats after 1958 demonstrates. This appeal can also be understood as a method of deflecting progressive domestic reform. If it is necessary to get wide-ranging agreement on an issue, then it is more likely that the *status quo* will be maintained. However, his increasing use of the veto after 1958 reflects Eisenhower's unwillingness to support legislation with which he disagreed.[85] His response to educational reform is a case in point. In certain circumstances, particularly when security was involved, Eisenhower could be persuaded to act, on virtually all other occasions when pure educational considerations were involved he prevaricated.[86] This is the limit of the non-partisan Eisenhower on social and economic issues. He remained committed to maintaining the line at the point when he entered office in 1953. This is part of the trade-off between left and right and is to be expected in any democratic system. However, it is a more serious question when the President is confronted with a divisive matter of principle in which major interests are involved. When Eisenhower had to take sides on an issue which divided the society he consistently refused to do so. In these circumstances his non-partisan stance disguised what was in effect a partisan position on the question, though it should be recognised that on McCarthyism or civil rights he did not publicly acknowledge his conservative position.

Eisenhower once described himself as 'liberal on human issues, conservative on economic ones', and while the latter claim is true the former is open to question.[87] If the cold war is interpreted as a struggle between two irreconcilable powers for dominance, then perhaps being liberal on security issues would be a luxury that a president could not afford to indulge in. Under threat from Communism internationally, the inclination to silence American communists and to harass them might be understandable. Nor is American behaviour exceptional at this time. Anti-communism was a central prop in most conservative ideologies in Western Europe. The Communist Party was outlawed in the Federal Republic of Germany, while the PCI was harassed by the Italian state until well into the 1960s. Yet this does not provide an adequate explanation for Eisenhower's refusal to publicly condemn McCarthy. Certainly he did not believe American Communists were a threat; he revealed to Churchill in 1954 that the government could detain most of the estimated 25 000 Communists without difficulty. He also acknowledged that Robert Oppenheimer, the controversial physicist, was not disloyal. Despite this and his statement (in private) the same year that 'I've made up my mind you can't do business with Joe and to hell with any attempt to compromise', Eisenhower never sought to publicise these views or to influence public opinion against McCarthy. He publicly identified with and appeared to endorse the prevailing right-wing ethos.[88]

There are a number of factors which contributed to Eisenhower's actions at this time. The first is very simply that Eisenhower's world view was permeated by anti-communism, a view shared by large sectors of an American public who certainly accepted a number of McCarthy's claims concerning communist penetration of government. Also McCarthyism and anti-communist witch-hunting was popular in the Republican Party and among administration officials. Nixon and Jerry Parsons counselled against presidential attacks on McCarthy, believing that he could be reconciled to the Administration.[89] Eisenhower appears to have had little concern for civil liberties in this area of government. The 1954 Communist Control Act accepted the McCarthyite version of the communist threat to the security of the United States. In contrast to the Truman administration, Eisenhower shifted the emphasis from loyalty to security; any individual could be a security risk without necessarily being disloyal. Oppenheimer is investigated and dismissed under pressure from McCarthy, and not from any belief in his disloyalty. The Truman administration may have initiated the original loyalty programmes, but they did so under pressure from their right, whereas the Republican administration entered into this with enthusiasm. Eisenhower's reluctance to act against McCarthy had little to do with a hidden hand strategy, as suggested by Greenstein, and more to do with the balance of power within the Republican Party. McCarthy's attack on Communists in government had been convenient when the Democrats were in office, but it became an embarrassment when Eisenhower won in 1952. There was also an ideological overlap between McCarthy and mainstream Republicanism represented by Eisenhower. The President may have disliked McCarthy, but he was in sympathy with the ideology which the latter promoted. Eisenhower's refusal to act decisively against McCarthy legitimised his approach to politics and reinforced a belief among the public that there were Communists in government, undermining the morale of public employees and their civil liberties. In this the classic conservative priorities come into play; sustaining order had primacy over liberty.[90]

Eisenhower evaded action until he was compelled to move by McCarthy's actions. It is only when McCarthy questioned the integrity of the military and challenged the prerogatives of the presidency that Eisenhower acted; even then it was a minimalist approach to a political threat rather than a principled defence of civil liberties. Eisenhower's behaviour on the issue is reactive, there is much private discussion and heart-searching, but action is taken only when the Administration is threatened. It is surely no coincidence that Eisenhower takes a more active interest in undermining McCarthy only after receiving a letter from Lodge:

> The Senatorial investigation of the army, while ostensibly aimed at making sure that the army is secure against communist penetration, is actually a part of an attempt to destroy you politically and it is wishful thinking, as well as imprudent, not to proceed on this assumption.

Lodge warned that public confidence in the army could be damaged, but conceded the substance of the McCarthy case by recommending that every department of government be put in order 'to meet a McCarthy type of investigation'.[91]

While there is room for some ambiguity and doubt concerning Eisenhower's stand on individual civil liberties and the McCarthy issue, there can be none on the question of civil rights. Here was an issue which was clear-cut after the Supreme Court issued its decisions in 1954, and it was a question which the Republican Party had been traditionally associated with the liberal view. Ambrose suggests that on civil rights Eisenhower was moderate or middle of the road, an evaluation which the President would have endorsed. Just prior to the 1960 election he affirmed that 'his administration had an excellent record on civil rights, that it had made the practical moves that were possible and desirable'.[92] This is not a claim that can easily be sustained. Eisenhower proved to be consistently unsympathetic to the demands for civil rights expressed by black Americans. His action (or inaction) may have prevented change on occasions, such as when he vetoed the Attorney General's request to provide an opinion on segregation to the Supreme Court. Nor was he anxious to pressurise white southerners into positive action on segregation.[93] Eisenhower's sympathies were clear even before the Supreme Court verdict in 1954, and thereafter he distanced his administration from it and its consequences. Gallup found in 1954 that a majority of those outside the South approved of the Supreme Court decision, but over 70 per cent of southern whites disapproved.[94] The President took a minimalist approach to desegregation, and at no time between 1954 and 1961 did he offer positive support for the integration of the black community into the mainstream of American life. His public remarks were such that the white South had some justification for believing that he actively supported their cause. In 1957 for example he seems to have publicly and deliberately called for the emasculation of the Administration's own civil rights legislation, an invitation quickly taken up by the Senate.[95]

Eisenhower's dilemma was that of a conservative leader unable to deal with an issue which was challenging the *status quo*. If he acted decisively he would undermine the stability which he was seeking to protect and therefore promote change which would have further destabilising consequences. In addition, Eisenhower held a very restricted view of the role of the federal government on such occasions. He believed that the government should not play an active role in ending segregation. In addition, the Republican Party was, in his opinion, now the party of states' rights; while on the issue of segregation he considered himself to be, 'more of a "States Righter" than the Supreme Court'.[96] Prior to the Republican Convention in 1956, Eisenhower insisted that the platform document be amended in order that his administration should not be directly associated with the Court decision; indeed, he threatened to boycott the convention if this was not done.[97] When the Little Rock confrontation occurred the President at first attempted to ignore the issue, only reluctantly committing troops to protect the school children. That he did so at all can be accounted for by his recognition that the Governor of Arkansas had not complied with a court order, not from any lack of sympathy with the objections raised by the white South. As he subsequently put it:

> A situation arose in Little Rock that distresses me as much as it does you. Many thoughtful Americans agree with you as to the unwisdom of the 1954 decision of the Supreme Court. But those Americans . . . respect our laws and know they must be obeyed. Those Governors emphatically agreed that I, as President had a *duty* of making certain that the Court's order was not obstructed.

This was the limit of Eisenhower's support for desegregation. He was however at pains to insist that he was acting because the constitution impelled him to:

> My biggest problem had been to make people see, particularly in the south, that my main interest is not in the integration or segregation question. My opinion as to the wisdom of the decision or the timeliness of the Supreme Court's decision has nothing to do with the case.'[98]

This type of response is similar to his actions on the McCarthy case and indeed on the economy. This is characterised by a reluctance to become involved; such involvement only occurring when he is forced to do so by other events. That he was forced to act on the issue of segregation simply highlights the seriousness of the problem to which Eisenhower's own prevarication contributed.

Eisenhower retained the opinion that the Court had acted precipitously on desegregation, yet a case could be made that this reflected the unwillingness of a politician to act. His distaste for judicial activism reflected a deeper unease concerning the relationship between political change and human nature. In 1959 he argued that: 'Coercive law is powerless to bring about [integration] when in any extensive region the great mass of public opinion is in bitter opposition.' This is an appeal to prejudice in the sense used by Burke and the nineteenth century conservatives, but it is also close to the sentiments being expressed by contemporary intellectual conservatives both on this specific issue, and on more general issues of the relationship between politics and community. Eisenhower was effectively claiming that any belief is acceptable if a majority believes it strongly enough: 'Law is not going to do it. We have never stopped sin by passing law; and in the same way, we are not going to take a great moral idea and achieve it merely by law.' While this is surely true it evades the more important question of what to do to address what was commonly believed to be a wrong. To accept that those who had perpetrated the wrong should be allowed to continue in the behaviour because of their strength of belief on the issue seems to pre-empt any possibility of change.[99] It is not as if Eisenhower was lacking in advice on this issue from his political associates: Brownell, Mitchell and to a lesser extent Nixon were in favour of an activist policy on civil rights, yet the President chose to ignore this and to associate with the right-wing of the party and with racist sentiment generally.

Conclusion

The difficulty for Eisenhower and the Republican Party by 1960 was quite simply that whereas they had addressed a desire for stability in 1952 and for change which would reinforce stability, this was no longer the case by the end of the decade. It is difficult to judge whether the American public had become more liberal in sentiment during Eisenhower's two terms. Ideological disposition is a complex phenomenon and individuals can hold what appears to be contrary views with relative ease. What had changed however was that sections of the public believed that change was necessary on a number of issues. The most volatile was segregation, but the economy, defence and the Soviet Union were also issues of deep concern. Eisenhower was ill equipped to mediate these new problems, because they required innovation not passivity. He may have been the appropriate president in 1953, but by 1961 his conservatism did not address the issues of the day.

This does not mean that the American public had become more liberal by 1960, indeed the available evidence suggests that opinion on most issues remained remarkably stable until the mid-1960s. Change can be detected on the issue of segregation, whereas on communism, military strength, government size and levels of taxation what might be described as the conservative position continued to be dominant.[100] The 1960 election between Kennedy and Nixon was a contest between liberal and conservative, but one in which each side modified its ideological appeal considerably. Whereas Nixon played down his right-wing identity, Kennedy had to be careful not to appear too liberal or left wing. The Democrats carefully nuanced strategy on race, and the economy and welfare had a liberal edge, but one marked by conservative rhetoric on the Soviet Union and the missile gap. In so far as a liberal constituency existed in 1960 for Kennedy, it was a weak and porous one. The narrow victory over Nixon demonstrated Kennedy's political weakness in what, despite the Republican defeat, was an environment still influenced by Eisenhower's conservatism.

Notes

1. Byron E. Shafer (ed.), *Is America Different?* (Oxford: Clarendon Press, 1991), for recent assessments of the exceptional thesis.
2. Alonzo L. Hamby, *Beyond the New Deal: Harry S. Truman and American Liberalism* (New York: Columbia University Press, 1973); Susan M. Hartman, *Truman and the 80th Congress* (Columbia: University of Missouri Press, 1971); Michael J. Lacey, (ed.), *The Truman Presidency* (Cambridge: Cambridge University Press, 1989).
3. Robert Griffith, 'Why they liked Ike', *Reviews in American History* 7:4 (1979), pp. 577–83, 583.

4. Samuel A. Stouffer, *Communism, Conformity and Civil Liberties* (Garden City, New York: Doubleday, 1955); George H. Gallup, *The Gallup Poll: Public Opinion 1935–1971* (3 vols), volume 2, *1949–1958* (New York: Random House, 1972), passim on opinion during this period.
5. Gallup, op. cit., pp. 901–05.
6. Samuel Lubbell, *Revolt of the Moderates* (New York: Harper, 1956), p. 3.
7. Fred I. Greenstein, *The Hidden-Hand Presidency* (New York: Basic Books, 1982).
8. DDE presidential Papers: Name series, Box 5, Eisenhower to Brigadier General Chynewith July 20 1954, which is a reply to letter of July 5 1954.
9. Barry M. Goldwater, *Goldwater* (New York: Doubleday, 1988), pp. 99–100.
10. DDE presidential papers: Name series, Box 11, Eisenhower to Edgar Eisenhower, 8 November 1954.
11. DDE presidential papers: Diary series, Box 3, Eisenhower to Milton Eisenhower, 9 October 1953. Eisenhower noted the retention of Excess Profits Tax, the outcome of the Immigration Bill and the Reciprocal Trade Act as examples of this. Nor would he make commitments to attend specifically partisan meetings on the grounds that 'the President is the President of everybody in the United States', adding significantly, 'and we need Democratic votes to win in most states just because there aren't enough Republicans'. Diary series, Box 3, Eisenhower to Milton Eisenhower, 21 October 1953 minute of meeting with Republican delegation from Michigan.
12. DDE presidential papers: Diary series, Box 3, Eisenhower to E.F. Hutton, 7 October 1953. Emphasis mine.
13. Ibid., Eisenhower to George Whitney, 24 June 1953.
14. Ibid., Eisenhower to William Phillips, 15 June 1953. Robert Griffith, 'Dwight D. Eisenhower and the Corporate Commonwealth', *American Historical Review* 87 (February 1982). Eisenhower was quick to contrast his position with that of Roosevelt, who at all times was leader of a majority party. Eisenhower was placed in the more difficult position of being a leader without the support of that majority:

   As of today, every measure that we deem essential to the progress and welfare of America normally requires Democratic support in varying degrees. I think it is fair to say that, in this situation, only a leadership that is based on honesty of purpose, calmness and inexhaustible patience in conference and persuasion, and refusal to be diverted from basic principles can, in the long run, win out.

   It was not, therefore, just the need to accommodate the opposition, but a belief that this was the most appropriate method of achieving the ends of his administration.
15. DDE presidential papers: Diary series, 4 February 1957. See also the analysis of the different usages of the term liberal in Samuel H. Beer, 'Liberalism and the national idea', in Robert A. Goldwin, *Left, Right and Center* (New York: Rand McNally, 1965), pp. 142–69.
16. DDE presidential papers: Administrative series, Eisenhower to Meade Alcorn, 30 August 1957.
17. DDE presidential papers: Name series, Eisenhower to Edgar Eisenhower, 2 May 1956. Although he at times played with the idea of starting a new party this was more a product of irritation over specific issues than a well thought out strategy on Eisenhower's part. Indeed he recorded his annoyance at the interpretation rendered by the press of his concept of 'modern Republicanism'. He believed it had been used by those anxious to divide the party and to highlight 'non-existent' wings of the party. (Eisenhower to Alcorn, 30 August 1957). See also Sherman Adams, *First-Hand Report* (London: Hutchinson, 1962), p.39.
18. DDE presidential papers: Administrative series, copy of speech 'Modern conservatism', Gabriel Hauge, 6 May 1955; Eisenhower to Hauge, 23 May 1955.
19. DDE presidential papers: Name series, Eisenhower to Edgar Eisenhower, 2 May 1956.

20. Stephen E. Ambrose, *Eisenhower, The President* (London: George Allen and Unwin, 1984), pp. 56, 68–9, 76.
21. DDE presidential papers: Administration series, Box 23, Lodge to Eisenhower, November 1953. See also memo by Lodge, 15 October 1953, which concentrates on the same themes. Lodge remained critical of the Republican National Committee: 'Main criticism of RNC is that it doesn't know what its function is. – It is in fact to promote the President – when an Eisenhower Democrat is elected in opposition to a Republican mossback – that certainly does not mean "we are in trouble". Administration series, Box 23. Lodge to Eisenhower, 30 December 1953.
22. DDE presidential papers: Diary series, Box 2, Eisenhower meeting with Governor Statten of Illinois with reference to the Senate candidature of Joseph T. Meek, 27 April 1953. The following day there was a meeting between the President and Meek, where the candidate gave Eisenhower the undertakings he required.
23. DDE presidential papers: Administrative series, Box 9, Arthur F. Burns to Eisenhower, 9 March 1954. Burns was the chairman of the Committee of Economic Advisors and a close confidant of the President. For discussions on the recession see Ambrose op. cit., pp. 24, 90, 158; Adams, op. cit., pp. 138–9. James L. Sundquist, *Politics and Policy: The Eisenhower, Kennedy and Johnson Years* (Washington DC: Brookings Institution, 1968), pp. 15–20.
24. Samuel Lubell, op. cit., pp. 126–9 provides a useful picture of Humphrey and his views. DDE presidential papers: Diary series, Box 3, Humphrey to Eisenhower, 26 October 1953, on the options for the forthcoming budget.
25. DDE presidential papers: Administrative series, Box 9, Eisenhower to Burns, 2 February 1954.
26. DDE presidential papers: Administrative series, Box 23, Lodge to Eisenhower, 16 February 1954; 19 February 1954. In a note sent to the President the previous year, Lodge had remarked that inflation remained popular with many groups in society and it would be difficult to adjudicate the contending claims on government expenditure which in turn were based on often incompatible demands: 'The farmer wants a low cost of living; industry wants high profits; and the well to do want tax reduction.' Diary series, Box 3, memorandum, 15 October 1953.
27. Eisenhower Presidential Library: Burns Papers, Box 99, Interdepartmental Committee: Advisory Board on Economic Growth and Stability, minutes 1 April 1954. The following day Burns presented the same set of proposals to the Cabinet, adding significantly that 'such activities, however, should be supplementary to rather than competitive with private enterprise'. DDE presidential papers: Name series, notes Burns to Cabinet, 2 April 1954.
28. DDE presidential papers: Name series, notes Burns to Cabinet, 2 April 1954.
29. Gallup vol. 2, op. cit., pp. 1207–23; 1257.
30. DDE presidential papers, Cabinet series, Box 2, 25 September 1953 for exchange; Box 3, 12, 19, 26 March 1954; 30 April ; 14, 21 May for detailed discussion of the recession as well as decisions taken.
31. DDE presidential papers: Name series, David McDonald to Eisenhower, 5 April 1954.
32. DDE presidential papers: Campaign series, Box 2, 'Public opinion survey on political Issues, 1954', no date but from internal evidence late 1954 or early 1955 at latest.
33. DDE presidential papers: Administration series, Box 23, Lodge to Eisenhower, 30 July 1954; John W. Sloan, *Eisenhower and the Management of Prosperity* (Lawrence: University Press of Kansas, 1991), for an evaluation of the impact of economic policy on Eisenhower.
34. DDE presidential papers: Cabinet series, Box 4, 5 November 1954.
35. DDE presidential papers: Administrative series, Box 9, Burns to Eisenhower, 7

November 1956.
36. Ibid., Burns to Eisenhower, 'Some facts on the current economic situation in the United States', 22 October 1956; Burns to Eisenhower, 'Three years of prosperity', 17 August 1956. Burns figures on the percentage of families and individuals owning certain consumer items are as follows:

	1952 (%)	1955 (%)
Automobiles	65	71
TV	38.5	76
Fridge	86.7	94.1
Vacuum cleaner	57.7	64.3
Electrical washers	73.5	84.1
Freezer	9.3	16.8

37. Adams, op. cit., pp. 138–9.
38. DDE presidential papers: Hall papers, Box 127, 'Public opinion index', September 1955, Tables A–32; A–41, A–44.
39. Sundquist, op. cit., p. 20 points out that not only did the Democratic Party not have an alternative policy in 1954, but Democratic victories in that election were extremely narrow, perhaps confirming Nixon's analysis.
40. DDE presidential papers: Administration series, Eisenhower to Hauge, 4 February 1953.
41. DDE presidential papers: Diary series, Box 3, Eisenhower to Gruenther, 4 May 1953.
42. Ambrose, op. cit., pp. 394, 433.
43. DDE presidential papers: Administrative series, Box 18, Hauge to Eisenhower 13 November 1952, on conservative appointments. Saulnier papers: Box 6, Saulnier to Hauge, 15 December 1952; memo by Saulnier on future of CEA, 21 November 1952. For a discussion on the CEA, E.C. Hargrave and S.A. Morley (eds), *The President and the Council of Economic Advisers: Interviews with CEA Chairmen* (Boulder, Colo.: Westview, 1984).
44. Saulnier Papers: Box 6, 'The broad strategy of economic policy in the present (February 1953) situation'; 'Long range economic goals and how to achieve them', 3 December 1954 for a discussion of the conditions necessary for growth after the recession.
45. Diary series, Box 3, 'Memo for Director of the Bureau of Budget' 5 November 1953.
46. Administrative series, Box 18, Hauge to Eisenhower, 11 November 1953. For a detailed discussion on the Administration's strategy for controlling spending and the extent to which this was successful, Iwan Morgan, *Eisenhower Versus the Spenders* (London: Pinter, 1989); Sloan, op. cit., pp. 133–43.
47. Griffiths, 'Eisenhower and the corporate commonwealth', op. cit.
48. Hauge Papers, Box 1, Hauge to Humphrey, 16 October 1954: 'The economy is operating at high levels but we must do better. We must move forward to find more jobs and to improve living standards.' Hauge also insisted that if growth could not be assured without 'a military WPA' then 'we had better turn in our suits right now'. Ibid., Hauge to Humphrey, 25 March, 1953.
49. Adams, op. cit., pp. 20–21; Ambrose, op. cit., pp. 116–18; Mitchell papers, Box, 106, Taft-Hartley Act, Revisions. Letter by Eisenhower 16 October 1953 on need for possible changes. The file includes a number of speeches by Mitchell on this question, but also reflects a shift away from possible amendments to focus on corruption within unions.
50. Name series, Box 26, Eisenhower to Robert Clifford, December 7 1954; Legislative Meetings: Box 2. 21 June 1955. Barry Goldwater dates his disillusionment with Eisenhower to this time and claims that in reality there was no difference between the Democratic and Republican administrations (Goldwater, op. cit., pp. 99, 109).

51. Reichard, *The Reaffirmation of Republicanism* (Knoxville: University of Tennessee, 1975) for a detailed discussion; Ambrose, op. cit., p. 116; D.D. Eisenhower, *Waging Peace* (New York: Doubleday, 1965), pp. 461–62.
52. Diary series, Eisenhower to G. Whitney, 24 June 1953. For a theoretical analysis of the policy choices involved, Douglas A. Hibbs, jr, 'Political parties and macroeconomic policy', *American Political Science Review* 71:4 (1977), pp. 1467–87.
53. Areeda papers, Box 6, Eisenhower to R.F. Rich, 8 July 1957; Diary series, Eisenhower to F. Altschul, 25 October 1957.
54. Administration series, Box 18, Hauge to Eisenhower commending Henry C. Wallich's article 'Eisenhower economics', and Eisenhower comment on this 7 September 1956.
55. Cabinet series, Box 5, 30 September 1955.
56. Administration series, Box 9, Burns to Eisenhower, 17 August 1956.
57. These data derived from *Public Opinion Index for Industry*, September 1955, Hall papers, Box 127, Polls 1955/40.
58. Saulnier papers, Box 6, 'Long range economic goals', 3 December 1954.
59. Stein, op. cit., p. 418. Saulnier papers, Box 6, 11 March 1957, expressing concern at expenditure and the need to control it.
60. Administrative series, Box 18, Hauge to Eisenhower, 20 June 1957; Hauge memorandum on *The Affluent Society* to Eisenhower, 3 September 1958.
61. Ibid., Hauge to Eisenhower, 28 July 1956.
62. Administration series, Box 9, Burns to Eisenhower, 1 August 1955.
63. Administration series, Box 9, Burns to Eisenhower, 10 July 1956; Stassen to Eisenhower 1 June 1956, Burns to Eisenhower, 25 June 1956, Burns to Eisenhower 15 October 1956, on easing of credit restrictions.
64. Mitchell papers, Political series, Box 186, polls and analysis for the 1956 elections.
65. Ibid., '1956 Campaign Issues.'
66. Administration series, Box 9, Burns to Eisenhower, 26 March 1957.
67. Administration series, Box 7, Notes on meeting, 7 October 1957.
68. Ibid., Saulnier to Eisenhower, 6 December 1957. Cabinet series, Box 9, 18 October 1957. In November General Bragdon was authorised to prepare plans for public works which could be implemented in the event of further deterioration (Ibid., Box 10, 15 November 1957).
69. Central files, Box 18, Saulnier to Adams, 20 December 1957; Administration series, Box 29, Mitchell to Eisenhower with memo on recession, no date but from content mid-December 1957.
70. Administration series, Box 29, Hauge to Adams, 28 January 1958, Name series, Dwight McDonald, United Steel Workers of America to Eisenhower, 9 September 1958; Eisenhower to McDonald, 24 September1958, where he promises nothing and claims that the economic situation is improving; Sloan, op. cit., pp.143–51.
71. Saulnier papers, Box 11, 'Employment and unemployment in March 1958'.
72. Legislative Meetings, Box 3, 25 February, 11, 25 March, 15 April 1958. Those present usually included, in addition to Eisenhower, Halleck, Knowland and Leverett Salstonstall.
73. Merriam papers, Box 11, *Saturday Evening Post*, 14 February 1959. Lubell adds that the most significant factor may have been the failure to control inflation.
74. Merriam Records, Box 5, Hamlin to Merriam, 6 November. 1958.
75. Diary series, Box 10, Eisenhower and Macmillan, 11 November 1958; Name series, Box 26, 'Memo for the Record'. 9 December 1958.
76. Name series, Box 26, Hagerty to Eisenhower, 9 December 1958.
77. Diary series, Box 26, Stassen to Eisenhower, 15 December, 1958.
78. Administration series, Box 1, Alcorn to Eisenhower, memo 2 September 1958

drawing on Cabinet discussion 28 August 1958; ibid., Alcorn to Eisenhower, 29 September 1958; Memo 'Observations on the 1958 Election', 15 December 1958. For an authoritative assessment of the impact of the 1958 elections, Sundquist, op. cit., pp. 441–66.

79. Adams, op. cit., p. 247 where he cites Eisenhower on Conservatism; Sundquist, ibid.; Ambrose op. cit., p. 460.
80. Cabinet series, Box 14, 22 June 1959; 11 November. 1959.
81. Administration series, Box 32, Saulnier to Eisenhower 6 October. 1960; Saulnier papers, Box 6, file 4 'Notes on economic development', October 1960.
82. George Gallup, *The Gallup Poll: Public opinions 1935–1971* (3 vols), volume 3, *1959–1971* (New York: Random House, 1972), p. 1676. This did not mean that opinion was moving in a uniformly liberal direction. Opinion was finely balanced during the 1960 campaign between moderate and conservative views: William G. Mayer, *The Changing American Mind: How and Why American Public Opinion Changed between 1960 and 1988* (Ann Arbor: University of Michigan Press, 1992).
83. Arthur M. Schlesinger Jr, *The Cycles of American History* (London: Penguin, 1989), p. 389; Name series, Box 26, Hagerty to Eisenhower, 9 December 1958; Robert Frederick Burk, *The Eisenhower Administration and Black Civil Rights* (Knoxville: University of Tennessee Press, 1984).
84. Greenstein, op. cit., p. 11.
85. Ambrose, op. cit., pp. 488–9.
86. Ambrose, op. cit., p. 250; Janet Kerr-Tener, 'Eisenhower and federal aid to higher education', *Presidential Studies Quarterly* XVII:3 (Summer 1987), pp. 473–86.
87. Ambrose, op. cit.., p. 115.
88. The conversation with Churchill is cited in W. F. Crandell, 'Eisenhower the strategist: the battle of the bulge and the censure of Joe McCarthy', *Presidential Studies Quarterly* XVII:3 (Summer 1987) pp. 487–502, 501. This article draws an unfavourable contrast between the strategies followed by Eisenhower on the second of these occasions. The other citation can be found in Greenstein, op. cit., p. 200, 24 March 1954.
89. Michael W. Miles, *The odyssey of the American right* (New York: Oxford University Press, 1980), pp. 123–221, for discussion.
90. Schlesinger, op. cit., pp. 389–92.
91. Administration series, Box 23, Lodge to Eisenhower, 23 February 1954. There are numerous explanations of the reasons for the strength of McCarthy. I have not sought to pursue them here. Status anxiety may have been a contributing factor, but a more realistic approach would be to explain it in terms of the crisis management of the immediate post–war years and the demagogy of the Republican Party during a war, as well as the irresponsibility of politicians such as Eisenhower in not standing up to McCarthy's authoritarianism.
92. Ambrose, op. cit., p. 308; Legislative meetings, Box 3, 16 August 1960.
93. Ambrose, op. cit., pp. 124–7.
94. Gallup, op. cit., pp. 1249–52.
95. Ambrose, op. cit., pp. 406–9.
96. Diary series, Box 8, Notes of conversations, 13/14 November 1956.
97. Ibid., 19 August 1956.
98. Diary series, Box 27, Eisenhower to W.T. Forbes, 8 October 1957; Eisenhower to S. Hazlett, 18 November 1957.
99. Cited in Ambrose, op. cit., pp. 528–9; these views are similar, though less ideologically structured, to those expressed in a *National Review* editorial in 1957, cited and discussed in P. Gottfried and T. Fleming, *The Conservative Movement* (Boston: Twyne, 1988), p. 10.
100. Mayer, op. cit., for a careful assessment.

7 Conservatism, the Politics of Affluence and the End of the Post-war Era, 1960–94

The Politics of Equilibrium, 1960–68

For the first time in the twentieth century, Western European states successfully institutionalised and stabilised liberal democratic representative government. By the early 1960s there was no longer any overt threat to the democratic representative system, as there had been throughout the history of representative government. A new equilibrium had been established which reinforced order and stability. The nature of this equilibrium was contingent on the resolution of the historic conflicts which had divided Europe throughout the first half of the century. This had in large part been achieved by 1960, following the conservative consolidation of European politics. Equilibrium is not inherently stable; it is more a state of balance, though in this context the bias was towards stability rather than dissonance.[1] It was in response to this equilibrium that Bell formulated the 'end of ideology' thesis, and though it has been criticised ever since, his approach does capture the fundamental changes in liberal democratic politics:

> In the Western world, therefore, there is today a rough consensus among intellectuals on political issues: the acceptance of a Welfare State; the desirability of decentralized power; a system of mixed economy and of political pluralism. In that sense, too, the ideological age has ended.[2]

The convergence between social democracy, Christian democracy and liberalism during the 1950s had ended the historic divisions between the major ideologies. In particular, the competing ideological commitments to transformation or reaction on the part of left or right had almost completely eroded. Consensus, convergence and social peace were valued, rather than the lethal conflicts of earlier decades. The end of ideology symbolises the completion of the revolutionary era which began with the French Revolution, and its inherent tendency to totalitarianism. It is most importantly the end of passionate politics, necessarily so if politics have become stable and routine (and democratic). Democratic politics requires an end to revolutionary passion and the elitism which it carries with it; indeed the history of democratisation has involved the ending of such elitist passion.[3]

A central assumption of this view is that political stability did not exist in 1945, political stability had to be re-established on new foundations. There was also uncertainty concerning the future of the European party system. By 1945 the party system in a number of states had fragmented, while the war time experiences challenged traditional alignments. The potential for disequilibrium was enormous, continuity had been broken by the war and the system had to be re-made. It is true that this was easier in some states than others but nevertheless the process was necessary. Mass electorates – some sections of which had been radicalised by the war, others traumatised – were available for mobilisation. The challenge to the political parties after the war and into the late 1950s was to attract an electorate which was more open to change than at any time since 1918, while simultaneously integrating its electorate into the democratic political process. In a number of cases this was done by new political parties with new policies by the end of the 1950s. Once that had been achieved a degree of predictability could be expected from the electorate and the parties.[4]

The second assumption and the most important one for the subsequent period is that stability is a dynamic process and not a stagnant one. Though it is possible to characterise a period or a moment as stable, the underlying process is in continuous flux. The tendency within modern political systems is in fact one of dynamic equilibrium or punctuated equilibrium which can often tend towards entropy. At certain moments there will be a convergence towards equilibrium, when the system meshes and a consensus emerges which gives expression to this stability. Built into these two assumptions is the conclusion that by 1960 a high degree of stability had been achieved in liberal democratic party systems, though there are exceptions to this claim. The form is also important, for stabilisation by 1960 was not the *status quo ante*, but a developmental sequence seeking to achieve objectives never achieved within the capitalist states.[5]

The conservative achievement in this context was considerable; the end of ideology and the post-war equilibrium had established an environment quite favourable to conservative politics. One reason for this was the flexibility of many conservative parties, but another was the positive conservative interaction with change. Left-wing parties have normally been associated with change and progress. Yet in the post-war environment, conservative parties could not simply be parties of order.[6] Conservative parties would not have survived in the post-war world without a degree of conscious motivation and intervention not normally associated with the right.

Conservative parties quickly discarded their association with the inter-war authoritarian right. By the early 1950s conservatism had revived and reformed and quickly demonstrated its capacity to compete electorally with the left.[7] Though the initiative for the post-war consensus had come from the left, in most cases conservatives accepted the changes while Christian democrats made a more positive contribution to the nature of the welfare state. However, conservatism did not merely develop an accommodationist strategy during the 1950s, it also acquired a positive appeal to the electorate. In most states economic policy was formulated by conservatives who emphasised not only economic growth and collective provision but administered both the transition from agriculture to industrial society and to affluence. By the early 1960s conservatives could benefit from association with affluence and prosperity in a large number of states. Furthermore in the form of the 'catch-all' or 'people's party', conservatives sought to widen their electoral appeal beyond their traditional right-wing or denominational electorate. In this it was successful, not only in attracting voters, but in forcing the left in a number of countries to adopt a similar appeal and strategy.[8] Conservative parties often benefit from stability and this proved to be the case during the 1950s. But in this case conservatism also contributed to the equilibrium associated with that stability. Outside of Scandinavia, Christian democratic or conservative parties remained the largest parties in most political systems, normally providing the main party for government formation, or in two-party systems ruling on their own. Indeed, by the 1960s it was possible to speculate on the waning of opposition as the differences between left and right narrowed so appreciably. Though it was an exaggeration, it did highlight the extent to which convergence existed.

The other significant feature of the early 1960s was the virtual disappearance of the radical right from the European political system. During the first half of the century authoritarian and radical right-wing parties had influenced the climate of politics in many states, but after 1950 they are noticeable by their absence. This can in part be attributed to the defeat of fascism, but an important contributory factor was the democratisation of the right and the successful mobilisation of rightist voters in support of democratic conservative parties. Indeed, by 1960 it may be inappropriate to use right-wing in its historical sense, as the main forces on the 'right' are in fact conservative parties with unquestioned support for parliamentary democracy. If historically the right is associated with opposition to modernity, capitalism and liberal democracy, this is no longer the case in principle. Conservatism becomes a critic within the system and does not engage in a principled, and lethal, rejection of the elements of modernity normally associated with 'backlash politics'. It might be urged that conservative politics now offered a guarantor of the system by its participation in it. In its various post-war forms, conservatism played a similar role to that of social democracy, providing the means to accommodate sections of the electorate which previously had a contingent view of the political system. The active participation of conservative parties in the parliamentary system helped to stabilise that system and contributed to the exclusion of extremist parties on the right in much the same way as social democracy excluded extremists on the left. Conservative politics were now intrinsic to the system and this presence guaranteed that political competition would take place within the limits of a constitutional order.

There were exceptions to this process, but the two major ones tend to confirm the general rule. While Italy fulfiled many of the criteria noted above, in one fundamental respect it did not. The Italian political system was transformed by the success of Christian democracy, by the establishment of a republican form of government and by the acceptance of a republican constitution. However, the exclusion of the Communist Party, PCI, Italy's largest opposition party, from participation in government, though not in itself undemocratic, was more reminiscent of the Dutch or Austrian inter-war political experience than the more pluralistic and tolerant convergence model of the 1950s and 1960s. Despite this, the Italian political system had stabilised by the early 1960s, in common with most other European states. However it was a stabilisation without social consensus and in this Italy differed from the general trend.[9] Likewise, the French case offers a counter-factual case to the general trend. The experience of France under the Fourth Republic, its collapse and the establishment of the Fifth Republic highlighted the difficulty of stabilising liberal democracy. Italy and France share a number of elements after the war including a high degree of governmental instability and the presence of a large communist party in permanent opposition. The striking contrast between the two states after 1945 is the extent to which Italy had a strong Christian democratic party which was the largest party in the political system, and which remained pivotal to government formation, whereas France did not. It is the absence of a strong party on the right committed to the constitutional system which distinguishes France from Italy. The stabilisation of the Italian political system, as distinct from its government, rested on the continuing willingness of the DC to administer the system. This was absent in France, though at first it appeared that the MRP could hope to bring about the democratisation and domestication of the right. This proved not to be the case and the failure of Christian democracy to become the dominant party on the right weakened the Fourth Republic.

The reason for this is Gaullism, which continued to challenge the existing constitutional structures. The contrast between France and Italy is clear on the question of government formation. The Fourth Republic and Italy had similar levels of governmental instability, yet there are significant differences. In France government formation was a reflection of political instability within the system, a weakness which the Third Force parties could never overcome except through manipulating the electoral system for their own ends. The DC attempt to manipulate the electoral system prior to the 1953 election failed in its objectives, but apparent government instability disguised a more fundamental pattern of stability in terms of the political culture and voting patterns.

The Fourth Republic in France was unable to stabilise even on the quasi-authoritarian basis represented by Italy. The actual collapse of the Republic is normally attributed to the Algerian question, but this crisis threatened the Republic because there was no conservative or right-wing anchor within the political establishment with the authority to secure the regime's legitimacy. The threat to French democracy in 1957 and 1958 came from the right.

Table 7.1 shows the extent to which electoral instability was prevalent during the Fourth Republic. The only party which maintained its vote was the PCF, and given its exclusion from the political process its contribution to stability was negligible. Table 7.2 examines the shifts on the right between 1945 and 1962 and shows the total right vote, the vote for Gaullist parties and the vote for the MRP. It also calculates the vote for the Gaullists and MRP as a percentage of the total right-wing vote. The main conclusion from these calculations is that the MRP, the main party on the right committed to democratic government within the Fourth Republic, suffered electoral eclipse between 1946 and 1958. Under pressure from its own right, and from Gaullism, the MRP proved unable to anchor Christian democracy as a major constituent part of the political system. Its appreciable weakness over this time contributed to the instabilities of the party system and contributed to the unstable nature of the right in particular. There may be some doubt whether the MRP can be considered a party of the right in a strict sense, but for electoral purposes it can be seen as competing for votes among an electorate which would be thus placed. The seriousness of the MRP's weakness

Table 7.1 France: elections, 1945–61

	*1945	*1946 (June)	1946 (November)	1951	1956	1958	1962
MRP	23.9	28.2	25.9	12.6	11.1	11.1	8.9
SFIO	23.4	21.1	17.8	14.6	15.2	15.7	12.6
Radicals	10.5	11.6	11.1	10.0	15.9	8.3	7.8
Conservatives	15.6	12.8	12.9	14.1	15.3	22.9	9.6
Gaullists	–	–	3.0	21.6	3.9	19.5	31.9
PCF	26.2	25.9	28.2	26.9	25.9	19.2	21.7

Note: * Election of a Constituent Assembly. *Source*: Rose and Mackie, 2nd edn. (1982).

can be better appreciated by an analysis of the right vote at the 1956 election, which was divided among at least four different tendencies all of which, with the exception of the MRP, were ambiguous about the Fourth Republic.[10]

The Gaullist potential had been strong but latent. De Gaulle's hostility to the Fourth Republic and his refusal to endorse it weakened the right's capacity to stabilise around the Republic. The fissionable nature of the right in electoral terms reflected both the attractions of de Gaulle and the right's own uncertainly about its commitment to democratic government. Without de Gaulle it proved impossible to generate the conditions for a stable governmental majority. In the absence of such a stable majority, the Algerian events provided the context for breakdown. De Gaulle's appeal increased as the popularity of the government diminished in the course of 1957 and 1958. Yet de Gaulle did not establish a military dictatorship as some feared. He used the threat of a *coup d'État* to undermine the Fourth Republic and establish the Fifth. By operating within the political system, but against the party system and the existing Republic he created the political conditions for establishing another system without recourse to authoritarianism.

Table 7.2 The structure of right–wing voting patterns in France, 1945–62

General Elections	Total right	MRP total	Gaullist total	MRP as % of of total right	Gaullism as a % of total right
1945	39.9	24.9	–	62.4	–
1946 (June)	41.3	28.1	–	68.0	–
1951	48.5	12.5	21.6	25.7	44.5
1956	46.5	11.1	–	23.8	–
1958	56.4	11.2	20.5	19.8	36.3
1962	55.6	8.9	31.9	16.0	57.4

Source: Johnson, adapted from Table 5.4; additional data Mackie and Rose.

Whatever misgivings there might have been about de Gaulle assuming power in May 1958, by August he received popular support from across the political spectrum, with the exception of the PCF.[11] Over the next three years de Gaulle was well placed to establish his personal supremacy, but more importantly to establish within the Fifth Republic the institutions he believed France required to have political stability. In addition, his own party the Union pour la Nouvelle République (UNR) became the dominant force in France during the 1960s. Throughout the 1960s the UNR and its successor parties captured over 30 per cent of the vote at each parliamentary election, accounting for between 55 and 63 per cent of the right's vote on these occasions. In addition to this the right increased its combined vote at parliamentary elections, but most importantly, in the light of the new constitution, at the crucial presidential elections. The left weakens appreciably in the face of the new Republic and de Gaulle's appeal. In the 1965 presidential election, de Gaulle's appeal was spread across the social spectrum. It has been noted that his support among farmers was relatively weak, whereas among the industrial working class he secured 42 per cent of their vote. He also did better among women than among men, and among the older rather than the younger. Gaullism exhibited many of the features of a catch-all party both in terms of its wide appeal and its ability to transcend traditional alignments. In this Gaullism is similar to Christian democracy elsewhere and succeeds likewise in anchoring the right in the liberal democratic system, albeit one which de Gaulle designs himself. However, Gaullism had potentially wider appeal than Christian democracy. The ideological emphasis was on nationalism rather than on denomination and consequently Gaullism could appeal in theory at least to everyone in France. The strength of Gaullism in creating a majority for the new Republic is attested to in the electoral victory for the right at the National Assembly elections in 1968 and in response to the student disorders of May and June of that year.[12]

The Return to Confrontation: 1968–74

By 1968 the historic conflict between liberalism and conservatism had been resolved in favour of the former. Whether through Christian democracy, conservatism or Gaullism the relationship between authoritarianism and conservatism ended, while the experience of the post-war decades established a new relationship between democratic constitutionalism and conservative politics. As noted earlier, in many states it was the new conservative parties which contributed to the legitimation of liberal democracy in the twenty years after 1945. However, difficulties existed for these conservative parties in the new era. Even at its most innovative, the attraction of conservatism is usually its commitment to normality, to the preservative function of politics. Thus, while displaying considerable flexibility in the face of a rapidly changing political environment, conservatism still had to maintain its ideological hold on an electorate which was often traditional. By 1968 the preservative function of conservatism outweighed any innovative one, for the parties agreed that what had been achieved between 1945 and 1968 constituted what should be preserved. Conservatives balanced precariously between innovation and preservation until the middle of the 1960s, but subsequently found it more difficult to achieve this balance.

The post-war equilibrium quickly came under strain as the decade progressed. However, as Bell pointed out in response to critics, these strains were new in terms of their social origin and the cleavages they generated. Ironically, the very changes promoted by conservatives for preservative purposes now seemed to undermine the consensus achieved by the equilibrium which the conservatives sought to facilitate.[13] Rapid change in the nature of European society raised quite fundamental questions concerning the nature of conservatism as an ideology and a political movement. Both problems are related. If conservatism had absorbed the main elements of modernity and liberalism, to what extent did conservatives differ from liberals. Alternatively, if conservatives were prepared to embrace the interventionist growth strategy of social democracy and the welfare state, what differed there as well? In the context of an end of ideology, catch-all parties and electoral competition, was there a continuing role for conservative parties, if all parties were parties of reform, was a party of order necessary? Furthermore, if a party of order was not necessary, was it possible for a conservative party to justify its existence? The danger for conservatism at this time was that if they continued to administer the welfare state and merged with the reformism of the social democrats they would cease to have a distinct ideology or political autonomy. Once conservatives had accepted democratic politics, their continuing success derived generally, though not universally, from their ability simultaneously to attract the support of its traditional electoral base and to convince them (and a significant section of floating and centrist voters) that conservative priorities rather than those of the left could achieve social and economic objectives of benefit to voters and to the society generally. The difficulty encountered by conservatives by the end of the 1960s was that electoral competition would push it to the left and alienate its core constituency while failing to attract enough voters on the left to win elections. This tension between vote maximisation and ideological maximisation was particularly strong as long as the politics of economic growth and the welfare state remained central to the post-war consensus.[14]

While the notion of a 'progressive-conservative' party may not necessarily be an oxymoron, it is a category which the right has generally eschewed. What is not expected of conservative parties is that they will promote change in a progressive fashion, a function historically of the left or radicalism. However, in the course of the 1960s conservative parties became increasingly bound by the terms of the post-war consensus which automatically presumed continuous change. There is a shift to the left in the course of the 1960s, associated as much with conservatives as the left. The 1960 Presidential campaign in the United States, though won by Kennedy, was illustrative of this. Nixon promoted a cautious reformist programme which he subsequently believed had been too conservative. In 1964 the right-wing campaign by Goldwater proved a disaster for the Republican Party due to its extremism and its repudiation of the post-war consensus. In the United Kingdom there appeared to be little to choose between the Labour Party and the Conservatives by 1964, which may be one of the reasons for the success of Labour in that election. Both parties eschewed the extremes of traditional ideology and the election was fought on instrumentalist and technocratic lines rather than on ideological ones. In Germany, the changes in the SPD after Bad Godesberg facilitated a 'waning of the opposition', which in turn lead to the Grand Coalition between the SPD and the CDU from 1966 to 1969. One of the reasons for this coalition was the belief that the prosperity associated with the post-war consensus was under threat, and that there was need for decisive action in response to it.[15] The German experience does, however, demonstrate the dangers of convergence as the coalition brought about the growth of extremist movements on the left and right. Less typically, Italy also shared in this process with the movement to centre-left governments in the early 1960s, leading in 1963 to the participation of the PSI in government for the first time since 1947. Moreover, the stabilisation of Gaullism in France also had a leftist element to it, to the extent that de Gaulle approved of economic expansion and welfare benefits for the working class. Elsewhere, the 1960s can broadly be conceived as reformist, a process which continued and expanded the original post-war changes in economic policy, welfare and social rights. Although there are differences in the way such reforms are introduced, what is important is the recognition on the part of the conservative parties that it was necessary to offer a reformist programme or face criticism by the electorate.[16]

This apparent convergence between the two main ideological blocks lasted well into the 1970s, though it came under increasing strain after 1974. Its foundations and success were based on a number of assumptions. The first was that expansion in the capitalist economy would continue into the foreseeable future and that the business cycle could be controlled if not actually abolished.[17] This condition enhanced the belief, quite widespread by the mid-1960s, that politicians and governments could and should assure prosperity and affluence. This in turn was based on the belief that the electoral differences between the parties in any given system were close and not open to radical shifts. This presumed further that social and economic change did not necessarily disrupt the political system. The evidence by the early 1970s seemed to confirm the view that long-term stability and continuity had been internalised in the European and other liberal democratic political systems.[18] Virtually every conservative party adopted policies which can be described as 'technocratic conservatism', a stance which attempted to define conservatism as modern and in line with the progressive mood of the 1960s. This development was most explicit in Germany and Austria where each of the conservative parties jettisoned the traditional association with Catholic corporatism, adopting a positive stance in relation to capitalism and the idea of economic progress. In the case of the ÖVP, Müller has noted the weakening of the party's commitment to moral conservatism, reflecting its acceptance of changes in the wider society. The 1972 Salzburg Programme adopted a more cautious relationship to modernity, yet the party could still consider itself to be 'the Party of the Progressive Centre'. This accommodation with modernity marked a decisive break with the conservative past in Germany also. Grande has noted the significance of this change:

Technocratic conservatism marked an important break with the ideological traditions of German conservatism. The conservative criticism of industry and technology, which had dominated conservative ideology since the Romantic period had been overcome and disregarding some undertones of cultural criticism, conservatism was reconciled with technology.

What is important about this accommodation in Germany, but also elsewhere, is that the initial impetus for the change comes from the success of capitalism as an expansionary force and the belief that the problems of the business cycle had been overcome. The acceptance of modernity and associated aspects of the liberal economic order was taken to be inevitable, given the nature of politics and the apparent success of economic planning. While an acceptance of capitalism did not necessarily involve the acceptance of consensus, the particular nature of the post-war order facilitated this outcome.[19]

Within the reformist consensus, it is possible to detect conservative parties reasserting a continuing commitment to order in the face of some types of change. Change without instability appeared acceptable to most conservatives by the end of the 1960s. Indeed, conservatives in many political systems continued to advance the agenda of the expansionary era. What conservatives opposed was the destabilisation which was associated with radical change. Instability or disorder were feared, while regulated change or limited progress were considered acceptable. Technological change could be justified, once conservatives were convinced that the main fabric of society would not be permanently impaired by it. In turn, once capitalism was accepted, it also proved imperative to accept technology. However to do so did not imply that all change was good or should necessarily be accepted. The conservative notion of change proved to be far more qualified that was the case for socialist politicians. The social changes consequent on economic changes raised the possibility of disorder. Conservatives successfully reasserted order in the face of radical insurgency politics at the end of the 1960s. The decisive electoral victory in 1968 confirmed the dominance of the right in French politics, marginalised the left, especially the student radicals, and led to the imposition of order after the upheavals of 1968. Likewise in the United States, Nixon's election victory was based on an appeal to order in the face of radicalism on the streets if not always in the Democratic Party. In Ireland, perhaps the most traditional liberal democratic state at this time, the incumbent government was returned to office in 1969 in part because of its emphasis on continuity and in part because it identified the Labour Party as the carrier of radicalism in a conservative state. The British election in 1970 can also be understood as a return to order by a conservative party in the light of trade union militancy and other elements of instability.[20]

Despite the successful electoral response to change on the part of conservatives, by 1970 a widespread challenge existed to liberal democratic political culture. The student movement was but one, and a minor, reflection of this challenge though its methods were confrontational and public. More particularly there was a reassertion of radical utopian objectives after two decades of 'normality'. Critics of the existing consensus argued that the 'electoral state' could not fulfil the needs or the expectations of society, which were better served by the radical transformation of the political and economic system.[21] Yet the radicalism of the 1960s was quite distinct from the old left, with its roots in Marxism and identifying with the Soviet Union. Politics and economics tended to take second place to personal authenticity, cultural expression and non-hierarchical and decentralised forms of organisation. The 'new left' absorbed the key Marxist concepts of alienation and liberation, but gave them a different, and often non-economic, interpretation. In ideological terms, revolution would bring about a fundamental rupture in the older and corrupt society which would lead to the emancipation of everyone. At the level of political practice the traditional working class was effectively ignored, because of its apparent complicity in capitalist exploitation, and utopian objectives were focused on racial, women's, gay or national liberation. Deriving its intellectual strength from the older tradition of romanticism, the new left was anti-liberal and anti-democratic as well as anti-capitalist. This is clearest in the electoral process, which was either ignored or despised by the activists. Majority electoral outcomes were ignored because a theory of false consciousness could be invoked, on the grounds that opinion was so constrained by the media or some other manipulative agency that only when true consciousness was revealed could the masses be trusted with political power. This in turn would be achieved by revolutionary action.[22]

Increasingly the liberal democratic political system moved away from the state of equilibrium stabilised at the beginning of the 1950s to one characterised by disequilibrium tending towards entropy. Political entropy occurs where change can have its greatest impact, for the routine and normal aspects of political life can be challenged while opportunities emerge which would be discounted in an age of equilibrium. Entropy is especially pronounced when the process is accompanied by a challenge to the legitimacy of the political culture and the existing governing structures.[23] Historically such periods have provided revolutionary elites with the opportunity to gain political power, the end of the Second World War being the last European example of such an opportunity. In contrast, by 1968 most liberal democratic states had experienced at least twenty years of stable constitutional government (even in the case of France ten years had elapsed). New traditions concerning the transfer of power had been absorbed by the political culture. Elections, rather than revolutionary intervention, had become the appropriate method of achieving influence and bringing about change. In the short term, the reassertion of order through elections reinforced the legitimacy of existing institutions and parties, deflecting the revolutionary urge and enthusiasm. Yet the existence of a democratic polity also meant that though radicalism may be deflected, accommodation to new forces have to be made. However, the likelihood is that accommodation will take time to work into the culture and radical change will be limited by this. In addition, the changes which do take place will be added to the existing mix within the political culture rather than transforming it in a radical fashion. Incorporation of insurgency is the main feature of democratic politics, a form of defence which limits the effectiveness of radical politics.[24]

If the conservative strategy was accommodationist, the challenge itself was radical in a number of ways, and particularly in some states. The liberal democratic structure was placed under pressure not only by the student movement, the counter-culture and by demands for greater participation, but also by labour militancy, by terrorism and by severe social upheaval in a number of cases. These and other challenges may not have been major threats to democratic government, but they did challenge the legitimacy of governing institutions. For the first time since the 1930s, significant minorities rejected the constraints imbedded in the liberal democratic political system and attempted to secure alternatives to this. Whether or not governance itself was in doubt, a new and crucial division emerged between left and right. With the consensus at an end, the left returned to its historic association with reform and change, seeking to mobilise a majority for such changes. The right, in response, insisted on the need for order and sought to generate a majority of its own. The ideological division between the left and the right widened between 1966 and 1976 as a consequence of the changes. There was also increasing disorder in many states which enhanced the polarisation. Successive British governments collapsed under pressure from trade unions, while terrorism in Northern Ireland placed a serious question mark over the future of the state. In Belgium the existence of the state was increasingly questioned as a consequence of widening divisions over language. In the United States the civil rights movement, followed by urban riots, the Vietnam war and later Watergate, contributed to doubts about government and its functions. Similar experiences can be recorded in other states, although not all were as severely challenged as these examples.[25]

In the less highly charged environment of elections, discreet changes can be seen over this decade. The period is associated with increased volatility, some dealignment though perhaps without realignment. The stability of the Danish political system was shattered in 1973 when the vote for the four major parties declined from a total of 84 per cent in 1971 to 58.4 per cent in 1973. A similar phenomenon is discernible in the Netherlands. Both the denominational block and the Social Democrat (PvdA) suffer severe losses in 1967. Though the PvdA subsequently recovers and increases its vote, the denominational parties' decline continues thereafter. In a more complex fashion the 1968 presidential election in the United States drew attention to a high level of volatility among the solid Democratic voting block in the southern states. Each of these cases demonstrated that the stable voting patterns, which had prevailed from the end of the 1940s, could no longer be assured. In a remarkably short period of time the stability associated with this was replaced by a high degree of volatility in voting patterns. Rose and Urwin found that stability had been the main feature of most electoral systems up to 1969, but subsequent research, while confirming this finding, suggested that volatility was becoming prevalent.[26]

If change and the response to it had become the predominant feature of liberal democratic states by the early 1970s, the pressures associated with these phenomena were reinforced by two additional features. The defeat of the United States in Vietnam and the crisis of the presidency associated with Watergate profoundly affected the global balance of power, or at least the perception of this balance by the major powers. American power was seen to be in decline, while that of its main antagonist, the Soviet Union, if only by default was seen to be on the increase. For most of the 1970s America's role as a global arbiter remained in doubt while the consequences of Vietnam and Watergate worked through the American political system. America's weakness was compounded by the oil crisis and the accompanying recession, circumstances which affected all industrial economies after 1974. The oil crisis was probably absorbable, but the recession questioned the capacity of governments to continue expansionary programmes which assured growth, full employment and affluence. Keynesianism, in whatever form, no longer offered the security of counter-cyclical policy to smooth out the business cycle. The prospect of affluence and growth was replaced by that of stagflation and the reality of higher inflation and unemployment. As a consequence of these two factors a strong note of uncertainty and indeed pessimism enters the intellectual culture of the industrial states. Pessimism and uncertainty about continuing economic growth also contributed to the growth of the anti-industrial environmental movement in the 1970s. Liberal democracy appeared to be challenged at a global level by the anti-liberal coalition block of communism and authoritarian nationalism in the Third World. In domestic politics, it was being challenged by the prospect of left-wing insurgency and stagflation.[27]

These threats to order, whether political, economic or global, provided an opportunity for conservatives to respond by reasserting the older values and also by asserting new ones. Yet what is surprising during the 1970s was the extent to which the post-war consensus remained in place, if in modified fashion. Overwhelmingly governments elected during this decade insisted on maintaining the main characteristic of the post-war era. In many cases left-wing governments were returned to power or continued in power. However, even when ostensibly conservative parties were in government the point of departure from the right was not significant. In the United States Nixon could declare himself a Keynesian and in the face of recession endorse expansionary policies. Although he did not maintain this policy indefinitely, he certainly sought to gain electoral advantage from a full employment policy. Nixon had clearly absorbed the post-war conservative fear that high unemployment would make him unelectable. Carter's election in 1976 was a qualified endorsement of the moderate Democratic approach to employment and the economy, and was a move to the left, albeit a narrow one in the circumstances. In the American case there is no clear evidence by the 1976 campaign that opinion had shifted to the right on the main economic issues associated with the post-war consensus and the opportunity for conservative innovation remained limited.[28]

The European experience had similarities with that of the United States, in so far as it showed the limits to conservative insurgency. In Britain Edward Heath's government in 1970 was formed on the basis of a radical restructuring of the British economy, its relationship to Europe and a more qualified approach to the main constituent parts of the post-war consensus. At first the new Conservative government appeared confrontational, questioning many of the political certainties of the previous twenty-five years. In particular, among its primary commitments was the market and a reassertion of the traditional liberal solution to British economic decline. The most remarkable aspect of this government, and perhaps its most naive aspect, was the decision not to give state aid to the so-called 'lame ducks', that is, companies which could not survive without state support or subsidies. For the best part of eighteen months the government remained intent on pursuing this course, but to widespread opposition. Increasing bankruptcy, unprecedented unemployment and labour militancy persuaded the government to change course in 1972, resulting in the so-called 'u-turn'. Within a year the original policy had been abandoned and Britain embraced a strong interventionist strategy based on reflation, wage control and corporatist intermediation.

Whatever the merits of the original policy, the new one was an attempt to extend and defend the consensus established in 1945. This involved a return to a policy framework influenced by the left rather than the right, and demonstrated the limited room for manoeuvre on the part of a conservative government at this time. However, Heath proved unable to build a corporatist majority block in Parliament, among interest groups, especially the trade unions, or in society generally. What is of interest is that the government could not sustain its original policy once unemployment was seen to rise above a psychologically unacceptable threshold. Once Heath accepted these limits he was an open target for the labour movement and particularly the National Union of Mineworkers in 1973–4. Once the oil crisis and the recession intervened the miners were in a strategically strong position to achieve their ends. However, the Prime Minister turned his conflict with the miners, and the trade union movement, into a major crisis of confidence in the government itself. The first 1974 election was fought on the question of who would run Britain: the elected government or the trade union movement. Although the opposition Labour Party refused to concede this point, it acknowledged it indirectly by displaying willingness to concede on all the demands of the labour movement, not only on the question of the miners' pay claim. The Labour Party was successful in the two elections of 1974 because they seemed to occupy the centre ground in respect of the post-war consensus, but also because voters recognised that a Labour government could reach agreement with the labour movement and this would restore stability after three years of instability. Paradoxically the Labour Party appeared in 1974 as the party of order and the Conservatives as the party of change. In October 1974 Wilson secured his government's position, and Heath's defeat by Margaret Thatcher in the leadership election in the following year was an overt rejection not only of the man, but of his policies. Whether at this stage the change within the Conservative Party represented a move to the right is open to question, but it and subsequent events up to 1979 provided the opportunity for such a move.[29]

It is possible to detect a leftward drift for much of the 1970s elsewhere. The end of the dictatorships in Greece, Spain and Portugal, expanded democracy to the south of Europe and though conservatives ruled in Spain and Greece for much of the 1970s the movement in these states was to the left rather than the right. The Historic Compromise in Italy during the 1970s was both a reflection of the democratisation of the PCI, and a recognition of the need to accept labour as part of the governing process in a state where it had traditionally been excluded. This period is important in Italy as it demonstrated the willingness of the PCI to dilute its own political objectives for the benefit of stabilising the democratic state. Although the PCI were criticised for, and in the medium term damaged by, this, and despite the benefits derived by the DC from the Historic Compromise, it did mark the end of the long-term exclusion of the Communists from Italian politics. In the case of the Netherlands the government led by the PvdA in 1973 shifts politics to the left between then and 1977 when, in coalition with the weaker KVP, there is an expansion of the left's agenda. Many of the ambiguities detected elsewhere on the right are also evident in France during the 1970s. The election of Giscard d'Estaing in 1974 was followed at first by a policy of deflation, yet in similar fashion to that of Heath in Britain once the recession deepened and unemployment increased there followed a u-turn and a policy of reflation followed. The latter policy was associated with the Gaullist Prime Minister Chirac, whose policy priorities differed to a considerable extent from those of Giscard. In 1976 he resigned and was succeeded by the more conservative and traditionalist Barré, whose policy was one of retrenchment in the face of inflation and recession. Despite his position as prime minister of a conservative government and the increasingly conservative basis of the presidential majority, the economic and social policies of the Barré administration were disapproved of by public opinion and by a section of its own electorate, the Gaullists.[30]

By the end of the 1970s, then, whatever opportunity was provided by the recession had not necessarily worked to the advantage of the right or the left. There was a political balance within the liberal democracies which can be characterised as a cautious, but conservative, maintenance of the consensus. All else being equal most governments were concerned with unemployment, yet with inflation accelerating in many states and a slowdown in world trade not all was equal and therefore governments were proving inept at dealing with the problems associated with the economic downturn. The Carter administration in America, the Wilson/Callaghan government in Britain and Schmidt's coalition government in Germany were all left of centre in composition, yet each was faced with an external environment hostile to left-wing innovation or policies which would affect unemployment. In these and other states by the end of the 1970s concern had shifted from unemployment to inflation as the main problem for economic policy-making and all the associated policies that went with it.[31]

The Impact of Social Change on Conservative Politics

It might be concluded that the social change which affected the liberal democratic states from the middle of the 1960s would place conservative parties at a disadvantage. In the short term, as at the end of the 1960s, conservatives might gain advantage from the fear of the new or the disruption of the unknown. However, long-term social trends seemed to place conservatives, and the right generally, at a disadvantage.[32] A number of features came to prominence during the 1970s which were unsettling to conservative supporters and which caused difficulties for conservative parties. One explanation for the reluctance of conservative parties to break with consensus can be based on the belief that to do so would impair an already weak electoral base. Secularisation posed a general threat to conservative parties given the historic dependence on church-goers.[33] If societies became increasingly secular, would this have an impact on support for conservative parties? A similar difficulty presented itself with the emergence of the feminist movement in the 1960s. Historically, women had been more likely to vote for the right than the left. If, however, women's position in society was changing, there was every likelihood that women's political role would also change. Furthermore, inter-generational change could compound these specific features. Younger and better-educated voters may not be as attached to traditional parties as had been the case. More specifically, Inglehart suggested that not only could inter-generational change be detected, but that the form it took increasingly divided voters between a more traditional or materialist voter and a post-materialist voter. The latter were inclined to the left and to identify with issues and values which could provide support for the left.[34] Furthermore, the drive to liberalisation in most states tended to reinforce the leftist commitment to personal autonomy and expression, rather than the more traditionalist views of conservatives. Modernisation in the 1970s presented conservatives with a challenge from the left, as change had done on every occasion since the French Revolution. How does a conservative movement respond to change which in many ways is aimed at the dilution of values which conservatives identify with? Modernisation proved threatening, whether it took the form of a challenge to patriarchy, to conventional sexual morality or to the structure of the family. Authority once again appeared to be under threat by an insurgent left. Furthermore, modernisation and change was even more threatening when the traditional electoral and social components of conservatism appeared to be eroding as a consequence.

Table 7.3 gives the membership of religious denominations in a number of European states in 1981, the percentage of regular church goers and the relationship between this and the vote for the main conservative party. As noted earlier there is no clear correlation between membership of a denomination and voting behaviour. However, there is a relationship between regular attendance at church and voting for conservative parties. The Irish case has unique characteristics, including almost universal church-going, and it is consequently difficult to draw conclusions from this relationship. However, in other states there is a much closer relationship between voting for the right and regular attendance at church. Broughton's analysis drew attention to this, and it is a feature which is further confirmed by Inglehart's more recent analysis of the correlation between frequent church-going and voting patterns. In most liberal democratic states some two-thirds of those who attend church regularly (once a week or more) vote for the major conservative party in the system. This is also applicable for the United States in 1984 and 1988. The exceptions are in Britain where the correlation is much weaker and in Ireland where, at least until recently, denomination did not provide an adequate predictor to voting.[35]

Table 7.3 Denomination and church-going, 1981

	Catholic	Protestant	Regular	Vote for right
Britain	11	74	14	43.9 (1979)
Germany	41	48	21	44.5 (1980)
Netherlands	32	26	27	30.8 (1981)
Belgium	72	2	30	26.4 (1981)
Italy	93	0	36	38.3 (1979)
France	71	2	12	48.2 (1981)*
Ireland	95	3	82	81.8 (1981)**

Source: Stephen Harding and David Phillips with Michael Fogarty, *Contrasting values in Western Europe: unity, diversity and change* (Basingstoke: Macmillan, 1986), pp. 36–7; Thomas T. Mackie and Richard Rose *The International Almanac of Electoral History*, 2nd Edn (London: Macmillian, 1982) for vote.

Notes: * Refers to presidential vote, second ballot.
** Total due to combining Fianna Fáil and Fine Gael.

Yet despite the real evidence of decline in church-going, this does not necessarily translate into changing voting behaviour. The process seems to be more complex than this in any event. In virtually every case the vote for conservative parties is higher than the percentage of the population that often attend church. While frequent church-goers are more likely to vote for conservatives, the secularisation of modern society has not necessarily disadvantaged the conservative parties. This can be appreciated in individual cases. The Dutch political system experienced volatility and deconfessionalisation from around 1967. Between 1959 and 1972 the denominational parties suffered serious erosion of their vote: it dropped from 49 per cent of the total to 31 per cent over this period. The KVP suffered most, but so did the Christian Historical Union (CHU), though the ARP maintained its overall level of support despite the pressures of change in Dutch society. The denominational parties in the Netherlands were further disadvantaged in that secularisation accompanied and perhaps prompted the de-pillarisation of the political system, the stability of which had been maintained by pillarisation[36]. The contrast can be appreciated from Table 7.4 which is derived from Irwin's analysis of this process.

The decline in support for the denominational parties can in large part be explained by the decline in church-going. This also helps to explain the increased support from Catholics for the PvdA. There is no great decline in church membership, what has declined is the level of intensity and the degree of de-pillarisation. In the 1977 Dutch National Election Study it was found that those who attended church at least once a week were more likely to continue voting for the denominational parties (either the CDA or one of the splinter religious parties), whereas those who attended infrequently voted for secular parties.[37] What seems to have occurred between 1967 and 1977 is that the stable

Table 7.4 Dutch voting and religious preference, 1954 and 1977

	Roman Catholic		Dutch Reformed		Gereformeerd		No Preference	
	1954	1977	1954	1977	1954	1977	1954	1977
KVP	87		1		–	*	1	
ARP	–		13		82		2	
CHU	–		27		2		1	
CDA	*	54	*	31	*	70	*	8
PvdA	7	24	41	35	4	6	72	57
VVD	1	12	14	20	2	7	13	16
CPN	–	1	1	–	–	–	10	2
Other	5	9	3	14	10	17	1	17

Source: G. A. Irwin, 'Patterns of voting behaviour in the Netherlands', in Richard T. Griffiths (ed) *The Economy and Politics of the Netherlands since 1945* (The Hague: Martin Nijhoff, 1980).
Notes: *CDA first appeared in 1977 as a consequence of the merging of the three denominational parties (see the discussion below).

bases of Dutch politics underwent rapid change, change which was not restricted to new entrants to the electorate. One consequence of this was the decision to establish the CDA in response to the weakening of the denominational vote in an attempt to stem the decline. In the unified structure of the CDA, the three denominational parties attempted to consolidate their vote by providing a more modern and Christian democratic appeal, in the hope of emulating the success of other Christian democratic parties in Europe.

The Dutch case was probably the most striking example of secularisation leading to considerable change in voting patterns, but secularisation is detectable in most European states throughout the 1970s. In France the percentage of church-goers declined quickly, and this was especially pronounced among women. By the end of the 1970s the gap in religious identification between men and women had narrowed appreciably. Likewise in Germany church attendance erodes, though there, as elsewhere, regular church-goers still identified most strongly with the conservative parties. However, the problem for the conservative parties was that a smaller proportion of the electorate was attending church regularly, though those who did constituted a stable element of the conservative constituency. Yet, if conservative parties were dependent on these traditional sectors of the electorate for votes then unlike the 1950s they were likely to lose elections.

Different strategies were adopted in response to this phenomenon. In Italy, the controversy surrounding the issue of divorce highlighted the extent to which Italian opinion had secularised, a process which extended to the DC itself. When Fanfani attempted to use the divorce issue to reconstitute a centre-right anti-communist block, his strategy failed, in part due to defections from his own party. It is estimated that at least 16 per cent of DC voters supported the retention of the divorce law in the 1974 referendum. The contrast between Italy and the Netherlands is quite striking. The DC refused to accept that social change affected its electorate, its influence or dominance in government. For most of the 1970s it manoeuvered to maintain its position within the power structure, without addressing the consequences of secularisation or possible dealignment. This is what the three Dutch parties did in response to similar conditions. While acknowledging the existing disadvantages, they responded positively by establishing the CDA and sought to provide a centre-right alternative to the centre-left block. The problem of secularisation was compounded by social change, especially among women and the young, yet for the most part, even during the 1970s, conservative parties maintained their electorate, if at times with difficulty.[38]

The Politics of Conservative Renewal, 1979–90

If the changes which occurred between 1960 and 1980 appeared threatening to the right, this did not mean that it was defenceless in the face of secularisation, dealignment or social change. Success for the left is not inevitable in these circumstances. In fact, the experience of the 1970s pushed conservative parties to the right by the end of the decade. One reason for this was the right's experience during the 1970s. Working within a consensus increasingly defined by the left proved uncomfortable to conservative parties. In addition to this the basis for such consensus was evaporating. Neither convergence nor corporatism seemed to benefit conservatism in electoral terms, nor did it provide a means to regenerate the economy during the recession. Within conservative parties there was pressure for a return to or a reassertion of key values on the economy, social order and morality. The recession in 1979 provided the trigger for this shift in many parties, though the unease was detectable earlier. This in turn led to growing confrontation between left and right which was increasingly defined in terms of ideological polarisation. This was the moment when the post-war social consensus finally collapsed and when conservative parties reasserted their political dominance and independence from the post-war influences. This was facilitated by the recession, by a loss of faith in Keynesianism and by the inflationary environment which characterised the end of the 1970s.[39]

A movement to the right on the part of conservative parties might not have been electorally advantageous if other conditions were not also met. The recessionary environment provided the main window of opportunity after Keynesian responses failed. Electorates were also involved in a learning curve. As the recession continued public opinion came to recognise that while it might not be possible to have full employment and low inflation, it might be possible to have the latter at the cost of the former. As a consequence policy priorities began to change, and inflation became the main concern of policy-makers and the electorate. The classic policy cleavage reasserted itself. Conservatives identified with anti-inflationary strategies, whereas the left continued to defend a full employment policy. With the notable exceptions of Austria and Sweden, appeals to the full employment consensus failed throughout the industrial world, as conservative governments were elected on the basis of counter-inflationary policies. The fear of inflation and the belief that reducing it should be the policy priority provided conservatives with their initial political and ideological success. This reaction against the left was also facilitated by the recognition that the business cycle had returned, and that this involved zero-sum consequences. If policy-making no longer benefited all sections of society, whether equally or not, then it could be assumed that electorates would vote to maximise their income and defend their status, but that not every group could succeed in this strategy.[40]

State intervention, progressive taxation and redistribution has, in historic terms, been favoured by the majority which would benefit from such policies. However, since the 1960s this relationship no longer held. As a consequence of the changes in industrial societies the majority now owned property, paid taxes and were affluent.[41] Increasingly, anti-inflationary governments were maintained in power by majorities who considered this to be the top policy priority. This entailed that the maintenance of prosperity for those in employment took priority over seeking to deal with unemployment. In effect, the majority benefited during the 1980s, while the minority (usually low-skilled workers, the lower paid and those dependent on state provision) bore the brunt of recession, unemployment and cut-backs in public expenditure.[42]

This was further reinforced by a return to order on conservative terms during the 1980s. The restoration of order coincides with and is a product of conservative success in the 1980s. After the rapid social changes of the 1960s and 1970s, the spiralling inflation, the collapse of public finances and the political uncertainties which characterised the latter half of the 1970s, a mood of pessimism prevailed at the beginning of the 1980s. In the context of this crisis, conservatives were in a strong position to reassert authority and to restore order. Nor was this unique: during the 1920s and the 1950s conservatism proved to be capable of mobilising majorities for order by placing itself against the progressive appeal of the left. The appeal to order was successful, following as it did a period of rapid change and confrontation. These majorities appear when the progressive drive has exhausted its potential, and a period of assimilation is required to digest the main thrust of the reforming era, while at the same time discarding elements considered unpopular or unnecessary. It is unlikely that conservatives could have been successful in the 1980s without the recession, but this does not provide a full explanation. The conservative appeal also rested on the need to restore order and on its ability to compete with the left. Moreover, it necessitated a balanced strategy by the conservatives, one which accepted some of the changes introduced by the progressive wing of politics, amending others but most crucially persuading its own right that this balance was necessary for conservative success. In the absence of a return to order in this fashion, conservative voters will be alienated. Elections allow the uneasiness or objections of the right to be mediated in a stable and peaceful fashion. These periods of order are similar in that on each occasion there is a rejection of the left's utopian expectations, but other reforms are assimilated and consolidated. These periods are also associated with deflationary economic policy, a decline in state involvement in the economy and a reduction in public expenditure. Such periods also involve a more confrontational foreign policy; until recently in the twentieth century this was often directed at the Soviet Union.[43]

A return to order on conservative terms involves paring back but not necessarily diminishing the reforms of the progressive decades. To be successful conservative parties need not only be elected, but re-elected. The most successful conservative governments in the 1980s have been in Britain, Germany and the United States. In each case, conservatives have been successfully re-elected on a number of occasions and have consequently imposed their ideological mark on policy and on government. The move to the right has taken different forms in each of these three states because of the nature of each political culture, but they all shared the conservative determination to contain the left, restore economic order and challenge the Soviet Union. Although not as clear-cut elsewhere, similar patterns do occur. Counter-inflationary policies become the main feature of economic policy in the Netherlands, Belgium and Ireland, but also in states more closely associated with social democracy, in particular Austria and Sweden. A movement to the right on the part of social democratic governments in France, Australia, New Zealand and Spain confirms this general observation.[44]

Conservatives also benefited from other tendencies during this decade. Not only did conservatism become popular, but it became possible publicly to articulate conservative ideology. In reasserting the politics of order, conservatives insisted that there was a need to protect what existed from new utopian designs on the left. There is little reason to believe that conservatism in the 1980s was particularly radical. Thatcherism, frequently seen as a new and radical form of right-wing thinking, had more in common with the preservationist democratic right that had traditionally characterised British conservatism. Conservatives defended a limited form of government and economy, though in some cases this defence was promoted actively. This conservative defence of the established order benefited from the emergence of new cleavage structures in liberal democracy and from the changes taking place in a number of electoral systems. The politics of the new social movements (ecologists, feminists, pacifists among others) increasingly colonised the traditional left by the 1980s. Social democracy moved to the left, absorbing the issues of the counter-culture.[45] In this way left and right restructured themselves as the carriers of progress and order. Crucial differences emerged between the old and the new politics. Inglehart suggested that these new cleavages were based on conflicting sets of values which he has described as 'materialist' and 'post-materialist'. A number of putative alliances emerge from this process of realignment. The most significant is the remaking of the left, incorporating social democracy, the green movement and other alternative politics. The other, designated new right or neoconservative, incorporated conservatives, liberals and some sections of the old left. Each of these alliances are potential and are realised in specific circumstances only. The new right programme involves a defence of the market economy, liberal democratic political institutions and a strong defence capacity. At an ideological level it also involves a defence of representative and limited government against participative democracy, acceptance of free trade and the priority of market solutions as well as the insistence on making a clear distinction between public and private.[46]

Changes in society have facilitated more open competition in the electoral arena. The traditional class composition of electorates has declined as a consequence of social change and as a proportion of the electorate. Class and religion are much weaker sources of political identification than before. In particular the two most significant electoral blocks, the working class and catholic subcultures, have been weakened, though they have not disappeared.[47] These changes have contributed to the ideological, political and cultural pressures which have affected virtually all political systems since the beginning of the 1970s and which appear to be accelerating in the 1990s. Furthermore, cleavages based on value orientation, rather than class, have increased in saliency since the 1960s.[48] Moreover there is evidence to suggest that materialists are more likely to vote for parties of the right or centre (whether conservative, Christian democratic or liberal) than for parties of the left (whether communist, social democratic or green), and this tendency appears to be increasing. In addition, in so far as a realignment can be detected this has occurred on the right with a number of conservative or Christian democratic parties attracting voters which in the past have not been attracted by the right. Evidence for this is available in the United states, Britain and Germany in particular.[49] These trends offered the right an opportunity to re-establish ideological dominance in a more confrontational electoral arena and to benefit from the confrontation.

There can be little doubt that conservatives have been remarkably successful in electoral terms during the 1980s, often in quite difficult electoral circumstances. One of the remarkable features of this decade has been the electoral success of conservatives despite mass unemployment. In addition, despite the potential threat of social change, conservative electorates have proved to be quite stable in many states. More surprising has been conservative success in receiving mandates to control inflation and spending, and often to impose strict austerity programmes as well. In most cases, conservative governments have been re-turned to power in subsequent elections, but where they have not the incoming government has tended to maintain its policies. Centre-right coalition govern-ments have become the most common expression of conservative dominance in the 1980s, reflecting a common area of policy agreement between liberals and conservatives. Participation in such governments by conservatives has lessened the impact of social change for them. Conservatives claim that their appeal is less sectional, broader and more national than that for the left. In most cases con-servative parties attract voters from a wider range of the social spectrum than does the left. It may be that dealignment facilitated the wider appeal of such par-ties. Conservative parties in the 1980s were well placed to balance their appeal between traditional conservatives and the requirements of modernity.[50]

The most dramatic appearance of a 'new' conservatism, occurs in Britain with the establishment of conservative hegemony after four general election vic-tories. The change in conservative voting success under Margaret Thatcher can be seen in Table 7.5.

Table 7.5 British general election results, 1974–92

	Conservative	Labour	Liberal	Nationalist	Other
October 1974	35.8	39.2	18.3	3.5	3.2
1979	43.9	37.0	13.8	2.0	3.3
1983	42.4	27.6	25.4	1.5	3.1
1987	42.3	30.8	22.6	1.7	2.6
1992	41.9	34.4	17.8	2.3	3.5

Note:* Liberal includes the Liberal Party, the Social Democratic Party, the Social and Liberal Democratic Party and the Liberal Democrats.

The conservatives have been so successful in winning elections since 1979 that the party can probably be seen as the predominant party in the political sys-tem.[51] The three Thatcher governments in particular have moved British politics further to the right than at any time since the 1930s, and more dramatically have changed the intellectual climate to a considerable degree. While public opinion remains ambiguous concerning many aspects of Thatcherism, especially its commitment to the market and neo-liberalism, nevertheless in each election the Conservatives have won a majority of the votes.[52] There are numerous ways of explaining Thatcher's success. The nature of the political system has certainly contributed to this. Once the Conservatives can remain the largest party, there is every likelihood that they will be returned to office. This is reinforced by the presence of a strong third party in the system, a factor which disadvantages both the other major parties. However, there is more to Conservative success that electoral considerations. The 1979 election was won because of dissatisfaction with the incumbent government rather than for any strong endorsement of the Conservatives. This was clearly not the case in subsequent elections. The 1983 election is of importance because, notwithstanding the debate over the 'Falklands Factor', there are other issues to consider. Whether or not there was a pro-Conservative majority, there was certainly an anti-Labour one. The move to the left, the split in the party and the formation of the SDP weakened the Labour Party, while offering the government an opportunity to maximise its own electoral position. Furthermore, in the absence of either the SDP or the Liberal party, it was highly unlikely that these votes would have moved to Labour.[53] There was also a more positive appeal in 1983. The Conservatives certainly benefited from the Falklands war and from the popularity of its trade union legislation. Success in the war demonstrated Thatcher's capacity to lead in a crisis and to fulfil objectives, even in difficult circumstances. In addition to this, council house purchases, law and order and some aspects of its economic policies contributed to the return of the Thatcher government in 1983.

Between 1983 and 1987, these trends were, if anything, reinforced by a renewed emphasis on safeguarding the proprietorial majority that lived in private housing, were employed and wanted low inflation. While the affluent tended to benefit more than other sectors, it is probably the case that the Conservative appeal had a wide resonance, even among those who did not vote for them. In 1983, 1987 and again in 1992 the Conservatives were favoured by their traditional electorate, but also by voters in private industry and by working-class home-owners. In addition, privatisation and share ownership proved popular while reinforcing the Conservative emphasis on individualism and the market. Opinion was never unreservedly in favour of the Conservatives, but the party was in a strategically strong position to achieve its ends in 1987 as in 1983. Concern with unemployment or the welfare state did not outweigh a continuing fear of inflation, or, if it did, it was not strong enough to move crucial sections of the electorate to Labour. Other contributory factors in 1987 included the defeat of the miners' strike, Mrs Thatcher's strong position on the European Community, her anti-communism and the generation of an expansionary monetary policy which bolstered the economy prior to the election.[54]

Following the 1987 election a new consensus emerged in Britain which was determined by the Conservatives. It clearly rejected the main elements of the post-war consensus and sought a return to a market-driven society similar to that of the 1930s. Increasingly, Conservatives considered the post-war consensus an interlude forced on a reluctant right which could now be discarded. The component parts of the new consensus include the demise of the corporate state which is replaced by the strong centralised, but minimalist state. Cabinet government is preferred to consociational consensus. Centralisation involves the weakening of other centres of power, whether these be trade unions, local government or universities. Efficiency becomes the norm for adjudicating success whether for individuals or institutions. Privatisation and the deregulation of the labour market became central pillars of economic policy, while a commitment to redistribution is replaced by limited government responsibilities for society, low taxation and reduced public expenditure. This has been accompanied by a renewed emphasis on law and order, a reassertion of national sovereignty in the face of European integration and an insistence on the privileged nature of Britain's relationship with the United States.

Thatcherism, if treated in isolation, might be explained in terms of specifically

British conditions. Conservative success elsewhere can also be accounted for in terms similar to those which prevailed in Britain. A right-wing response to crisis management laid the basis for conservative success in many states. In Britain, Thatcherism may be the most recent example of a majority being mobilised by the right in response to economic adversity. A conservative-led neo-liberal response to economic crisis is not merely a British phenomenon, the key elements appear in a number of other states. While continental conservatives remained reluctant to use the term conservative or to be identified with Thatcher's high profile and confrontationalist style, the policies adopted by other right-wing governments do not depart radically from those of Britain. It is more a matter of nuance than substance.[55]

The reason for this is that the circumstances in most liberal democratic states are similar and policy change is circumscribed by this. Even in societies with consociational or consensual political cultures there had been a distinct move to the right. The limits and the opportunities involved in the move to the right can be detected in Germany. The CDU/CSU had been out of government since 1969, losing elections in 1972 and 1976. The social liberal government presided over a fairly successful response to the recession during the 1970s. However, deteriorating conditions at the end of the decade gave the CDU the opportunity to challenge the government in 1980. This they failed to do by mistakenly promoting Franz Joseph Strauss as their candidate for Chancellor, a decision which cost the conservatives votes. Despite this strains appeared in the government and by 1982 the coalition had disintegrated, the liberal FDP defected and formed a new coalition government with the CDU, which was returned to office in 1983. The CDU and the FDP had moved to the right as a consequence of the recession and the expansion of the Soviet Union at the end of the 1970s. This proved to be the basis of the coalition, which quickly implemented new and austere economic policies. The budget deficit was halved between 1983 and 1986, while public expenditure was controlled and the welfare system limited. On foreign policy the new government also promoted the twin track decision to locate cruise and pershing missiles despite the opposition of the left, now including the divided SPD.[56]

The success of the conservative-liberal government can be measured by its overall success in elections. As can be seen in Table 7.6 the coalition has proved to be successful on three occasions at Federal elections. While 1990 might be considered an exceptional election, government success can be attributed to Chancellor Kohl's ability to pursue the unification option, despite misgivings from other parties. With this caveat, the CDU has maintained its overall strength into the 1990s. There is little variation in the CDU vote, and what there is has not affected its ability to form a government. It is the SPD which has suffered a decline in its vote throughout the decade. This may in part be attributable to its stance on unification, but it seems to maintain a trend. The irony in Germany, as in Britain, is that it is the social democrats who have suffered most from electoral and social change with increasing fragmentation on the left. In an analysis carried out after the 1983 election Klingemann produced evidence to suggest that between 1976 and 1983 most social categories were moving towards the Christian democrats and away from the SPD. Out of eleven social categories the CDU/CSU had a majority in six and a plurality in a further three, while the SPD

Table 7.6 Vote at German elections 1976–90

	1976	1980	1983	1987	1990
CDU/CSU	48.6	44.5	48.8	44.3	43.8
SPD	42.6	42.9	38.2	37.0	33.5
FDP	7.9	10.6	6.9	9.1	11.0
Grünen	–	1.5	5.6	8.3	3.9
Others	0.9	0.5	0.5	1.2	7.7

Note: In 1990, Other includes the former Communist PDS which, due to allowances for parties organised in the former East Germany, were allowed representation without meeting the national 5 per cent threshold. The PDS received seventeen seats in the Bundestag.

had a majority in only two. Of particular significance is the move by the working class (especially the Catholic working class) back to the CDU/CSU and less surprisingly by those who either attend church regularly or occasionally. In each case there is a 10 percentage point movement in favour of the CDU/CSU, which helps to explain the revival of its vote after 1972.[57]

Germany has experienced dealignment, a weakening of partisan identity and electoral volatility similar to a number of other states. Yet the CDU has been quite successful in maintaining its voting levels, while those of the SPD have continued to decline. More importantly, the fragmentation of the left's vote, coinciding as it does with a decline in some core sectors of the SPD's support base, has made it much more difficult for the left to form a government. On statistical grounds the SPD and the Greens together could not have formed a government; this could only have been achieved if the Freie Demokratische Parteie (FDP) had joined the government. As this option remains highly unlikely, it secures governmental control for the centre right. The move to the left by the SPD, the success of the Greens and the growing influence of the new social movements provided the opportunity for the centre right to create the conditions for a governmental majority. One consequence of this has been the movement back to the centre by the SPD since the 1990 election, a phenomenon found in a number of societies after the right's success. In a sophisticated discussion of these trends Minkenberg has suggested that the new cleavage structures prompted by conflicts over materialist/post-materialist values have facilitated the generation of the new conservative majority. This conservative majority reflects a realignment to the right against the new-left and a defence of actually existing society which is considered to be under threat by post-materialist politics. Moreover, in Germany as in Britain and the United States this new conservatism attracts support from the majority of the electorate which has benefited from the policies of the new right. In much the same way as in other liberal democratic societies in the 1980s German conservatism has successfully appealed to a majority on the grounds of protecting income and by providing a limited approach to crisis management.[58] The CDU has also probably benefited from the growth of a new German pride (or patriotism) during the 1980s and enhanced by German unification. Moreover, the government has benefited in the short run from unification, but also from flexibility on other issues such as the environment and nuclear power.

Similar patterns to those in Britain and Germany are detectable in the United States. The Republican Party won three presidential elections, pushing federal policy well to the right in comparison to the 1960s or 1970s. There is also a detectable shift in a conservative direction on a number of issues, including law and order, the economy and taxation. Furthermore, the Democratic Party suffered electorally from its move to the left and its identification with the programme of the new left. Though the United States is often seen as liberal society par excellence, this has not been incompatible with strong conservative social and political trends.[59] Since the late 1970s the Republican party has successfully mobilised support around conservative issues, but also benefited from concern with the deteriorating economy, crime and foreign policy. The foundations for conservative success in the United States were similar to those in Europe, and while the 1980 presidential election sent mixed signals, Reagan's victory reflected a move to the right and provided a limited mandate on economic and foreign policy.[60]

The Reagan administration was the most right-wing presidency since the 1920s, even more so than that of Eisenhower in the 1950s. Reagan's re-election in 1984 reflected his popularity, but also the strategic hold which the Republican Party held over the presidency. This strength was confirmed by Bush's election in 1988. While this success was helped by the weakness of the Democratic Party at the federal level and by poor performances by Democratic presidential candidates, an acceptance of conservative values by many Americans has also contributed to the party's success. Throughout the 1980s the Republican position on the economy and on foreign policy has been generally favoured by significant majorities. On some social issues, such as welfare and positive discrimination, the Republicans have also acquired an advantage. However, on other issues such as abortion opinion remains divided, and Republicans have not proved successful in mobilising opinion in favour of the conservative position.[61] The Republicans have also benefited from dealignment, weakening partisan identification and greater electoral competitiveness in the South. White voters in the once Democratic South have moved to the right over the past thirty years and now provide the most consistent support for Republican presidential candidates.[62]

George Bush's election in 1988 confirmed the conservative trend in presidential elections. In some ways this election was more significant than Reagan's re-election in 1984 because it secured the political achievements of the previous eight years. In part it was a vote of confidence in Reagan, but it was more than this. It was not a foregone conclusion that Bush would win the election; at first Dukakis was well ahead of Bush in the polls.[63] However, Bush retrieved the position by emphasising a number of factors which became salient. He stressed the party's success on economic issues and on foreign policy, emphasising the commitment not to increase taxation, which became a major consideration in voting intentions. However, the campaign was not fought essentially on economic or foreign policy grounds, but on ideology. Bush successfully portrayed Dukakis as a liberal and increasingly those who considered him to be a liberal voted for Bush. By stressing ideological values the Bush campaign was well placed to cross-cut any appeal which Dukakis might be able to make on economic issues.

On the death penalty, drugs or related issues the Republicans were closer to majority opinion than Dukakis. In addition, Bush emphasised issues such as school prayer, the pledge of allegiance and national security in such a way as to imply that Dukakis was in some way 'un-American'. Bush successfully reasserted the traditional Republican identification with the politics of morality, as in the 1920s, and juxtaposed conservative moral norms against the moral liberalism which he attributed to Dukakis. Taken together, these issues, the Reagan legacy and the endorsement of the Administration's economic and foreign policy assured Bush of victory in 1988.[64]

The shift in a conservative direction was not restricted to these states. Elsewhere, similar trends were evident. This is most pronounced in economic policy. In Ireland, which has a strong tradition of state intervention, economic crisis at the end of the 1970s led to a dramatic shift in policy during the early 1980s and the generation of a deflationary consensus which was maintained throughout the decade. Likewise in France, despite socialist incumbency in the presidency, left-wing policy was discarded and deflation endorsed. More surprisingly, the Gaullist Rassemblement pour la République (RPR), traditionally an interventionist party, endorsed many of the Thatcherite and Reaganite policies when in opposition, and seriously attempted to implement them once in power again in 1986. While the right suffered defeat at the 1988 presidential elections, the policy package pursued by the incoming socialist government did not depart dramatically from that promoted by Chirac. Similarly in the case of Belgium, though increasingly bound up with the dispute over language, the coalition government pursued policies which were little different in emphasis from those imposed elsewhere.[65] The revival and success of the CDA in the Netherlands offered further confirmation of these trends. From a weak beginning at its foundation in 1977, the new party stabilised its electoral strength in the course of the 1980s, successfully establishing a centre-right government with the Liberal party and strengthening its position at the 1986 and 1989 elections. The centre-right governments were based on the need to impose order on the public finances and to pursue a moderate foreign policy. The opposition of the left to 'twin track' contributed to the government's success, allowing it to confront the utopianism of the left and associate it with the PvdA. In the course of the 1980s the CDA strengthened its position, while policy moved gradually to the right with a growing emphasis on issues invoked by conservative parties elsewhere.[66]

The Prospects for Conservatism in the 1990s

Conservatism proved to be remarkably successful during the 1980s. During the early 1990s its prospects appear strong, though the political terrain has become more complex and indeed threatening. Conservatives remain in governments in many liberal democratic states, whether alone, in coalition with liberals or even on occasions with social democrats. Conservative ideas and policies have been translated into legislation throughout the industrial world, a process which extends well beyond the right. The continuing weakness of the social democratic left is testament to the continuing ideological dominance of conservative ideology. Economic policy continues to be the main feature of conservative influence, though it extends into foreign policy and certain social matters. The collapse of the Soviet Union and the demise of communism has further enhanced conservative influence, though it may be premature to conclude from this that liberal democracy will become a universally attractive political model. Even in Eastern Europe the stabilisation of liberal democracy is as yet incomplete, while in Russia its prospects have diminished appreciably.[67]

Nevertheless a number of factors remain important in explaining the continuing success of conservatism specifically and the centre right in general. The first is that liberal democracy won the cold war politically, economically and militarily. As a consequence the liberal democratic model has become extremely influential, though as noted in previous chapters the possibility of stabilising it will be difficult for most former communist states. Furthermore, the market has become the icon of the 1990s, reinforcing the strong link between democracy and capitalism. The relationship between liberalism, democracy and capitalist industrialisation remains complex but it does appear that it is this mix which secures democratic legitimation in capitalist societies. It is not axiomatic that conservatism or the right would benefit from these successes. However, the circumstances of the 1980s have facilitated the right in doing so, because it was the right rather than the left that identified most closely with the political forms which secured the end of communism.

Conservatism may also have benefited from the relative success of its own policies in the 1980s. The current recession has lasted twenty years (1974–94), this is a longer period than that of the 1930s (eleven years) or that of the last century, in 1879–96 (seventeen years). The safety net of the welfare state has assured that conditions are not as difficult during the current recession as previously. It is likely that these conditions will continue and that the economic environment will remain a difficult one. Long-term unemployment has not yet disadvantaged the right, indeed the misery index has declined since its high point during the 1970s. The reason for this is the successful anti-inflation strategy of the right, which has virtually eliminated inflation in most OECD states (average around 3 per cent for 1993). The problem in the 1970s was compounded by high unemployment and inflation, whereas by the 1990s unemployment is the main difficulty. Even this has not proved electorally damaging on most occasions, as electorates have learnt to live with it or to believe that nothing can be done about it.[68] To date conservative governments have been able to persuade electorates that 'there is no alternative' to low tax, low spending and restrictive economic policies, a claim which continues to have saliency in the 1990s. The re-election of the Conservative government in Britain in 1992 is a case in point. Despite a poor showing in the opinion polls during the campaign, there was a final swing to the Conservatives which secured them victory. The reasons for this were complex, but concerns over taxation and personal prosperity certainly contributed to Conservative success, as did the belief that it was the recession rather than Conservative policy which weakened economic performance. By way of contrast the Democrats won the presidential election in the United States, because the Bush administration was blamed for the difficult economic conditions being experienced. Bush maintained a significant lead on foreign policy, but on the economy he failed to attract support. Sections of the Republican majority of previous years defected to the independent candidate,

Ross Perot, while former Democratic voters returned to that party. Economic policy was the key factor in explaining Bill Clinton's victory, yet it was not a mandate for radical change. On most issues, Clinton successfully presented himself as a centrist candidate and it proved impossible for the Republicans to make salient the ideological issue in 1992. Indeed, Bush was affected by the movement to the right of the party during the primaries and nomination process, there was a widespread belief that the party had been captured by the extremist right. In part, Clinton benefited from the rejection of Bush, but his policies have been carefully framed to address the conservative centre-ground of politics. On crosscutting issues Clinton will be able to push policy to the left, on abortion for example, but on the crucial areas of the economy or foreign policy he remains a captive of the move to the right under the Republicans. This does not mean that he will be helpless in the face of this, but that his policy choice will be circumscribed that this reality for some time to come.[69]

While the balance remains right of centre, the 1990s remain more uncertain than the previous decade. At the moment when the right had reimposed order on the industrial states, disorder returned. The end of the cold war has not brought stability to Europe, but has inaugurated a new period of instability. While this stability may be short lived, there are also signs suggesting the opposite. The end of the cold war and communism have also brought to an end the post-war era in Europe and the certainties that have gone with this. All the stabilisers which characterised that era have now collapsed, including economic stability, the European balance of power and affluence. In addition, the European party system is coming under increasing strain from nationalism, right-wing extremism and political fragmentation. The Belgian and Italian party systems have virtually collapsed, while in France the 1993 election demonstrated the weakness of the socialist vote. It is too early to draw conclusions from these events. Italian Christian democracy has collapsed under the pressure of the end of communism and the scandals have shattered its legitimacy along with that of the socialists. Although the DC has been dissolved, there remains a strong centre-right consituency to be mobilised. This is already happening under the success of the Forza Italia led by the millionaire Silvio Berlusconi and the National Alliance (formerly the neo-fascist party). The Italian party system is now realigning in quite radical fashion, though prediction remains difficult as a new electoral system is also in place. Whether this will threaten parliamentary democracy in Italy is questionable as change continues to be mediated through the democratic process. However, the challenge in this case is to the right, which is currently experiencing an unprecedented crisis. Conservatives will also be challenged by the growth of nationalism among its electorate. In most states this takes the form of growing hostility or scepticism to the European union and European integration. The growth of anti-European sentiment in Germany, France, Britain and elsewhere is concentrated on the right and if it continues will cause difficulties for conservatives, especially Christian democrats who identify most enthusiastically with the concept of European union.[70]

It is likely that change will be the main feature of the coming years and that conservative politics will be challenged by some of these. This can work to the advantage of a conservatism which maintains its ability to maintain order in the face of instability. This has been the historic task of conservatism since before the French Revolution. However, there are difficulties involved in this process. Order cannot be reconstituted on an authoritarian or fundamentalist basis. Pope John Paul II remains the only major figure in liberal democratic society who continues to insist on a consistent anti-modernist politics for the 1990s. But even within the right there are serious points of tension between liberals and conservatives, especially on issues concerned with individualism and personal morality. While conservatives have been liberalised to a considerable extent in respect of these issues, there remain key conceptual differences between liberalism, which is ultimately based on an individualistic ethic, and conservatism which has an ethical conception of the collective moral good. In practical terms liberals join with the left on issues such as abortion, whereas conservatives continue to oppose it on principle. In Italy and Belgium centre-right majorities have divided on these issues. But there is more to practical politics in this. The issues of freedom and the market highlights these differences. There is a distinction to be drawn between the conservative view of freedom for the individual which implies limits and that of individual freedom which is universal in application and derives from Mill and classical liberalism. A similar distinction can be drawn over the market. Although liberals and conservatives agree on the importance of the market, conservatives see it as a disciplinary force, while liberals believe it is a force to liberate and extend freedom. While the right may unite around common themes there remains considerable space for disagreement. The collectivism of conservatism establishes limits to its acceptance of liberalism; such a stance offers it a choice of partners on the left and right depending on the circumstances. In such a context the prospects for conservatism remain good.[71]

Notes

1. Charles S. Maier, *In Search of Stability* (Cambridge: Cambridge University Press, 1987), pp. 261–73 It should also be noted that both stability and equilibrium are relative terms. However equilibrium allows one to appreciate more fully the dynamic nature of politics in particular. Adopting the criteria noted above would exclude the United States from the post-war democratic order due to discrimination against blacks, while Switzerland could also be excluded because of its denial of the vote to women. In addition France has to be excluded from this model until the late 1960s and under different circumstances.
2. Daniel Bell, *The End of Ideology: On the Exhaustion of Political Ideas in the Fifties*, rev. edn (Cambridge, Mass Harvard University Press, 1988), pp. 393–407. The original was published in 1960; the 1988 edition includes an 'Afterword, 1988 The End of Ideology Revisited' which contains a defence of the original thesis.
3. Albert O. Hirschman, *Shifting Involvements* (Oxford: Martin Robertson, 1982); Gabriel A. Almond and Sydney Verba, *The Civic Culture: Political Attitudes and Democracy in Five Nations* (Princeton: Princeton University Press, 1963); Hirschman explores the pacifying effect of the franchise while Almond and Verba suggest implicitly that this lack of passion is necessary for stable democracies.
4. Seymour M. Lipset and Stein Rokkan, 'Cleavage structures, party systems, and voter alignments: an introduction', in Lipset and Rokkan (eds), *Party Systems and Voter Alignments* (New York: The Free Press, 1967), pp. 1–64, for an analysis which suggests that the stable nature of the party system has deep roots. For a recent

qualified endorsement of this position Stefano Bartolini and Peter Mair, *Identity, Competition, and Electoral Availability: The Stabilisation of European Electorates 1885-1985* (Cambridge: Cambridge University Press, 1990).

5. Richard Rose and Derek W. Urwin, 'Persistence and change in Western party systems since 1945', *Political Studies* 18:3 (1970), pp. 287–319.

6. Maier, op. cit., pp. 271–2, where he describes the break with normality in heroic and intentionalist terms, whereas that of the imposition of normality lacks this intentionalist content.

7. In this chapter conservative parties include the Christian democratic parties, the Republican Party in the United States, the Conservative Party in Britain and the various versions of Gaullist parties in France. Conservative here does not normally refer to other parties on the right or to liberal parties.

8. Otto Kirchheimer, 'The transformation of the Western European party systems' in Joseph La Palombara and Myron Weiner (eds), *Political Parties and Political Development* (Princeton: Princeton University Press, 1966), pp. 177–200; Karl Dittrich, 'Testing the catch all thesis: some difficulties and possibilities' in Hans Daalder and Peter Mair (eds), *Western European Party Systems* (London: Sage, 1983), pp. 257–66; Gordon Smith, 'Core persistence: change and "people's party"', in Peter Mair and Gordon Smith (eds), *Understanding Party System Change in Western Europe* (London: Frank Cass, 1990), pp. 157–68.

9. Paul Ginsborg, *A History of Contemporary Italy: Society and Politics 1943–1988* (London: Penguin, 1990) for a detailed history of exclusion and inclusion; Stuart J. Woolf (ed.), *The Rebirth of Italy* (London: Longman, 1972); Severino Galante, 'The genesis of political impotence. Italy's mass political parties in the years between the great alliance and the cold war' in Josef Becker and Franz Knipping (eds), *Power in Europe?* (Berlin: Walter de Gruyter, 1986), pp. 185–206.

10. R.E.M. Irving, *Christian democracy in France* (London: George Allen and Unwin, 1973); Frank Giles, *The Locust Years: The Story of the Fourth French Republic 1946–1958* (London: Secker and Warburg, 1991).

11. Jean-Pierre Rioux, *The Fourth Republic, 1944–1958* (Cambridge: Cambridge University Press, 1987), pp. 298–307. Jean Lacouture, *De Gaulle: The Ruler 1945–1970* (London: Harvill, 1991), pp. 164-81. A useful comparison might be made between the behaviour of de Gaulle in the Fourth Republic and that of de Valera in Ireland between 1927 and 1937. In each case these leaders worked within a constitutional structure with which they fundamentally disagreed, while seeking to undermine it and establish a new constitutional structure which each believed would be more appropriate to the requirements of the society. In each case this was achieved. Whether it is possible to see these cases as examples of reformist conservatism within a democratic political culture is a question I am currently exploring in an unpublished paper.

12. Institut Charles De Gaulle, *Approches de la Philosophie Politique du Général de Gaulle* (Paris: Éditions Cujas, 1983) which explores some of the aspects of de Gaulle's thought which generated this support.

13. Bell, op. cit., pp. 409–47.

14. Noël O'Sullivan, *Conservatism* (London: J.M. Dent, 1976). Interestingly O'Sullivan titles his last chapter 'The crisis of conservative ideology in the twentieth century' and concludes by identifying the dilemma for conservatism in a liberal or corporatist polity, pp. 150–54.

15. Brian Girvin, 'The United States: conservative politics in a liberal society' in Brian Girvin (ed.), *The Transformation of Contemporary Conservatism* (London: Sage, 1988), pp. 164–192; Otto Kirchheimer, 'Germany: The vanishing opposition' in Robert A. Dahl (ed.) *Political Opposition in Western Democracies* (New Haven and London: Yale University Press, 1966), pp. 237–59; David Butler and Donald Stokes,

Political Change in Britain: The Evolution of Electoral Choice (London: Macmillan, 1969).

16. Francis G. Castles (ed.), *The Impact of Parties: Politics and Policies in Democratic Capitalist States* (London: Sage, 1982) for an important contribution to the discussion on parties and the competitive arena.

17. For a cautious, but optimistic, version of this view, Andrew Shonfield, *Modern Capitalism: the Changing Balance of Public and Private Power* (London: Oxford University Press, 1969).

18. Rose and Urwin, op. cit., quantified these data building on the 'freezing' thesis of Lipset and Rokkan, op. cit.; for an assessment Peter Mair (ed.), *The West European Party System* (Oxford: Oxford University Press, 1990).

19. Wolfgang C. Müller, 'Conservatism and the transformation of the Austrian People's Party'; in B. Girvin (ed.), *The Transformation of Contemporary Conservatism* (London: Sage, 1988), pp. 98–119. See also Müller's analysis of the role of the political parties in the Austrian form of social partnership which explains in part at least why there is an accommodation with modernity. 'Die Rolle der Partein bei Entstehung und Entwicklung der Sozialpartnerschaft', in Peter Gerlich, et al, *Sozialpartnerschaft in der Krise* (Wien: Hermann Böhlaus, 1985), pp. 135–224. While Germany does not have the same relationship between the political parties and consensus, nevertheless the emergence of technocratic conservatism can be seen as having its origins in a similar need to achieve accommodation and consensus, see Edgar Grande, 'Neoconservatism without neoconservatives? The renaissance and transformation of contemporary conservatism', in Girvin, op. cit., pp. 55–77; 'Neoconservatism and conservative-liberal economic policy in West Germany', *European Journal of Political Research* 15:3 (1987) pp. 281–96.

20. Richard M. Scammon and Ben J. Wattenberg, *The Real Majority* (New York: Coward, McCann and Geoghegan, 1971); Kevin P. Phillips, *Post Conservative America* (New York: Vintage, 1983), pp. 31-62; Michael Gallagher, *The Irish Labour Party in Transition 1957–82* (Dublin: Gill and Macmillan, 1982), pp. 86–103.

21. David Caute, *Nineteen Sixty-Eight: The Year of the Barricades* (London: Hamish Hamilton, 1988); Herbert Marcuse, *One Dimensional Man* (London: Sphere Books, 1968); Gerald Howard (ed.), *The Sixties* (New York: Paragon House, 1991).

22. Marcuse, op. cit., is the most articulate representative of this view.

23. Ghita Ionescu, *Centripetal Politics: Government and the New Centres of Power* (London: Hart-Davis, Macgibbon, 1975); Samuel P. Huntington, *American Politics: The Promise of Disharmony* (Cambridge, Mass: Harvard University Press, 1981), pp. 167–220.

24. Examples of this during the 1960s and 1970s might be the reduction of the voting age to 18 in many instances, the growing acceptance of racial and sexual equality, and the extension of new social rights across the social spectrum. Hirschman, op. cit., has already been cited to the effect that universal suffrage has normally a conservative effect on society.

25. Gabriel A. Almond and Sidney Verba (eds) *The Civic Culture Revisited* (Boston: Little, Brown, 1980) surveys the threats and instabilities since the original 1963 edition; Bell, op. cit. for a review of these decades.

26. Rose and Urwin, op. cit.; Maria Maguire, 'Is there still persistence? Electoral change in Western Europe, 1948–1979' in Daalder and Mair (eds),*Western European Party Systems* (London: Sage, 1983) pp. 67–94; Steven B. Wolinetz, 'The transformation of Western European party systems revisited', *West European Politics* 2:1 (1979), pp. 4–28.

27. Huntington, op. cit.; John H. Goldthorpe, 'The end of convergence: corporatist and dualist tendencies in modern Western societies', in Goldthorpe (ed.), *Order and Conflict in Contemporary Capitalism* (Oxford: Clarendon Press, 1984), pp. 315–44;

Paul Kennedy, *The Rise and Fall of the Great Powers* (London: Unwin Hyman, 1988), pp. 533–64.

28. Girvin, op. cit.; A. James Reichley, *Conservatives in an Age of Change* (Washington, DC: Brookings Institute, 1981), pp. 56–78; Stephen Ambrose, *Nixon: The Triumph of a Politician, 1962–72* (London: Simon and Schuster, 1989); William G. Mayer, *The Changing American Mind: How and Why American Public Opinion Changed Between 1960 and 1988* (Ann Arbor: University of Michigan Press, 1992), pp. 448–55 for assessment of polls.

29. Samuel H. Beer, *Britain Against Itself* (London: Faber and Faber, 1982); James Alt, *The Politics of Economic Decline* (Cambridge: Cambridge University Press, 1979); Martin Holmes, *Political Pressure and Economic Policy: British Government 1970–1974* (London: Butterworth, 1982).

30. Already in 1974 Giscard had lost most of the working-class support which had been attracted to de Gaulle in the 1960s. In contrast to the Gaullist presidential majority, that of Giscard in the 1970s was more traditional and right-wing; R.W. Johnson, *The Long March of the French Left* (London: Macmillan, 1981), p. 93 for the data; Volkmar Lauber, *The Politics of Economic Policy: France 1974–1982* (New York: Praeger, 1983), pp. 5–16; Ginsborg, op. cit., pp. 348–405.

31. The impact of inflation is comprehensively traced in Leon N. Lindberg and Charles S. Maier (eds), *The Politics of Inflation and Economic Stagnation* (Washington, D.C.: Brookings Institute, 1985); Mayer, op. cit., pp. 93–5.

32. Butler and Stokes, op. cit., offered this model for Britain; Johnson, op. cit. also suggested that the left had acquired a sociological majority.

33. David Broughton, 'The social bases of Western European conservative parties', in Girvin (ed.) *The Transformation of Contemporary Conservatism* (London: Sage, 1988), pp. 193–224, for an assessment of this relationship providing data for the late 1970s and early 1980s.

34. Ronald Inglehart, *The Silent Revolution* (Princeton: Princeton University Press, 1977).

35. Broughton in Girvin, op. cit., pp. 193–224; Ronald Inglehart, *Culture Shift in Advanced Industrial Society* (Princeton: Princeton University Press, 1990), pp. 458–60

36. Pillarisation is used to describe the method by which the different denominational and political groupings organised the distribution of power and resources through a system of interest accommodation. The main pillars are Catholic, Protestant, Socialist and Liberal. Each pillar was based on the homogenity of its membership, though the Catholic pillar was the least porous. Each pillar was in theory self contained and autonomous, with a member never having to encounter members of the other pillars. During the 1960s these structures began to erode and a process of de-pillarisation began which led to significant changes in the nature of Dutch politics. Rudy B Andeweg and Galen A. Irwin, *Dutch Government and Politics* (Basingstoke: Macmillan, 1993), pp. 23–49.

37. G.A. Irwin, 'Patterns of voting behaviour in the Netherlands', in Richard T. Griffiths (ed.), *The Economy and Politics of the Netherlands since 1945* (The Hague: Martin Nijhoff, 1980), pp. 199–222 for discussion and assessment of the other contributory factors; G.A. Irwin, J. Verhoef and C.J. Wiebrens (eds) *De Nederlandse kiezer '77* (Voorschoten: VAM, 1977), pp. 150–63.

38. Johnson, op. cit., pp. 103–15; Ian D. Connor, 'Social change and electoral support: the case of the CDU/CSU, 1949–87', in Eva Kohnsky (ed.), *The Federal Republic of Germany: The End of an Era* (New York: Berg, 1981), pp. 85–93; Ginsborg, op. cit., pp. 350–51; Sandro Magister, *La Politica Vaticana e L'Italia 1943–78* (Rome: Riuniti, 1979), pp. 418-20; Leonardi and Wertman, op. cit., pp. 173-80; Paola A. Farnetti, 'Patterns of changing support for Christian democracy in Italy: 1946–1976', in Bogdan Denitch (ed.) *Legitimation of Regimes* (London: Sage, 1979), pp. 249–72.

39. The contributors to Girvin, *The Transformation of Contemporary Conservatism*

(London: Sage, 1988), trace many of these developments; John H. Goldthorpe, 'Problems of political economy after the postwar period', in Charles S. Maier (ed.) *Changing Boundaries of the Political* (Cambridge: Cambridge University Press, 1987), pp. 363–407.

40. These problems are analysed in Lindberg and Maier op. cit.
41. These are relative concepts. However, while a majority of citizens are not wealthy, in contrast to the first half of the twentieth century an increasing majority do own property, usually a home, and possess significant material goods formerly only associated with the wealthy minority. In this sense the majority have a stake in the society and usually seek to defend it.
42. John Kenneth Galbraith, *The Culture of Contentment* (London: Sinclair-Stevenson, 1992); Wessel Visser and Rien Wijnhoven, 'Politics do matter, but does unemployment?' *European Journal of Political Research* 18:1 (1990), pp. 71–96; Charles S. Maier, 'Democracy since the French Revolution', in John Dunn (ed.), *Democracy: The Unfinished Journey 508 BC to AD 1993* (Oxford: Oxford University Press, 1992), pp. 125–54; 151–2 for discussion.
43. Maier, 'Democracy since the French Revolution', op. cit., pp. 151–54.
44. Francis G. Castles, 'The dynamics of policy change: what happened to the English-speaking nations in the 1980s', *European Journal of Political Research* 18:5 (1990), pp. 491–513.
45. Frances Fox Piven (ed.) *Labour Parties in Postindustrial Societies* (Cambridge: Polity Press, 1991), for a comprehensive overview of this process.
46. The classic statement of the older model is Gabriel A. Almond and Sidney Verba, *The Civic Culture:* op. cit., published in 1963. In 1980 another volume of essays on the concept and implications of original debate was published: *The Civic Culture Revisited* op. cit. The contrast between the two books can be detected in the critical approach taken to the concept by a number of the contributors to the second volume; Carole Pateman, 'The civic culture: a philosophic critique', pp. 57–102. For a comprehensive discussion of the new social movements and their impact on the cleavage system of the liberal democratic states see Claus Offe, 'Challenging the boundaries of institutional politics: social movements since the 1960s', in Charles S. Maier, *Changing Boundaries of the Political* op. cit., pp. 63–106; Inglehart, *The Silent Revolution* op. cit., on the relevance of the distinction between materialist and post-materialist.
47. Russell J. Dalton, Scott C. Flanagan, and Paul Allen Beck (eds), *Electoral Change in Advanced Industrial Democracies: Realignment or Dealignment?* (Princeton, N.J: Princeton University Press, 1984); Ivor Crewe and David Denver (eds) *Electoral Change in Western Democracies* (London: Croom Helm, 1985); Stefano Bartolini and Peter Mair, *Identity, Competition, and Electoral Availability: The Stabilisation of European Electorates 1885–1985* (Cambridge: Cambridge University Press, 1990).
48. Ronald Inglehart, *Culture Shift* op. cit., for the strongest statement of this claim.
49. Ronald Inglehart, 'Value Change in industrial societies', *American Political Science Review* 81:4 (1987), pp. 1289–1303; Ivor Crewe, 'Has the electorate become Thatcherite?', in Robert Skidelski (ed.), *Thatcherism* (London: Chatto and Windus, 1988), pp. 25–50; Brian Girvin, 'The United States: conservative politics in a liberal society' in Girvin (ed.), *The Transformation of Contemporary Conservatism*, op. cit., pp. 164–92; Michael Minkenberg, 'The New Right in Germany: The transformation of conservatism and the extreme right', *European Journal of Political Research* 22:1 (July 1992), pp. 55–82. A distinction should be made between the decline in the working class as a proportion of the electorate and an increase in the proportion of working-class voters who vote for the right (however defined). Both factors help the right, but clearly the latter where it occurs is of greater significance.
50. Paul Lucardie and Hans-Martien ten Napel, 'Between confessionalism and liberal conservatism: a comparative analysis of Christian democratic parties in Flanders,

Germany, Italy and the Netherlands', (paper presented at European Consortium for Political Research Joint Sessions, University of Limerick, 1992.

51. Anthony Seldon and Stuart Ball (eds), *The Conservative Century: The Conservative Party since 1900* (Oxford: Oxford University Press, 1994), for a comprehensive assesment; Ivor Crewe, Neil Day and Anthony Fox, *The British Electorate 1963–1987* (Cambridge: Cambridge University Press, 1991) for the structure of opinion and voting intentions.

52. Lindsay Brook et al., *British Social Attitudes Cumulative Sourcebook* (Aldershot: Gower, 1992).

53. Anthony Heath, Roger Jowell and John Curtice, *How Britain Votes* (Oxford: Pergamon, 1985); Peter Riddell, *The Thatcher Government* (Oxford: Basil Blackwell, 1983).

54. Harold Clarke and Paul Whiteley, 'Perceptions of macroeconomic performance, government support and conservative party strategy in Britain 1983–1987' *European Journal of Political Research* 18:1 (January 1990), pp. 97–120; Andrew Gamble, *The Free Economy and the Strong State* (London: Macmillan, 1988), pp. 110–39; Peter Jenkins, *Mrs Thatcher's Revolution: The Ending of the Socialist Era* (London: Jonathan Cape, 1987), pp. 317–79, Brook, et al., op. cit., Table F-2; Crewe, Day and Fox, op. cit., passim, for issues and voting trends.

55. For this reluctance in the case of the Netherlands, Paul Lucardie, 'Conservatism in the Netherlands: fragments and fringe groups' in Girvin, *The Transformation of Contemporary Conservatism*, op. cit., pp. 78–97; for comparison between different states in Europe, Visser and Wijnhoven, op. cit., passim.

56. Kenneth Dyson, 'Economic policy', in Gordon Smith, William E. Paterson, Peter H. Merkl (eds) *Developments in West German Politics* (Basingstoke: Macmillan, 1989), pp. 148–67; Edgar Grande, 'Neoconservatism and conservative-liberal economic policy in West Germany' op. cit., pp. 281–96.

57. Hans-Dieter Klingemann, 'West Germany', in Ivor Crewe and David Denver (eds), *Electoral Change in Western Democracies* (London: Croom Helm, 1985), pp. 230–63 for the presentation of data and discussion of these.

58. Minkenberg, op cit. for discussion of these trends; Connor, op. cit.; Russell J. Dalton, 'The German Voter' in Smith, Paterson and Merkl, op. cit., pp. 99–121.

59. Girvin, *The Transformation of Contemporary Conservatism*, op. cit., pp. 166–69; Irving L. Horowitz, *Ideology and Utopia in the United States 1956–76* (London: Oxford University Press, 1977).

60. Sundquist, *Dynamics of the Party System*, op. cit., pp. 412–36; Mayer, op. cit., 19–134.

61. In this respect Mayer, op. cit., pp. 329, 339, concluded after a careful review of public opinion in the 1980s that: 'The American people are basically conservative on social issues, but they are not reactionary.' While Republicans might acquire a window of opportunity on social and cultural matters, it would be dangerous for them to push this too far to the right.

62. Martin P. Wattengerg, 'The building of a Republican regional base in the South: the elephant crosses the Mason–Dixon Line', *Public Opinion Quarterly* 55:3 (Fall 1991), pp. 424–31; Earl Black and Merle Black, *The Vital South: How Presidents Are Elected* (Cambridge, Mass: Harvard University Press, 1992); Austin Ranney (ed.), *The American Elections of 1984* (Durham: Duke University Press, 1985).

63. White House personnel in 1988 were convinced that Bush was in a weak position and could lose the election (Source: personal interviews).

64. Barbara G. Farah and Ethel Klein, 'Public opinion trends', in Gerald M. Pomper (ed.), *The Election of 1988: Reports and Interpretations* (Chatham: Chatham House, 1989), pp. 103–28; Paul R. Abramson, John H. Aldrich, and David W. Rohde, *Change and Continuity in the 1988 Elections* (Washington, DC: Congressional Quarterly,

1991); Mayer, op. cit., pp. 315–40 for an evaluation of the weakness of the liberal position.

65. Brian Girvin, 'The Campaign', in Michael Laver, Peter Mair and Richard Sinnott (eds), *How Ireland Voted 1987* (Dublin: Poolbeg, 1987), pp. 9–29, which traces the evolution of policy; John Tuppen, *Chirac's France, 1986–88* (London: Macmillan, 1991), pp. 129–200; Ella Searls, 'The French Right in Opposition 1981-1986', *Parliamentary Affairs* 39:4, (October 1986), pp. 463–76.

66. Lucardie, op. cit., pp. 78–97; Lucardie and ten Napel, op. cit.; Bart Tromp, 'Party strategies and system change in the Netherlands', in Mair and Smith, *Understanding Party System Change in Western Europe*, op. cit., pp. 82–97; Central Bureau voor de Statistiek, *Nationaal kiezersonderzoek 1989*, Vol. 1 (The Hague: SDU, 1990), pp. 21–2.

67. Francis Fukuyama, *The End of History and the Last Man* (London: Hamish Hamilton, 1992); Brian Girvin, 'Political change, political culture and the end of history', paper prepared for Annual Conference of Political Studies Association of Ireland, October 1992; John Gray, 'From post-communism to civil society: the re-emergence of history and the decline of the Western model', *Social Philosophy and Policy* 10:2 (1993), pp. 26–50.

68. It may be more accurate to say that electorates are not prepared to pay the price of dealing with unemployment, which might require increased taxation.Visser and Wijnhoven, op. cit., pp. 71–90; Galbraith, op. cit.; *Economist*, 30 October, 1993, pp. 19–20 for report on inflation levels.

69. Anthony King et al., *Britain at the Polls, 1992* (Chatham: Chatham House, 1992); *The Gallup Poll Monthly* 311 (August 1991), pp. 33–48; *Times Mirror* poll, May/June 1992; *New York Times* 8 July 1992; Gerald M. Pomper et al., *The Election of 1992* (Chatham: Chatham House, 1993).

70. John Fitzmaurice, 'Belgian paradoxes: the November 1991 election', *West European Politics* 15:4 (October 1992), pp. 178–82; Mark Donovan, 'A party system in transformation: the April 1992 Italian election', *West European Politics* 15:4 (October 1992), pp. 170–77; Francesco Sidoti, 'The Italian political class', *Government and Opposition* 28:3 (Summer 1993), pp. 339–352; James L. Newell and Martin J. Bull, 'The Italian referenda of April 1993: real change at last?', *West European Politics*, 16:4 (October 1993), pp. 607–615; Howard Machin, 'How the Socialists lost the 1993 elections to the French Parliament', *West European Politics* 16:4 (October 1993), pp. 595–606; Peter Fysh, 'Gaullism today', *Parliamentary Affairs* 46:3 (July 1993); pp. 399–414.

71. John Gray, 'A Conservative disposition: individualism, the free market and the common life' John Gray, *Beyond the New Right: Markets, Government and the Common Environment* (London: Routledge, 1993), pp. 46-65.

Index

Gadamer, Hans Georg, 17
Galbraith, J. K., 174
Galileo Galilei, 9
Gambetta, Léon-Michel, 41
Garibaldi, Giuseppe, 45–6
Garraty, John A., 81, 85–6
Gaulle, Charles de, 194–5, 197
Gaullism, 193–5, 197, 215
Gellner, Ernest, 10–11, 96, 99
Germany, 38, 62, 67, 68, 73
  conservatism in
    inter-war, 69, 70
    19th Century, 37–8, 46–9, 52
    post-war, 110–22 *passim*, 138, 196-7, 208,
      212–14
  First World War and, 59–60, 61
  Nazism in, 66–7, 77–80, 81–2, 94, 101
  secularisation in, 204, 206
  socialism in, 47, 52, 69, 70, 78, 212–13
  unification of, 46–7
Giddens, Anthony, 11, 12
Giscard d'Estaing, Valéry, 202
Glorious Revolution, 8–9
gold standard, 69, 162–3
Goldwater, Barry, 162, 163, 164, 196
government intervention in the economy
  UK study of, 127–54
  US study of, 159–79
Grande, Edgar, 197
Gray, John, 13
Great Britain *see* United Kingdom
Great Depression, 74–80, 81–2, 84–7
Greece, 66, 202
Greenstein, Fred I., 180, 181
Grenada, 2

Hagerty, Jim, 178, 179, 180
Hall, Sir Robert, 145
Halleck, Charles, 177
Hamilton, Alexander, 28
Hamilton, Richard, 79
Hamlin, John, 177
Hauge, Gabriel, 145, 164, 170, 171, 174–5, 176
Heath, Edward, 201–2
Heathcoat-Amory, , 138
Hegel, Georg, 36, 38
Hirschmann, Albert O., 40, 63, 98
history, subjectivism of, 17
Hitler, Adolf, 77, 80, 82, 87
Hobbes, Thomas, 3, 10
Hobsbawm, Eric, 31
Hoover, Herbert, 71–2, 84–5, 161
housing policies, 135, 136–8
Humphrey, George M., 165, 166, 167, 168
Hungary, 66, 67

ideology, 19–20, 49–50, 108–10, 161, 190
incomes policies, 139–41, 143, 146
individualism, 108, 163

industrial capitalism, 11–12, 45, 48, 109–10, 198
inflation, 207, 216
  UK, 132-3, 143, 146, 151–2
  US, 168, 177
Inglehart, Ronald, 203, 209
Ireland, 61, 63, 66, 67, 69, 83–4, 204, 208, 215
Ireton, Henry, 8
Italy, 60, 62
  conservatism in
    19th Century, 45–6, 49
    post-war, 104–5, 106, 110, 112–22 *passim*,
      138, 192–3, 197, 217
  fascism in, 66, 67, 76–7, 94–5, 101
  secularisation in, 204, 206
  socialism/communism in, 202
  unification of, 45–6

Jackson, Andrew, 29
James I and VI, King, 5
James II, King, 9
James, Harold, 81
Jews, 38, 94–5
John Paul II, Pope, 218

Kant, Immanuel, 10
Kennedy, John F., 179, 184, 196
Kersbergen, Kees van, 109
Kershaw, Ian, 66
Keynes, John Maynard, 74
Keyserling, Leon, 170
Klingemann, Hans-Dieter, 212
Knowland, William, 163, 176
Kohl, Helmut, 212

Labour Party (UK), 69, 70, 73, 86, 127–32, 136,
    141, 145, 149, 151, 153, 154, 202, 211
labour unions *see* trade unions
land and property, 7–9, 15, 28, 32, 108–9
Lapua movement (Finland), 82–3
Latvia, 66
Law, Andrew Bonar, 53
left-wing politics *see* liberalism/radicalism;
    socialism/communism
Legitimists, 35
Leo XIII, Pope, 100
Lepsius, M. Rainer, 78
Levellers, 7
Liberal Party (UK), 69, 129–30
liberalism/radicalism, 1
  conservative conflicts with, 14, 20, 37–49,
    206–15
  conservative consensus with *see* consensus
  modernity and, 13
  nationalism and, 45–9, 50
  origins of, 7–9
  revival in 1960s/70s of, 198–200, 203, 209
  revolutionary movements and, 24, 32
Lilburne, John, 7
Lithuania, 66